Interdisciplinary perspectives on modern history

Editors
Robert Fogel and Stephan Thernstrom

Family time and industrial time

"It takes just 23 minutes for the operatives employed in the factories at the Amoskeag Corporation to 'skidoo' through the mill gates after the clocks strike 6, the first whistle blows, and the first bell gives its warning that the day's work is done . . . just as the clock in the tower announced the hour, there was the sound of a whistle, answered by a hoarse-tuned steam gong. This was followed by the clanging of the bell but it had struck three times before whirring of the machinery ceased. Almost at the same instant the big gates flew open. The first to leave the plant were men and boys, some with dinner pails and some with bicycles. Then came a steady stream of men and women, boys and girls . . . Many of the younger women were attractively dressed, several even stylishly attired, while the hats they wore were no home-made affairs, but the creation of Manchester milliners. Many of the older women dragged themselves along wearily, with wan faces, showing that the struggle for existence was costing them something.

The great majority of the younger of toilers were chatting amiably, and appeared to be thoroughly happy and contented with their lot. Then the workers came in groups of dozens or more, then by threes and fours, then couple followed couple, and lone stragglers brought up the rear, the last to leave their daily duties being women . . .

Meanwhile the watchmen stood like sentries at the gates, but though it required but 23 minutes for the great drove of humanity to pass but 30 minutes had elapsed before the gates were closed . . . Fifteen thousand people had issued forth from those great gateways and from others leading to the West Side. Except for the noon hour they had been busily engaged from 6:30 o'clock in the morning until 6 o'clock at night and collectively they had earned in the vicinity of $18,335."

Manchester Mirror, June 15, 1907

Photograph courtesy of the Library of Congress

Family time and industrial time

*The relationship between
the family and work in a
New England industrial community*

TAMARA K. HAREVEN
Department of History, Clark University
Center for Population Studies, Harvard University

CAMBRIDGE UNIVERSITY PRESS
Cambridge
London   New York   New Rochelle
Melbourne   Sydney

Published by the Press Syndicate of the University of Cambridge
The Pitt Building, Trumpington Street, Cambridge CB2 1RP
32 East 57th Street, New York, NY 10022, USA
296 Beaconsfield Parade, Middle Park, Melbourne 3206, Australia

First published 1982

Printed in the United States of America

Library of Congress Cataloging in Publication Data
Hareven, Tamara K.

Family time and industrial time.

(Interdisciplinary perspectives on modern history)

Bibliography: p.

Includes index.

1. Textile workers – New Hampshire – Manchester –
History. 2. Amoskeag Manufacturing Company – Employees –
History. 3. Family – New Hampshire – Manchester – History.
4. Manchester (N.H.) – Social conditions. I. Title.
II. Series.
HD6956.T42U65   305.5′6   81–3903
ISBN 0 521 23094 2 hard covers   AACR2
ISBN 0 521 28914 9 paperback

To Randolph Langenbach
and to John Modell

Contents

Preface

Family and work, the two most central commitments in most people's lives, have emerged as themes in recent social history, but the relationship between these two areas has not been closely considered. The specialization of historical studies has fostered a sense of the division of these two worlds and a neglect of the ways in which they inevitably interact. Social and economic developments in the larger society, economic constraints, and changes in industrial organization affect the family's ability to respond to labor markets, organize migration, and influence work processes. In turn, internal changes within the family, as well as the family's priorities, which are dictated by its needs and cultural traditions, affect labor supply, motivation for work, and social relations in the production process. In short, family behavior can be better understood in relation to the workplace, on which its survival and success depend; similarly, workers' behavior must be seen as founded on familial traditions and expectations, which, along with external forces, shape the patterns of labor response.

This book begins to examine more closely the role of the family in the adaptation of immigrant laborers to factory work and life in an industrial city. It focuses on the experience of the laborers who worked for the world's largest textile corporation and the city it built – the Amoskeag Mills in Manchester, New Hampshire – at some point during the first three decades of this century.

Conventional wisdom in sociology and history has maintained for some time that industrialization destroyed the traditional family and that the migration of individuals from nonindustrial to industrial settings resulted in the severing of community ties and the destruction of traditional culture. Recent research has begun to reverse these stereotypes, but questions remain: Under what historical conditions was the family able to control its environment and influence work relations, and under what conditions was the family's control weakened or lost? How did the family adapt to changing work processes and conditions? What resources did it draw on in this process, and at what internal cost? In attempting to answer these questions, I have followed patterns of behavior as well as the

xi

actors' own perceptions of their lives and the historical forces affecting them.

Essentially, this book sets out to explore the interrelationship between three different kinds of time: individual time, family time,
and industrial time. An understanding of how these kinds of time
reinforced each other or conflicted provides insight into the interaction of individuals with the larger historical processes. Under what
circumstances did the family respond to external clocks, and under
what conditions did it function in accordance with its internal
clocks?

The abundance of Manchester's surviving records and the vitality
of its people have provided a rare opportunity to examine these
larger questions. I first became involved with Manchester in 1971,
when I took my urban history class from Clark University to visit
the giant mill complex along the Merrimack River. I was struck by
the drama of its urban space and the presence of many former mill
workers in whose memories almost a century of Manchester's industrial history still lived.

Manchester also offered one of the richest combinations of historical sources, including corporation records and photographic and
architectural materials. The more than seventy thousand career files
kept by the Amoskeag Company, which recorded the numerous
comings and goings of each worker, provided an opportunity for
reconstructing work careers over time and individual and family
histories by linking these records with other sources. The linkage of
this unique set of records enabled me to reconstruct entire family
groups and extended kinship networks through time. This made it
possible to escape the usual limitations imposed by historical records and to study individuals and families longitudinally, rather
than at one point in time.

While reconstructing the work and family histories (a four-year
process), I began interviewing former Amoskeag workers and their
relatives. Initially intended as a modest exercise to supplement the
documentary and quantitative information, it emerged as an ab-
sorbing and moving experience. I embarked, therefore, on the
publication of a separate book of select oral-history narratives while
most of the interviewees were still alive: *Amoskeag: Life and Work in
an American Factory-City* (New York: Pantheon), was written in collaboration with Randolph Langenbach and published in 1978.

The current book weaves the oral histories into the quantitative
analyses of the workers' career histories, kinship networks, and
corporation records in an effort to explore patterns of behavior as
well as people's own perceptions of their lives and the historical

circumstances affecting them. Oral-history interviewing provided access to human experiences and to perceptions of their own lives and historical conditions that documentary material alone rarely does. Oral history has been criticized because of its subjectivity, but when used discriminately as a source for perceptions, rather than "facts," its subjectivity becomes its strength. I hope this book will demonstrate the potential in integrating various approaches in the reconstruction of a multi-layered reality. Most important, I hope it will suggest that different dimensions of historical experiences can be reconstructed from different kinds of sources; that these dimensions are sometimes mutually reinforcing and at other times contradictory, thus contributing to an understanding of the complexity of historical reality.

The relationship among individual time, family time, and industrial time considered against the backdrop of larger historical changes is complex, especially when examined through the historical reconstruction of discrete lives. The major challenge was to retain the complex interplay among individual careers, family patterns, corporate policy, and behavior on the shop floor. In this effort, I encountered the awesome task of trying to separate into strands and analyze the many components of family and work and industrial behavior without losing sight of ways in which they shaped each other. The organization of this book reflects an attempt to follow these different strands while conveying the complexity of their interaction.

Chapter themes move back and forth between family and work and from individual careers to workers' collective behavior. Thus, in chapters that focus on the family, the world of work and the corporation are pulled into the background, and vice versa. This thematic organization does not permit chronological construction but, rather, allows historical time to cut across each chapter. Only the second and last chapters provide an overall chronological framework.

It is my hope that this integration of quantitative and qualitative sources, beyond making a contribution to the theoretical understanding of the family's role in the process of industrialization and in immigrant workers' adaptation to industrial conditions, will also convey some of the depth of the human experience that has been a neglected dimension in the study of the process of industrialization.

The making of this book required the dedication of many people. I would like to express my gratitude first to the people of Manchester, New Hampshire, whose histories inspired this study and whose life stories added richness and depth to my understanding of the way people confront social change. I am grateful to the Manchester Historic Association for making their rich collection available to me, for their continued assistance over an eight-year period when they housed my research project in its earlier stages, and for acting as a conduit for a grant from the New Hampshire Charitable Funds and Affiliated Trusts. The librarian, Mrs. Elizabeth Lessard, in particular, assisted me in many ways, by guiding my research assistants and generously sharing with me her rich knowledge of Manchester's history. I am also indebted to the Manuscript Division of the Baker Library at the Harvard Graduate School for Business Administration, especially to former archivist Robert Lovett, whose generous help greatly facilitated my research in the Amoskeag records, and more recently to Florence Bartoshevsky.

In addition to the main depositories of records at the Manchester Historic Association and the Baker Library, I am indebted to the librarians at the Manchester City Library, the Merrimack Valley Textile Museum, the Clark University Library, the American Antiquarian Society, Widener Library at Harvard University, the Boston Public Library, the Massachusetts State Library, the State Library of New Hampshire, the National Archives, particularly Joseph Howerton, and the Library of Congress.

I am grateful to the Office of the City Clerk in Manchester, New Hampshire, for permission to research vital records; to Gerald Robert, former president of the Association Canado-Américaine, for permission to research in the society's collections; to the National Archives of the Province of Quebec; and to the McCord Museum, particularly Stanley Triggs and Nora Hague for access to their ample photographic collections.

Dr. Thomas Leavitt, director of the Merrimack Valley Textile Museum, provided the initial support for this project. The museum's research grant enabled me to launch the project and seek additional funding.

The following agencies and foundations provided generous support during this project: The National Endowment for the Humanities, Research Grants Division, with matching funds from the New Hampshire Charitable Funds and Affiliated Trusts, the Amoskeag Industries, and the Cogswell Benevolent Trust. The New Hampshire Council for the Humanities and the Sol O. Sidore Fund, the United Textile Workers, the Merrimack Valley Textile Museum, the New Hampshire Charitable Funds and Affiliated Trusts, and the

Rockefeller Foundation supported the collection and transcriptions of the oral histories.

A sabbatical leave from Clark University in 1975 and a fellowship from the Ford Foundation for one term in 1976 enabled me to embark on intensive data analysis and to launch the writing of this book, and the generous support of Clark University provided clerical and research assistance. Crucial to the writing and revision of this manuscript has been the support of the National Institute on Aging through a Research Career Development Grant.

During the past three years the Center for Population Studies at Harvard University has provided the ideal setting for data analysis and writing, as well as clerical assistance and warm support. Colleagues at the center provided continuing encouragement, especially Nathan Keyfitz and William Alonso, who as previous directors of the center had greatly facilitated my work. I am also grateful to George Masnick and Doug Ewbank for their advice in demographic analysis. The staff members of the center were extremely helpful at every stage.

During the initial writing stages I benefited from the Rockefeller Foundation's gracious hospitality in its Center for Scholars in Bellagio, Italy. I was in residence with the Ossabaw Island Foundation's project, where I greatly appreciated the supportive and inspiring environment while completing my writing.

During the years of research, analysis, and writing, many research assistants and secretaries have provided expert help. I am grateful to my research assistants from St. Anselm's College, especially Dan D'Antonio, and to Mary DuBois and Kathy Hynes. Most important, the work of Louise Perreault, Robert Perreault, and Denise Arel provided the backbone for the coding of the Amoskeag employee files in the Manchester Historic Association and the data linkage for the reconstruction of kinship networks. Robert Perreault, who also served as the chief interview assistant on the oral-history project and who translated the French interviews into English, generously helped me later in his capacity as librarian of the Association Canado-Américaine. Ronald Petrin and Sally Boynton succeeded Robert Perreault as interview and research assistants, and Frank Skrzysovsky provided valuable assistance in documentary research, as did Jean Ferguson. I am also grateful to Agnes Godbout, Jean Evangelauf, and Sidney Ellis for transcribing the oral-history interviews and to Joanne Jacobs, Laurel Forcier, Wanda Fisher, Joyce Ingham, Kathy Larson, and Madelyn Priestly, who provided clerical assistance at Clark University at different stages.

Steven Shedd was the major computer programmer. Without his sustaining help and skill, the fate of this project might have been dramatically different. In the final stages, Judy Bates also provided expert programming.

Brian Benson, Yale Bohn, Merle Sprinzen, and Barbara Wiget provided statistical assistance, and William Harris provided valuable advice in the final editing of the tables. The assistance of Arnaud Friedlander and Tom Flynn, in the editing of final versions of the manuscript and in library research, was equally valuable. Also, Kelly Cameron, Jeanne Merino, Anna Brown, and Barbara Watson were extremely helpful in library research and proofreading, as was Karen Ulbin in her research in Manchester. Catherine Ellis executed the technical design of the kinship charts of the Anger family.

The bulk of the typing and retyping was the responsibility of Linda Speare, who handled it with heroic patience, intelligence, and humor; she was assisted by Barbara Sindegrilis, Ann Scanlon, and members of Clark University's typing pool, especially Terry Reynolds.

Howard Litwak, more than anyone else, worked on every phase of this project, first as research assistant and subsequently as editor of several versions of the manuscript. Both he and Joan Rosenstock dramatically improved the style and coherence of the manuscript and provided valuable advice at various stages.

Many colleagues and friends have encouraged and guided my work and offered constructive criticism. Most important initially was Richard Bushman's encouragement to embark on this study. John Modell, Maris Vinovskis, and Howard Chudacoff generously shared their methodological expertise. My collaboration with each of them on various articles on the history of the family in other communities helped shape my methodology for this study and provided important comparative patterns.

Two colleagues in particular influenced my thinking and provided me with new ways of interpreting my evidence: David Montgomery, who patiently tutored me in labor history, helped me to see the connection between the Amoskeag experience and general patterns of working-class behavior, and Glen Elder, who introduced me, along with other historians, to the life-course approach to the study of the family, was, with his continuing advice, a great help in the formidable task of analyzing longitudinal data. John Modell and Glen Elder read the manuscript in its entirety and made valuable organizational and substantive suggestions, and Stanley

Engerman read a major part of the manuscript and offered significant methodological and substantive criticisms. David Montgomery, Robert Wheaton, Claude Fischer, Alfred Chandler, Ron Walters, Howard Chudacoff, Brian Palmer, Randolph Langenbach, and David Grimsted provided valuable comments on individual chapters. Jean-Claude Robert and Jacques Rouillard shared their insights on the social history of Quebec and thus facilitated my understanding of the background of French-Canadian immigrants to New England. I am solely responsible, however, for the final form of the manuscript.

I am indebted to Robert Fogel for valuable advice in earlier stages of writing and to Stephan Thernstrom for his constructive criticisms and for setting aside his own work to meet tight editorial schedules.

Steve Fraser at Cambridge University Press provided encouragement and support throughout the completion of this book and helped improve its quality. Sandra Graham coped with the mammoth task of production with expertise and patience. Ann Ivins greatly improved the readability of the manuscript by her sensitive copyediting.

I am grateful to Kathleen Adams, who stepped in at the most difficult moments during the final stages of this work. In addition to contributing an anthropological perspective, she provided help and encouragement in numerous ways. I am indebted beyond words to David Grimsted for his insights and sustaining friendship.

Finally, I am deeply grateful to the two people to whom this book is dedicated: John Modell, with whom collaboration on a variety of projects has been a stimulating experience and whose inspiration and encouragement are ever present, and my husband, Randolph Langenbach, who has made me sensitive to the visual and environmental context of history and with whom collaboration on the study of the Amoskeag became inseparable from our lives.

Cambridge, Massachusetts *Tamara K. Hareven*

A note on citations

Oral histories

Excerpts from oral-history interviews that were published in Tamara K. Hareven and Randolph Langenbach, *Amoskeag: Life and Work in an American Factory-City* (1978), are cited as "name of the interviewee, *Amoskeag*, page number." Interviews that were not included in *Amoskeag* are cited as "name of the person, interview." With several exceptions, the names of the previously unpublished interviewees were changed to ensure privacy. Whenever an unpublished segment of a previously published interview is cited, the original name is used. For example, Cora Pellerin's published interview is cited as "Pellerin, *Amoskeag*, page number." Her previously unpublished segment is cited as "Pellerin, interview."

Tables and figures

Unless otherwise specified, the tables in Chapter 5 are based on a sample of individual employee files from the Amoskeag Company records and their linkage with vital records; the tables in Chapters 9 and 10 are based on the same sample; all tables and figures in Chapters 7 and 8 are based on a sample from the 1900 United States Federal Manuscript Census. See Appendix B for a description of sources. Unless noted otherwise, all tables were tested for statistical significance.

1 *The theoretical context: the family in the process of industrialization*

Industrialization and urbanization have often been cited as the forces that transformed Western society, radically reshaping people's lives. In his now classic analysis of working-class culture in early industrial England, E. P. Thompson dramatized the traumatic effect that industrialization had on the family: "Each stage in industrial differentiation and specialization struck also at the family economy, disturbing customary relations between man and wife, parents and children, and differentiating more sharply 'work' and 'life' . . . Meanwhile the family was roughly torn apart each morning by the factory bell" (1963:416).

Until recently, most sociological research on the family, guided by the theory of social breakdown, argued that industrialization led to the disruption of traditional family patterns. The theory of social breakdown is based on two arguments. The first is that industrialization fragmented the traditional three-generational extended family and led to the emergence of an isolated nuclear family. According to this view, the family became increasingly nuclearized to fit the requirements of the new industrial system and as such was the unit most compatible with that system (Parsons 1955). The second argument, made frequently by the Chicago School of Sociology and some of its followers, maintains that through the history of industrial development migration from rural to urban centers uprooted people from their traditional kinship networks, and that the pressures of industrial work and urban life caused a disintegration of the family unit. Adaptation to industrial life thereby stripped migrants of their traditional culture (Thomas and Znaniecki 1918–20, Wirth 1938, and Linton 1959).[1]

Even sociologists such as William Goode who disagree with the notion of social breakdown have claimed that there was a "fit" between the nuclear family and the requirements of industrial society. Some claim that because the occupational system is based on achievement rather than ascription, the detachment from rigid rules of extended kin renders individuals more mobile and therefore more adaptable to the labor demands of modern industry. It should be noted, however, that Goode views the conjugal family's

1

integration with the industrial system as one that serves industry but at the same time places workers at the mercy of the factory system. "The lower-class family pattern is indeed most 'integrated' with the industrial system" writes Goode, "but mainly in the sense that the individual is forced to enter its labor market with far less family support – his family *does not prevent industry from using him for its goals*. He may move where the system needs him, hopefully where his best opportunity lies, but he *must* also fit the demands of the system, since no extended kin network will interest itself greatly in his fate" (Goode 1963:12–13).

During the past decade, various historical studies have convincingly refuted the claim that industrialization destroyed the three-generational family, and this study will question the assumption concerning the "fit" between the nuclear family and the industrial system. The myth about the existence of a three-generational extended family in the preindustrial past, which Goode rightly called "the classical family of Western nostalgia" (1963:6), was exploded by demonstrating that the nuclear household had been the dominant preindustrial form of family organization and that it had experienced a continuity in Western society for at least the past two centuries (Laslett 1965, Demos 1970, Greven 1970, and Laslett and Wall 1972).[2]

The assumption that families and kin groups break down under the impact of migration to urban industrial centers and under the pressures of industrial work has also been challenged. Neil Smelser, in his study of the family in the early stages of the industrial revolution in Britain, documented the recruitment by textile factories of entire family groups as work units. Fathers contracted for their children, collected their wages, and often disciplined them in the factory. Entire families depended on the factory as their employer; the factories, in turn, depended on the recruitment of family groups to maintain a continuous labor supply (Smelser 1959). Smelser argued, however, that the family working as a unit in the factory was limited to the first phase of the industrial revolution, that by the early 1830s, the development of new machinery had introduced specialization, so that families no longer worked together in the factory. As Anderson (1971) shows, however, among textile workers in mid-nineteenth-century Lancashire, recruitment of family units in the textile industry continued.

Most important, Anderson stressed the survival of vital kinship ties and the continuity of the role of kin in migration and adaptation to industrial conditions. Thus, the family as a work unit, which

Smelser identified for the early industrial revolution, survived in different forms throughout the nineteenth century and, as this study shows, was also present in the United States in the twentieth century.[3]

The family functioned as a crucial intermediary in recruiting workers from rural areas, not only in the initial phases of industrialization but actually throughout the nineteenth and twentieth centuries. Thus, families who were prepared to leave their rural communities and enter industrial employment or to send some members to the factory were essential to the early development of the industry. Changing conditions in the rural economy, as well as the internal changes within rural families, were therefore essential conditions for releasing a labor force for industry. The very success of the early industrial system depended on a continuous flow of labor from the countryside to the newly industrializing centers. Most of the migration of workers to factory towns was carried out under the auspices of kin. Kinship ties with communities of origin were reinforced by the back-and-forth migration of individual members and the transfer of resources.

This continuity was evident as the factory system emerged as a major force in New England in the early nineteenth century. It can be seen in both styles of recruitment of rural laborers for the emerging textile mills – the "family system" and the "mill girl" system. The family employment model, which was imported from England by Samuel Slater in the late eighteenth century, was most prevalent in, but not restricted to, small company-owned industrial villages in Rhode Island and southern Massachusetts.[4] In the late eighteenth and early nineteenth centuries, rural New England families often sent one or more members to work in nearby textile mills. Factory wages were low, and family survival often depended on the employment of the maximum number of members. However, families did retain some choice and control over their economic endeavors by maintaining subsistence farming as a backup if the factory failed. Even when entire families moved to industrial centers, they did not completely abandon their rural base; they worked in factories for a time, then returned to their villages, and at a later point migrated back to industrial work, often in accordance with the agricultural seasons.

The second model, the employment of "mill girls" – young women from rural New England – emerged as the dominant labor base of the planned large-scale textile towns founded and developed during the first half of the nineteenth century. The system was perfected in Lowell, Massachusetts, the prototype for this model, and was followed in its sister communities, including Manchester, New Hampshire.[5] For most young women, factory work represented a transitional phase – usually one or two years – between domestic work in their parents' farm homes and marriage. The savings they accumulated from their factory labor were sent back to their families on the farm. Again, the interdependence of the countryside and the factory was maintained through back-and-forth migration; family ties still linked factory workers and rural communities into a common social system.

In the mid-nineteenth century, however, as mill girls were replaced by a cheaper labor force, family employment emerged once again as the dominant pattern – but with a difference. New immigrant families, Irish, French Canadian, Portuguese, and East European, were recruited, replicating, in some respects, the experiences of the earlier family-type employment system. Unlike the New England and French Canadian factory workers, however, European immigrants could not return easily to their communities of origin for supplemental support. However, even long-distance overseas migration did not entirely sever the links of immigrants with their native bases. Relatives on both sides of the Atlantic maintained ties and transmitted assistance.[6]

The nineteenth-century experience of family recruitment into the textile industry thus suggests the continued role of the family as an active agent in its interaction with the factory system. Being an active agent does not imply that the family was in full control of its destiny; nor does it mean that workers and their families were successful in changing the structure of industrial capitalism. Recent revisions of the stereotypes of family passivity and breakdown have exaggerated the strength of the immigrant and working-class family in American society. Such a neoromantic interpretation of the role of the family could easily generate another extreme stereotype, as removed from historical reality as its predecessor.

The crucial historical question is not merely whether the family was an active or passive agent, but rather under what historical conditions was it able to control its environment and under what circumstances did its control diminish? How did the family reorder its priorities to respond to new conditions, and how did this reordering affect internal family relations?

To answer these questions, it is necessary to look not only at the ways in which industrial work affected family organization and work roles but also at the way the family affected conditions in the factory by linking an examination of family behavior to industrial work processes.

This is where the studies of labor history and family history converge.[7] Until very recently, the "new labor history" and family history have gone their separate ways, with little attention to the interplay between the two spheres. Labor studies have concentrated on unions and work relations on the shop floor and on the dynamics of working-class culture; family studies have tended to examine the domestic unit in isolation from other institutions. Even studies of the family economy are concerned primarily with work roles, especially those of women, or with household budgets, rather than with the family's relationship to the workplace.

An important discovery in labor history has been the workers' carry-over of premigration customs and traditions into the modern industrial system and their use as a resource in the adaptation process (Gutman 1976 and Montgomery 1979). What was the family's role in this transmission? To what extent did family background and ties handicap or advance workers' adaptation to industrial conditions, and conversely, how did changing work relations affect family traditions and roles? An exploration of the interaction between family and work has to be both contextual and dynamic, taking into account that workers' behavior, work procedures, and industrial organization are not constant over time, just as the internal organization of the family changes over the life course of its members and in response to external conditions.

Any examination of the family's interaction with the workplace must also consider the role of extended kin. Historians' concentration on the household, in part to prove the persistence of nuclear family patterns, has gradually led to a limited view of the family as strictly a residential unit and has caused a confusion of "family" with "household." Also, because historical analyses of nineteenth-century family structure are based primarily on the household schedules in the census, they have not taken into consideration kin outside the household. Recent scholarship has thus tended to reinforce the notion of the "isolated nuclear family" in modern society, which has been so prevalent in family sociology.

Revisionist sociological studies by Litwak, Sussman, and others have documented the pervasiveness of informal kin relations in contemporary American society outside the confines of the nuclear family. Sussman has identified patterns of mutual assistance between married children and their aging parents; Litwak has demonstrated the survival of kinship ties in a highly mobile society and the positive role of kin in social mobility (Sussman 1959, Litwak 1960, and Sussman and Burchinal 1962).[8] These studies emphasize the continuity of generational exchanges of goods and services between the nuclear family and extended kin over the life course of the family and its members.

"Family" has many meanings and "families" take many forms. This study views the family both as a domestic group and as a kinship system that extends beyond the household. Most historical studies have treated the family as a static unit, but in reality, individuals fulfill various roles and find themselves in a variety of familial configurations over their life course.[9]

A life-course perspective views the interrelationships between individual and collective family behavior as they constantly change over people's lives and in the context of historical conditions. The life-course approach is concerned with the movement of individuals over their own lives and through historical time and with the relationship of family members to each other as they travel through personal and historical time. As Elder defines it, the life course encompasses "pathways" by which individuals move through their lives fulfilling different roles sequentially or simultaneously (1978). In following such movements from one role status to the next, or in the simultaneous balancing of roles, individuals synchronize their activities with those of other family members and in response to historical conditions. The crucial question is how people plan and organize their roles over their life course and time their transitions both on the familial and nonfamilial level in such areas as migration, starting to work, leaving home, getting married, and setting up an independent household. How are these individual transitions related to collective family timing?

The metaphor that captures best the interrelationship of individual transitions to changing family configurations is the movement of schools of fish. As people move over their life course in family units, they group and regroup themselves. The functions they adopt in these different clusters also vary significantly over their lives. The multiplicity of familial relationships in which individuals are engaged changes as well, and along with these changes individuals' transitions into various roles are also timed differently. In this respect, family status and work roles are as important in defining individual and collective timing as is age, the most commonly used variable.

The life-course approach thus converges on the issue of timing – an understanding of the interrelationships of family, individual, and historical time (Hareven 1975, 1977). "Family time" designates the timing of such life-course events as marriage, the birth of a child, a young adult's departure from the home, and the transition of individuals into different family roles, as the family moves through its life. "Individual time" and family time are closely synchronized, because most individual life transitions are interrelated with collective family transitions. In the historical context of this study, in particular, the close integration of individual moves with collective family needs made individual timing dependent on collective family timing. For example, embarking on a career, leaving home, and getting married, now considered acts of individual timing, were historically much more closely synchronized to collective family needs and schedules and often a major source of pressure and conflict in the family as well.

Family time and individual time are affected by "historical time" – the overall social, economic, institutional, and cultural changes in the larger society. For example, demographic changes, economic constraints, and legal changes have all affected patterns of family and individual timing.

"Industrial time," an aspect of historical time, refers not only to production schedules but also to changes in industrial work organization and relations in the overall context of industrial capitalism. Specifically in the context of this study it includes the historical changes in the textile industry under the impact of business cycles and their effect on working conditions and labor relations. More broadly defined, industrial time encompasses the industrial culture governing behavior and relations in the workplace and industrial communities.[10]

An understanding of the synchronization of these different levels of timing is essential to the investigation of the relationship between discrete lives and the larger process of social change.

From a life-course perspective, the most crucial aspect of timing is the point in an individual's or a family's life at which he or they intersect with historical forces. For example, the age, the career stage, or the family stage at which individuals encountered the Great Depression affected their ability to cope with adversity. Such timing is conditioned by the historical moment, as well as by the culture and experience from earlier life that individuals bring with them to those conditions, and the networks in which they are enmeshed at that particular moment.

Timing provides a way of understanding how individuals and families ranked their priorities in their daily lives as well as in their

encounter with social and economic developments in the larger society; how they revised their experiences to meet new circumstances;
what kind of choices they made even under severe constraints,
when few options were available to them. This is precisely where
people's cultural backgrounds played an important part in determining patterns of timing and in shaping individuals' and families'
responses to external historical conditions. The cultural heritage
that people brought with them into a situation guided their preferences, the priorities they followed, their coping with adversity, and
their strategies in responding to changing needs or constraints imposed by external historical conditions. How individuals and families were guided by the dictates of their cultural preferences on timing, how they revised and modified their transitions to meet new
conditions, is a crucial question underlying the issue of people's
adaptation to changing circumstances in their own lives within the
larger context of historical conditions.

2 The historical context: the Amoskeag Company and the city it built

The Amoskeag Manufacturing Company and Manchester, New Hampshire, the city it had planned and developed starting in 1837, were products of the new industrial order launched in New England by a closely knit group of Boston-based entrepreneurs. The newly created town, strategically located by the Amoskeag Falls on the Merrimack River, was named after Manchester, England, already famous as the world's largest textile city. Half a century later, when Manchester, New Hampshire, emerged as the site of the world's largest textile factory, it had managed to avoid some of the environmental problems of its English namesake. In 1902 a British traveler wrote:

> None of the manufacturing towns in New England pleased me as much as Manchester, in New Hampshire. Unlike its great-grand-mother, it has clean air, clear water, and sunny skies; every street is an avenue of noble trees . . . Perhaps the handsomest, certainly the most impressive, buildings in Manchester are the Amoskeag and Manchester Mills. They are built of worn red brick, beautifully weathered, and form a continuous curved facade . . . nearly half a mile long. Rising sheer out of a deep, clear, swift-flowing stream (the Merrimack), upon the other bank of which are grass and trees, they need little more than to be silent to masquerade successfully as ancient colleges (Young 1903:35–6).

The Amoskeag Manufacturing Company dominated the city of Manchester for almost an entire century. Between 1838, when construction began, and 1936, when the mills shut down, hardly a person in Manchester was not in some way affected by the Amoskeag Corporation. To the people who lived and worked there, the Amoskeag was a total institution, a closed and almost self-contained world.[1]

Manchester was modeled on the factory town of Lowell, Massachusetts, founded two decades earlier and developed by the Boston Associates. These entrepreneurs established the headquarters of their new company in Boston, where it remained throughout the corporation's life.[2] During the 1830s, the Boston Associates pur-

9

chased the water power of the entire length of the Merrimack River, New England's second-largest river, and assembled a fifteen-thousand-acre plot opposite the Amoskeag Falls as a site for the planned city. The development of the city's real estate was never entirely divorced from the company's operations. Ownership of water resources and the land on which the city grew gave the company control over not only Manchester's initial development but its economic life during the century of Amoskeag's existence. A new industrial city was thus superimposed upon the rural countryside, a reluctant neighbor of the rapidly expanding corporation.[3]

Manchester's urban plan reflected the social program of its Boston developers. Although it never matched Lowell's reputation as a city of mill girls, like Lowell, Manchester founded a community of young women working together in the mills and living together in boardinghouses, within the social system of corporate paternalism, a philosophy of benevolent control, which treated workers as the "corporation's children" and permeated every aspect of life: the organization of work, the management of the boardinghouses, the founding of charities, and the endowment of churches. In the mid-nineteenth century, when the majority of the labor force consisted of young, unmarried women from rural New England, the company also regulated their behavior after working hours to reassure their parents, who might otherwise have been reluctant to let their daughters engage in such work. The boardinghouses were closed and locked at 10 P.M., church attendance was compulsory, and alcoholic consumption was prohibited.

This so-called utopian period came to an end for most of the planned New England industrial communities shortly before the Civil War. Irish immigrant families willing to work for lower wages replaced the mill girls, and speculative housing gradually replaced corporation boardinghouses. Lowell, the "glorious" city of spindles and mill girls, diminished to an ordinary industrial town.[4] The utopian period also came to an end in Manchester but with a difference: Whereas management had become fragmented among many small factory units in Lowell, it was consolidated in Manchester. With T. Jefferson Coolidge as treasurer, the Amoskeag Company, during the last two decades of the nineteenth century, began to annex mills that had originally been constructed as separate corporations, though these too had been founded by the Boston Associates and managed by overlapping directorships. Thus, by 1905, the Amoskeag Company had become the only large textile corporation in the city (Brown 1915, Blood 1948). The Stark Mills, the sole exception to the Amoskeag's dominance, were annexed in 1922.

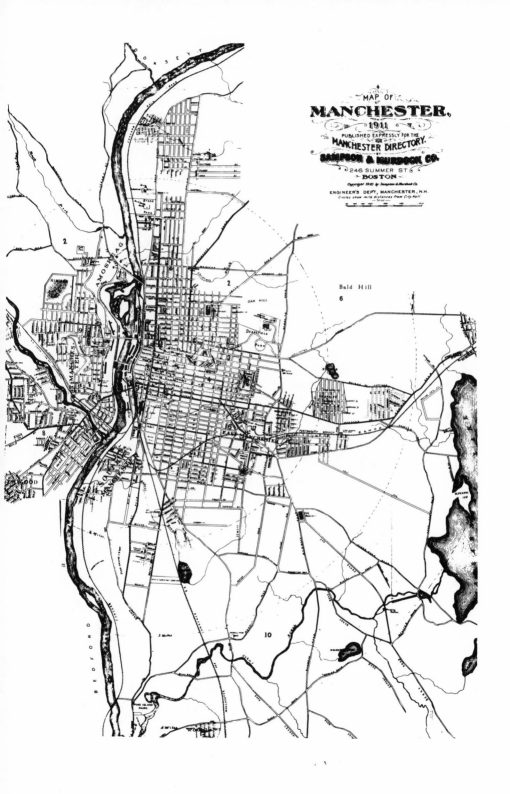

MAP OF
MANCHESTER,
1911
PUBLISHED EXPRESSLY FOR THE
MANCHESTER DIRECTORY.
BY
SAMPSON & MURDOCK CO.
246 SUMMER ST
BOSTON

Copyright 1910 by Sampson & Murdock Co.

ENGINEER'S DEPT, MANCHESTER, N.H.
Circles show mile distances from City Hall.
Scale

By any standard, the Amoskeag was a giant. At its peak, in the early twentieth century, it was the world's largest textile plant, employing up to seventeen thousand workers. The Amoskeag encompassed approximately thirty major mills, each equivalent to an entire textile mill elsewhere. Combined with numerous related buildings, these mills covered a total of eight million square feet of floor space, an area almost equal to that of the World Trade Center in New York City. The Amoskeag housed a total of seventy-four separate cloth-making departments, three dyehouses, twenty-four mechanical and electrical departments, three major steam power plants, and a hydroelectric power station. The company was almost totally self-sufficient in its operations and carried out all of its own design and construction, even of the largest mills. For a time, it also manufactured locomotives and Civil War rifles, as well as textile machinery. In 1906 the Amoskeag employed seven thousand women and six thousand men and it produced four million yards of cloth per week of a great variety, including tickings, denims, stripes, ginghams, and cotton flannels (*Manchester Union*, August 27, 1906). By 1915 it turned out cloth at the rate of fifty miles per hour.

The Amoskeag Mills, more than the mills in any of the sister communities, were distinguished by the integrity of the spaces and the splendor of their architectural design. It is the front of the mill yard, facing the city, that dramatically underscores the architectural and social designs behind the Amoskeag. The front wall along the canal is pierced by archways, bridges, and wrought-iron gates. It is punctuated by the conspicuous bay window that marked the agent's office, the symbol of the Amoskeag's immediate center of control. A large cluster of boardinghouses, constructed in the style of federal town houses and owned by the corporation, faced the solid wall of mills. The resulting design resembled a walled, medieval city, with the mill yard reinforcing the sense of enclosure. The most striking aspects of the Amoskeag mill yard were its organic unity and visual continuity, products of more than seventy-five years of almost continuous construction by the corporation's own engineers and craftsmen. It was a rare example in the United States of a large-scale, long-term, coordinated approach to urban design. Even the bricks used in later additions were carefully matched in color to those of the earliest buildings.

The mill yard was open at each end, with tree-lined canals and railroad tracks running its entire length on two different levels above the river. Instead of a long, straight avenue, however, a gentle curve softened the rigor of the design, dividing the mill yard into identifiable spaces. "These carefully designed and meticulously maintained spaces were a supreme expression of the unbounded confidence of the Victorian age, rooted not only in the belief of continuing material progress but also in the conviction that no social problem could stand in the way of the headlong rush for industrial improvement" (Langenbach 1968). The bell towers, which were deliberately aligned with the city streets so as to be visible from all directions, were the most prominent expression of the corporation's sense of pride. Their visual domination of the city's skyline and internal space, combined with the sound of their bells symbolizing the corporation's power, made a lasting impact on the workers. But as Tommy Smith, a former superintendent in the dyehouse, recalled, the most unforgettable sight was that of the thousands of people pouring out of the gates at the sound of the bells:

> Each of the mills had its own bell tower; and when the signal came over the electric wire, the bell ringers would jump onto the ropes. I used to watch them to see how high they could jump. They'd pull the rope down with all their weight. The ropes went up through all the floors to the bell tower, and all the bells would ring.
>
> When the bells rang, it was time to go home. The people flocked out of the mills. All the gates on Canal Street would be opened, and the people would come across the bridge. That was something to see. Picture the people coming out of the main gate on Stark Street! They'd be hustling and joking – nine thousand people trying to get out of those gates to get home as quickly as possible [*Amoskeag*, pp. 223–4].

The rush of the crowd leaving the mill yard when the bells rang was imprinted in the memories of many workers. It also frequently impressed visitors to the city. In 1905, a reporter compared the rush of workers from the mill to the rush of bees from their hive: "Never have I seen such a way of life as takes place from the Manchester Mills at the noon hour or at 6 o'clock" (*Manchester Mirror*, November 8, 1905).

To encourage the development of business and private housing in Manchester, the Amoskeag auctioned off land to private buyers for stores and residences and, at the same time, endowed churches and ethnic social clubs with land, all according to a master plan conceived in the 1830s. The plan went beyond a mere layout for streets and houses to include an elaborate set of restrictions and rules that controlled the nature of private development. The deed restrictions included limitations on the number and size of the houses in the residential areas ("to avoid overcrowding") and even on the types of materials allowed for the construction of buildings in the commercial areas. These plans and restrictions were followed in subsequent developments during the entire history of the company.[5]

As the corporation grew and consolidated production under one centralized management, the city itself expanded and diversified. Yet two-thirds of Manchester's employment opportunities remained dependent on the Amoskeag Company. In fact, until the 1930s, no new industry could be established in Manchester without the Amoskeag's permission because the company controlled practically all the available industrial land. To many people, the Amoskeag was Manchester.

The Amoskeag's control of Manchester was different, however, from that of the Pullman Corporation in Pullman, Illinois, or of southern mill villages.[6] Manchester was not a company town in the strict sense of the word. At the beginning of the twentieth century, only about 15% of all the workers' housing was owned by the corporation. There was no company store. Manchester was a lively city full of private shops, movie houses, and dance halls. It had grown into one of the largest industrial cities in New England, boasting a population of fifty-five thousand. Between 1888 and 1891, three shoe shops opened in Manchester, and the 7-20-4 Cigar Factory opened in the 1890s. Most cigar workers were Belgian, and only a few of their relatives worked in the Amoskeag. The shoe factories, on the other hand, fulfilled an important backup function for the Amoskeag workers, providing an alternative source of employment in the city's limited occupational structure. The workers perceived the Amoskeag's control of their lives. As a former weaver, William Moul, put it: "It seemed like you were locked in when the Amoskeag owned the mills" (Amoskeag, p. 11).

The Amoskeag Company's domination of the economic life of the city gave it great influence over its political life as well. Amoskeag overseers and other officials served on the board of aldermen; Herbert A. Salls, for example, overseer in the worsted department, was on the board of aldermen in 1911. Management retained close ties with the police force, which proved a most useful connection during the strikes of the 1920s and 1930s.

Although the Amoskeag bestowed certain advantages on the city, its dominance also exacted heavy tolls. This was particularly true for workers and their families during the long and bitter strike of

1922 and during the subsequent period of the corporation's decline, when employment opportunities became almost nonexistent. The shutdown of the mills in 1936 devastated the entire city.

Absentee management and remote control also affected the spirit of both the mill and the city. At no time did Manchester residents own a significant portion of Amoskeag stock. The Amoskeag Company was managed by a board of directors, many of whom were prominent Boston financiers. Few had more than small investments in Amoskeag securities; most had little familiarity with the Amoskeag plant. The treasurer, the man almost solely in charge of the management of the Amoskeag, ran the mills out of the Boston office and had little contact with the workers and managers in Manchester. The agent – a local, salaried official – represented the board of directors and was in charge of executing, and to some extent planning, most aspects of production and handling all matters concerning personnel and labor relations. The agent was the corporation's top executive and representative in Manchester. He exercised a good deal of authority but received his instructions from the Boston office and was ultimately accountable to the treasurer (Creamer and Coulter 1939).

The Amoskeag Company had only six agents in its entire history. Three agents were from three generations of the same family: the Straws. Ezekial Straw, who later became governor of New Hampshire, became agent in 1856, having worked as an engineer for the company since 1838. He set the pattern for corporate paternalism, which his son, Herman, later retained and adapted to a newly arrived immigrant labor force. Herman Straw, whose tenure as agent represents the peak period in the Amoskeag's development, retired in 1919 but continued to act as a consultant for the company until his death in 1929. William Parker Straw failed to command the same loyalty and respect his father had, particularly during the period of the corporation's decline and the labor struggles of the 1920s. The integrity and loyalty of the Straws were such that to most workers, the Straws were the Amoskeag. Some workers even thought that the Straws owned the company. F. C. Dumaine, who succeeded T. Jefferson Coolidge as treasurer in 1906, did not really enter the employees' lives until the nine-month-long strike of 1922.[7]

As the Amoskeag emerged as a major modern corporation in the post–Civil War period, the composition of its labor force changed. In the decades after the Civil War, the New England mill girls were replaced by immigrant workers. The first to arrive were Irish family groups who came to Manchester in the 1850s and 1860s, despite the

Amoskeag's initial reluctance to allow them into the city. By 1870 there was almost an equal number of men and women in the Amoskeag's labor force. There was thus a double implication to the transformation of the work force: The transition from native to immigrant workers was coupled with a transition from the mill girl as the base of the textile mills' labor force to entire family units. In 1860, the foreign-born constituted 27% of Manchester's population. Of the 5,480 foreign-born residents, 3,976 had come from Ireland. By 1890 the foreign-born constituted 45.5% of Manchester's population. Among the foreign-born, the French Canadians constituted the largest single group, 28%; the Irish had dropped to 10%. Although the proportion of foreign-born dropped slightly to 45% in 1900, it remained constant throughout the next decade (Hanlan 1979).

The influx of larger numbers of immigrants in the three post-Civil War decades resulted in the emergence of immigrant neighborhoods, differentiated by their ethnic character and clustering around their respective churches. The first major immigrant neighborhood had developed near St. Anne's Church, the first Catholic church in Manchester, which the Irish had established. In this neighborhood, one-half of the population were listed as foreign-born in the 1870 census, although virtually all native-born residents in that neighborhood had parents of foreign birth. The Amoskeag also began to absorb German and Swedish immigrants in small numbers, mainly as skilled craftsmen, as well as skilled textile mechanics and dye experts from Scotland. The Scots were recruited to teach various skills to local workers. The Amoskeag brought approximately eight "Scotch girls," who were skilled gingham weavers, to Manchester after a thorough search in different villages around Glasgow.[8] Skilled and semiskilled Scots immigrants followed in the wake of the gingham weavers and the dye experts in the late nineteenth and early twentieth centuries. And they, in turn, were followed by less skilled immigrants. The ties between Glasgow, the center of the Scottish emigration, and Manchester were so close that the same family owned one boardinghouse in Glasgow and another in Manchester (Tommy Smith and Lewis and Virginia Erskine, interview).

French-Canadian immigrants, driven from rural Quebec by land scarcity, depleted farms, and poverty, began in the 1870s to enter the labor force of the Amoskeag mills, as well as those in various other New England industrial towns.[9] An interviewee, repeating her father's deathbed admonition, expressed the despair shared by many Quebec farmers: "When I'm gone, don't keep this land. *Sell it*" (Lena Saucier, interview).

By the turn of the century, in addition to French-Canadian farmers, the Amoskeag and other New England mills began to attract textile workers who were driven out of the mills in eastern townships in Quebec by cheap labor imported by mill owners from northern Quebec (Harvey 1978). By 1900 the steady recruitment of French Canadians into the Amoskeag had significantly altered Manchester's population. Priests in Quebec, who had earlier resisted their parishioners' immigration to New England, now succumbed and proceeded to establish parishes in Manchester. The first French parishes were founded in the 1870s and 1880s.[10]

The Amoskeag Company, like other New England textile corporations, soon concluded that French Canadians were the ideal labor force and proceeded to recruit them systematically. In the late nineteenth century, mill agents from New England became a well-known phenomenon in the Quebec countryside. The editor of the New England newspaper *Le Travailleur* testified before the Massachusetts Bureau of the Statistics of Labor about the pervasiveness of this practice:

> I have a letter from an agent of the Boston and Maine Railroad who says he is ready to testify that since two years, no less than one-hundred superintendents or agents of mills have applied to him for French help, one mill asking for as many as fifty families at a time [Massachusetts Bureau of the Statistics of Labor 1882:17].

The Amoskeag had a special advantage in the recruitment of French Canadians because of its location on the direct railroad route between Montreal and Boston. In addition, the Amoskeag's advertisements in Quebec newspapers – elaborate descriptions of the fine working conditions and attractive opportunities, accompanied by photographs of the mill yard – were convincingly designed to attract farmers as well as industrial workers. The typical advertisement read:

> More than 15,000 persons work in these mills that border on both sides of the river. Their wages allow them comfort and ease and all seem to be content with their lot. It is true that the larger company to which they sell their labor treats them as its own children . . . [The article here proceeds to enumerate the welfare activities of the company.] That is the reason why the Amoskeag Company has never had any trouble with its employees. It treats them not as machines but as human beings, as brothers who

Table 2.1. *Amoskeag Mills, ethnicity and sex of employees by department and workrooms*

Department	American		Irish		English		French		German		Scottish		Polish		Greek		Other	
	M	F	M	F	M	F	M	F	M	F	M	F	M	F	M	F	M	F
Cotton																		
Carding	37	21	29	71	7	15	176	116	12	3	9	2	359	180	129	20	89	23
Spinning	18	42	21	56	6	5	372	665	9	1	6	1	7	19	275	168	27	16
Dressing	86	109	53	138	9	11	150	344	14	15	14	20	4	2	14	1	10	12
Weaving	107	84	84	202	16	25	730	1,074	192	111	31	87	514	666	142	67	98	56
Cloth rooms	130	58	92	43	34	7	211	22	28	15	29	11	28	2	2	—	59	6
Dye houses	22	—	115	—	13	—	30	—	9	—	51	—	97	—	23	—	33	—
Yard	25	—	20	2	4	1	91	—	1	—	2	—	34	—	9	—	22	—
Mechanical power	207	3	221	4	37	—	172	—	35	—	43	—	1	—	—	—	50	—
Land/water power	64	—	83	—	5	—	151	—	6	—	15	—	7	—	—	—	3	—
Miscellaneous	94	8	66	8	15	1	70	3	24	4	7	1	16	—	6	—	14	4
Clerical	66	81	6	22	6	2	6	4	6	6	2	3	1	—	1	—	1	3
Overseers and officials	88	22	11	—	4	—	4	—	8	—	5	—	—	—	—	—	3	—
Total cotton	944	408	804	546	156	65	2,143	2,224	342	156	214	127	1,068	868	591	257	405	121
Total males and females, cotton	1,352		1,350		221		4,367		498		341		1,936		848		526	

Worsted

Wool sorting	31	1	17	1	9	—	24	—	3	—	—	—	5	—	3	—	3	1
Carding, combing, French drawing, mule spinning	27	4	23	19	23	1	22	6	12	1	—	—	5	—	316	28	15	3
English drawing	7	8	4	123	6	3	3	33	—	—	1	3	3	—	17	43	1	—
Spin, twist	19	26	33	68	3	3	83	187	2	27	2	1	1	4	42	114	4	3
Dress, warp spool	13	17	8	45	1	4	12	141	4	36	1	7	—	—	9	—	4	5
Weaving	10	25	22	156	11	15	126	174	16	22	1	11	4	—	25	14	11	1
Wet dye, finishing	15	—	113	—	3	—	19	—	14	—	9	—	3	—	—	—	4	—
Cloth rooms	56	80	60	108	38	15	61	136	26	36	17	13	4	—	—	—	7	16
Miscellaneous	6	11	2	37	—	—	9	18	1	—	1	2	—	—	1	—	—	1
Clerical	5	25	1	10	1	2	1	—	1	2	1	2	—	—	—	—	—	—
Overseers and officials	13	—	—	—	—	—	—	—	1	—	1	—	—	4	—	1	1	—
Total worsted	201	199	303	567	95	44	361	695	79	124	33	44	16	4	413	202	51	30
Total males and females, worsted	400		870		139		1,056		203		77		20		615		81	
Total cotton and worsted	1,145	607	1,107	1,113	251	109	2,515	2,920	422	280	248	171	1,084	873	1,004	459	456	611

Note: A dash indicates there were no people in that group.
Source: Amoskeag Records, BLH.

have a right not only to wages but also to the pleasures of life . . .
Its employees work not only to earn a wage but to please their
employers, who know how to treat them well. It has resolved
with justice to itself and its workers the problem of the relations
between capital and labor [*Le Canado-Américaine*, November 10,
1913].

Although French Canadians migrated to other New England industrial towns as well, Manchester was exceptional in the size and
cohesion of the French-Canadian community that developed on its
west side beginning in the late nineteenth century. Even today, this
section of the city is often referred to as Little Canada ("La Petite
Canada"). By 1910, French Canadians comprised 35% of the
Amoskeag's labor force and 38% of the city's population.

Because management characterized the French Canadians as
"docile," "industrious," and "stable," they were especially wel-
come. In addition, they were considered desirable for the textile
industry because of the large number of children in their families.
By contracting with one worker, the Amoskeag frequently enlisted
an entire family, with the likelihood that additional kin would follow later with their own large families.

Their emergence as a critical majority of the mill's labor force by
no means gave the French Canadians a position of power, though
they did fill a significant portion of the skilled and semiskilled jobs.
(For a complete ethnic breakdown of the Amoskeag Company, see
Table 2.1.) The ranks of overseer and second hand were confined,
by and large, to native-born Americans, English, Scottish, and second-generation Irish, with an occasional sprinkling of Germans
and Swedes. The French Canadians drew their strength from sheer
numbers. In many workrooms, the bosses were forced to learn
some French in order to maintain smooth operations.

Later immigrants, particularly Poles and Greeks, came in smaller
numbers and never achieved the same strength and influence.
Poles started coming to Manchester, first from other New Hampshire and New England communities and later directly from Poland. In 1902 the 850 Poles in Manchester founded their first parish.
By 1920 the city's Polish population had grown to two thousand,
with Poles comprising approximately 10% of the Amoskeag's labor
force. The Greeks began to appear in Manchester around the turn of
the century; they were first recruited into the shoe factories and
eventually entered the textile mills as well, and by 1920 they constituted as large a proportion of the Amoskeag's labor force as did the
Poles (Creamer and Coulter 1939).

As a result of the influx of immigrants into Manchester, neighborhoods were transformed from the 1870s on. In 1882 almost half the population was foreign-born in two of the city's census districts. Only two of the city's wards had a predominantly native population – in Ward 6, 82% and in Ward 7, 72%. In Ward 4, on the other hand, 80% of the residents were French Canadians, and in Ward 3, 42% were French Canadians. Ethnic differentiation of most neighborhoods had also become prominent. In 1882 the city marshal, in taking a special census, classified the ethnic groups in Ward 5, the city's first Irish neighborhood, surrounding St. Anne's Church, as consisting of 43% native-born, 25% Canadian, and 28% Irish. Except for immigrants from the British Isles, who comprised 2% of the population, other ethnic groups were of inconsequential proportions.[11]

Within the neighborhood stretching from the immediate mill yard into the downtown area (Ward 5), the Irish, the French Canadians, and the Scots clustered in specific city blocks along Elm Street, Manchester's main downtown business street. The French Canadians constituted 60% of the residents of one part of Elm Street, and the Irish, who had previously dominated this section, now constituted only 10%. Along Park Street in the same ward, 47% of the residents were native-born, 36% were Irish, and 13.5% were French Canadians. A considerable proportion of the natives were of foreign (especially Irish) parentage.[12]

Initially, the immigrant population lived in mixed neighborhoods stretching into the central city and downtown area beyond the corporation's district, although within each neighborhood ethnic groups clustered in specific blocks. In what had been the original Irish neighborhood, French Canadians lived in separate blocks around St. Augustine's Church. The Poles on Manchester and Merrimack streets gradually replaced the Irish, who had moved farther southeast of the mill yard, and Spruce Street became "Little Greece." As one Greek woman reminisced about the richness of the "little cities within a city":

> Manchester was divided into an amazing network of ethnic communities. Cedar Street was the Middle East in all its splendor, mostly, Syrians. Little Greece was on Spruce Street one thoroughfare away. The French in west Manchester were so ethnic that you needed an interpreter to enter. The Chinese, with their impeccable laundries, had scattered throughout the city [Vasiliki Georgeopolis Chambers, *Manchester Sunday News*, November 16, 1980].

German immigrants clustered in individual and two-family houses in a newly developed section of the West Side following the sale of land by the Amoskeag. The major part of the West Side emerged, however, as "Little Canada." It was Manchester's largest and most homogeneous ethnic neighborhood, with the homes of most residents aligned with the steeple of St. Marie's Church and towers of the mills.

Not only mill workers lived on the West Side. The French-Canadian community imported its own middle-class crust: shopkeepers, attorneys, doctors, and teachers. This segment of the population grew over time, as local members of the community made their entrance into it. [13]

Because the West Side emerged as a homogeneous community with its own churches, schools, social clubs, and shops, it experienced less ethnic conflict than the mixed neighborhoods, particularly in the area where the Irish were being displaced by newly arriving Poles and Greeks.

Ethnic hostilities fermented in both the neighborhoods and the mill and erupted from time to time into open conflict. Hostility toward newcomers fed on both the fear of the deterioration of one's neighborhood and the fear of the loss of one's job to the newcomers. The appearance of Greeks and Poles in the Irish area triggered a pattern of neighborhood succession. Merrimack Common, one of the central green spaces in Manchester, which had been designated by the Amoskeag to be a park, was frequently the site of fistfights between Irish and Poles.

At the same time, the entry into the mills of workers prepared to accept unskilled jobs at low pay caused anxiety over the deterioration of wages and working conditions. The experience of the shoe factories in Manchester and other neighboring textile mills had also warned the Amoskeag's workers that new immigrants could be potential strikebreakers. On a number of occasions French-Canadian workers were attacked by Irish workers on their way to work. Later, Greek workers complained that other workers were throwing rocks at them from the top of the gate at the entrance to the mill yard. One Greek worker expressed his frustration to Agent Herman Straw:

> I take up the liberty to write to you few lines stating my complain with it.
>
> I am a Greek workman, working almost two years in your Mills but I do not think that I used right in some ways.
>
> The other day when I was entering the gate and was walking down the Mill I was almost near the door of Building that I work

some one from the roof throw stone on me, not only on me but on all the Greeks and not only that day but always.

I told to the boss of my room who seems to me does not pay any attention to me forever, and so I beg your kindness to investigate the matter, or else you see us some day with broken heads.

Trusting that you may pay more or less attention,

I am,

John L——[14]

As suggested earlier, residents of corporation housing were generally native-born until the 1880s. But by 1900 considerable numbers of immigrants had penetrated this enclave as they gradually replaced the native-born and the Irish in semiskilled and skilled occupations. At the same time, the corporation dwellings were transformed from boardinghouses, substantial and attractive structures with high ceilings and hardwood floors that accommodated large numbers of individuals, into family flats, and additional "corporations" (the nickname for the corporation tenements) were built in three-to-four-story row-house family units.[15] To meet the needs of the increasing numbers of workers with large families recruited to work in the mills, the Corporation, in the 1880s and again in the 1910s, supplemented the earlier structures with additional row houses built in a similar style.

Even though the corporations were ethnically diverse, clustering along kinship and ethnic lines occurred within them. Applicants on the waiting list learned from friends or relatives about an opening and then used their connections to obtain that flat. Thus, despite the random character of the availability of openings, foresight, careful planning, and luck made ethnic and kinship clustering possible in the corporation housing. A former worker who grew up in the corporations recalled that teen-age boys had actually staked out specific ethnic boundaries and often waged gang fights over the protection of those boundaries (Mitchell Skrzyszowski, interview). But most interviewees who had lived in the corporations remember them as ethnically diverse in comparison with the homogeneous ethnic neighborhoods. Those who preferred to live in ethnic neighborhoods traded well-maintained, inexpensive housing for ethnic cohesiveness.

Although the corporations were not explicitly differentiated along ethnic lines, they were divided along job status hierarchies. The imposing brick row houses of the overseers and second hands were more spacious, better appointed, and separated by several blocks from the workers' housing. But these residential patterns did not lead to complete social segregation. The sense of the corporation as a "family" was expressed in the residence of lower skilled workers, overseers, and the agent in virtually the same neighborhood. Overseers' children went to the same schools as workers' children and all played together in the Amoskeag playground. The agent's house was located in the vicinity of the overseers' housing and was thus in proximity to the workers' housing as well. Although the Straw family owned a mansion in Manchester's North End – the exclusive upper-class neighborhood where wealthy businessmen, Amoskeag superintendents, and bankers lived – Agent William Parker Straw lived in the agent's house near the mill yard during his tenure of office.[16]

In 1903 T. M. Young described a typical Amoskeag-owned boardinghouse:

> First let the reader visit a boarding-house for mill girls which stands close to one of the mills and belongs to the mill company. It is an old block three or four stories high, and Mrs. Smith, the lady who receives us, is the lessee and manager. Her mother, who preceded her in the business, conducted it for twenty-five years, so Mrs. Smith has a good deal of inherited experience . . .
>
> Mrs. Smith occupies the house, she tells us, at a nominal rental – probably not more than one-fifth of its value – runs it as a commercial enterprise, and, as she says, "makes it pay." There are many similar boarding-houses round about the mills, and the only qualification required by the mill-owners of their tenants is a certificate of good character.
>
> The ground-floor of this house contains at one end a parlour cosily furnished with carpets, curtains, armchairs, lounges, a piano, pictures, and bric-à-brac. The girls are now all at work, but in the evenings they use it as a reading and sewing room. Next to the parlour is Mrs. Smith's office and private room, and at the opposite end of the building is a dining-room capable of seating eighty-five persons. Two classes of workpeople are allowed to use this room – first, women living in the house, who pay from 8s. 4d. to 9s. 4d. a week, and have private bedrooms, the use of bath-rooms and sitting-rooms, and three meals a day; and, secondly, other employés, men or women, who board only, and pay 9s. 4d (men) and 8s. 4d. (women) a week. Mrs. Smith says that she has eighty girls living in the house, and could let many more rooms if she had them; she serves meals to 150 people three times a day, and, as there is not room for all at once, every meal is served twice.

The bedrooms have every appearance of middle-class comfort and refinement. They are prettily carpeted; each one has its own radiator to warm it in winter. The bedsteads are brass-laquered, with white coverings. The furniture – a dressing-table, chairs, and a writing table – is of American oak, and most of the rooms have been decorated with some taste by their occupants with pictures, photographs, and knick-knacks. Only a wardrobe is missing, but you will find its substitute in the form of a substantial American trunk in the corridor outside the bedroom door.

The mill company stipulates that the fare provided in its boarding-houses shall be sufficient in quantity and in quality varied and good. The following bill of fare provided at this house does not strike one as erring on the side of parsimony:

Breakfast, from 5.30 to 6.30, always consists of porridge and milk, two kinds of hot meat, baked potatoes, hot rolls and butter, tea or coffee, and condiments.

Dinner, from 11.30 to 12.30: Soup; three kinds of hot meat; potatoes, tomatoes, corn on the cob, or other vegetables; pastry, and tea or coffee. Eight bushels of vegetables are usually needed for one meal, and the housekeeper says that to-day fifty-three tins of marrowfat peas were used at dinner.

Supper: Tea or coffee, bread-and-butter, cold meats, jam and jellies, and an iced sweet-cake something like a jam sandwich. Sometimes hot dishes are substituted for the cold meat. To-night, for instance, there is to be "clam chowder," a delicacy in high favour with Americans of all classes.

The girls are at liberty to spend their evenings where and how they please, provided they are in by ten o'clock. If they are out later than ten a satisfactory explanation is required. They arrange for their own washing, which they may do in the house (where facilities are provided) or they may send the clothes out.

Seventeen servants are employed to do the housework, and the kitchens, cold store, and ice-room are well appointed and clean. Sixty tons of coal, says Mrs. Smith, were used in the large boiler in the basement for heating the coils last winter.

It may be urged, however, that the fare in these boarding-houses is partly a gift from the mill-owners in lieu of wages; and, in so far as the rents paid for the houses are less than their value, that is in a sense true [Young 1903: 38–9].

From its inception, the Amoskeag was a paternalistic corporation, similar to its sister companies that founded Lowell and Lawrence, Massachusetts, and other planned New England industrial

Table 2.2. *Comparison of five Merrimack valley textile cities, 1903, and general manufactures in the Merrimack valley, 1905*

Town	Capital in mfg. ($)	Wage earners	Wages ($)
Haverhill	10,305,960	9,574	4,817,892
Lawrence	60,063,192	21,900	8,907,784
Lowell	54,809,638	29,393	11,580,724
Manchester	25,248,460	17,579	7,322,904
Nashua	9,405,109	6,159	2,508,135
Total	158,832,359	84,605	35,137,459

Source: Dumaine Papers, Manchester Historic Association.

communities. Unlike these other corporations, however, the Amoskeag remained under the same management over its entire existence and experienced continuity in its paternalistic policies into the beginning of the twentieth century.

Continuing its nineteenth-century tradition the Amoskeag launched a new program of corporate welfare in 1910. Introduced simultaneously with efficiency measures, the welfare program was devised to attract additional immigrants to the city, to socialize them to industrial work, to instill loyalty to the company, and to curb labor unrest and thus prevent unionization. As will be seen in Chapter 3, the program was only partly successful in meeting those objectives. As many workers were aware, despite its corporate welfare programs, the Amoskeag's wage scale was lower than that of its sister corporations in other New England towns (Table 2.2).

Wage rates and the length of the workweek fluctuated dramatically in the Amoskeag during the first two decades of the twentieth century. In 1937 economist Daniel Creamer, in association with Charles Coulter, carried out a detailed analysis of the Amoskeag's wage and hour policies in the pre–World War I period. The unweighted average full-time wage in the seventeen most important textile occupations in the mills was $9.53 a week in 1911, at about the same time that the Amoskeag launched its welfare program. A 10% increase in 1912 brought this average up to $10.55. In the succeeding two years the average wage amounted to $10.38 and $9.93, respectively. This computation was based on full-time wage rates; in reality, many employees worked only part-time or intermittently and therefore did not earn even this amount (Creamer and Coulter, 1939:182–3).

Between 1911 and 1918 the length of the workweek and wage

rates fluctuated in the Amoskeag, often involving intermittent production followed by layoffs. Prior to 1914 the official workweek was 58 hours. Although the New Hampshire state legislature established a 55-hour week in January 1914, the Amoskeag retained the wages of the longer week. In an editorial in the *Amoskeag Bulletin*, management was self-congratulatory about this act in the midst of a "nationwide industrial depression" and at the same time cited its largess as a justification for increasing discipline and production. In "Happenings," the company's announcement of events, overseers were instructed to stop the "straggling of employees from different departments through the yard and congregating in the hall and stairways just before noon and night . . . With the new 55-hour law it becomes more than ever necessary that employees work and that machines be kept running the full-time required by the rules of the company" (January 5, 1914).

Many of the average weekly wage rates described above were actually based on piece rates rather than hourly wages. By 1910, most of the major textile occupations in the Amoskeag had been placed on a piece-rate system – a method of compensation in which the worker is paid by a defined unit of output. In some jobs the workers were paid strictly by the unit; in others they had to meet a set quota each day in order to earn the standard rate (see Chapter 11).

In the winter of 1914–15, as a result of depressed conditions in the industry, production was reduced and entire departments shut down temporarily. When they reopened, a 40-hour workweek was instituted and the average weekly wage in the manufacturing departments sank to $7.37. In the mechanical departments, the comparable figure was $9.62. However, in 1916, under the impact of wartime production and in response to a wage increase in neighboring mills, the Amoskeag twice raised wages by 5%, and with a return to full production the workweek was once again 55 hours in some departments and 50 hours in others. The cost of living had also increased. Food in Manchester was 12.9% more costly in 1916 than in 1913, and the wage increase over that period was 14.9% (Creamer and Coulter, 1939:184).

Between 1913 and 1916, as neighboring mills in the Merrimack valley granted wage increases to keep up with the cost of living, the Amoskeag's wage increases continued to lag behind those of other mills by 12.5%. When the Amoskeag increased wages by 7.5%, the other mills increased them by 10%.

The workers were well aware of the meaning of those wages and hours. "When we first came [in 1895] we worked six days a week. We'd start at 7 A.M. and work till 6 P.M., on Saturdays till 4 P.M. That made it a long day, but in the mills we had an hour to eat," recalled Antonia Bergeron, who earned $6 a week. "When I was earning a dollar a day, it didn't take me long to get rid of it . . . You'd buy a piece of Indian cotton, 5 cents a yard" (*Amoskeag*, p. 61).

Marie Proulx, who started work in 1906, was paid $4.20 a week. "I had to resign myself to working there," she recalled. "It was not enough for our expenses . . . Four dollars and twenty cents per week – I couldn't go far with that." Her earnings contrasted dramatically with the corporation's profits. "And you earned $8,000 per day for the corporation," her husband, Omer, suggested to her. "The spindles that you ran took $11 per pound. Marie had 125 spindles per frame, and she ran six of those" (*Amoskeag*, p. 68).

As a young boy, Raymond Dubois worked as a doffer in the spinning room about 41 hours a week earning 38 cents an hour, or $15.58 a week: "For a young boy, this was adequate pay." But the older women who mounted the empty bobbins on the spinning frames were paid $12 a week. "They used the older women to put the empty bobbins on because they were cheaper labor" (*Amoskeag*, p. 153). Anna Schmidt, a former burler, recalled being paid $14.15 every two weeks. "That's sixty hours a week – imagine!" (*Amoskeag*, p. 213).

In June 1918, when six other mills granted 15% increases versus the Amoskeag's 12.5%, the discrepancy provoked a strike by the United Textile Workers' Union, which had succeeded in organizing the workers and in establishing itself officially under the regulation of the War Production Board. This strike was the first led by a trade union in the Amoskeag since an 1886 strike led by the Knights of Labor. The strike halved production in the mills. Because the Amoskeag was working primarily on war orders, the secretary of war dispatched an arbitrator, who granted the workers their demand for a 15% pay increase instead of the 12.5% the Amoskeag had offered. The strike was settled within five days, but in the process the union had added five thousand new members (Creamer and Coulter 1939:191–2).[17]

The union's foothold in the corporation remained limited, however. The main concession that it succeeded in obtaining was the formation of an adjustment board, composed of representatives of management and labor, to investigate and rule on grievances filed by individual workers or groups of workers through "grievance" committees.

Under the impact of war production, the Amoskeag, along with other mills in the region, acceded to a number of wage increases at the request of the Textile Council of the United Textile Workers. The first, in May 1919, was a 15% wage increase to remain in effect without change until the third Monday in April 1920. In December 1919 an additional advance of 12.5% was granted. The last wage increase in the postwar boom period occurred at the end of May 1920. After that, a depression set in and was reflected in curtailments in different departments. Production in the cotton division was cut down to three days a week. After a two-week complete shutdown in January 1921, production was resumed with a 22.5% reduction in the wage scale.[18]

The 20% wage reduction announced in February 1922, which triggered the first major strike in the Amoskeag's history, eliminated the real wage gains made during the years 1918–20. The return to the 54-hour week shortened the workweek by only one hour since 1914. These changes were accompanied by an increase in work loads. Similar wage cuts in most New England textile cities at the same time also precipitated strikes.

The Amoskeag strike of 1922, the first long-term general strike in the company's history, marked the turning point for both the workers and the mills. The nine-month-long strike ended after the strikers accepted the corporation's restoration of the pre-strike wages, but the workers lost their battle for the 48-hour week.

The Amoskeag's decline began in the post–World War I period and ended with its final shutdown in 1936. Ironically, the seeds of the company's decline were hidden in its success. Its enormity was both a factor in its durability and a cause of its ultimate collapse. To save on the cost of making each yard of cloth, the Amoskeag had added spindles, thus increasing its production beyond the capacity of the market. In the long run, southern competition, antiquated machinery, inefficiency, changing fashions in the textile market, and high labor costs defeated the New England textile mills. By the 1920s, when workers in other areas of the United States were experiencing prosperity, the workers in the Amoskeag were rehearsing for the Great Depression. The 1921–3 recession was thus only a prelude to a period of calamitous decline for New England's textile industry. Inevitably, the recession of the early 1920s led to the closing, before World War II, of most large cotton mills in the region. A significant number of mills in Lowell, for instance, either relocated in the South or simply liquidated during the 1920s; and few believed that a future existed for New England cotton mills.

The Amoskeag found it difficult to modernize because of the

enormous costs entailed in retooling a plant of its size, although the Boston office did take several steps deemed crucial to the continued operation of the mills in order to secure its investment. The most important step was the reorganization of 1925. After several years of increasingly large losses, Treasurer F. C. Dumaine moved to protect the $18 million cash reserve that the corporation had accumulated during times of affluence. To accomplish this, he divided the Amoskeag Manufacturing Company into two companies: a holding company, called the Amoskeag Company, and the Amoskeag Manufacturing Company, which became a subsidiary of the holding company. The plant in Manchester and all the stock in trade were transferred to the Amoskeag Manufacturing Company; the liquid capital was almost entirely retained by the holding company (Creamer and Coulter 1939). Under this so-called Plan of Reorganization Dumaine effectively sealed the fate of the Manchester operation. By leaving the manufacturing company with insufficient cash for modernizing and properly maintaining the large plant, he made its eventual shutdown almost a certainty. The cash reserve, rather than being distributed, was isolated in the holding company and controlled by Dumaine himself, protected from further losses in the manufacturing division (Creamer and Coulter 1939).

In 1927 the Amoskeag Company warded off an attempt by a group of New York entrepreneurs to purchase a controlling interest, with the object of liquidating both companies and distributing the assets, which were at that time of greater value than the market value of the stock. Dumaine devised a plan that allowed disenchanted stockholders who wanted to sell to exchange their stock for twenty-year, 6% bonds, with the debt resting on the Amoskeag Manufacturing Company. This action consolidated Dumaine's personal control of the manufacturing company by replacing the payment of dividends (which is done only when a profit is made) with the payment of 6% interest (which is a legal obligation). This bond debt figured most prominently in the reorganization attempt prior to liquidation. Because the holding company held 31.6% of the bonds, the manufacturing company was, in effect, continuing to pay the holding company after its capital had been stripped away.

The meaning of this financial manipulation did not escape the attention of the Amoskeag workers. The $18 million withdrawn from the manufacturing company was, they claimed, a surplus created by their labor, funds that should be used to keep the plant running in hard times. In fact, the distrust and antagonism on the part of the workers became major obstacles to the continued running of the plant, and the subsequent hearings investigating the closing of the mills had to be transferred to Boston because local hostility in Manchester was too intense.

By then, the anger was directed at F. C. Dumaine, although as late as October 1935, Dumaine reportedly said that there would be no liquidation of the plant "as long as there is a breath in my body." However, by December the corporation had applied for reorganization in the New Hampshire bankruptcy court, and on July 10, 1936, Arthur Black, the special master in the bankruptcy proceedings, recommended liquidation. Ten days later the federal judge ordered the plant liquidated. The flood of March 1936 had all but precluded the possibility of reopening the mill on a reorganized basis because the cost of repairing the damage would have exceeded the available capital.

Following a U.S. Senate investigation into the financial structure of the Amoskeag Company, the special investigator announced that "the activities of the holding and manufacturing companies savor of nothing short of financial sabotage" (*Manchester Leader*, September 17, 1936). Later his assistant was quoted in the October 2, 1937, *Manchester Leader* as saying: "The evidence here shows . . . a willful disregard of the public moneys invested, to say nothing about what is happening to the mill employees and the community of Manchester."

Despite the evident signs of decline, the repeated threats to shut down the plant, and the financial maneuvering, many workers appear not to have read the writing on the wall. In the week ending March 8, 1935, the Amoskeag employed 11,014 workers; by the end of June, the number of employees had been reduced to 6,000 and by September 15 to fewer than 1,000. Even when all work stopped later in September, the workers viewed the shutdown as temporary. The company had been operating for one hundred years; it was inconceivable that it would suddenly go out of business. During the flood of 1936, when river bridges were destroyed and a great deal of the plant's equipment was threatened, former employees, still expecting the Amoskeag to reopen, worked around the clock to rescue the machinery.

The ranks of the unemployed continued to grow. In 1935, 6,272 workers registered with the State Employment Service. By 1938, 11,072 were registered. Prior to the Amoskeag's shutdown, the burden of relief had been greater on Manchester than on other New England industrial cities; after the shutdown, relief facilities were totally inadequate to cope with the staggering unemployment rates.

By November 1935, 22.8% of Manchester's families were on relief. The Work Projects Administration (WPA) started employing people in the city that fall. By February 1936, 3,753 persons were employed on WPA projects and 3,160 were receiving general relief (Creamer and Coulter 1939:99–104).

During the months following the shutdown, one-quarter of the Amoskeag's former workers left the city. Emigration from Manchester in 1936 exceeded by 53% the annual average of emigration over the preceding five years. For former Amoskeag workers there was a 93% increase. Many sought jobs in neighboring New England towns or returned to Quebec (Creamer and Coulter 1939:96).

Recovery after the shutdown was a slow process. In 1936 Arthur Moreau, onetime mayor of Manchester, and a number of concerned citizens, including William Parker Straw, formed the Amoskeag Industries, a corporation designed to buy the Amoskeag properties and attract new companies to Manchester through the sale of mill space and machinery. Beginning in 1936, companies began buying or renting space in the mill yard to start new operations, and in the following years, the Amoskeag mill yard became the site of a number of smaller textile mills and other businesses, most of which were short-lived. Many of these businesses were branches of companies headquartered elsewhere; others were newly established small plants, including dyeing mills, garment factories, shoe factories, a rayon knitting mill, a finishing plant for broom handles, and a casket company. (The Amoskeag industries also bought the corporation tenements, where many former workers continued to live.)

By 1938, seventeen companies were operating in the mill yard, employing, however, fewer than two thousand people. Some of these companies, which employed former Amoskeag workers, shut down again during the recession of 1938. Two more stable mills – the Chicopee, a branch of the Johnson & Johnson Company, which wove gauze, and the Waumbec, which specialized in synthetic fibers –became major employers of former Amoskeag workers.[19]

Each time a new textile plant opened, former Amoskeag workers rushed to the gates, hoping that a former boss would recognize and hire them. Many who found jobs were soon unemployed once again. Lucille Bourque summarized the long history of uncertainty: "After the Amoskeag I went to the Raylaine and the Raylaine closed. I went to Textron, and that closed. So I went to Forest Hills . . . Well, that closed. And then I quit. I used to go in and out. I'd quit and go back" (*Amoskeag*, p. 306).

The Amoskeag tower and view of the millyard, 1968. (© Randolph Langenbach, 1978.)

The burling room, 1910. (Courtesy of the Manchester Historic Association.)

Albanel, Lac St. Jean, Quebec, ca. 1904. (Courtesy of the William Notman Collection, McCord Museum of McGill University, Montreal, Canada.)

Amoskeag strikers, 1922. (Courtesy of the Manchester Police Department.)

Unemployed loom fixers, after the Chicopee Mill shut down in Manchester, February 1975. (© Randolph Langenbach, 1978.)

3 The corporation's children: continuities and change in corporate paternalism

> The Amoskeag was a continuation of the old feudal system, where the lord of the country, or whoever it was, took care of hundreds of people that worked for him or were connected with him. The attitude was there.
>
> Tommy Smith, *Amoskeag*, p. 233

The Amoskeag's corporate welfare program

In the beginning of the twentieth century, the Amoskeag embarked on a corporate welfare program consistent with its earlier philosophy, and an efficiency program and new personnel policies. The company's historian identified 1911, the year of the establishment of the Amoskeag's Textile Club, as "the beginning of a movement towards a better understanding and appreciation of the condition and relation between employers and employees" (Browne 1915: 163).

The Amoskeag's corporate welfare program was by no means unique. Starting in the 1880s, a number of major American corporations and railroads had introduced a variety of employee welfare programs. Such programs grew dramatically between 1910 and 1917. Most corporations shared the same goals as the Amoskeag. The Ford Motor Company, for example, had developed an elaborate welfare system, including a profit-sharing plan and ambitious programs to supervise the employees' personal conduct and mold their character. The architectural distinction of Ford's Highland Park plant designed by Albert Kahn, played a role in the company's policy, just as the design and maintenance of the Amoskeag's much older mill yard was partly intended to keep up the morale of its labor force.[1] But despite its similarities with other companies, the employee welfare program in the Amoskeag distinguished itself by its links with the corporation's nineteenth-century paternalistic traditions.

On one level, the Amoskeag's welfare program was indigenous to the Amoskeag and represented a continuity with the corporation's traditional paternalism of the nineteenth century. It fostered an

Amoskeag "spirit," which served as an important source of identity for both workers and management. At the same time, it was representative of what John D. Rockefeller, Jr., proclaimed as the dawn of "a new day . . . in industry" (Fosdick 1956:185). The movement of welfare capitalism was intended to improve employer-employee relationships, socialize new immigrant workers to industrial mores, which were often considered synonymous with Americanization, avert or diffuse employee discontent by providing amenities, and foster workers' loyalty to and identification with the employer. In 1919 the United States Bureau of Labor Statistics defined "industrial welfare" as "anything for the comfort and improvement, intellectual or social, of the employees, over and above wages paid, which is not a necessity or required by law" (U.S., Bureau of Labor Statistics 1919:8). Under this category the bureau surveyed and analyzed 431 establishments that had introduced a variety of employee welfare measures in American industries, ranging from profit sharing to kindergartens for workers' children.

Programs in different industrial establishments carried different labels, such as "sociological work," "fellowship work," "advance work," and "industrial betterment" (Brandes 1976:10). Some industries embarked on welfare and scientific management simultaneously; others launched welfare programs only; still others concentrated on efficiency, either along Taylorist lines or by focusing exclusively on personnel management.

Spreading rapidly, welfare capitalism attracted support from religious and civic organizations, social reformers, universities, and state and federal departments of labor. Several universities, including the University of Chicago and Yale University, introduced courses in industrial welfare. Industrial welfare programs received outright endorsement and encouragement from President Theodore Roosevelt. President Taft, in cooperation with the National Civic League, was instrumental in introducing welfare programs for government agencies. President Wilson adopted industrial welfare to stimulate industrial production during World War I (Brandes 1976).

The National Civic Federation, founded by Marcus A. Hanna, a Cleveland businessman and President McKinley's adviser, and Samuel Gompers, president of the American Federation of Labor, stimulated welfare programs in industry and also served as a clearinghouse for the dissemination of information. In July 1904 the Civic Federation brought together representatives from many prominent corporations that had already introduced welfare measures and organized a committee to promote welfare work throughout American industry. In the pre–World War years the Civic Federation enjoyed the support of both union leaders and anti-union business leaders (Brandes 1976:21–6).[2]

Within the wide spectrum of programs introduced in various industrial establishments, the Amoskeag's program was modest. Except for the corporation housing, an institution as old as the company, its major focus was on social and recreational activities and to some extent on health services, rather than on overall improvements in the workers' lives. The Amoskeag never introduced a profit-sharing plan and its employee retirement program provided only a limited pension plan. Its image as a company that supported major welfare programs nevertheless survived in workers' memories because of the elaborately maintained corporation housing, the social activities sponsored by the corporation, and the overall grandeur and scale of the mill yard.

The Amoskeag's industrial welfare programs fit into three strategies of managerial reform that, according to Montgomery (1979), distinguished the transition of American industry into the modern factory and corporate management: institution of employee welfare plans, professionalization of personnel management, and scientific management in the strict sense of Taylorism. Although the Amoskeag made a major commitment in the first two areas, it only flirted with Taylorism, introducing "scientific management" on a limited scale. But efficiency and welfare became important slogans in the Amoskeag during this time, and the two programs were intertwined.[3]

The Amoskeag's effort to professionalize and centralize personnel management was introduced simultaneously with the employee welfare program. At its core was the employment office, established in 1911 and modeled on similar offices that were coming into being at this time throughout the United States.[4] Most welfare activities were administered through the employment office, and William Swallow, its director, was in charge of both.

The major function of the employment office was to centralize all employee appointments, transfers, and dismissals. Previously, each overseer had hired and fired his own workers, but under the new system a worker seeking a job first applied to the employment office.

The major purpose of this procedure was to set up a rational hiring process by controlling the flow of workers into different departments, by matching up workers' skills with job openings, and by counteracting the overseers' favoritism. The employment clerks maintained a cumulative file for each worker, which included severance slips that recorded the worker's conduct, as well as his or her reason for leaving. In addition to placement, the employment office analyzed workers' employment patterns and employee turnover.

The new system was intended to curb labor turnover, which plagued the Amoskeag and most other major corporations in this period. Management believed that the systematic registration of hiring and firing would limit the flow of workers in and out of the mill in search of other jobs and curb their tendency to take off during the hunting and fishing seasons.

An important aim of the employment office was to flag "troublemakers" and "agitators" in an effort to prevent strikes. The employment office kept blacklists and investigated workers systematically, including in their files additional materials such as court records or newspaper clippings on former workers' whereabouts and arrests of current and former workers. Lists of "agitators," "communists," and "troublemakers" were generated systematically by the employment office in the 1920s.

Joseph Debski, who worked as a clerk in the employment office from 1911 until 1929, recalled the procedure:

> I kept the records of the people employed and the people that left the company. We had a daily report to make out on everybody that was hired that day and everybody that left. If an overseer fired somebody, he'd put a reason down on his final check. There'd be a stub there to say why, and we'd keep that as a matter of record. In the record we had everybody that ever worked in the Amoskeag. We therefore had a running account of just what they could do and what they couldn't do.
>
> When we were interviewing people, the first thing we would ask them was what job they were looking for. Then I'd say, "Where did you work before?" They'd say, "Here." "What's your name?" We'd go to the dead file and get their records. If the record warranted that they were good, we'd hire them. If they weren't so good, I'd say, "I can't hire you today," or "There's nothing for you." In other words, if they're all right – if they worked in another department and the boss said they were good – I'd give them a job if I had it . . . If a guy didn't get along with his boss, we'd give him a job in some other department, but we

> wouldn't send him back to him. You'd have to give the guy an-
> other job or else you'd run out of help . . . He might be a good
> worker for one fellow but not for another [*Amoskeag*, p. 126–7].

Once a worker was blacklisted in the Amoskeag there was almost
nowhere else in Manchester he could go.

> The boss had the power to blackball you for the rest of your days.
> The only way you could get a job there again was if you dis-
> guised yourself. Some of them did that. They would wear
> glasses, grow a mustache, change their name . . . It was either
> that or starve to death. [William Moul, *Amoskeag*, p. 11].

By attempting to counteract informal procedures in the hiring
and placement of workers, the efficiency program tried to subject
both workers and overseers to the discipline of a rational corporate
structure. This effort clashed with both the overseers' traditional
autonomy in the hiring and firing of workers and with the workers'
own customary reliance on friendship and kinship ties in obtaining
jobs or transfers. Consequently, the employment office, from its
inception, had only limited success; the older ways appealed to too
many people. Its major accomplishment was the centralization of
the flow of labor and bookkeeping; it could not totally replace the
older system of hiring and placement.

As long as jobs were open and available, the system did help to
protect workers from ruthless overseers, but in other respects, the
employment office never achieved the efficiency that had been its
aim. Overseers continued to make most of the decisions in hiring
and firing. Informal family and friendship ties continued to govern
hiring preferences. Workers who knew the "boss" approached him
directly, either on their own behalf or to find a job for a friend, and
the boss issued a request to the employment clerk, who rubber-
stamped the procedure.

Tommy Smith, former superintendent of the dyehouse, recalled
how the formal procedures were circumvented:

> Before they had an employment bureau, people would go in and
> see the overseer for a job. Then a couple of overseers down in the
> mill got caught taking bribes. It was right after they built the
> employment office. With an outfit like that, it was hard to do
> something out of the ordinary. The employment office didn't
> have to let the overseer pick his own people if they didn't want
> to, but in most cases they did. Ahern, in the employment office,
> was an extrovert Irishman, inclined to be a politician as well.
> He was a good fellow. He knew everybody around the city
> [*Amoskeag*, p. 233].

The system also worked in reverse. If the employment clerks needed a favor in placing someone, they called the overseer.

> I remember Archie Smith, the boxer. He had kidney trouble,
> couldn't walk straight or anything, and Mr. Ahern [employment
> clerk] was friendly with him. He needed a job, and Mr. Ahern
> called me up in the dyehouse and asked if I could give this man a
> job, which I did do. I took care of them, and they took care of me
> [Tommy Smith, *Amoskeag*, p. 234].

Family and ethnic ties survived as an almost undisputed principle in hiring. Smith insisted that the practice of the "Scottish" Dyehouse to hire only its own was repeated with various ethnic groups:

> As far as the dyehouse was concerned, it was run by Scotsmen all
> my life. That's my solution right there. The Scotsman that was in
> authority would hire a Scotsman over a Frenchman.
>
> Ethnic groups really did control a great percentage of the jobs –
> like if I wanted to or could use a man, and a Scotsman was in
> need of a job, I would call Mr. Swallow up and tell him I was
> sending Mr. So-and-So in to see him and to please send him
> down to the dyehouse, that I had a job for him [*Amoskeag*, p.
> 234].

The company's employee welfare program consisted of two elements: One was oriented primarily toward overseers, with the expectation that loomfixers and eventually less skilled workers would
also participate, and the other was aimed directly at the rank and
file and was intended to reach their families as well.

A key feature of the overseer program was the Amoskeag Textile
Club, which the corporation founded on June 29, 1912. The Textile
Club was intended "to advance the acquaintanceship of the employees of the Amoskeag Manufacturing Company with each other,
to provide social recreation and amusement for its members; to promote athletics and healthy sports" (Browne 1915:168). The club
sponsored annual outings to the beaches, organized baseball teams
and lessons in photography, and produced shows with employee
talent in its own theater. The Textile Club was largely financed by
proceeds from the mill remnant store; the Amoskeag also turned
over a park to the club. Converted to a sports field, the park became
"the largest and finest resort of athletic sports in New England outside of Boston" (Browne 1915:168). The elaborately designed "Textile Field," one of the corporation's wonders, a symbol of its efforts
to advance worker health and morale, was admired by outside
visitors and Amoskeag workers alike. To supply recruits for the
Amoskeag Baseball Team, which played against the Boston Red Sox

and other professional teams, the corporation even enticed professional baseball players to work in the mill. Not unlike the way colleges use football scholarships today, the Amoskeag gave athletes easy jobs and corporation housing in the overseers' section.

> Now Jack Howard had a very good job in the mills, but he was brought here because he was a baseball pitcher, just like they bring people to college because they are good players. Exactly! He was the Amoskeag's star pitcher. He had been to Holy Cross, and from Holy Cross he went to the Philadelphia Athletics and threw his arm out. He recovered enough so that he was still a good pitcher, but they didn't want him back again. He used to take care of the dress room in the mill. He'd supply them with the warping tickets. He floated from mill to mill, seeing what they had in process and what was to be taken care of. He had that job until the mill went out [Dorothy Moore, *Amoskeag*, p. 178].

The Textile Club's publication, the *Amoskeag Bulletin*, which appeared bimonthly between 1912 and 1922, was a major propaganda vehicle for the corporation, publishing its social announcements, recording amusing anecdotes, fostering high standards, and preaching the work ethic. From its first issue, the *Bulletin* published biographical sketches and portraits of overseers, thereby providing models for the workers of the men who had risen to the most coveted of accessible ranks within the corporation's structure.

The Textile Club also sponsored contests for poems about the Amoskeag. William Swallow, director of the employment office, won the contest for a poem entitled "Amoskeag, old Amoskeag,"[5] to be sung to the tune of "Maryland, My Maryland":

> Thou wert so rich and strong of yore
> > Amoskeag, old Amoskeag.
> Thy size the world n'er saw before
> > Amoskeag, old Amoskeag.
> Thy trade mark, emblem of the best,
> Thy fabrics spread from East to West,
> Thy spindles whirled with n'er a rest,
> > Amoskeag, old Amoskeag.
>
> Through all the years thy name has stood
> > Amoskeag, old Amoskeag.
> For honest worth and nation's good
> > Amoskeag, old Amoskeag.
> When threatening storms and foes arise
> To dim thy splendor, dwarf thy size,

Thy stalwarts will not yield the prize
    Amoskeag, old Amoskeag.

The breaking dawn reveals the way
    Amoskeag, our Amoskeag.
Co-operation wins the day
    Amoskeag, our Amoskeag.
Thy sons and daughters with their might
Will keep thine emblem ever bright.
Success and fame are thine by right
    Amoskeag, our Amoskeag.

For rank-and-file workers, the most significant and continuing Amoskeag contribution to welfare was the "corporations." The rent, approximately $1 per room per month, was substantially lower than the market rate for the rest of the city, and the buildings were carefully maintained by the Amoskeag's maintenance crews (see Appendix E). An inspector from the Labor Department who visited the tenements concluded:

> The corporation tenements demonstrate that their owners have a sense of responsibility, a regard for the condition of the homes in which the operatives live. The tenement houses, instead of being great ill-shaped, rambling structures, are solidly built and comfortable, and, as a rule, have never more than three families to one entrance. An effort seems to have been made to secure the privacy of family life, which is so essential to happiness. The presence of a front door bell is of itself a mark of civilization [*Manchester Mirror*, August 22, 1889].

In their recollections, most former workers consistently praised the corporation's housing and especially its maintenance of good housing conditions. They noted the sturdiness of the buildings and the consistently low rents:

> They had six rooms with a basement, a bath, and central heat. They were very well cared for by the company, which had a department of tenement maintenance who would come out and knock on your door every springtime and ask if maybe there wasn't a room to be painted or a floor to be fixed or something to do. It only cost me $9.25 every month for rent. I could heat it on four or five tons of coke, and coke only cost $4 or $5 a ton. So you see, we lived differently than we do now [John Jacobson, *Amoskeag*, p. 141].

Another worker recalled the difference that the corporations made as far as modern conveniences were concerned:

> In the buildings where I grew up they didn't have modern con-
> veniences at all. They had what they called a shed out in the
> backyard, an outhouse. You'd look down in the hole and you'd
> see rats running around. Some people would throw a cat in
> there; they used to clean them out once a year, with pumps that
> had to be worked by hand. When we moved to the corporation
> tenement and they had modern conveniences, I felt just like a
> millionaire – we didn't have to run outside [Ernest Anderson,
> *Amoskeag*, pp. 144–5].

To qualify for housing, workers had to have large families, prefera-
bly with more than one member working in the mills. Their names
were often kept on waiting lists for months, sometimes years, before their turn came. As with getting a job, personal connections
with the employment office through relatives or friends could
speed up the process, often by jumping the waiting list:

> You went to Mr. Swallow to get into the corporation tenements.
> He had charge of the employment office, the accident depart-
> ment . . . and the tenements. If you were a conscientious worker
> and you had worked there faithfully a good many years, and you
> had a family and didn't ever cause any trouble anywhere, you'd
> get one, if you waited long enough. Your boss would speak to
> you or something like that. It wouldn't make any difference if
> you were skilled or not. What Mr. Swallow'd go by is how many
> of your family work in the mills, are you a clean-living family,
> and so on. When you came in to apply, they had a pile that high
> there of names, what kind of place they want, how many rooms,
> how many children they got, all that stuff. If you got one in two
> years you'd be lucky. But then you could keep it indefinitely
> [Joseph Debski, *Amoskeag*, p. 135].

Prior to the establishment of the employment office, workers wrote
to the agent directly, pleading for a corporation tenement:

> May 31, 1905
> Sir: Will you be kind enough to give me a paper and give a good
> word for me. So that I could get a tenement in the Corporation
> the is one on Arkright Street, no. 16 the family ar to moved away
> soon and I would like to have it I you please give me a paper
> and good word and tell how long I ave been working in the
> Amoskeag Co.
>
> Your Joseph Fianchetto[6]

Of all the Amoskeag's programs and amenities, the corporations
most directly touched the workers' lives and affected the largest
number of people. The low rent for well-maintained housing eased

the sting of low wages. For many families, the corporation housing made the difference between survival on low wages and slipping below the poverty margin, especially for families with many children:

> The only thing that enabled us to live was that we had a corporation tenement. We lived at 313 Canal Street, on the corner of Middle and Canal. There were nine rooms there, four stories. There were two large rooms on the first floor; the living room, kitchen, two large rooms, and a bathroom on the second floor; two large rooms on the third floor; and two attic rooms upstairs [Alice Olivier *Amoskeag*, pp. 257–8].

For mothers who wanted to keep in touch with their infants during the workday, corporation housing offered another advantage – it eliminated a one- to two-mile walk to work. Housing in the corporations gave workers a sense of permanence as long as they worked in the mill. By supplying inexpensive and well-maintained housing, the corporation succeeded in providing certain portions of the working population with an incentive to continue working in the Amoskeag. In many situations, gaining access to a corporation flat was a reward for stability and a further inducement to remain at the mills. During the bitter strike of 1922, workers were not evicted from the corporations even though they were unable to pay their rent; but the rents were deducted from their pay after the strike.

The pervasiveness of the corporation's housing should not be exaggerated. Whereas in the first half of the nineteenth century most of the labor force lived in company boardinghouses, by 1910 such accommodations housed only about 15% to 20% of the Amoskeag's workers. The majority of workers rented city housing, and some owned private homes.

The workers who chose not to live in the corporation housing – French-Canadian, Polish, and Greek workers – preferred their own ethnic neighborhoods, near their churches and especially the parish schools. Some preferred a separation of the family's residence from the world of the mill. Many workers wanted to own private homes, which they hoped to purchase in the developing ethnic neighborhoods.

Although the Amoskeag's welfare program provided an ownership plan that offered workers house lots and mortgages conditional on continued employment with the Amoskeag, most homeowners purchased in the private market. Workers of five years' standing were permitted to buy from the corporation plots of land 50 feet by 100 feet located on the west side of Manchester. Suitable building plans were available without charge, but specific restrictions were attached to construction, such as a two-family limit on houses, as was true also of other developments in Manchester located on corporation land. First and second mortgages were available, each for one-half the purchase price of the land. The first mortgage was interest free if the employee remained in the company's employ and built the structure. If the worker stayed for five years, the second mortgage was waived. If he remained on for yet another five years, the first mortgage was waived. Only about two hundred workers availed themselves of this plan.[7]

In addition to providing amenities attractive to the workers, the corporation reached outside the mill yard to offer incentives to stay in the mill. In launching such services – designed to instill values of cleanliness, health, and modern housekeeping – the Amoskeag's policy was consistent with that of other business corporations in the twentieth century (U.S., Bureau of Labor Statistics 1919). Through these programs, which were intended to foster loyalty and identification with the corporation, the workers and their children were connected to the total environment of the mills whether they lived in nearby corporation housing or in the French section on the West Side.

To socialize and Americanize workers, the corporation provided evening English classes for workers and special courses for women in sewing, cooking, and gardening. In 1914 approximately 250 young women were enrolled in these classes. Almost all eight visiting nurses, who instructed mothers in housekeeping and "modern" childrearing methods and provided medical aid, were hired under Treasurer F. C. Dumaine's personal supervision; some had actually been interviewed by him. The nurses routinely visited the homes of the sick and the helpless elderly to provide food and assistance. In addition, the Amoskeag's charity department sent visitors to the homes of all those requiring assistance and, if investigation warranted it, arranged for deliveries of coal and food. Occasionally the charity department also supplied needy workers with cloth. The deliveries usually took place within twenty-four hours of the "investigation." Most of the recipients were widows with large families or children caring for sick and elderly parents. However, there were several cases of widows without large families whose husbands had died recently from injury on the job or who were former employees. The Charity Department denied assistance to one individual because he had refused work. Workers from the British Isles and Greece represented nearly two-thirds of all the cases for assistance. French Canadians and East Europeans composed the bulk of the remaining cases. There were only two cases of aid to American families.[8] As the following report from the federal Bureau of Labor[9] indicates, the Amoskeag welfare program was extensive:

> The Company maintains a thoroughly equipped Accident Ward, with a doctor and trained nurse in attendance during working hours, where all accidents to employees are treated and proper medical attendance given until full recovery, without charge to employee. The Company provides, free of expense, a dentist for the children of employees under fourteen. The Company further maintains three visiting nurses whose duties are to visit the sick among the families of any of its employees (whether they live in Corporation tenements or elsewhere). They are ready at all times to call at the home of any employee of the Company in whose family there is sickness and to do any work that may naturally and rightfully be expected of any trained nurse. The social and domestic welfare of the employees is cared for chiefly through the offices of the Amoskeag Textile Club and the Amoskeag Woman's Textile Club with a present combined membership of almost 2000 to which all employees are eligible and the dues to which are $2 per annum. These clubs provide a Cooking and Sewing School, also Domestic Science Classes, all under competent teachers, for the families of its members, free of charge. Courses of entertainments (lectures and Concerts) are given in their season, together with annual Spring and Fall Field Days. The Clubs also give their members an opportunity of joining the Camera Club, the Glee and Orchestral Clubs and the Gun Club. A Boy Scout movement is carried on among the boys and the Children's Gardens have turned out numerous successful exhibitors at local Fairs. All these movements are carried on without further expense to the members. Textile Field, where baseball and football are played and various Athletic meets held, is one of the finest athletic fields in New England with a grand stand seating capacity of 4000. There is further the Recreation Grounds with its baseball diamond and Tennis Court, where the Field Days are held, thoroughly equipped with kitchen facilities lavitories [sic] and shower baths. A Children's Playground has been provided equipped with swings, slides, swimming pool and a pavilion for the Mothers with attendants to look after the children. Efforts are made to care for the welfare of the employees in every way.

The playground, on the site of the old railway depot, offered children supervised play, a swimming pool in the summer, and an ice rink in the winter. The garden plots, primarily for children, were also cultivated by adults. The dentist's office was located in the same building as the employment office. The annual Christmas party for the employees' children, a special event, is well remembered by many former workers. Unlike the International Harvester Company, the Ford Motor Company, and smaller industrial establishments, the Amoskeag did not develop a formal Americanization program, except through the various classes for young women and housewives and the English classes. Americanization seemed to have been less of a goal for the Amoskeag than fostering loyalty and identification with the corporation.[10]

The paternalistic ideology underlying these programs permeated the Amoskeag's entire managerial structure. The agent personified the paternalistic system. He had to have what F. C. Dumaine's son later defined as "It": the ability to relate to workers, to show interest in their personal lives, to be fair and considerate, and, at the same time, to be firm and insist on performance and discipline (*Amoskeag*, p. 337). These were also the qualities expected from overseers. Although the agent was clearly identified with the structure, he remained at a distance; the overseers were the bosses with whom the workers had direct contact, from whom the workers took their orders, and to whom the workers went for help in times of trouble. Workers depended on overseers for their continued employment and smooth working relationships. A worker in conflict with a second hand normally took the problem to the overseer for resolution. Prior to the introduction of the union and its grievance committee in 1918, workers had no other recourse. Particularly in cases of unfair treatment by overseers, the grievance mechanism provided little satisfaction for the worker.

The overseers were the pillars of the Amoskeag's paternalistic system. Although most overseers had worked their way up, as bosses, they identified with management. Most men did not become overseers until their late thirties and even more commonly their forties. They were singled out for their ability to handle staff and manage production. From the corporation's point of view, the ideal overseer was an enlightened despot – exacting and compassionate at the same time. In addition to managing daily production in his department and maintaining discipline, the overseer was to foster among the workers a spirit of loyalty to the corporation, to socialize the workers to industrial procedures, and to exemplify by his own conduct the Amoskeag's commitment to efficiency and employee welfare. With a continuous influx of new immigrants and teen-agers embarking on their first jobs, the overseers had to educate workers to maintain production schedules, to handle the machinery, and to conform to rules. Overseers took this task seriously because production and safety depended on effective socialization of the workers. Some also fulfilled these tasks with a degree of sympathy and tolerance toward workers' needs. Marie Proulx, for instance, recalled the gentle treatment from her first boss when she started work at age 12:

> So the next day when I went back to the mills with my curls, that old boss there took hold of my hair and said, "Tie back." "Me?" I said. I asked why in French. So he brought someone who spoke French, and he said it was too dangerous, that my hair could get caught in the straps of the machinery [*Amoskeag*, pp. 67–8].

Newly arrived workers rapidly became familiar with the details of the Amoskeag's hierarchical structure. Most workers never had a sophisticated conception of the flow chart of authority within the Amoskeag, but they understood the paternal role of the "boss." They learned quickly that currying favor with the boss was important for survival or advancement and that obedience and discipline were the keys to their relationship with bosses. Letters that new immigrant workers wrote to their bosses, and occasionally to the agent, reveal their perception of the bosses as paternalistic figures and their own position as obedient "children." Many of these letters were dictated to the neighborhood grocer, who then translated them and sent them to the agent or a specific overseer. During the first decade of the twentieth century, the overseers and the agent received numerous such letters from workers and former workers.[11] Written in an almost unintelligible scrawl and broken English, these letters generally requested adjustments in pay and improvements in working conditions; occasionally they included a plea for personal help:

> Dear Sir: March 27, 1906
>
>   I am kind enough to please you if you can give me more pay because I not got no enot in this work . . .

Some responded subserviently to harsh and unfair treatment:

> My dear foreman:
>
>   I told you day before yesterday to let me have a little more money to meet my expenses and you fired me out. I did not mean to quit my job. I simply asked you. I worked for you for 2 years and I do like to work for you. Please let me have my posi-

tion and if you think that is right make my pay $6.25 per week, or you can do anything, but please let me have my job. Thanking you for all you kindness, I am yours most faithfully, George Giacos, 10 October 1909.

Manchester, N.H.

Mr. George Officer: Received Nov. 29, 190?

I please to you very much.

Forgive me job because I am sick about one month and I go in the doctor Will Sir if you like give mie job because I aim poor Boy. I spend to my money of my sick and I like very much to you Work. You know mi I am Workman. I working before seven months in this mill in this shop and I don't take never off of this shop.

Well, Dear George, you know to my need. Will excuse my for that I can't speak English for speak to you my name.

Zises J.

Others requested a better job.

Sir Officer   Received Dec. 1, 1909

I am pleased so you if you like make me change because it too Small pay for me. Well, if you can put me in the other work and put other boy here in this Work and put me in New Work because must I take almost seven dollars a week because I have big family here and is too hard for me.

I have a little sons and one girl And my Wife and if you can make me change you know to my need

My officer

I am poor man

Well excuse me Sir because I do not speak English.

Often workers wrote asking forgiveness for past violations, especially for stealing cloth.

Mr. Straw plese this $7.00 in the funds of the Amoskeag C. as I have taken or received equal to that amount from corporation for years in these stock or goods authorized to pay back by the priest in confession. (3/21/1919)

Dear Sir:

Please accept this money. 23 years ago I worked for McCarty on the driers a small engine. The cloth goes on roolers hot and then moves upstairs. I seen some of the help take cotton cloth. I wet it, ring it out and put it and pack it in these pail or dinner box. I done the same enough to make a dress for my wife, but

when she found out how I got it, she never wore it and burnt it
up and then I left Manchester to come to Florida and from that
day to this I always wanted to pay for the cloth. So, here it is. ($3
sent in 1918)

And some involved the bosses in personal family squabbles, using
the arrangement to get at erring relatives.

Dear Sir,   Manchester Oct. 5, 1896
Please take notice at once my wife Philman T____ is working at
Amoskeag Mill no. 9 weaver please. Discharge her for she is a
common drunkard she has been taken once to the West Manchester Police Station for drunk and once to the City Farm for
Drunkness was there 2 months. She only works one or two payments then go on a spell. I want her to stay at home she has three
name to go by. She is a French woman about 34 years old. Her
Names are

        Philman T——
        Pleby E——
        Phieby F——

You will do me a great favor by doing so at once oblige,
                          J. Francis T——

These letters, filled with subservience and eagerness to please,
reflect neither a sense of collective group identity among workers
nor a recognition of collective group needs. Management continued
to encourage these paternalistic one-to-one relationships between
workers and their bosses, because paternalism was viewed as the
most efficient means to counteract union fraternalism. The origins
of paternalism, however, go back to a much earlier time.

Nineteenth-century roots of the Amoskeag's paternalism

The Amoskeag's foray into corporate welfare programs at the beginning of the twentieth century had its roots in the early nineteenth century. The ideology of corporate paternalism as it first
emerged in the planned New England towns provided the moral
justification for the new industrial order. It was most clearly articulated in Lowell, Massachusetts. The American manufacturers who
created those communities were intent on proving that "the introduction of manufacturing was in every place a harbinger of moral
and intellectual improvement to the inhabitants of the vicinage,
and the numerous operatives from remote and secluded parts of the
country" (White 1836:107–8; Appleton 1858). By developing these
carefully planned and socially controlled communities, their found-

ers thought to avoid the horrors associated with industrialism in Britain. Furthermore, as Caroline Ware observed:

> The introduction of a humane, paternalistic regime into an early American factory was essential for the recruitment of desirable workers, because of the scarcity of a suitable labor force. In America, as opposed to other places, even the most docile labor was so scarce that manufacturers had to draw on a higher type. The exploitation of the worker was checked by the need of attracting the higher type, and the concentration of the population was only temporary because of the ever present possibility of returning to the land [1931:15].

The Boston Associates, who planned and developed the first large New England industrial communities, extended their ideal of paternalism into the realm of architecture and town planning. Francis Cabot Lowell, who established the first fully mechanized textile factory in Waltham, Massachusetts, in 1814, devised an employment system for attracting young women from rural districts to work in the mills. The mill yard in Waltham resembled a country village, with grass, trees, and a belfry on the mill. The design of the boardinghouses imitated traditional New England white clapboard farmhouses (Ware 1931).

Later, in Lowell and Manchester, a more substantial brick architecture was used, but the conscious landscaping and provision for greens, parks, and wide tree-lined streets reflected the founders' firm belief that they could create a successful industry without the squalor for which Britain had become notorious (Coolidge 1942; Langenbach 1968). They realized that without their paternalistic approach to the planning of living and working environments they could neither attract sufficient workers to fill the newly developed large-scale units nor socialize a rural labor force into useful working members of the new industrial order. Partly aimed at young women, the philosophy of paternalism viewed the corporation as a responsible but strict parent and the workers as obedient and diligent children. As in feudal society, the relationship involved reciprocity but not equality. In return for minimal pay, workers were expected to provide their labor and their obedience and loyalty to the corporation. Enlightened management was expected to provide protection and adequate working and living conditions, as well as moral supervision, whether the workers wanted it or not.

The relationship between management and workers was thus not strictly defined around an exchange of labor for pay. It was enmeshed in a network of services and obligations that transcended the work relationship in a narrow sense. As a result, workers hardly experienced any separation between work and private life. Corporate control engulfed the workers' entire existence, including their moral behavior and religious life, as a typical broadside to Lowell employees indicates:

> Every kind of ardent spirit (except prescribed by a legal physician) will be banished from the limits of the corporation, and . . . intemperate, immoral, prodigal persons, if they succeed in obtaining employment, will be discharged unless they reform, after admonition. All persons employed by the Company, will attend some place of public worship on the Sabbath, when practicable.[12]

This formula was repeated in many other industrial establishments and was kept alive in Manchester into the 1870s and 1880s. The family model was incorporated into the industrial system, with the agent (who was the chief manager) filling the father's role. The same model was also expressed in the hierarchical management structure of the newly developing textile industry. The overseer was the "father" of his workroom and was expected to treat the workers like his children. In this way the factory acquired an image not entirely alien to workers from rural backgrounds. Its paternalistic environment was intended to assure young women workers and their parents that the boardinghouses in Lowell and Manchester were observing some of the traditional values of rural society. Enforced by elderly matrons, the employers' strict rules of behavior in the boardinghouses – a 10 P.M. curfew, required church attendance on Sunday, and the prohibition of smoking and gambling – mirrored the values that parents guarded in rural life.

The most persistent feature of nineteenth-century paternalism was its concentration on the family unit as the linchpin of the industrial order. Although industrial development would shift the focus of production from family to factory, the family was still the primary unit of production at the beginning of the industrial revolution in the United States. It was also considered the base of morality and stability and the socializer of the young. The founders of industry justified the factory's role as carrying on the family's work in a broader social center. If the factory was to be a surrogate family, its hierarchy would have to be modeled on the organization of the family – a notion that persisted even after the influx of foreign immigrants had transformed the labor force and planned communities had become ordinary industrial centers.

The family model was central to the management of early planned industrial textile towns, both ideologically and because it fit the historical developments of the time. The factory assumed some production functions previously held by the family. Because the planned industrial communities provided the first experience of an institutionalized workplace for rural workers removed from the farm, the new system tried to model itself on the institution it was replacing. The factory's role as surrogate family was not unique; other institutions that developed in the same period, such as reformatories, hospitals, and public schools, which also replaced functions previously performed by the family, similarly used the family as their model (Rothman 1971).

However, the founders of the early industrial communities in New England went beyond the family's activities in their effort to socialize young laborers, and to some extent adults, into a stable, industrial labor force. The advocates of early industry had promised to end idleness and poverty by providing steady employment to women and children of the poorer classes and by teaching them industrial habits, namely, to be precise, orderly, and productive. This was to be accomplished through careful supervision in the workplace and at home and the introduction of Sunday schools. Samuel Slater, the Rhode Island textile industry pioneer, was as proud of his Sunday school as he was of his newly established factory (White 1836). By the middle of the nineteenth century, Manchester's Pastor Henry Dexter was able to claim that the factory "may not inaptly be termed one great boarding school where the pupils remain from four to nine years" (1848:7).

Paternalistic control of the workers' lives in the Amoskeag prior to the Civil War was not as all-encompassing as the agent and the clergy would have liked. The successive land sales by the company in the 1840s and 1850s cleared the way for private development of neighborhoods adjacent to the corporation housing. In response to a severe housing shortage in the 1850s, private developers increasingly made housing available, especially to new immigrant workers.

In reality, two boardinghouse systems coexisted in Manchester: the corporation's own boardinghouses and the private ones, in which increasing numbers of immigrant workers tended to reside. In his analysis of the housing arrangements of the Amoskeag's workers in the 1860s, James Hanlan found that of 352 workers hired by the Amoskeag in 1860, all of whom signed a contract agreeing to live in corporation housing, fewer than half actually did so (1979:133). In 1870, in a memorandum to the overseers, Agent Straw reaffirmed the requirement that workers live in company housing or in housing approved by the company. Overseers were required to enforce these rules and workers were to affirm by their signature that they would adhere to the corporation's housing and moral guidance policies (see Appendix E). Nevertheless, only 23% of the 661 workers sampled by Hanlan in 1870 actually proceeded to live in company housing. Of the foreign workers hired in 1870, only 34 out of the 229 sampled lived in corporation housing. The addresses of the employees in the Amoskeag's register of workers suggest that by 1878 the requirement for residence in corporation housing was no longer enforced.[13] During the remainder of the nineteenth century, as the Amoskeag's labor force was transformed from rural New Englanders to foreign immigrants and as the city's population both expanded and became diversified in its ethnic neighborhoods, the corporation's direct control over the workers' residential arrangements and personal conduct dwindled.

But the more significant and wide-reaching influence of the Amoskeag's paternalism was in its control and supervision of the city's development. The Amoskeag continued to control Manchester's growth through strict deed restrictions on the land it sold to private owners, as it had during the first phases of Manchester's growth in the 1840s. The Amoskeag Company also tried to keep the community in its social debt by donating sites for parks, schools, and churches. The mill agents continued to give the impression that they were providing moral leadership and were overseeing the moral life of the city. When Frederick Smyth, mayor of Manchester, testified before the Senate Committee on Education and Labor, he described the agents of the Amoskeag and the other, at that time separate, corporations as

> men who understand human nature and who understand how to
> get along with their help. We have no men in Manchester who
> take more interest in the religious and moral character of the city
> than our mill agents. They come out here with the boys, and
> parade the streets with the firemen and with the soldiers when
> asked, and they all go and sit down at their banquets [U.S., Senate 1885:117].

Continuities and new directions in the twentieth century

The nineteenth-century paternalistic tradition survived in the Amoskeag after it collapsed in Lowell and the other sister communities. Whereas the original corporate management fragmented in Lowell, Lawrence, and other New England mill towns, the Amoskeag entered the twentieth century under its original management,[14] and was thus uniquely able to perpetuate its paternalistic policies. The continuity in management facilitated the corporation's control over the city and the introduction of the new welfare programs of the twentieth century.

The Amoskeag launched its new efficiency and welfare program at a critical juncture in the history of the northern textile industry. Then at the peak of its physical expansion and consolidation as the world's largest textile mill under one roof, the Amoskeag's new-found prosperity was tempered by two nagging anxieties: the threat represented by the expanding southern textile industry and the fear of labor unrest in the face of the Lawrence strike in 1911 and the growing strength of the International Workers of the World in New England.

Strike prevention was a major goal underlying the Amoskeag's program of paternalism. Unrest and protest in neighboring New England towns prompted F. C. Dumaine in 1910 to authorize a 5% wage increase because he felt he had to keep up with the other textile mills: "It is like a pile of bricks," he wrote. "If you pull out one brick all the others follow and the entire structure collapses."[15] In 1911 Amoskeag workers publicly expressed sympathy for the Lawrence strikers by holding solidarity demonstrations in the main square in Manchester and by providing temporary homes for the children of the Lawrence strikers. But the Amoskeag workers did not go on strike. The corporation, however, in order to maintain close observation of the workers' actions, hired the Burns Detective Agency of Boston to send spies into the clubs and tenements. Although the detectives concluded that the workers' mood was placid and that the Amoskeag had no reason to fear labor insurgence, there seems to have been some concern nevertheless on the part of management.[16] Launched prior to the Lawrence strike, the Amoskeag's playground was soon supplemented by various other programs, implemented because of management's desire to foster loyalty and to avert strikes. The simultaneous establishment of new welfare incentives and a more efficient screening of workers indicates that management was not blind to the expression of sympathy for the Lawrence strike. When IWW organizers visited Manchester, they were run out of the city by police, whose chief worked in close collaboration with the Amoskeag's agent and treasurer.

The alleged threat of potential strikes provided management with a convenient explanation to stockholders who viewed the welfare program as a luxury. "I understand the Company has built a base-ball grand stand that cost near $40,000," wrote one stockholder from North Andover. "It does not seem right to spend money on sports instead of manufacturing, when the Common Stock pays only 3 percent."[17] In reply to such criticisms, Dumaine and Straw suggest-ed that the alternative to the playground was the IWW. A typical newspaper article in 1914 headlined the Amoskeag's welfare pro-gram as "the finest answer to IWWism, – as Revealed by Amoskeag Manufacturing Company in Handling its 14,000 employees – Play-grounds and Garden for Our Children, Ball Park and Outings for Young Folks, Co-Operative Home Building Proposition, and Care of Sick for All Operatives." In a description of a Flag Day parade in Manchester, a journalist expressed his surprise at the

> absence of red IWW flags from the line of 25,000 marchers, En-glish-born, Scotch-born, Irish-born, Jewish-born, Greek-born, Polish-born, Scandinavian-born . . . all loyally wearing or wav-ing or carrying the stars and stripes to show the pride they felt in their American citizenship. There were the thousands of non-English speaking foreigners such as are found in other cotton mill centers of New England, but where were the IWWs with their red flag and their motto, NO GOD, NO COUNTRY?

The writer concludes that only an uninformed stranger would ask such a question in Manchester:

> Had he known of the manner in which this, the biggest cotton manufacturing corporation seeks to help them better their eco-nomic condition and to enjoy life, he would not have wondered that IWWism has not gained a foothold nor that even old line unionism has failed to take root in this community [Sunday Standard, New Bedford, July 5, 1914].

Like other corporations that plunged into welfare programs, the Amoskeag was partly stimulated by civic organizations and the so-cial reform movements of the Progressive era. Correspondence be-tween F. C. Dumaine and leaders of some of those organizations suggests that Dumaine tried to steal their thunder. In particular, Dumaine felt pressure from the National Civic Federation's Welfare Department and the Civic Federation of New England, as well as from local philanthropic and reform organizations in Manchester, such as the Young Men's Christian Association and the Settlement House Association.

The Amoskeag followed the models of some programs initiated by these national organizations and copied some of the programs proposed by the local reform organizations in Manchester. Leaders of the Civic Federation of New England, for example, kept tabs for some time on the Amoskeag's activity and corresponded with Dumaine. They offered their help to improve sanitary conditions in the Amoskeag: "Our New England Committee, devoted to workshop improvement, gives special attention to sanitary and health conditions in the mills, and only coincidentally goes into more elaborate phases such as club work, recreation facilities, etc."[18] But Dumaine politely declined their offer.

Similarly, when Gertrude Beeks, secretary of the National Civic Federation, who had been the architect and first director of the elaborate corporate welfare program at the International Harvester Company, wrote to Dumaine offering assistance in the development of welfare programs in the Amoskeag, Dumaine replied that "the best way for us to do something for the comfort and welfare of our people" would be to set up a clubhouse for which the YMCA was agitating.[19] Undaunted, Beeks offered to counsel Dumaine on the erection of the clubhouse. Although that offer was also rejected, Beeks finally obtained permission to visit Amoskeag in 1909 to see various types of manufacturing and the "conditions under which your employees live and work." In thanking Dumaine for his hospitality, Beeks asked if his "people were pretty well unionized." This was of interest to her, she explained "merely because it is so often stated that employers, who are doing so much in the way of welfare work, do not believe in unions."[20] She was right, of course, in her assumption.

The Settlement House Association of New Hampshire also agitated with Dumaine and Herman Straw to promote an Amoskeag day nursery and a home for working girls.

> The object of this institution is to furnish a place where girls employed in the factories and mills who have no homes of their own may live at reasonable cost under healthful and moral conditions, also to furnish a day nursery at which the mothers of small children who are employed in mills and factories may leave their babies during their hours of labor, with the assurance that they will receive proper care and attention.[21]

The association raised $7,000 for the construction of the building but needed assistance from the Amoskeag to see it through. They first approached Herman Straw, who suggested they send the application to F. C. Dumaine. Dumaine replied that it "is absolutely impossible for me to subscribe to work of this kind, no matter how much I might believe in its usefulness."[22] The Settlement House Association persisted, however, and opened its own home for girls, taking in forty residents. It then once again asked Dumaine for help. Dumaine replied that the Amoskeag would rather open its own day nursery than aid the association's endeavors. Although the Amoskeag never opened a day nursery, it did establish a playground.

In dealing with settlement workers and the Civic League's welfare department, Dumaine was explicit in stating his preference for an Amoskeag welfare program rather than the reforms initiated by the civic associations. His strategy was clear: He was concerned that a welfare program offered by another organization might divert the workers' loyalties. Rather than support these organizations, Dumaine thought it better to launch an Amoskeag program and get credit for it.

It is clear that the family-oriented programs introduced at the Amoskeag, in addition to resembling those of other industrial corporations, were modeled on some of the programs that progressive reformers and social workers had introduced into immigrant slums in major American cities by the beginning of the twentieth century. Adequate housing, playgrounds and parks, vocational training for immigrant children, clubhouses for working girls, visiting nurses, and homemakers all were part of the progressive reformers' response to immigrant problems.[23] Despite the drastic differences in their respective perceptions of the rights of labor, working conditions, and reform goals, especially industrialists' opposition to unions, progressive reformers and captains of industry nevertheless had some goals in common: the improvement of working and living conditions in industrial establishments and the education of immigrant workers (Wiebe 1962). Both recognized the significant role of the family and home in the process of Americanization and endeavored to socialize new immigrants to "American" ways.

A comparison of the Amoskeag's nineteenth-century and twentieth-century paternalistic programs reveals both continuities and discontinuities. In the nineteenth century the goal was to assimilate native-born rural workers into industrial life; now the corporation had to deal with foreign immigrant workers. But despite the foreign background of its labor force at the turn of the century, the Amoskeag succeeded in maintaining something of the nineteenth-century sense of a "corporation family." In this respect, there was a clear continuity between the "old" paternalism and the "new." There were also, however, major differences.

In the new paternalism, the emphasis had shifted from socialization and protection of young New England girls to housing and welfare provisions for entire immigrant families. The new paternalism was also distinct in its concern with efficiency and centralized administration. Coinciding with the Amoskeag's consolidation and expansion into the world's largest textile mill, the new paternalism was as committed to efficiency as its predecessor had been committed to moral purity.

Effectiveness of the paternalistic program

The Amoskeag welfare program collapsed in the wake of the 1922 strike. Only the physical amenities, the corporation housing and the playground, survived. More dramatic than the disappearance of its programs, however, was the death of the Amoskeag "spirit," although the elaborate paternalism of the corporation remains vivid in the minds of many former workers to the present day.

How effective was the Amoskeag's welfare program in meeting the corporation's goals? Both native-born workers of rural origin and later groups of foreign immigrants found certain aspects of paternalism compatible with their own premigration traditions. Although the factory system appeared alien at first, the hierarchical authority structure and the authoritarian but benevolent father image of the boss were models familiar to the workers in their family and religious life. As a former worker described it: "It's like a family, the father is the big boss . . . the mother is the second hand" (Eveline Brousseau, interview). The view of the family as a corporate unit, as an entity working together collectively, also fit the world of the textile mill, because the corporation encouraged family employment and because individual adaptation to the world of work and to survival in a factory system depended on each member's ability to function as a member of a collective family unit. Many corporation policies were family oriented. The Amoskeag recruited its workers through family and kinship ties and encouraged their placement in the workrooms in family clusters. It often relied on relatives to socialize and discipline family members in the factory setting and to assist them in learning work processes. The corporation thus used the workers' traditional reliance on kin and family members to serve its own purposes. The workers' tendency to migrate along kinship lines to new communities and to work in family units, their reliance on their kin for finding work, and their custom of assisting each other also served the corporation's needs for recruitment of a large and stable labor force. Reliance on kin also saved time and money in the training of new workers, as relatives and friends performed this function, even under the new paternalism. Ironically, management launched family-oriented programs outside the mills at the same time it attempted to curb the quasi-familial informality that reigned inside the mills by introducing centralized hiring. Most workers preferred the opposite: They wanted to retain some degree of familial control within the world of work and be left alone with their families after work.

Nevertheless, the workers found some of their traditional migration and familial work patterns encouraged by corporation policy. From their point of view, labor recruitment along family lines and the opportunity for relatives to work together was essential, because it enabled them to obtain employment for a significant portion of their family members and facilitated their own adjustment to the factory system. The prospect of living in the corporations was a particular inducement to come to Manchester, because workers' housing at most other New England textile firms had long since been replaced by private speculative tenements.

The other services the Amoskeag offered benefited a much smaller proportion of the working population. The Amoskeag's Textile Club remained an elitist institution, with the majority of its members being overseers or second hands and the office staff. As a report on Textile Club membership assembled by the corporation suggests, only a small proportion of the rank-and-file workers actually participated in its activities. However, a large number of workers participated in the club-sponsored recreational activities such as picnics on the shores of Lake Massebissic, Christmas parties, and sports events. As Tommy Smith pointed out:

> I belonged to the Amoskeag Textile Club. It was a good move to open up sociability among the workers and give them an outlet, a way to meet each other more often; but the bulk of the membership was really the more important men in the company. The others didn't go into it too much . . . They'd walk around with their neighbors, even go visit relatives and friends on the West Side after supper, and walk home [*Amoskeag*, p. 234].

Most club members who held jobs with lower status were native-born or of English, Scottish, and Swedish origins. Fellow workers suspected those who joined of trying to ingratiate themselves with the bosses. The club did succeed in fostering loyalty and identification among the upper echelons, especially because Agent Straw was its president.

Similarly, only a small proportion of the work force took advantage of the cooking school, the sewing classes, and the services of visiting nurses and the dentist. The participants in these activities were more likely to be of English, Scotch, Irish, and German origins than the newer immigrants, who were dissuaded by language difficulties and distance from the mill.[24] But beyond such practical problems, many workers were actually reluctant to be involved or to expose their children to the Amoskeag's programs. They preferred to center their social activities around their churches and ethnic clubs. The playground, with its wading pool, swings, and ice-skating rinks, was an exception, however – it touched the lives of the workers' children much more than any other welfare program. Hundreds of Manchester children, even those whose parents did not work in the Amoskeag, played each day under the huge AMOSKEAG CO. PLAYGROUND sign. In some ways, the playground was also an important equalizer, for it provided a meeting ground for the children of both overseers and rank-and-file workers. Even Agent Straw's daughter sneaked out from her fenced-in garden to play there when her mother was not looking:

> My parents didn't let me play in the corporation playground, which was way down near the station. I guess they thought I had plenty to do up where I lived. But they never objected to the children from around there coming to our yard. Never. My mother didn't think there was anything wrong with the other children, but she thought that the playground was meant for those who didn't have as many opportunities or the yard that I had. We had everything right there. We had the baseball grounds, and we had the skating rink in the wintertime. The only thing we didn't have was slides.
>
> Once in a while I disobeyed but not very often. One time I went to the Amoskeag playground, and I ripped my dress. My friend's mother stitched it up for me so my mother wouldn't know. She was a seamstress and her husband was a mill worker [Mary Straw Flanders, *Amoskeag,* pp. 250–1].

With the limited exception of the corporation housing, welfare programs developed by the Amoskeag improved the workers' lives and conditions only minimally. Although some services, especially dental care, were used by a cross section of the workers, most beneficiaries of the Amoskeag's welfare system were the "old reliables," especially the workers of Yankee, English, Scottish, Irish, and German origins. These ethnic categories also provided the most overseers and second hands, as well as some of the more highly skilled workers, such as the loomfixers. Nevertheless, the Amoskeag's welfare and social activities were widely known among most workers.

The programs were clearly successful in generating an image of corporate care for the workers' lives outside the mills, an impression held even by workers who did not participate. Those programs that appealed to children and youth – the playground, Christmas party, and picnics – lingered significantly in people's memories.

The Amoskeag's welfare programs also left a positive impression, because, unlike those in Pullman, Illinois, and other company-controlled mill towns, they were not compulsory. The Amoskeag owned neither churches, schools, nor company stores – except for a remnant shop, where workers were allowed to buy cloth at reduced rates. After the early nineteenth-century period, workers could choose where to live, where to shop, and, except for those renting corporation housing, did not depend on utilities and services from the corporation.

It is doubtful whether the welfare program succeeded in curbing labor turnover and molding the workers into a more stable labor force. A more effective measure for the prevention of labor turnover, particularly among women, would have been a nursery and kindergarten for children of working mothers, but management never pursued this idea and did not seriously entertain the request of the Settlement House Association to set up such an institution. Most women who took advantage of the cooking and sewing lessons were English-speaking second-generation immigrants, born to parents working in the mill, who enjoyed greater economic security. New French-Canadian or Greek immigrants rarely took part in these activities.

Nor did the pension plan affect a large number of workers. During the period 1916–23, only 137 workers with a minimum service record of thirty years were granted pensions, although 290 workers qualified. Most beneficiaries of the pension plan were overseers and second hands rather than shop floor workers (Creamer and Coulter 1939, pp. 177–8).

Although corporation housing tended to foster stability for the fraction of the labor force that had access to it, the Amoskeag, like other industrial establishments in this period, continued to be plagued by labor turnover (Chapter 9). Employees' stability depended on a more complex combination of factors including family considerations and needs, wages, and the prospect of alternative jobs in the city. In the post–World War I period the corporation itself intensified turnover by frequent firings and layoffs.

The Amoskeag workers nevertheless experienced a loyalty and identification with the corporation that was by no means exclusive to the overseers and agent. This identification was derived from the fame and pride in the Amoskeag product rather than the various services provided by the corporation. The dramatic architecture of the mills themselves, the meticulous maintenance of the mill yard and the housing, and the care for minute details in the pre–World War I period contributed to the sense of corporate identity and concern for the work force that has survived in the workers' memories as one of the Amoskeag's great distinctions. To what extent did the Amoskeag's welfare program diffuse workers' discontent and help prevent unionization? Most interviewees perceived the Amoskeag's welfare programs not as a substitute for the higher wages to which they were entitled but as a supplement. Some referred to these programs as "fringe benefits." But in the post–World War I period, some workers like Ernest Anderson, a former loomfixer, began to see through the trade-off: "They were trying to make it easier one way, make you more satisfied for the small wages that you were making" (interview). In the twenties and thirties younger workers, especially, would not accept playgrounds as a substitute for decent wages. As Cora Pellerin, a former weaver, put it:

> Dumaine . . . said, "I've always been fair to my help, and I don't need the union. They have a union in Massachusetts, and they don't do what I do for my help." It was true in a way . . . but the newer generation wanted more money, and they wanted someone to represent them . . . We needed the union [*Amoskeag*, pp. 207–8].

Why it took so long for a union to obtain a foothold in the Amoskeag is still an open question. The corporation's own explanation that playgrounds and picnics tended to keep out the IWW and to prevent unionization is highly unlikely. That the corporation prevented strikes by intimidating the workers is a more likely explanation. In addition to the special detectives who were hired for a onetime survey during the Lawrence strike, the Amoskeag had detectives on its permanent staff:

> They had a watchman at every gate, and they had two detectives walking the yard. Some wore civilian clothes. Some workers knew who they were; some didn't . . . The Amoskeag also had the Manchester Police Department behind them [Joseph Debski, *Amoskeag*, p. 133].

But despite the corporation's watchfulness and intimidation, labor unrest bubbled under the surface and occasionally erupted into open conflict even before the strike of 1922. In 1912 a group of weavers demanding higher wages walked out and returned only after the company had announced a wage increase of about 5% to all operatives. This increase, following the previous 5% increase on March 11, granted in reaction to the Lawrence strike, restored the 10% wage cut of 1908. Management reported the walkout in "Happenings," the Amoskeag's public diary, without editorializing.

> The weavers on 640 looms in No. 3 Upper Weave Room, Southern Division, walked out yesterday and today [refused] to weave A. C. A. tickings for the same price that is paid the weavers on [the] same work in Jefferson Weave Room.
>
> [They were joined by] the weavers on 200 looms in No. 3 Upper Weave Room, Central Division [who] walked out this afternoon, refusing to weave 19,000 range for 24.2 cents per cut but demanding 28 cents.
>
> The coiler boys and strippers on the cards in No. 9 Lower Card Room, Central Division, refused to work this morning on account of dissatisfaction with their pay, but the matter was adjusted and they resumed work after a shutdown of two hours.[25]

Two additional walkouts occurred between the inauguration of the welfare program and the strike of 1922. On January 8, 1913, twenty-eight Greeks in the No. 4 Upper Spinning Room, Central Division, walked out at 6:30 A.M., because two Greek workers had been discharged, and on March 16, 1914, ten weavers in the No. 11 Mill walked out. The *Amoskeag Bulletin* reported:

> An unfortunate misunderstanding occurred with the weavers in one of the No. 11 mill weave rooms last Thursday by reason of which they were induced to make a demonstration that is not in accordance with Amoskeag traditions and is in violation of the principles of the employees of the company. It is regrettable from every standpoint that any Amoskeag people, without proper notification, and before all other means had failed, should walk out from the mills, because it gives a false impression to those outside of the mills who cannot be acquainted with the true conditions.[26]

Even though these spontaneous, sporadic strikes and walkouts, which erupted in different departments, were stopped before they could spread, their occurrence tends to dispel the image of Manchester as the "strikeless city." They suggest, rather, that worker discontent existed before World War I and that spontaneous collective action occurred before the introduction of the union in 1918.

Although corporate paternalism and intimidation could not prevent unions and strikes, they may have been effective in delaying their appearance in the Amoskeag. An identification with paternalism so pervaded the outlook of most workers that the effectiveness of the union when it did arrive was undermined. In generating an Amoskeag consciousness in the workers, paternalism delayed the development of their collective awareness as workers. This strong identification was consistent with the pattern identified by David Brody (1968) as common in industry nationwide. Had it not been for the Great Depression, Brody claims, workers would have continued to favor welfare capitalism, as evidenced in the decline in strike activity and labor turnover during the 1920s.[27]

Even though Amoskeag workers identified with paternalism, there was an undercurrent of discontent. Some workers, who were prepared to insist on rights rather than accept handouts from the corporation, had begun to form a collective identity separate from management. It was not, however, until the strike of 1922 that workers presented a concerted challenge to the paternalistic balance.

4   *The meaning of work*

We were proud. We thought we were somebody. Oh yes, we were.

Mary Cunion, interview

A Scottish weaver who spent her entire work life in the Amoskeag, Mary Cunion thus summed up her identity as a worker. From the perspective of today, when industrial work is commonly viewed as an isolating, alienating experience and when routine jobs are thought of as dehumanizing and debilitating, it is difficult to recognize a world where workers were deeply attached to exhausting jobs that provided little pay in return for endless hours.[1] Among the interviewees, even those employees who had worked for the Amoskeag for only a limited time considered themselves "Amoskeag men" and "Amoskeag women." Such loyalty and identification with the company and the attachment that workers expressed toward their jobs seem especially puzzling in light of the conflicts and disappointments that followed the strike of 1922 and the subsequent decline in the Amoskeag.

This is not to say that the workers were not ambivalent in those attitudes. The very people who expressed attachment to their work experience also questioned why they worked there in the first place. For example, 80-year-old Mary Cunion began her interview with the declaration: "I spent my happiest times in the mills. Could you beat that?" Later in the interview, however, she confessed: "If I had my life all over again, I wouldn't be in the mill. No, I wouldn't be in the mill. I'd rather be outside . . . It was drudgery there; of course, it paid well, but it's regular drudgery." (*Amoskeag*, pp. 43, 48).

Few workers had any alternative to working in the mills. Most had migrated to Manchester specifically to work in the mill or were born into the world of the Amoskeag. "I was brought up in the area of the mill . . . We didn't know anything else existed, really . . . We lived near the mills, we carried dinners for our parents [to the mill], and we just were accustomed to the mills," recalled Raymond Dubois, a former spinner (*Amoskeag*, p. 152). "It was the way I earned

69

my living; it was like a trade," recalled one man who had worked as a doffer all his life (Charland Valerian, interview).

Marie Jean, who began as a spinner at age 16 and worked in the mill all her life, loved her job and was proud of her accomplishment: "The boss said that I was the best spinner in the room." But Marie had few options other than the Amoskeag. "I didn't like to work in a shoe shop. I was not educated to work in a store. So I went into the mills and I did the same thing my sister did. I spin" (interview). And Irene Wilson recalled: "That seemed to be the only place I could get steady work. Also some of the head men in the Amoskeag were my friends" (interview).

When Mary Cunion tried to escape the mill at a much earlier point in her career, she quickly discovered that to obtain a pleasant job she would have to give up a survival wage:

> I used to work days weaving, and the pay I made at weaving paid for the business college. It was right up here on Elm Street. I went to Bryant and Stratton Business College way back when I was only fifteen or sixteen years of age. I studied shorthand, and I studied typewriting in a regular course. I took the course, and I got a diploma. Mr. Chase of the Chase Tea Company wanted to hire me for the stenography; but when he showed me the price he was going to pay, I said I couldn't do that. I said "They pay three times as much as that with my board at the Amoskeag!" He didn't send for me again [*Amoskeag*, p. 47].

Others had similar experiences – "nicer" jobs did not pay well. Many excursions into the outside world ended in a return to the Amoskeag. One worker recalled the serene beauty of a small mill town in western Massachusetts, where he went to work after leaving the Amoskeag. He enjoyed the pastoral surroundings, the opportunity to cross the stream and pick apples and run back to the mill. But the pay was much lower than in the Amoskeag, and he eventually returned to Manchester.

Many young workers who started out in shops or as vendors in ice-cream parlors quickly switched to the Amoskeag because of the better pay. Melinda Landry, for example, first worked at Woolworth's. She was paid very little and was also concerned as to whether her job would last after the holidays. "I'd been putting my name in at Amoskeag for a long time, and after I had gotten my job at the store, they [Amoskeag] called me." She worked there continuously afterward even though she was short and slight and had to stretch constantly to reach the spinning frame (interview).

The workers' dependence on the Amoskeag was compounded by

their lack of both education and professional training. For example, Thomas Bergeron, a weaver, disliked his work, particularly because of the piece rates, but had to resign himself to it. "I never learned a trade to work outside. My father told me I had to go to work, so I worked there" (interview).

In analyzing the motivation of immigrant workers at the beginning of the century, John R. Commons concluded: "Partly fear, partly hope, make the fresh immigrant the hardest . . . worker in our industries" (1907:126–7). Newer immigrants clung to their jobs in the Amoskeag because of fear of poverty, insecurity, and isolation in declining rural areas and of poverty and unemployment in urban centers. Attracted also by regular pay and decent housing, they hoped to keep their children in school longer, eventually own a home, and advance, perhaps, to better-paying, stable positions, if not for themselves, for their children.

Such fears and hopes were effectively exploited by management in its attempts to transform immigrant workers into a stable, obedient labor force. Awe of the boss and the threat of being fired and blacklisted were constant reminders to workers who might be tempted to disobey or perform less assiduously. The general fear of being unemployed, without resources and chronically poor, no doubt helped keep workers in line.

Like many other enterprises in this period, the Amoskeag effectively exploited the worker's hopes and fears as incentives for work. Fast workers were rewarded with higher pay; steady workers who produced high quality materials were often singled out as models. Some were rewarded with more satisfying and easier jobs. Good workers also had a better chance to place their relatives in desirable jobs.

The Amoskeag held up the example of the man who had "made it" as proof that steady work would be rewarded with advancement. It never failed to extol the promise of advancement, although in reality the opportunities for advancement were rather limited.

Fear and hope alone, however, do not explain all the feelings of workers for their jobs. Rather, such commitment derived from their self-respect, their sense of competence as workers, their faith in the fairness of the process, and their pride in the quality of the goods they produced and the community setting of their work. The workers' self-respect and sense of community was expressed even in the clothes they wore. As the photographs taken by Lewis Hine and many other contemporary photographers demonstrate, both men and women and even young boys went to work attired in proper street clothing. Men wore suits and women sported fine dresses and fancy hats. They kept their overalls and smocks in lockers in the mill and changed after arriving. When asked about their attire, workers expressed the sense of dignity that their clothing symbolized: "We were proud we were weavers and we dressed well" (Cora Pellerin, interview).

The identification of workers with their jobs can be partly explained by the process of making textiles itself. Even though they worked on only one aspect of the operation, most textile workers understood their work and product as part of the entire process. Whether they were spinners, carders, weavers, or dyers, most interviewees described the whole process of textile making in detail, even when their own work had been limited to one small aspect of the operation.

Both men and women workers had a sense of belonging to a community. Workers were loyal to their jobs, to their workrooms, and often to their bosses. As Emily Renoir recalled: "It hurt me most when the bag mill stopped, to leave the mill where I learned it all . . . that hurt me the most" (interview). They often identified a workroom by the overseer's name. Even today, many workers speak of "Mr. Cram's room" or "Mr. Flynn's room" rather than of "Weave Room No. 2" or "No. 5." Despite the giant size of the mills, work in the Amoskeag produced a sense of familiarity both among workers and bosses. Jean Chagnon, a former second hand, recalled the feeling of integration:

> You knew they spent more time in the mill with those people than they do at home with their family. Just like a brother and sister. I hated to leave my job; I was afraid they were gonna push those people out. They were all my kids. I had girls start with me when they were 18 years old. When I left, some of them were grandmothers. I cried when I left [interview].

"We were all like a family" was the recurring description that workers attached to their social connections in the mill. Lydia Masters, a former weaver who left Manchester to work temporarily in an automobile factory in Detroit, compared the experiences: "I liked working in the mills better . . . we had our friends in that mill, and it was just sort of a way of living" (interview). John Jacobson, an overseer in the weave room, recalled the close ties he had formed with fellow workers prior to becoming an overseer:

> You've got to remember that I grew up with most of these people when I was a regular worker. As I walked through the mills it was all people that I know quite well; and I'd stop and talk with

them . . . and you could learn a lot about your work and a lot about how things were going by talking a lot to the employees [interview].

The workers' attachment to each other made them reluctant to change jobs or rooms unless they were dissatisfied or had prospects for a better job. Marie Proulx, who had worked with her husband most of her life, recalled: "At age 15, I went to No. 4 mill. We were there when we were married, and we stayed there. I was twenty years without going out of that room" (*Amoskeag*, p. 66).

Ever since the Western Electric studies, the role of informal group relations in the workplace has been recognized in social psychology and industrial sociology as significant for good worker-to-worker relations and industrial productivity (Mayo 1933, Roethlisberger and Dickson 1939, Whyte 1951, and Sayles 1963).[2] In summarizing the Western Electric studies, Arensberg emphasized the significance of informal organization in the workrooms:

Out of Mayo's watching these, worker-to-worker relationships of a new sort unite the lonely, embittered, apathetic workers of the mule-spinning room, the doctrine of "informal organization" or "teamwork" seems to have been born (Arensberg 1951:339).

In the Western Electric case, informal group cooperation was stimulated and reinforced through the special attention accorded individual workers by the research team's investigators. The remarkable aspect of the work relationships in the Amoskeag was that the informal groups were generated by the workers themselves through their informal networks and operated independently of the formal structure of the factory. Informal groups emerged in the Amoskeag from social networks formed by kinship and ethnic ties that were carried over into the workplace from the cohesive neighborhoods.

For children of Amoskeag workers attachment to the mill started in childhood, even before they were old enough to work. Even though they were not actually entering factory work before age 14, children were socialized to the work experience in the mill at an early age. Industrial labor became part of their lives even before they actually worked. The experience of their parents, and the proximity of their homes to the mills, prevented any real separation between the world of childhood and the world of work. Children carrying lunch pails to the mills at the noon hour were a familiar part of the Manchester scene, where schoolchildren earned their first money by bringing lunches from the boardinghouses to the mills. Most youths attending high school worked regularly in the mills during the summer. The expectations that children would have to work as soon as the law permitted were strongly impressed on them from an early age by their parents. The family economy was built on the assumption that children would contribute to the family's effort from the earliest opportunity, and the family's work ethic required it.

By the time they entered the mill, young people had become familiar with the work process. Parents and older brothers and sisters provided a variety of models of occupational behavior. Most young boys and girls commencing work in the mills learned initial tasks from relatives rather than from strangers. An informal family apprenticeship system was thus infused into the formal structure of the world's largest textile mill.

When they came to take their first job, the children were already familiar with the names of overseers and second hands, knew the gossip about various transactions in the workrooms, and were familiar with a number of shortcuts and tricks. They also knew from an early age that the Amoskeag Corporation was the single largest employer in the city and that they could not afford to be blackballed because it would be difficult to find work anywhere else in northern New England.

For workers who started as teenagers, the Amoskeag symbolized their transition to adulthood. It was tied up with their youth; it was the place where they first learned their jobs, where they became "workers." Commencement of work was a rite of passage, separating the grown-ups from the kids. To even those youngsters who lived with their parents and contributed most of their pay to the family economy, starting work provided a sense of independence. For boys, the beginning of work meant money to buy their first suit, permission to begin smoking and stay out later. For girls, it meant buying a new dress, permission to go to dances and movies, and the right to put up their hair. For both boys and girls it involved joining peer groups of other workers. Although many regretted leaving school at such an early age and feared the drudgery and pressure of a workday, they nevertheless looked forward to becoming a wage earner. The sociability of the workrooms and the occasional dances and games were additional enticements.

Some scholars, particularly Shorter (1971), have argued that industrial work offered young men and women independence from parental control. And Anderson (1971) argued that by becoming wage earners, sons and daughters were placed in a bargaining position with their parents. But these views have been challenged by

Scott and Tilly (1975, 1978), who have argued for a continued inter-dependence between working daughters and their families of origin.

As this study shows, those who lived at home habitually contributed most of their wages to the family collectivity. Even those who migrated to work in cities still maintained ties to their families and communities of origin and continued to send a portion of their wages home. A commitment to a collective family economy continued to tie young men and women to their families of origin, even if they were not living in the same household.

In the world described here, holding down a job did not necessarily convey independent adulthood (see Chapter 7). After starting to work, many young men and women continued to live in their parental homes, the homes of relatives, or boardinghouses, still subject to strong familial supervision and discipline. But work in the mill did confer a degree of independence, particularly to younger women. It provided a partial escape from their mothers' supervision and from domestic chores and enabled them to follow a separate schedule determined by factory time. It also gave them a sense of managing their own lives, albeit a limited one.

For young women, mill work was an alternative to domestic service or work at home. It gave them pride in a new skill and the ability to earn money. As Cora Pellerin reflected on the advantages of mill work:

> If I wanted to go back on the farm, I'd have had to go work in private houses in Montreal and Quebec, take care of the house, wash clothes, help with the food, and whatever there is to be done. Housemaid. My mother didn't want that because we were brought up in the States, and she knew that if her girls were going to go wrong, they were going to do it away from home also. So she said, "At least if they work in the mills, they work a certain hour, they get paid, they do what they want" [*Amoskeag*, p. 203].

Although some young men and women already knew each other from their immediate neighborhood or through friendship and kinship ties, work in the mills nevertheless provided an important transition from a family orientation to a peer orientation. Fellow workers often introduced new workers to their jobs, thus easing the initial adjustment to work. Occasionally, relationships were prejudiced by previous grudges and dislikes lingering from childhood, but new workers were more often aided by friends and were also able to meet new ones. Good peer relationships in the mill were essential to ease a new worker's adaptation to the demanding work processes, to aid in the development of skills and in learning shortcuts, and to provide reinforcement and assistance.

Assistance from fellow workers extended beyond the immediate work environment to personal life, such as the advice older women gave to young women about courtship and marriage. Older men and women often provided advice on sexual behavior. Some adolescent women learned the facts of life by eavesdropping on the conversations of older women or by asking for information directly. Some lessons provoked anxiety; others allayed it. Ora Pelletier learned some of the facts of life the hard way:

> My mother never explained anything to me about the facts of life. When I started to work, I was fifteen, and a guy who used to go to school with me was there working in the same room . . . One day I was right at the end of the frame, and I suppose one of the older guys must have said something to him, because he came over and started speaking to me. All of a sudden, he kissed me on the cheek. I turned around, and SLAP! I slapped his face, and he went flying. He started to cry. At the other end, they were laughing like hell.
>
> For two weeks I couldn't eat, I couldn't sleep – I thought I was pregnant. My mother always said, "Don't ever let a boy touch you." He had touched me; he kissed me. I was too afraid to tell anybody . . . I had heard from one of the girls that if a girl was pregnant, she shouldn't menstruate; so after two weeks, when I saw I was menstruating, I knew I wasn't pregnant [laughs]! So I started to eat like a horse . . .
>
> I remember the girls in the mill saying that one of the girls was going to have a baby. I couldn't believe it. They said, "Yes, it's true." She was always sitting with us, so I asked her if it was true. She said, "Yes," and she started to cry because nobody would talk to her. She said, "It isn't my fault." She told me she had been raped in the woods [*Amoskeag*, pp. 243–4].

Some friendships that were formed in the mill lasted a lifetime and would frequently overlap kinship ties. Many young workers met their future spouses in the mill, either on the job or through their friends. "There were those who weren't married and they got married during the time they worked together and it was like a family. We all knew each other and we'd have parties" (Angelique Laplante, interview). During their breaks, young men often visited their girlfriends at their looms and spinning frames to help them with their work, a common practice that was tolerated by bosses as long as work was not interrupted.

Young men and women in the Amoskeag could behave on the job in a way rarely possible in their own homes. They enjoyed joking, singing, and carefree talk, teasing and bantering, which alleviated the pressures of the job and the drudgery and thus made the twelve-hour grind more bearable. "I enjoyed every one of my jobs," recalled Amelia Gazaille, a spinner. "We worked a long day but we enjoyed ourselves. We'd get together during our dinner hours. And when . . . the circus used to come to Manchester, they used to close down and let us see the parade" (interview).

In the spinning rooms, where many teen-agers were first trained for their jobs, young workers socialized and even played games despite the heat and the dirt. "I had a good time. It was very easy for us. We use to dance in the noontime and we used to jump rope. We use to bring our lunch or something. Even after I was married we'd go out into the alley at noontime and dance" (Laplante interview). The burling room, in particular, provided the perfect opportunity for sociability during work hours – it mirrored the experience of the Lowell girls in the nineteenth century: carefully dressed young women, working together, socializing, joking, aiding each other, planning mischief, sharing secrets, gossiping, and learning from older women.

But the similarity of the world of the Amoskeag and that of Lowell stops here. For most young women in Lowell, working in the mill represented only a transitional phase into adult life. In early twentieth-century Manchester, however, work in the mill was a career that, even if frequently interrupted, engaged considerable numbers of women for the better part of their lives. The home environment of women workers in Manchester was more tightly organized along family lines than the home environment in Lowell. Whereas the boardinghouses of the Massachusetts town provided a surrogate family of fellow workers, the Manchester world consisted of real families.

The structure and pace of textile work enabled women to work intermittently, to align their work periods to the rhythms of family life. Those women who continued to work after marriage dropped out for childbearing and later reentered the mill. As long as the Amoskeag retained its flexible employment policies, women who dropped out for childrearing did not risk permanent loss of a job. Even when a job was lost in one department, they could always find another job in another workroom. In the 1920s, however, this flexibility disappeared; women found it necessary to return to work as soon as they were able to after childbirth. Given the instability of industrial employment and the general insecurities of workers' lives, women were often the major supporters of their families, especially when their husbands were ill or injured.

Although economic necessity was a major factor in driving women to work, it was not the only reason. Like men, women developed attachments to their jobs. Women who started working in their teens when they were single were especially likely to continue after marriage because of the ties they had formed and the sociability the job offered.

There was, nevertheless, a difference between men and women in their orientation to work. Even though women developed a strong identity as workers, they continued to see themselves as standbys, whereas men considered themselves the chief breadwinners. In their role as standbys, women, who were more security-conscious, consented to take the undignified jobs that men avoided. In this respect, women were prepared to swallow their pride when their family's survival or economic security was at stake, which was ably demonstrated during the strike when the fear of starvation prompted anxious women to return to work. For example, because money was scarce and because they thought that they would be less vulnerable to pickets, Maria Lacasse and her fellow women workers decided to return to the mill during the 1922 strike:

> It was the men who didn't want to go back during the strike, because there were pickets. They were afraid they were going to get killed. There was another woman on the block who said, "How about us women going to work? If we go to work, they're not going to attack us because we're women." So I decided I was going to go back because fall was coming, and we didn't have any money. We didn't know how we were going to live. That's what the strike was all about: they didn't give the workers enough money. But I knew they were not going to win; so when that woman asked me, I had the children kept, and I went in to work. I told my husband to stay home; I was afraid he would be hurt by the pickets [*Amoskeag*, pp. 260–1].

Acute family need drove Maria to swallow her pride and principle of self-reliance, whereas her husband avoided the humiliation of poverty:

> During the strike, the union didn't give us much money, but they gave us food. My husband didn't want to go to the union

> store, so I said, "I'll go. Maybe they'll give us a little something."
> The woman in th store said to me, "If you can carry a twenty-four
> pound bag of food, I'll give it to you because you have a large
> family." So the woman filled the bag, and I carried it from the
> corner of Chestnut and Bridge down to Canal [which is almost
> one mile] [*Amoskeag*, p. 260].

For most women workers, as for men, mastery of a job, no matter
how simple, was a source of pride and self-esteem. Both men and
women valued their work for the personal and group satisfaction it
offered. Workers developed a fondness for their jobs and rarely forgot the operations involved. Even a simple job that required relatively little skill provided a worker with a sense of competence, a
sense that one had the knowledge and ability to carry out one's
tasks properly. After working on the same job for fifty-four years,
Eveline Brousseau still felt proud of her work. She remembered her
pleasure when she became skilled enough at the age of 13 to do her
job without supervision:

> The woman who teach me how to weave, I stay with her for
> about two weeks. Then I do everything by myself. Then every-
> body was proud of me because I do the job perfectly good. That's
> why I keep a long time over there. For me, I'm proud of it; I do
> my job well. I'm proud of my life" [interview].

The challenge of a more complex and demanding job was essential for the self-esteem of many workers. In spite of mechanization,
certain jobs still required workers to exercise their judgment.
Weavers, burlers, and yarn sorters, for example, often set their own
production standards. Such responsibilities reinforced the workers'
sense of being skilled craftsmen. Her ability to perform the complex
procedures involved in weaving and matching samples of cloth
gave Anne Beauder a sense of competence: "I was proud. I was a
good sample weaver. They had a commission for cloth and the
overseer asked me to come and match samples on Sunday. It was all
right. I was learning all the tricks in the mill" (interview). Love of
one's work encouraged a sense of perfection: "And when you like a
job and you're a perfectionist, you want to do that job right, say 'I
did that job!' You want others to say, 'when he sets a card, it's set.'
You couldn't do that in Chicopee," said Henry Carignan (interview), who had worked in both the Amoskeag and the Chicopee
Mill – the Johnson & Johnson plant that opened in Amoskeag's
former Coolidge Mill in 1938. Cora Pellerin, a weaver all her life,
expressed the pride she felt: "You have to have it in you to be a
good weaver. You either fit or you don't" (interview).

Mary Cunion was another who liked weaving best because of its complexity and the many challenges it held:

> We used to have warps in five or six colors. It was not just in your hands. It was in your head too. You had a pattern. You had to watch your pattern . . . Sometimes when the loom would get out of order, a bobbin would drop and sprout a whole warp, and the warp would have to be cut out and you'd have to start all over again . . . in fact, you never learn it all. My aunt Susan was a weaver in the old country before she came here . . . She used to say, "you never in your lifetime learn it all because every warp you get in is a new one; a new color" . . . Weaving was the best thing in the mill work [interview].

The worker's sense of perfection was reinforced by the corporation's insistence on high standards. "Amoskeag was serious about work being perfect," reminisced Omer Proulx. Although the extremely complicated assignments offered by No. 4 Mill deterred many workers, to Marie Proulx, Omer's wife, they provided both a challenge and self-esteem. As a yarn tester, she had developed an unusual expertise in sorting different shades of yarn. She would not trade her job for an easier one, even though her fellow workers warned that "it's all kinds of colors that you're in . . . It doesn't make sense." Marie did not agree: "It did make sense to me. We were raised in that." The boss appreciated her ability and placed her in the front row, where she worked for twenty years, despite the strain. "I lost my eyes in No. 4 Mill" (*Amoskeag*, p. 68).

The corporation's pride in the product was internalized by the workers. That their particular skill was needed to make a product that was appreciated by outsiders contributed significantly to their attitudes toward work. Management constantly reminded the workers that the cloth they produced was famous, that the "world was knocking on the door to buy Amoskeag cloth," and that even the Ford Automobile Company used it for its cars. Workers were well aware of the Amoskeag's reputation. "They were making the best cloth in the whole world at the Amoskeag. You can't buy cloth no more like the Amoskeag was making" (James Burton, interview). Workers cherished samples of the Amoskeag cloth long after the mills had closed. Later, when they worked in mills that produced a much poorer quality of cloth, they looked back to Amoskeag products with admiration and a sense of loss.

Antoine Pelletier, a yarn sorter, recalled that Henry Ford's agent once waited in the lobby to approve the color for a yarn to be used

in a giant order – a million and a half yards – of automobile uphol-
stery cloth:

> I remember one time in 1927 . . . they came up and got me, one
> morning, at 2 o'clock. Mr. Manning told me to blend and to
> match a sample as much as I could. I worked from 2 o'clock in the
> morning . . . We had 86 colors to work from. We had red, brown,
> maroon, green, olive, taupe – they were all dyed in vats. That
> color needed about six to seven blends. It was a hell of a job. We
> finally got the order . . . a million and a half! [interview].

Even though workers felt a profound attachment to their jobs,
they were equally aware of their limited opportunities for advancement, both in status and monetarily. Both Marie and Omer Proulx,
who referred to their experience in the mills as a "life of glory,"
also confessed that they had hoped for better opportunities and
more rewarding jobs. "Fifty years ago when we worked in the
Amoskeag, it was an experiment for me, much more than anything
else," said Omer Proulx. "Weaving cotton was merely trifling away
the time." Omer worked his way up to second hand, but he did not
want to stop there. In his own basement he experimented constantly with new inventions in an effort to improve machinery and thus
advance the hope that "I would wear a white shirt someday"
(*Amoskeag*, p. 68). At the same time, as a French Canadian, he was
also painfully aware of the improbability of advancing beyond the
ranks of second hand, at least not without Scottish, Irish, and
American friends.

Even years later the very word *Amoskeag* still evoked intense
emotional responses – both a sense of pride and a sense of loss – in
its former employees. When unfolding layers of memory, experiences and reactions as they were perceived at their occurrence are
often confused when viewed with hindsight. In addition, the despair that followed the shutdown in 1936 and the difficult working
conditions and inferior products of the mills that opened in Manchester afterward may have led workers to idealize the Amoskeag.
The positive feelings now expressed could result from loneliness in
old age and the consequent glorification of an earlier "golden age,"
a nostalgia enhanced by distance in time. Yet when work is an almost all-encompassing experience, there is little other justification
for one's life:

> When you work twelve hours a day, you have to find pleasure in
> work. There's nowhere else to find it. You can't look forward to
> going home or going out in the evening. I remember my father

and my aunt talking about the good time they had [Virginia Erskine, *Amoskeag*, p. 231].

But the retrospective character of these statements alone does not account for the strong attachment felt by workers in the next generation. Bette Skrzyszowski, who worked in the Chicopee Mills in Manchester until the last minute of their unexpected shutdown in 1974, but who had never worked in the Amoskeag, expressed a sense of loss the day the mill shut down.

> You go up and down the aisle, and you say, "I used to have all these looms to fill." Now you don't have anything. Now it's so empty, you can almost hear the stillness come across the room. You go through a section where a lot of them are running, and then you come to where it's awful quiet. Only a few are running. And it's a lot colder, too . . . But there's just no place to go. After you put that many years into a place, it's like a second home. You go every day, you know how much time it's going to take you, and you come home at a certain time. Just a nice routine. You knew what to do and how to do it, and you knew how long it would take you. Nobody bothered you. You knew you had a job to go to. It was a good feeling. Now you know your time has come, and you feel lost. You just have no place to turn. I've spent half my life in the mill [*Amoskeag*, pp. 381–2].

Former workers did not simply idealize their experiences, however. In recounting their work histories, they remembered both the good and the bad. The very people who expressed their sense of attachment and pride were equally vocal about their feelings of entrapment and discontent. Even committed workers were not oblivious to the low status accorded mill work even in a community whose economy was so heavily dependent on industrial activity. "A lot of people think it was a disgrace to work in the mills . . . If you worked in the mills you just didn't have any education . . . That's why people started sending their children to high school and college" (Helen Robinson, interview). When Arthur Morrill rushed to the Amoskeag exhibit in Manchester in 1975, he described himself as an "Amoskeag man" and spontaneously demonstrated the use of a "kiss of death" shuttle he had brought from his personal collection. But later, in his interview, he exclaimed: "I don't know to this day why I went to work in a stinking cotton mill" (*Amoskeag*, p. 105).

The work ethic in American society had been considered the unique property of the Yankee upper class. Thrift, sobriety, and hard work have been defined as the essential elements of the Protestant ethic.[3] Much of the historic tension between labor and capital has been cast as a conflict between a preindustrial work ethic and the demands of the modern industrial system. But this dichotomy might not be the correct model. The Amoskeag's immigrant workers, like many of their contemporaries in other American industrial establishments, behaved in a way often considered characteristic of the Yankee work ethic. Their commitment to hard work and faith in work as a redeeming feature was the very center of their survival. Their sense of the inherent value of work – of getting one's job done and doing it well – was inculcated at an early age. Their basic dedication to work was inherent in the values and traditions that immigrant workers had first learned in rural society, as was their sense of fair play and their expectations of just treatment by bosses and fellow workers. Their acceptance of industrial discipline did not reflect blind submissiveness. They accepted difficult conditions and the bosses' authority not because they had no standards of their own but because they had no choice.

Immigrants from nonindustrial backgrounds had to adjust not to working per se but to the regulation and scheduling of their labor and leisure by others.[4] Newly arrived workers were willing to "sell their labor" to the corporation and to work for a demanding boss and an invisible master because industrial work offered them a way out of rural poverty. The major conflict between their nonindustrial values and the work ethic of the industrial system did not involve the need to work but whom they were working for, at what pace, and by whose standards.

At the same time, their work ethic incorporated a commitment to high standards and a product of quality. A good product, they felt, reflected not only the corporation's standards but also the workers' own sense of competence. They worked not merely out of submission to authority but out of respect for the work process itself and the product. For that very reason, when veteran workers taught newcomers industrial work procedures and discipline they also imparted criteria for good performance.

The standards adhered to by Amoskeag workers were thus, at least partially, internally generated. In this respect, at least in the earlier part of this century, the workers' point of view coalesced with that of the corporation. Later, when the corporation began to decline, workers often guarded those standards more zealously than the bosses. Whereas the corporation was willing to produce an inferior product in order to remain afloat, workers sustained their commitment to the perfection of the product and the mutual understanding in work relations that had developed earlier.

The sense of family and community responsibilities workers carried over from rural backgrounds also shaped their commitment to work as a collective enterprise. In the industrial arena, workers were limited by the pace of machinery and the pace of other workers. The collective nature of industrial work dictated a communal work ethos. The industrial work ethic contained therefore two different and often conflicting components: doing one's job well and meeting one's responsibilities to fellow workers. Codes of collective behavior governed the workers' relations to each other, both on the shop floor and in their families.

Work careers did not spring entirely from individual choices. The family offered its members some of the main incentives for work. Even the metaphor by which other organizations and aspects of life were perceived and judged was based on the family. Workers often compared good working relations to good family relations: "We were all like a family" was a recurring summation of work experience. It is not surprising, therefore, that the shutdown of the mill was perceived as not only a personal catastrophe but also the breakdown of the mill family.

5 *The dynamics of kin*

This chapter examines the variety of roles played by kin in workers' migration to Manchester and their adjustment to industrial conditions. It focuses on three interrelated activities: the Amoskeag's use of kin in the recruitment of immigrant workers; the role of kin within the factory in hiring, job placement, and the control of work processes; and overlapping both areas, the vital functions of kin in providing assistance in critical life situations. In this discussion, the term *kin* includes both members of the nuclear family and relatives residing elsewhere.

The discussion of the interaction of kin with the corporation covers both a period of relative stability as well as one of crisis. During the earlier years of labor shortage, when the corporation relied heavily on kin as labor recruiters, the influence of kin on the placement of workers was extensive. In the subsequent period of labor surplus, when unemployment and the deterioration of work relationships reduced the effectiveness of kin in influencing the workplace, kin continued to carry the major burden of assistance.

The function of kin in the factory

From the late nineteenth century through World War I, workers brought their relatives to the factory, assisted in their placement, and taught them industrial work processes and schedules, thus fulfilling the corporation's expectations. In particular, when the Amoskeag Company began to recruit French Canadians systematically, it utilized the workers' own informal ties by encouraging those already living in Manchester to recruit their Canadian kin and provide the necessary support for newly arriving relatives. The corporation could thus restrict its own efforts to organizing transportation; it did not need to concern itself with assistance to new workers.

This chapter is an expanded version of "The Dynamics of Kin in an Industrial Community," *American Journal of Sociology* 84, Supplement, 1978 by permission of the University of Chicago Press.

The trainloads of potential workers arriving from Quebec were generally not crowds of helpless people moving into completely un- known territory. Most had already received firsthand descriptions of both the town and the factory. Most likely, someone greeted them upon their arrival. They often had relatives still in Canada, so if things failed in Manchester, they could always return to the fa- milial environment of their place of origin.

Their movement from Quebec villages and towns to Manchester followed a pattern of chain migration.[1] First a son or daughter or married couples without children came. After they found work and housing, they sent for other relatives. Workers without relatives in Manchester joined former neighbors who were already living there.

As Antonia Bergeron summarized the process in her own family:

> So when my neighbors went to the U.S., I decided to go with them. It cost [my parents] a little to let me go (not money cost, but feeling cost) but they knew the people well and they had faith in me . . . I didn't know anyone when we arrived . . . Then I met a woman who had taught me school in Canada when I was small. She worked in the mills here. She helped me, found me a job in the mills . . . My mother came up later with my little brother and my little sister . . . As time went on, we'd have an- other person come up, and another, and finally the whole family was here [*Amoskeag*, p. 60].

The Simoneau family provides a typical example of chain migra- tion. In the 1880s Eugene Simoneau and his wife migrated to Lis- bon Springs, Maine, where their first three children were born. Af- ter working in the Lisbon Springs textile mills for a time, the family subsequently returned to Canada where their other four children were born. After his mother's death, the oldest son migrated to Manchester in 1908 and started working as a weaver. He then brought his father and all his younger brothers and sisters. The father entered the same weaving room in which the son was work- ing; subsequently, each child entered the mills upon reaching age 14 except for the youngest son, who became a barber and worked in the shop that his father set up after he left the mill (Figure 5.1).

Chain migration was not limited to Manchester: French Canadi- ans followed their kin into other New Hampshire and Maine facto- ry towns as well. Although the major migration route led from Que- bec to Manchester, a good deal of back-and-forth migration also occurred. Jean Dione articulated the migratory character of kin this way: "Our family was five minutes in Canada, and five minutes here . . . One child was born here, one in Canada" (interview). Dione did not refer, of course, to the entire family unit but rather to

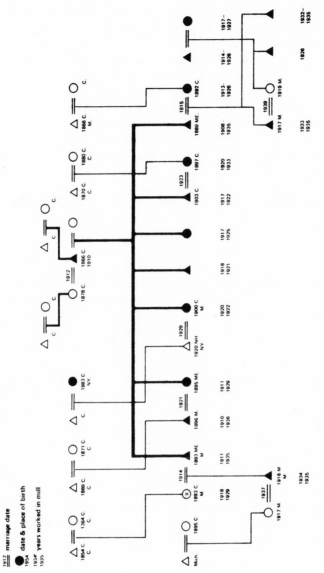

Figure 5.1. Kinship chart of the Simoneau family.

different individual family members moving back and forth. But in his mind, this movement of individuals or of smaller segments of the kinship group was part of a continuing pattern of family movement connecting both sides of the border.

In addition to facilitating the flow of workers to New England towns, chain migration also tied families in Manchester and Quebec into one social system. Kin assistance continuously flowed back and forth between Manchester and the communities of origin. Those who went to the United States spearheaded the migration for other relatives, locating housing and jobs, and those who remained in Quebec often took care of the family and property responsibilities. In order to migrate, individuals needed not only assistance upon arrival but also psychological and economic support in preparation for departure. A backup system in the community of origin was especially important, because French-Canadian immigrants to New England industrial towns during the early part of the century did not consider their migration final. Ties with the relatives remaining behind had to be maintained to ensure that the property or the farm (often still functioning) would be taken care of while the owners migrated on a provisional basis. The knowledge that relatives remaining behind would assume those responsibilities provided a needed sense of security to the migrants.

The role of kin in labor recruitment and the placement of workers started with simple assistance in finding employment for newly arrived immigrants or young relatives coming of age and later developed into more complex assistance, such as placing relatives in preferred jobs and departments. As Mary's letter suggests, the practice of kin recruitment was common even in New England:

> Dear Birt,
>   Before you come up go and get your permit to go to work. You will work with me all day and a boss over you. I hope you can come up before Sat. I know you will like it. Millie send her love to Kit and Rufie. I hope they will come up soon. Nell hates to go home. Love from all. Come up soon.
>
>   Mary B.[2]

Workers at the mill often exploited their good relations with the overseers to place their kin. As the following letters suggest, this practice was not limited to French Canadians:

>   June 22, 1904
>   Please mister if possible you get job to give it that man because he is my cousin and he is family man for family holder.
>
>   no signature[3]

Sept. 16, 1904

Dear Sir (Mr. Foreman)

I am sure that you know that my Brother is working here quite long while now all most six months since, and I hope you be kinde if you Please, and give him another one which with little more Pay to satisfing his own Poor self and he will be very much obliged to you.

Very truely yours,

E. Piter[4]

This was especially important in finding jobs for young relatives in rooms where the bosses were known to be more considerate and flexible and where parents need not fear their children's exposure to bad habits. These informal patterns of workers' placement through kin eventually affected the composition of workrooms as well as the work processes. Even after the employment office was introduced in 1911, the ability of workers to influence hiring persisted.

After the centralized personnel system was created, overseers retained the right to request a specific worker through the employment office. If a worker did not immediately find an appropriate place, he or she took an interim position while relatives continued to look for a better work situation. When an opening appeared in a suitable workroom, the worker was informed and requested a transfer. The size of the corporation, with its many departments and several workrooms for each operation, allowed such movements from workroom to workroom or from department to department. Workers in a desirable room interceded with the overseers to request their relative from the employment office. The pervasiveness of family influence over the employment process is expressed by Joseph Debski who, having been appointed to introduce a centralized and depersonalized hiring system in 1911, proceeded to hire his own relatives, one after another. His description of that process contradicts his raison d'être: "I was the first in my family in the mills. Then I got my brother in, my other brother, my sister, and my wife [laughs] . . . But they don't make jobs. But if there's one job and three people looking, naturally you can give it to your own" (*Amoskeag*, 136–5). This practice was commonly followed by most workers, regardless of their levels of skill.

Overseers supported recruitment through kin because they were thereby assured of employing someone they could trust. They could also rely on workers to teach newly arrived relatives their jobs and to assume some responsibility for new workers. As a result of this

Table 5.1. *Percentage of French-Canadian workers with relatives working in the mill at any time*

Relatives ever in the mill	Percentage ($N = 717$)
None	24.4
1	29.9
2	17.5
3	9.9
4	5.9
5	3.5
6	3.1
7	2.1
8	1.8
9 and more	1.9
Mean N relatives ever working in the mill	2.0

Note: Includes people who worked before 1912 as well.

informal recruitment process workers naturally tended to cluster in the mill along kinship and ethnic lines.

Analysis of the kinship networks of French-Canadian workers reveals the pervasiveness of kin clustering: Out of 717 French-Canadian workers in the original sample of the individual employee files, 75.6% had relatives working in the mill at any time (not necessarily at the same time; Table 5.1). Although this figure is conservative, because it does not include all kin working in the mill but only those kin who could be traced and linked (see Appendix C for details of this process), it nevertheless gives some idea of the magnitude of kin clustering in the Amoskeag mills. Of the 121 clusters of workers for whom kin relationships were established, 20.7% consisted of husband and wife, 28.1% consisted of couples and their parents, and 24.0% consisted of extended kin as well as members of the nuclear family (Table 5.2). The most frequent correlation, two members of the same kin group working in the same department, occurred 93 times and constituted 61.6% of all coincidences of kin (Table 5.3). These figures represent kin working in the same department, though not necessarily at the same time. The oral histories confirm the pervasiveness of this practice. Once a family member was established in a particular department, other relatives followed, even when the original family member was no longer working there.

Table 5.2. *Kinship clusters working in the mill*

Cluster	N	Adjusted percentage[a] (N = 121)
Original informant only	31	25.6
Husband and wife only	25	20.7
Husband and/or wife and their parents	34	28.1
Husband and wife and their children	2	1.6[b]
Nuclear and other members	29	24.0

[a] Total number of kinship clusters working in the mill for which exact relationships of all members are known. The reconstruction of the kinship clusters is explained in Appendix C.
[b] The small percentage of children working with their own parents is a result of the linkage and trace process. Because marriage and employment records were used predominantly for the trace, it was impossible to retrieve larger numbers of sons and daughters who were still unmarried and living at home.

Table 5.3. *Percentage of times members of kinship clusters worked in the same department at any time*

Kin in a department	Times this occurred	Percentage of times this occurred (N = 151)
2	93	61.6
3	23	15.2
4	18	11.9
5 or more	17	11.3

Even more significant for socialization and mutual assistance was the tendency of relatives to work at the same time in the same workrooms (Table 5.4). Of 103 instances of kin overlapping in the mill during the same period, 65 instances (63.1%) involved two members and 21 instances (20.4%) involved three members. Of the 105 kin clusters working in the mill analyzed, 59% had two or more members working at the same time (Table 5.5). Members of two generations in the same kin group coincided or overlapped frequently; of the kinship clusters with known relationships, 65.7% consisted of two generations of the same family working in the mills at the same time (Table 5.6).

The tendency of relatives to drift to certain workrooms was com-

Table 5.4. *Percentage of times members of kinship clusters worked in the same department at the same time*

Kin in a department	Times this occurred	Percentage of times this occurred ($N = 103$)
2	65	63.1
3	21	20.4
4	7	6.8
5 or more	10	9.7

Table 5.5. *Percentage of relatives coinciding in kinship clusters with members working in the same department at the same time*

Members coinciding	Clusters	Percentage ($N = 105$)
1	43	41.0
2	31	29.5
3	17	16.2
4	14	13.3

Table 5.6. *Generations in each cluster working in the mill at the same time*

Generations working in the mill at the same time	Clusters	Percentage ($N = 105$)
None	6	5.7
1	29	27.6
2	69	65.7
3	1	1.0

mon to most of the family clusters analyzed. Of 151 instances of departmental overlap, the highest incidences occurred in the weave room (31%) and the spinning room (34%). This high frequency reflects the character of these two departments: They had the highest concentration of semiskilled workers, and they attracted French Canadians in large numbers. They were also the departments to which sons and daughters were typically sent for their apprenticeship. The dress room, the card room, and the spool room accounted for 7.6%, 5.3%, and 8%, respectively, of all instances of overlapping. Kin also overlapped in the boiler room (6%), in the yard (2.6%), and in the bleach room (6%).

In assessing the significance of these patterns, it is important to note that the large number of French Canadians in the mills is in itself merely the outcome of the dependence of a major part of the working population on the Amoskeag. Although a high proportion of French Canadians in the work force could account for the overall presence of larger kinship clusters in the mills, the high degree of clustering that occurred in the same workrooms suggests that clustering was deliberate. There were, in fact, some family-specific workrooms, rooms to which members of the same family tended to return again and again. And this was not limited to French Canadians. The Scottish dyehouse was a case in point. Clustering was also reinforced by ethnic ties, and kin and ethnic clustering often overlapped. Certain departments and workrooms tended to attract members of certain ethnic groups and were known, in fact, for the ethnic group most commonly within them. Thus kin and ethnic clustering were mutually reinforcing. Virginia Erskine recalled ethnic and family clustering in the dyehouse:

> My uncle Johnnie Carlin was superintendent in the dyehouse . . . My aunt also worked as a clerk in the dyehouse office, and practically all of my mother's family worked there. Their father had come over to work in the dyehouse and when their children grew up they went to work there. My father was Swedish, but he went to work there after he married my mother by virtue of her family connections [*Amoskeag*, p. 222].

In the Anger family, for example (Figure 5.2), eight siblings and their spouses overlapped in various configurations over their work careers in several departments. In a twisting department, ten incidents of overlap of different durations occurred, involving different pairs of Anger siblings at various points in time, followed by in-laws and brothers and sisters of in-laws. At one point, Florida (Anger) Gelly, her brother Henry, and the aunt of Henry's wife worked in the same room (Figure 5.3). At another point, Florida Gelly, her

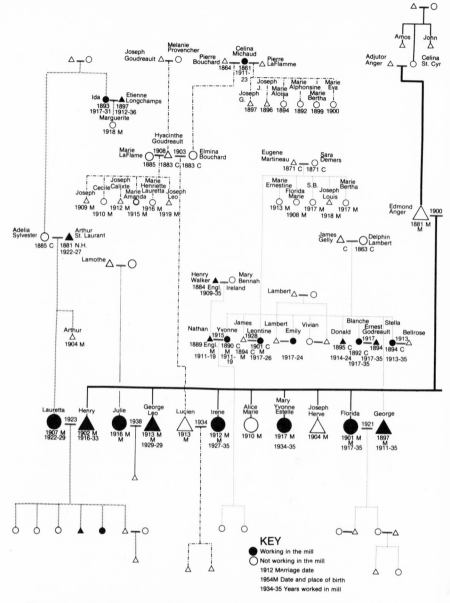

Figure 5.2. Kinship chart of the Anger family.

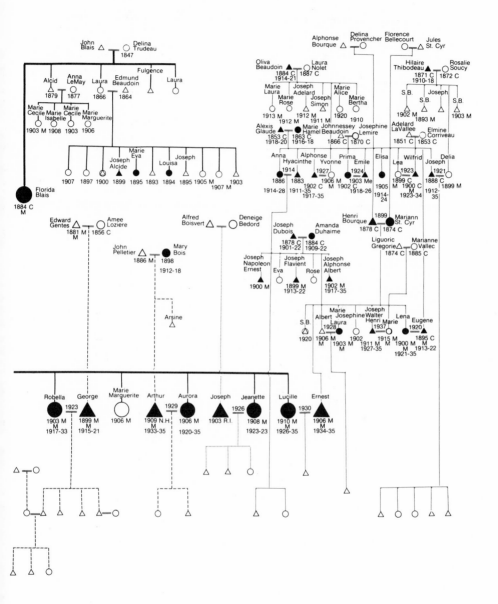

95

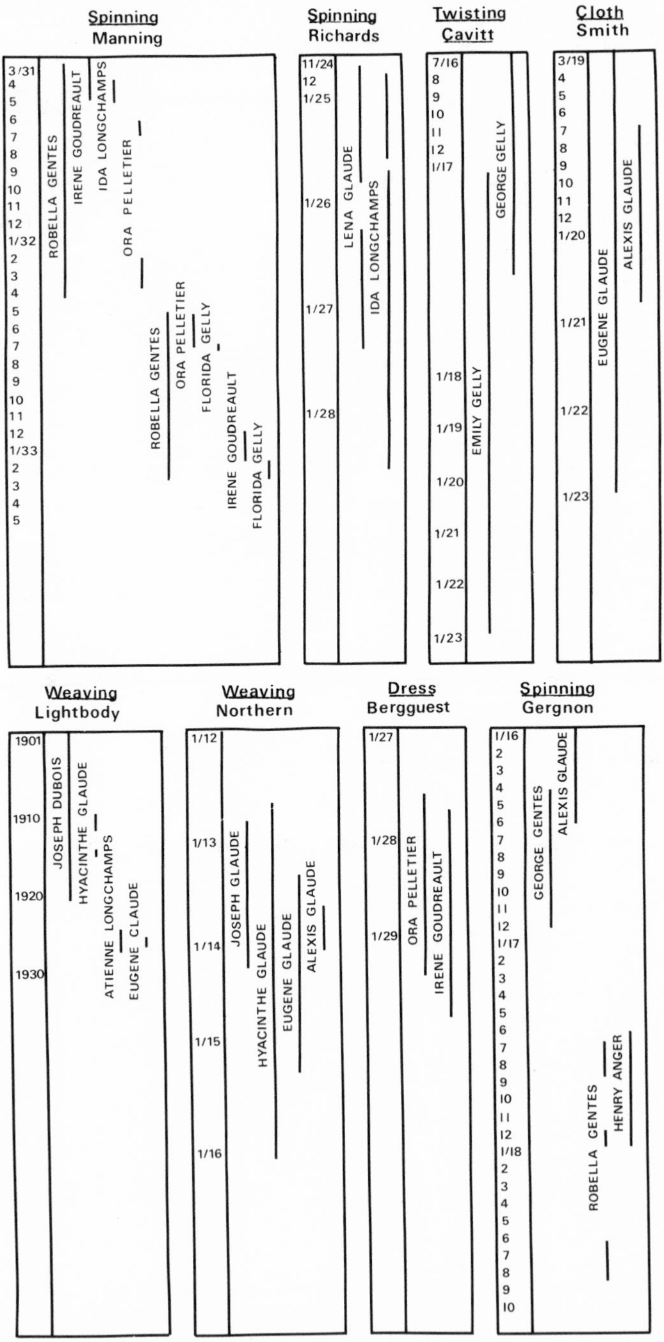

Figure 5.3. Work configurations of Anger family members and extended kin in the Amoskeag Mills over time. For relationships see Figure 5.2.

Spinning
Lynch

3/32
4
5
6
7
8
9

GEORGE GELLY

Weaving
Sanborn

1/25
2
3
4
5
6
7
8
9
10
11
12
1/26

1/27

1/28

EUGENE GLAUDE

HYACINTHE GLAUDE

ATIENNE LONGCHAMPS

Spinning
Dorney

7/31

1/32

1/33

1/34

1/35

ORA PELLETIER

FLORIDA GELLY

HENRY ANGER

ORA PELLETIER

LUCILLE BOURQUE

YVONNE ANGER

Spinning
Sweetser

1/17

1/18

1/19

1/20

1/21

1/22

GEORGE GENTES

HENRY ANGER

GEORGE GENTES

ROBELLA GENTES

ORA PELLETIER

GEORGE GENTES

ORA PELLETIER

Twisting
Blain

1/17
1/18
1/19
1/20
1/21
1/22
1/23
1/24
1/25
1/26
1/27
1/28
1/29
1/30
1/31
1/32
1/33
1/34

BLANCHE GARCEAU

IDA LONGCHAMPS

LAURA DUBOIS

GEORGE GELLY

FLORIDA GELLY

BLANCHE GARCEAU

EMILY GELLY

LAURA DUBOIS

IRENE GOUDREAULT

Dress
Van Vielt

1/26
2
3
4
5
6
7
8
9
10
11
12
1/27
2
3
4
5
6
7
8

FLORIDA GELLY

WILFRID LAVALLIERE

Weaving
Miller

1/21

1/22

1/23

1/24

ELISA GLAUDE

EUGENE GLAUDE

Weaving
Molloy

1/23
2
3
4
5
6
7
8
9
10
11
12

EUGENE GLAUDE

JOSEPH GLAUDE

Note: Name at top of each column is of overseer in charge.

97

husband, George, and George's sister and brother-in-law worked there. The next case of overlap occurred when two of George's sisters and one of Florida's sisters joined the room. At another time one of Florida's sisters and her sister-in-law overlapped; and on another occasion, one of Florida's sisters and the brother-in-law of another sister overlapped. The Anger siblings and their extended kin offer numerous other configurations as well. In addition the configurations repeated themselves in different forms in other workrooms. For example, in a spinning room, Ora (Anger) Pelletier overlapped with her sister Robella and Robella's husband, George Gentes. At another point George Gentes overlapped in that room with his wife's brother Henry Anger. During a period of almost forty years, the members of the Anger family, their in-laws, and their in-laws' relatives moved through the various workrooms in different configurations.

Ora Pelletier's account sheds some light on those movements: Initially, all the siblings old enough to work started work together. "My brothers and sisters and I would go down to the mill together. We'd work together all day and come back home together." Ora was initiated to work by her sister Robella. "Bella had got me a job working with her at the Langdon Mill [part of the Amoskeag] spinning, and Henry [her brother] was working there, too, in the room upstairs." Ora then moved to the warp room, where she got her sister Irene a job as a tie-over girl. "We sisters were always working with one another. We used to exchange our lunches" (*Amoskeag*, pp. 242, 186, and 189).

A new worker with relatives in the mill did not walk into a social vacuum on his or her first day. Relatives were present to help, to instruct, and to prod. The presence of kin in the mill was particularly important at the beginning of a career when they not only facilitated finding a job but also offered guidance and support to young relatives on their first entry into the factory. Relatives helped initiate new workers into the techniques of the job and the social regimen to be observed. The development of a successful career in the mill depended, however, on more than the mere presence of kin. The climb up the ladder depended on how well connected the worker's kin were, their reputation, and their status in the mill.

Typically, a relative accompanied young men and women on their first venture to the employment office or a workroom. Relatives instructed young people in their first jobs, thus saving time and money for the corporation and obviating the need for special training and apprenticeship programs. Workers were able to perform their own jobs while teaching their relatives, at least in the period preceding the speedups and the intensification of the piece-rate system. Parents, older brothers and sisters, aunts, uncles, and cousins invested in the training of their progeny or other young kin because the work was essential to the family's economy and because they wanted their relatives to succeed in the factory without violating cherished family attitudes toward work or compromising the reputation that other family workers had achieved.

Beyond the immediate practical assistance extended by relatives, kinship ties provided an identification and a reference for new workers. New workers bore the label of their kin. An individual was identified and often judged by the family to which he or she belonged or by association with other known relatives in a department. Incoming workers were immediately labeled as Joe Dubois's daughter or Anna Gagnon's niece. The status of relatives present in the mill sometimes descended to the shoulders of a new worker. The sins of the fathers were not necessarily visited upon the sons, nor was a worker uniformly treated as an independent agent. In this respect, kinship ties bestowed disadvantages as well as advantages.

Learning jobs from relatives and carrying out the first few weeks of work under their supervision had the tremendous advantage of enabling the new worker to obtain tips on shortcuts and "tricks" in established work procedures. By imitating the techniques of other workers or by adapting them to one's own tempo, a worker had some control over the pace of work and was even able to secure some leisure time while tending to machinery. Older relatives in the mill also provided comfort, reassurance, and a sense of belonging. The unspoken, but clearly conveyed, code of behavior in the workrooms and the presence of more experienced workers from one's family group made new workers – particularly young women – less vulnerable to work hazards, fatigue, and pressure from bosses. Parents considered these factors in choosing the room to which they would send their children.

Relatives were also instrumental in setting limits on work loads or improving conditions that could not be achieved through regular channels. Although the following example was unsuccessful, it does illustrate how such maneuvering might have achieved a desired result. Marie Houde wanted to be assigned a set of window looms because she had problems with her eyesight. Her boss said she would have to wait until such a set of looms became available. One day she asked permission to switch with her son, who had window looms. The next morning her son gave notice. The overseer saw through the timing of the switch and eventually ordered Marie to return to her original looms. He then turned the window looms over to a woman who had been waiting for a chance to work near the windows because she wanted to be near her husband.[5]

Relatives present in the same workroom provided some protection from accusations of misconduct by second hands and from misunderstandings and conflicts. This was true particularly when a formal grievance was involved, because relatives were able to support each other and corroborate each other's statements. Susan Gagne was dismissed by the boss because she had missed one day without notifying him that she was sick. When she reported for work the next day the second hand asked her to leave. Her sister, who spoke English, interceded on her behalf and filed a grievance with the Adjustment Board. As a result, Susan was reinstated.[6] When workers lost their tempers with one another or with the bosses, relatives acted as intermediaries to smooth things out, effect apologies, or bring about compromise. The presence of relatives or close friends was particularly important when the work processes were structurally interconnected and the speed of one worker depended on that of his fellow workers.

Relatives alternated running machinery and taking breaks, substituted for each other during illness, childbirth, and trips to Canada, and often helped slower kin complete their piece-work quotas. Out of consideration for each other, they rarely exceeded the production quotas that had been informally agreed upon. This type of family work pattern also allowed older workers to hold on to their jobs for a longer period. Those in speedier and more exacting jobs traded their know-how for assistance from younger relatives. When family groups worked together, as in the case of the Scottish dyehouse workers, older workers could stay on the job as long as younger relatives were willing to perform the more physically taxing tasks. Relatives thus provided mutual support in facing supervisors and in handling the work pace. The presence of kin in the same workroom, especially relatives who were well respected or in supervisory positions, sheltered workers from fines, layoffs, and, in certain circumstances, mistreatment by management or conflict with other workers.

It is not surprising, therefore, that workers with kin present in the workrooms or with strong kin connections were more likely than others to advance up the ladder of skill. Workers whose parents or other relatives had developed stable careers in the mill were more likely to have alternative job options available in the mill, which often aided their advancement, slight as it was (see Chapter 9).

To a limited extent, kinship ties served as a surrogate for labor unions. Family manipulation of the work process provides a partial explanation for the absence of unions from the Amoskeag until World War I. As long as the corporation's paternalism harmonized with the workers' attitudes and with familial orientation, and as long as the flexibility in the system enabled the workers to exercise controls informally, workers showed little enthusiasm for union membership. Perhaps it is no coincidence that the union was successful in recruiting larger numbers of workers and in calling a strike during a period when family groups were beginning to lose their influence over the work process.

Kin assistance in critical life situations

The interdependence of kin in the factory was part of a larger role that kin fulfilled as the very source of security and assistance in all aspects of life. Within the family, relatives provided major support over the entire life course, both on a routine basis and in times of stress. Kin assistance was essential both in coping with the insecurities dictated by the industrial system, such as unemployment and strikes, and in coping with personal and family crises, especially childbirth, illness, and death.[7]

The basic axis of kin assistance both in the nuclear and the extended family was that of siblings with each other and parents with their children. Most mutual assistance among kin was carried out between brothers and sisters and between adult children and aging parents, even after they had left their common household. Older brothers and sisters were expected to care for their younger siblings as a matter of course, even to act as surrogate parents in the event of the death of one parent. Given the wide age spread of children within the family, it was not unusual for the oldest child to be about the age at which he or she could have been a parent of the youngest child.

Grandmothers and aging aunts cared for grandchildren and for nieces and nephews, without necessarily living in the same household. They also cooked meals, cleaned house, and mended clothes when a mother was working.

Older female relatives assisted young women in childbirth and took care of the other children in the family while the mother was recovering. Relatives cared for each other during illness (at a time when people rarely stayed in hospitals). Relatives reared orphans, along with their own children, and also took in invalids and retarded family members.

Male relatives helped each other in the repair and maintenance of their apartments or homes; when they owned farmland outside the city, they cooperated in planting and harvesting. They shared tools and implements, traded services and transportation.

As siblings left home and established their own households, modes of assistance in the nuclear family were broadened to include extended kin. In addition to this basic interaction of the core siblings and parents, nuclear families were enmeshed in larger kinship networks that often spanned two or three generations and were expanded through marriage. The distance of the relationship affected, of course, the intensity of the interactions. Instead of close involvement with childrearing, health care, and the collective work and maintenance of the household, assistance was more of a casual nature. The level of obligation varied depending on how closely kin were related. In times of crisis, or in the absence of other sources of support, however, more distant kin often took on major responsibilities as well. Even though nuclear families resided in separate households, they extended their reach beyond the household by sharing and exchanging resources and labor with their kin. Autonomous nuclear households drew their strength and support from extended kin. Living in proximity to one's kin was essential for survival, particularly in periods when transportation was difficult or when a shortage in housing occurred. Despite the predominance of the nuclear household, relatives opened up their homes to each other during periods of transition or need. Some newlywed couples initially lived either with their parents, usually the wife's parents, or with an older brother and sister. Couples often shared housing temporarily with relatives after their arrival in Manchester or during periods of scarcity.[8] Generally, however, they adhered to the custom of separation of the nuclear household from extended kin. They lived near each other, often in the same building, separate but available in time of need.

The social space of the Simoneau family in Manchester illustrates the conscious effort of kin to reside near each other and the flexibility kin exercised in extending to each other temporary help with housing. When the oldest son first arrived to settle in Manchester in 1908, he lived in a boardinghouse. When his widowed father and younger siblings joined him two years later, the family lived in a tenement close to the mills. Shortly thereafter, they moved to the West Side to be near other relatives. His father married a woman from his hometown who lived nearby in Manchester. She brought her niece, who had been living with her, into the household. The niece later married the oldest Simoneau son.[9]

As each of the sons and daughters married, they set up separate residences within several blocks of their father's house. When only two unmarried teen-age children remained, the father moved to the nearby village of Goffstown. Because commuting to work in the mill was difficult for the young daughter still living at home, she moved in with her married sister in Manchester. The father lived in Goffstown until his death, at which point the youngest son moved to Boston. The other siblings continued to live in proximity to each other. Two brothers and their wives shared housing temporarily, first during the 1922 strike, when a brother lost his home because of unemployment, and again after the shutdown of the Amoskeag, when another brother sold his home and moved to Nashua to seek work. Upon his return, he and his family moved in with the oldest brother for a limited period while looking for their own place to live.

The experience of those without relatives to assist them demonstrates the bitter price paid for isolation from kin. Lottie Sargent's father, for example, had no relatives in the city. After his wife died in childbirth, he took Lottie as a baby to bars and clubs, where the "ladies of the night" kept an eye on her. Eventually he placed her in the orphanage until he remarried, when he took her into his newly established household. Another example of the consequences of isolation from kin is provided by Cora Pellerin, who had no relatives in Manchester to care for her two daughters. When both she and her husband were working in the mill, she had a housekeeper. But during her husband's prolonged illness, she had to place the children in the Villa Augustina, a Catholic boarding school. To both Cora and her daughters, it was a heartrending experience:

> I had never been to a school with the nuns. It was hard for me to put them in there. It is a big, big building, and it seemed that it was just like a jail. That's the way I felt inside. I used to go and see them every Wednesday night, and they'd come home every Saturday. They'd have supper with me and leave every Sunday afternoon at four o'clock. If they didn't come, it was because they'd been bad and were being punished. I used to cry on my way home. I wiped my eyes before seeing my husband because if he'd notice it, he'd take the girls out [*Amoskeag*, p. 211].

Even though a systematic measure for the consistency of kin assistance is not available, it is clear from the interviews that assistance from distantly related kin was frequent. The interviewees were conscious of kinship ties that often included extended kin to whom one might be related through in-laws or cousins. Thus, in addition to the actual communication with kin, the mental kinship map, which was often reinforced by an elaborate genealogy, encompassed distantly related kin as well.

The fluidity and informality in the functions and roles of kin in Manchester was characteristic of the overall kinship structure in American society. Normatively defined in American culture, rather than legislated, the obligations among extended kin have always been flexible and voluntary (Parsons 1943:22–8). The boundaries for extended kin were loosely defined, centering on the nuclear family as a focus.

Goode characterizes kin in contemporary American society as "ascriptive friends." Kin are involved in mutual reciprocity as friends but "they may not intrude merely because they are relatives" (Goode 1963:76):

> There is no great extension of the kin network . . . Thus the couple cannot count on a large number of kinfolk for help. Just as these kin cannot call upon the couple for services . . . Neither couple nor kinfolk have many *rights* with respect to the other, and so the reciprocal *obligations* are few . . . the couple has few moral controls over their extended kin, and these have few controls over the couple [1963:8].

As opposed to more generationally defined kinship systems in traditional agrarian societies, where the place of each member was more clearly determined within the kinship system and where obligations among kin were more rigidly legislated and defined, the extended kinship system in Manchester (and in the United States generally) was loosely defined. Kin relations and obligations revolved around individuals or the nuclear family.

In Quebec, for example, the opportunities and obligations of children were ranked in relation to inheritance practices.[10] French Canadians in Manchester, on the other hand, adopted a more flexible and voluntary system. They followed, however, several basic implicit rules governing kin assistance, which also specified that nuclear family members (and later parents and their adult children) were first in priority for assistance. Customarily, couples also drew a line between in-laws and their family of orientation. The closest kin connections followed a mother-daughter dyad – adult women usually were engaged in closer exchanges with their own mothers than with their mothers-in-law and drew explicit boundaries with their husbands' families.

This sequence of priorities usually led to a multi-layered pattern of kin interaction over the life course. As younger children grew up, older siblings helped them find jobs. They aided younger sisters, especially, in preparing for marriage and in setting up households. In addition, they cared for aging parents and often continued to assist their siblings later in life. Older children thus sometimes were caught in a squeeze between helping siblings and caring for aging parents simultaneously. Marie Anne Senechal, for example, had no sooner finished rearing her younger siblings when she encountered the responsibility of caring for her aging father and continuing to aid her siblings in their adult years.

Within each family or kin group, one member, usually a woman, emerged as the "kin keeper." Larger networks had several kin keepers, but within a nuclear family the task usually fell upon one member. Most commonly the oldest daughter or one of the older daughters was cast in the role of kin keeper when a crisis arose, such as the death of the mother. Ora Pelletier viewed herself as a kin keeper (even though she was not the oldest daughter):

> But if they need me, if they have any trouble or you know they're in trouble or they're worried about something or if they need a recipe or something they always call me like if I was the mother . . . No matter what happens you know they will call me and ask me. Ask me for advice, or, "Do you remember how Mom used to do this or that?" [Interview].

Kin keepers usually retained their role throughout their lives. Although the needs and responsibilities changed, their centrality to the kin group as helpers, arbiters, and pacifiers continued and became even more pivotal with age. They were at times designated by parents in advance or were thrust into that position by circumstances and by their skills and personalities. Given the wide age spread of children within the family, designating the oldest or middle children as kin keepers was an important strategy for large families.

Some kin keepers remained single because the responsibility of care extended and escalated as they grew older. They commanded greater authority among their siblings, nieces, and nephews and were in the center of family communication. Kin keepers kept track of different family members who immigrated or who married and left town; they scheduled family reunions and celebrations of birthdays and anniversaries. When adult siblings were in conflict with each other, kin keepers tried to resolve the feud by acting as intermediaries.

Kin keeping thus carried with it prestige and respect, in addition to the many tasks and services. For a woman, in particular, this position also bestowed a power and influence she rarely held within her nuclear family, where the father was the source of authority and the final arbiter. But kin keeping was also confining and bestowed many obligations on the person so designated.

Marie Anne Senechal explained how she became a kin keeper. The oldest daughter, she was left at age 20 with eleven children, including two infants, when her mother died. She opposed her father's plan to place the non-working children in an orphanage, and, along with her work in the mill, she took charge of them. Committed to rearing her siblings, Marie Anne allowed her sister, two years her junior, to get married, knowing that this decision sealed her own fate – the entire care of the home would be on her shoulders forever. "It's my fault that my sister got married. I should have told her not to. She was 18, and she was the one who was taking care of the house. She asked for my advice, and I said, 'Well, an old maid doesn't have a very good name' . . . I pushed my sister to get married." But the sister's departure was not free of guilt. "When she left with him [her husband], all of us were at the window. All the little kids. She never forgot our faces in the window. As long as she lived, she always said, 'Marie Anne, why did I get married and leave you all by yourself?' " (*Amoskeag*, pp. 280–1).

Florida Anger, the oldest daughter, helped with the rearing of her younger siblings even though both parents were alive. She and her sisters and brothers worked together in the mill, and her parents assigned her the task of making sure her siblings actually went to work and stayed with their jobs. She also helped at home with childrearing and housework. After they married, her younger sisters turned to her for assistance, especially during the illness and death of a child of one of her sisters. Throughout their adult lives, her brothers and sisters sought her help. She mediated the quarrels over the use of their father's insurance money and his car after his death and subsequently tried to reconcile her feuding siblings when petty conflicts arose.

How were the multiple patterns of kin assistance that extended over the entire life course and flowed back and forth across a wide geographic region enforced? Why did kin assist each other over long time periods? What prepared them to pay the high personal cost of self-sacrifice that often led to the postponement or denial of marriage for women?

The most eloquent explanation advanced for kin assistance has been the theory of exchange relations, which Michael Anderson employs in his study of nineteenth-century weavers in Preston (1971). His emphasis on instrumental relationships is particularly relevant to this study. Using economic exchange theory, Anderson argues that the basis for kin assistance was exchange in services and in supports during critical life situations. The motives that led kin to help each other, he argues, were calculative: Parents aided their children with the expectation of receiving assistance in old age; more distant kin helped each other in the hope of receiving returns when they were in need. These calculative relationships were reinforced by strong societal norms dictating mutual obligations among relatives. Anderson thus sees kin assistance as a series of exchanges revolving around self-interest and reinforced by social norms.[11] Although the time period is different, the Manchester workers share several characteristics with Preston's laborers. In both communities kin provided the almost exclusive source of assistance for a low-resource population with a high proportion of migrants. However, the interviews of former Manchester workers, which provide crucial information on their own perceptions of instrumental relationships, make it clear that certain aspects of kin assistance cannot be entirely explained by economic exchange theory.

In the context of Manchester, instrumental relationships fell into two categories: short-term routine exchanges in services and assistance in critical life situations and long-term investments in exchanges along the life course. In addition to those forms of assistance previously discussed, kin provided money on a short-term basis and traded skills, goods, and services. For example, mill workers supplied their relatives with cheap cloth and received farm products in exchange. Plumbers and masons traded services with each other, and storekeepers exchanged merchandise for medical or legal assistance from relatives.

Long-term investments were more demanding and less certain in their future returns and the most pervasive exchange along the life course was that between parents and children – old-age support in return for childrearing. Under conditions of frequent migration, exchanges across the life course also occurred among aunts and uncles and their nieces and nephews, with the former frequently acting as surrogate parents for their newly arrived young relatives in Manchester. Such exchanges were horizontal as well as vertical. Horizontally, aunts and uncles were fulfilling obligations to, or reciprocating the favors of, brothers or sisters by taking care of their children; vertically, they were entering into exchange relationships with their nieces and nephews who might assist them later in life. Godparents also represented long-term exchanges. Because godparents assumed obligations of future assistance to their godchildren, well-to-do relatives or at times non-relatives were preferred.

Although the benefits of short-term exchanges are easily understandable, it is difficult to accept calculative motives as the exclusive base of long-term kin assistance, especially when the rewards were not easily visible. For example, those women who substantially delayed or even sacrificed an opportunity for marriage to fulfill their obligation to care for younger siblings or aging parents did so for no apparent reward. Men and women supported members of their nuclear families even when a more distant relative might have been a better long-term contributor to an exchange bargain. These forms of kin behavior exceed benefits that could be measured by economic exchange.

Young family members who subordinated their own careers to family needs did so out of a sense of responsibility, affection, and familial obligation rather than with the expectation of eventual gain. Within this context, kin assistance was not strictly calculative. Rather, it expressed an overall principle of reciprocity over the life course. Reciprocity, as Pitt-Rivers (1973) defines it,

> is undifferentiated in that it requires that a member of the group shall sacrifice himself for another, that kinsmen shall respect preferential rules of conduct towards one another regardless of their individual interests. Such reciprocity as there is comes from the fact that other kinsmen do likewise. Parents are expected to sacrifice themselves for their children but they also expect that their children will do the same for theirs. The reciprocity alternates down the chain of generations, assuming that the grandparental generation will be repaid in the persons of the grandchildren.

The sense of duty to family was a manifestation of family culture – a set of values that entailed not only a commitment to the well-being and self-reliance or survival of the family but one that took priority over individual needs and personal happiness. The preservation of family autonomy was valued as a more important goal than individual fulfillment. Family autonomy, essential for self-respect and good standing in the neighborhood and the community, was one of the most deeply ingrained values: it dictated that assistance be sought among kin. Few of the interviewees turned for help to the church, ethnic mutual-aid associations, public welfare, or charity. (It must be remembered that given the stigma attached to receiving charity, many may not have admitted they were aided in this manner.) The first large-scale acceptance of public welfare occurred in the 1930s when workers turned to the federal Emergency Relief Administration and the Work Projects Administration after enduring weeks of unemployment and the subsequent shutdown of the mill.

In a regime of insecurity, where kin assistance was the only continuing source of support, family culture by necessity dictated that family considerations, needs, and ties guide or control most individual decisions. Migrating to Manchester, locating jobs and housing, and leaving the mill and returning to Canada were all embedded in family strategies, rather than individual preferences.

At times, such family decisions ignored individual feelings to a degree that would seem callous from the vantage point of our times; Mary Dancause, for example, was at age 4 sent by her parents back to live with relatives in Quebec when she had an eye disease. When she reached age 12, her parents uprooted her from a loving environment in Quebec to bring her back to Manchester to take care of younger siblings. She recalled her bitterness and loneliness: "I was so lonesome, I cried so much, you won't believe it. My mother would be working in the kitchen and I would be talking to myself: 'I want to go back, I want to go back'" (interview).

Her older brother, who had also been left behind, but who was not summoned back, decided to strike out on his own for Manchester. When he knocked on his parents' door, his father did not recognize him.

> There was a knock at the back door. "We don't want anything," Father said, and he banged the door. So my brother went around to the front. He rang the bell, and my father said, "It's you again." My brother said, "Wait a minute, can I talk to you?" He told him, "I'm your son" [*Amoskeag*, p. 51].

Both career choices and economic decisions were made within the family matrix. Families might be described as being composed of units that were switched around as the need arose. Each unit was relied upon and used when appropriate. Following such strategies, families timed the movement of members in response to both individual schedules and external conditions. Family strategies revolved around a variety of decisions: when to migrate, when to return, when those who were left behind should rejoin the family in Manchester, who should be encouraged to explore other working opporunities, who should be encouraged to marry, and who should be pressured to stay at home.

Collective family needs were not always congruent with individual preferences. Nor did the subordination of individual needs to family decisions take place without conflict. Many interviewees who had made personal sacrifices expressed long-repressed anger and pain during the interview. Anna Fregau Douville, for example, as the last child of working age who could support her parents, left school and started working at age 14 and postponed her own marriage. When Anna finally announced she was going to get married, her sisters pressured her to cancel her engagement, claiming that her fiancé was a drunkard. Actually, "they were scheming to get me to support my folks until they died . . . But my mother told me, 'Anna, don't wait too long. What if I die or your father dies? Then you'd insist on staying with me, and you'll lose your boyfriend.' " She got married and lived two houses away from her parents. Although Anna had been determined to live her life independently of her family, she was never quite free of guilt:

> They [her parents] were on the city welfare . . . even with the hard times I had during my life, I never stopped for sympathy for myself, because I knew about my mother's life . . . Sometimes when I'm sitting here all alone, I wonder what Pa and Ma would do if they could come down and see all the funny things I'm watching [on TV] all by myself. A lot of things go through your head when your folks are gone . . . You don't realize it when they are living. You want to live your own life; but when your folks are gone and you think of all the good things that you have today, you wish they could share them [*Amoskeag*, pp. 289–90].

Having grown up in a large family where she experienced first-hand the pressures imposed by kin, Anna subsequently set strict boundaries with her husband's family immediately after marriage: She refused to pay her mother-in-law's debts and made it clear to her husband and her in-laws that they could not rely on her to compensate for their extravagances:

> I put my foot down the first year that I got married . . . When his parents used to come and visit me and ask to borrow money . . . I said, "Listen, I don't go down to your house to bother you. I'm happy with my husband and get the hell out. Don't ever come here and try to borrow anything from him or from me" . . . My husband agreed with me. He said, "I'm glad that you can

open up with them. I couldn't talk that way to my own family"
[*Amoskeag*, p. 291].

Interestingly, despite her resentment of extended family obligations and her own bitterness toward her siblings, Anna Douville
keeps the most complete family albums and follows the traditional
Quebec custom of maintaining a family genealogy. Her personal
resentment of the intrusions of kin into her own privacy was divorced from her ideological commitment to keeping a complete
family record for posterity.

Anna's rejection of assistance for her husband's family represented a common pattern among women who had been deeply enmeshed in responsibilities with their own kin. Once they married,
they refused involvement with their husbands' relatives to avoid
taking on new obligations, having just emerged from their own
families' burdens. Cora Pellerin, for example, postponed her marriage until the death of her fiancé's ailing mother rather than join
his household and take on the responsibility of caring for her.
When she married, Cora closed her home to her husband's older
sister. She allowed her housekeeper to give her husband's sister an
occasional meal, but she did not admit her as a regular member of
the household even though her sister-in-law could have acted as a
baby-sitter and a housekeeper. Eventually her sister-in-law moved
to a convent (interview).

Marie Anne Senechal, who spent most of her life rearing her own
siblings and finally married when she was in her sixties, drew a
firm line with her husband's sister. Even though she allowed her
own siblings to live in her house, she would not tolerate her sister-
in-law. Marie Anne drove her out of the house, finally, after pro-
voking a quarrel.

Ora Pelletier, whose six older sisters worked in the mills, was
ostracized by her siblings ever since she cashed in their father's
insurance policy after his death and used the money for her own
needs. She felt entitled to the money because she was the last remaining daughter at home and had taken care of her father until his
death.

Alice Olivier still resented being sent to work in the mill at age 14
while her two brothers were sent to the seminary at Trois-Rivières.
At age 60, she returned to high school to fulfill her old dream of an
education. During the interview, just at the point when she was
about to graduate from high school, she finally expressed the resentment she had harbored since childhood (*Amoskeag*, pp. 268–9).

And Marie Anne Senechal, who defended her lifelong sacrifices for her family without any aura of martyrdom, finally wiped away a tear at the end of the interview and said: "I thought I'd never marry. I was sixty-seven years old when I got married . . . It was too much of a wait, when I think of it now, because I would have been happier if I'd got married . . . I knew I wasn't living my own life, but I couldn't make up my mind" (*Amoskeag*, pp. 281–2).

Limitations of kin assistance

Paradoxically, the very source of strength of kin in the factory and in family relations was also its source of weakness. The integration of kin with the factory was a potential source of conflict and problems in both the workplace and the family. In a setting where relatives were considered responsible for each other's performance and where new workers were hired on a relative's recommendation, workers often had to deal with a relative who did not conform to factory discipline or who violated some of the basic rules of work behavior. How far should loyalty to kin go? Although workers were not held responsible for the misconduct of a relative, their access to the boss was diminished when relatives hired on their recommendation proved unsuitable. Their own standing was affected as well by a relative's conflict with bosses or with other workers. Competition with one's own kin presented another dilemma. Did one hide the fact of being a better worker? Did one slow down and sacrifice a bonus to protect a slower relative or give up one's lunch break to fix the warps for a young relative?

Some workers chose to enter the mill as free agents to avoid the stigma of kinship ties. Several young men quit because they did not want to work with their fathers. To allay any suspicion of receiving more favorable treatment, children and close relatives of overseers preferred working in different rooms. Marie Proulx, for example, first worked in the room where her husband was second hand. But she decided to transfer after a while: "I was afraid there would be conflict. They'd say that I get sugar and the others get dirt . . . I'd rather leave instead" (*Amoskeag*, p. 70).

The piece-work system and the speedup of production imposed additional strains on kin. Because time was no longer available to teach younger relatives, it had to be guarded jealously. Anna Douville's sisters, for example, did not want to be saddled with teaching her spinning. She started work, therefore, in another room. After she had learned how to spin, she asked to be transferred to work with her sisters (*Amoskeag*, p. 286). The anxieties expressed by Anna's sisters are consistent with many grievance cases that were instigated by workers who objected to teaching other workers without the proper adjustments for loss of piece-rate time (see Chapter 11).

Identification with a kinship group whose reputation was less than ideal made work relations more difficult. In addition, family loyalties and the use of kinship ties for advancement conflicted with the principles advocated by the union. The use of kin to get a job, to escape layoffs, to be rehired, and to advance in the mill clashed with the principle of seniority, which the union struggled to introduce as the basis for rehiring and promotions. Workers accustomed to using kinship ties were reluctant to surrender their access to patronage for an objective system of seniority. Even though management itself had tried to replace the informal family patronage system with a rational personnel policy, it, too, opposed the union's demands for seniority, claiming the principle would undermine the traditional practice of rehiring and promotion on the basis of merit.

Ironically, in some situations the union was inconsistent on the principle of seniority, suggesting that workers' relatives have priority in hiring. But management refused to be committed to any specific hiring policy. When the wool sorters' local, for example, insisted in 1920 that families of wool sorters should have priority in the hiring of apprentices, Agent Straw unequivocally rejected the proposal. Although he agreed that giving preference to families of wool sorters was a nice idea when feasible, he would not accept a ruling that only a son or brother of a wool sorter could be hired.[12]

The ability of kin to influence the factory system fluctuated with changes in the fortunes and policy of the factory itself. Kinship ties were most effective when labor was in short supply and prior to World War I, when hiring was more loosely organized. During periods of labor surplus, which became increasingly common in the 1920s, kinship ties continued to be useful in finding a job, particularly as the lines at the employment office became endless. The strike of 1922, the subsequent decline of the mill, and particularly its final shutdown in 1936 revealed the insecurities inherent in a one-company-dominated town.

When most family members worked for a single employer, the family unit was vulnerable to the vicissitudes of the company. Because of the dependence of a major portion of a family group on one employer, relatives were unable to assist each other when layoffs occurred, and especially during the strikes and the final shutdown.

Unable to save on their subsistence budgets, they had few or no reserves left to share during the strike and shutdown.

The strike itself set relatives at odds. Whether or not to strike divided some families and caused conflicts that took years to overcome. Some relatives, in fact, have not spoken to each other since their split over the strike in 1922.

During periods of unemployment, the effectiveness of kin as migration agents continued, though the route of migration was reversed. Kin outside Manchester enabled unemployed Amoskeag workers to find temporary or more permanent work elsewhere in New England or to migrate back to Canada. As the economic crises in the city and the resulting unemployment rendered local kin assistance ineffectual, workers in Lowell, Lawrence, and, to a lesser extent, Rhode Island found jobs for unemployed Manchester relatives and shared housing with them.

Some workers commuted to jobs in other New England industrial towns. With a mother or aunt nearby to care for her children, a woman was able to work outside Manchester. In many instances, an older female relative cared for the children for the entire week while the parents shared housing with kin and worked in Lawrence or in other industrial towns. Young women who returned to Quebec during the strike worked on the family farm or as waitresses or maids in restaurants and hotels while residing with their relatives. The existence of relatives in these communities and in Quebec thus provided access to employment and housing when local kin were unable to extend such help.

Migration and the continuity of the kinship system

Although historians and sociologists have long recognized the importance of kin in communities of destination in facilitating migration and settlement, less attention has been paid to the role of relatives remaining in the communities of origin. Kin who remained in Quebec fulfilled a crucial function in providing backup assistance and security for the migrating family. Availability of continued support in the community of origin was therefore an essential consideration in the decision to migrate.

The networks of relatives, besides serving as important backup systems, also enabled workers to experiment with different employment opportunities, to send their sons to scout for better jobs, and to marry off their daughters. "Long-distance" kin, like those nearby, were sources of security and assurance in times of crisis and often served as a refuge.

Some people who worked until their later years of life retired to their villages of origin. Some unmarried pregnant women, for whom life in Manchester was unbearable because of shame and social pressure, went to live in convents in Quebec until their children were born and then either remained there or returned to work in Manchester. Some parents left young children with relatives in Quebec until they found jobs and housing in Manchester. Sick children were sent to Quebec to recuperate with relatives.

This interaction between immigrants in Manchester and their kin in Quebec leads to a revision of existing models of the territoriality of kin. Most recent historical studies of kinship in the industrial environment have focused on geographic proximity as the chief measure of kin interaction. Elizabeth Bott's (1957) important model of urban networks emphasizes residence in the same neighborhood as the most salient feature of kin interaction.[13] Although the Manchester data offer important examples of the interconnectedness of kin with neighborhood, which is central to Bott's model, they also reflect kin as mobile units transcending the specific boundaries of one neighborhood or community.

Manchester's French-Canadian textile workers had many of the same characteristics listed by Bott as generally conducive to the formation of strong kinship networks: neighborhood proximity; similarity in work (particularly where one industry dominates the local employment market), occupational status, and migration patterns; and lack of opportunity for social mobility. Despite their common characteristics, Manchester's French-Canadian workers differed considerably from London's East Enders in their interaction with kin. The Manchester study reveals that strong ties over several generations can still be maintained under conditions of kin dispersion.

In Manchester, as in mid-nineteenth-century and twentieth-century East London or Preston, kinship networks were embedded in the city's neighborhoods. But the social space of French-Canadian kin extended from Quebec to Manchester and spread over New England's industrial maps. French-Canadian kinship behavior in Manchester thus demonstrates the importance of intensive kin networks in one's immediate neighborhood and workplace, as well as the persistence of distant kinship ties laced through a larger geographic region.[14] Geographic distance did not disrupt basic modes of kin cooperation but led, rather, to a revision of priorities and forms of assistance. Under certain conditions, migration strengthened kinship ties and led to new kin functions, which evolved as changing conditions dictated.

The historic pattern of long-distance kinship ties found in Manchester has many contemporary parallels, most notably among Appalachian migrants to Ohio. In their study of Beech Creek, Ohio, Schwarzweller, Brown, and Mangalam (1971) concluded that the kinship structure provided a highly pervasive line of communication between kinsfolk in the home and in the urban communities. It channels information about available job opportunities and living standards directly and therefore tends to orient migrants to those areas where kin groups are already established. In this context, their definition of a "migration system" is particularly pertinent to this study: "Two subsystems together form the interactional system in which we wish to consider the adjustment of a given group of migrants, individually and collectively. We have then one migration system to consider, namely, the Beech Creek–Ohio migration" (pp. 94–5).[15]

Continuities and discontinuities in the functions of kin

To understand fully the role of kin in twentieth-century Manchester, one must place it in historical perspective. Ideally, the kinship patterns of French Canadians in Manchester should be compared to those of their communities of origin in rural Quebec. Unfortunately, only two studies of kinship in Quebec are available for comparison: an ethnographic study of the village of St. Denis, by Horace Miner (1939), and a more recent study of urban kinship ties in Montreal by Philippe Garigue (1967).[16]

Were the kinship patterns of St. Denis transported to Manchester? In the absence of a full-fledged comparison of family structure, demographic behavior, women's labor-force participation, and family economy for Manchester and the Quebec parishes of origin, it would be impossible to answer this question conclusively. This discussion is limited, therefore, to a comparison with the kinship patterns found in Quebec by Miner and Garigue, respectively. In rural St. Denis, kin were at the base of the organizational structure. They controlled the channels of land transmission and all major aspects of assistance and discipline. Symbols of kin permeated religious life, and reverence for ancestors constituted an important component of socialization. Even marriage partners were chosen within the kinship network. Kin directed and dominated most important career decisions. In outlining the stages of the family cycle in rural Quebec, Miner stressed the farmer's perception of the inter-relatedness of generations: "Life is like a turning wheel. The old turn over the work to the young and die, and these in turn get old and then turn the work to their children. Yes, life is like a wheel turning" (p. 85). Particularly important for comparative purposes is Miner's emphasis on the interchangeability of sons for inheritance, rather than on primogeniture. The father decided which son would inherit the farm and launched the other sons into the outside world by providing them with assistance to migrate to the towns to find jobs or by helping with their education. After the father's death, the other brothers customarily left the household, because it was considered a disgrace to live in a brother's home. Also important, for comparative purposes, was the prevalence of mutual assistance and shared effort, especially among brothers who farmed in the same village or in nearby villages.

Migration to Manchester shifted the economic base of the family from landholding to industrial work. It disrupted, therefore, the basic territorial continuity and the interlocking of generations within the family cycle. The move to an industrial economy obviously exposed the French-Canadian immigrants to different occupational careers and economic organization. Accordingly, it necessitated a reorganization of family roles and a redefinition of kinship rules. The stem family structure found by Miner in St. Denis was not present in Manchester.[17] As indicated earlier, sons and daughters in Manchester tended to set up their own households after marriage even though they did not move far away from their parents. At most, some spent the first two years of marriage in their parents' household. Once removed from the land, fathers in Manchester lost the bargaining power and control they had held by virtue of their estates. Thus, the move to industrial cities may have weakened the patriarchal authority of traditional rural families.

However, despite this major change, migration to Manchester did not result in a breakdown of kinship ties. Traditional family structures were not disrupted through the migration of sons and daughters. Migration was an essential component of the family cycle in Quebec. Non-inheriting sons left home to work in cities, often in textile towns such as Trois-Rivières. Daughters usually entered domestic service or textile work. Migration to Manchester was, therefore, part of the larger historic pattern of rural-urban migration of Quebec sons and daughters at specific stages of the family cycle.

The factory system in some ways reinforced family ties. Industri-

al work allowed adult sons and daughters to remain in the parental
household until marriage and to establish their own households
nearby after marriage. In this respect, life in an industrial town
(provided the entire nuclear family had migrated) offered greater
opportunities for cohesion and contact among relatives throughout
their lives. The dispersal of children by inheritance practices did
not affect families in Manchester. As long as employment in the
mills was available, children and parents continued to work in the
same place, thus allowing continued interaction with not only parents but also siblings.

Life in the industrial town added new functions to an already
long repertory of kin interaction. The legacy of rural Quebec to industrial Manchester, the principle and practice of kin solidarity,
was extremely significant in the adaptation of rural workers to industrial conditions. Once villagers left the land, their kin ceased to
be the exclusive organizational base of social life and lost many of
their sanctions. However, a corporate view of family life and an
orientation to a collective family economy was maintained in Manchester, at least in the first generation. The principle of resource
exchanges across the life course took new forms, such as the provision of housing, child care, the teaching of skills, and brokerage
within the factory.

A comparison of the organization and behavior of kin in Manchester with that of kin in urban Quebec communities is also illu-
minating. Garigue (1956) found large kinship networks in Montreal, which were vitally linked with relatives in their rural community
of origin, as well as in a number of other French-Canadian communities. These networks did not contain scattered nuclear families
but, rather, concentrations of kin clusters in each location, who, as
part of a larger network, maintained contact with each other in several different communities. Individuals and nuclear families generally migrated to join a specific cluster. Migrants often moved to a
certain urban community because other relatives lived there. The
pattern outlined by Garigue places kinship ties in Manchester into
a larger world of French-Canadian networks, a cell in a larger series
of clusters – many located in Quebec.

The crucial historical questions are: What changes in kinship patterns resulted from migration and settlement in new communities?
What behaviors were transferred with modifications and which remained intact? Answers hinge on an overall understanding of the
transmission of premigration organizations and traditions to new
settings. A systematic distinction between complete transfers of

traditional patterns or their modification and new adaptation will considerably advance our understanding of the role of kin in the process of modernization.

The French-Canadian case in Manchester suggests that what has been considered a survival of premodern patterns may also represent modern responses to new industrial conditions. French-Canadian immigrants initially transported kinship ties and traditional practices of kin assistance to Manchester. They subsequently adapted their kin organization to the industrial system by developing new modes of interaction and new functions.

Although the basic kinship ties had been imported from rural Quebec, their functions, responsive to the demands of industrial production, were different from those customarily performed by kin in rural society. Functioning in an industrial environment required a familiarity with bureaucratic structures and organizations, adherence to modern work schedules, planning in relation to the rhythms of industrial employment, specialization in tasks, and technological skill. The roles assumed by kin – hiring young relatives and manipulating the pace of production – required a mastery of "modern" processes, a high level of expertise and sophistication. The role of kin in these areas, as well as in the more personal areas, such as housing, required a comprehension of the complexity and diversity inherent in an urban industrial system. The selective use of kinship ties by the workers of Manchester represented, therefore, both earlier practices and their modification.

The selectivity used by immigrants in adapting their traditional ties and resources to industrial conditions is most significant in this process. Modernization theory has frequently viewed integration with kin as an obstacle to geographic mobility and adaptation to modern ways (Moore 1965, Inkeles and Smith 1974).[18] The Manchester case suggests, rather, that kin not only facilitated migration to industrial communities but also served as agents of adaptation and modernization by providing role models and offering direct assistance. Under the insecurities of the factory system, the selective use of kinship was part of survival strategy and under certain circumstances also facilitated mobility.

6   *Adaptation to industrial work*

"So they took me to the employment office, and I went there, and the man who hands out the jobs sent me to the spinning rooms. There I don't know anything about the spinning. I'm a farmer. I don't know anybody when I get in there. Just like a lost sheep I feel there. Everybody, especially the women, they talk to me nice but I don't know what the boss is talking about" (John Mekras, interview). When John Mekras arrived in Manchester from Greece in 1912 he did not know a word of English. He did not last long in the Amoskeag. "I quit. I want to be the boss myself. Instead, there were too many bosses. And by gosh! I did it too" (interview). The factory was a winnowing, as well as a socializing, agent. Like Mekras, many workers fled the factories immediately after their first encounter, never to return. Others were fired and did not have the necessary connections to be rehired. "The people didn't know the language at that time, and besides that, they didn't know their job correctly . . . but anything you misunderstand and you don't do the job right you'd get hell – you'd be out. Those days with no work, the boss didn't like you, you were out . . . no more" (Mekras, interview).

Other workers came determined to stay. The Amoskeag inspired in them a sense of hope for stable jobs and for a new life for their families; they were prepared to pay the price to achieve it, to endure the hardship imposed by a novel way of life. "All the families from Canada who came up here to Manchester, if there were two in a family who could get to work here, it was marvelous. Just seeing the size of the mills was enough. They all made big sacrifices to be able to go work in the mills" (Melina Landry, interview).

Because many of the Amoskeag's workers at the turn of the century, especially those from Quebec, had migrated to Manchester from subsistence farms or lumber camps, they did not have a sense of having lost a golden, rural world. They did not look back with nostalgia at their rural past and did not complain about the loss in status encountered by preindustrial craftsmen when the factory system took over their jobs, seized control of their time, and ren-

120

dered them dependent on capitalist owners to provide the market for their skills.

Many were driven into the factory system by the deprivations and tedium of farm life. Although they might have had some freedom in setting their own time schedules, they had no power over the change of the seasons, the failure of crops, the fluctuations in market prices, and their social isolation in remote villages. Those who worked in lumber camps lived long distances from their families and were subordinate to bosses. Textile work, on the other hand, offered fairly regular employment at set wages; because jobs were available for the entire family, the family could stay together as a unit; there was some chance for social and occupational advancement.

Willing to trade their rural "freedom" for the industrial confinement of the textile mill, immigrants were prepared to endure long hours of work at low wages. Those who were unable to tolerate the pressures and the conditions either were dismissed or left voluntarily. Those who stayed learned quickly, because they came with a commitment to hard work carried over from their rural backgrounds where work and life were inseparable and survival depended on the collective work of the entire family.

The process by which immigrants from preindustrial backgrounds were transformed, willingly or grudgingly, into industrial workers is part of the history of working-class life throughout a century of industrialization in Europe and the United States. A large body of historical literature, following in the wake of E. P. Thompson and his followers in England and the United States, particularly Herbert Gutman, has documented the stress and conflict inherent in the adaptation of workers from preindustrial settings to the pressures of new work processes and schedules and authority relationships within industrial capitalism.[1]

In adapting to the industrial environment, immigrant workers in American factories continued to hold on to their traditions. For most of them, adjustment to industrial time and discipline, to the pace of machinery, to the authority of the bosses, and to peer pressures from fellow workers was a taxing process. But it was by no means a one-way process, for the workers, in turn, introduced some of their own traditions and work habits into the modern factory system. This transition from a nonindustrial to an industrial work setting is still being experienced today by some segments of American society, with the influx of each new immigrant group.

As Herbert Gutman puts it: "The American working class was continuously altered in its composition by infusions from within and without the nation, of peasants, farmers, skilled artisans, and casual day laborers who brought into industrial society ways of work and other habits and values not associated with industrial necessities and the industrial ethos" (1976:15). What happened to these traditions and practices in the workers' encounter with the factory system? Did workers abandon these earlier ways in response to industrial imperatives? Did the transition of workers from preindustrial settings to the factory system entail, as E. P. Thompson (1967:57) claims, "a severe restructuring of work habits – new disciplines, new incentives, and a new human nature upon which these incentives could alight effectively"?

Studies of labor history over the past decade have rejected the earlier view of new immigrant workers as helpless peasants in the factory setting and the view that immigrants to industrial centers were shorn of their traditions and cultures. The work of Herbert Gutman emphasizes the continuity between preimmigration cultural traditions and the industrial system. The customs and work habits that workers brought with them, argues Gutman, were a "resource" actively used by new immigrants in adapting to industrial conditions.[2]

The responses of the Amoskeag workers to the factory setting show that they called upon their traditional cultural resources and associations in their efforts to adapt to the pressures of industrial time and discipline. Rather than allow themselves to be completely shaped by the system, they devised their own ways of coping with pressures by drawing on their traditional customs and family ties. The new form of behavior that emerged was a hybrid of earlier customs and industrial modes.[3]

In addition, not all aspects of their traditional culture clashed with the factory system. A tradition of family integration with work, and among Catholic workers an acceptance of a hierarchical world order, facilitated their adaptation to the authority system in the factory.

Gutman's emphasis on the "preindustrial" backgrounds of workers who came into American industry may have presented too homogenous a picture of their origin. Even though it would be impossible to quantify specifically the variety of backgrounds those workers came from, there is a good indication that many of the "rural" Quebecers who came to the Amoskeag had already worked in industry at some point in their lives, either in Canada or during their earlier peregrinations in New England. Most Polish workers had come from Łódź, a major textile city, which had a tradition of union activism. The expert British and Scottish recruits already had industrial experience. Although the dramatic contrast between their own backgrounds and the Amoskeag industrial giant was imposing, the trauma associated with the transition may have been far less dramatic than previously thought.

Actually, whether an "industrial" and "preindustrial" dichotomy adequately reflects the social reality of the late nineteenth and early twentieth centuries needs to be questioned. By the late nineteenth century, both rural and industrial communities in the United States and Canada were already aware of industrial time, even though the rural economy and organization of work followed nonindustrial forms. Even immigrants from rural communities in Quebec had been exposed to industrial time schedules, through the employment of other family members. Thus it is unrealistic to refer to rural communities in an industrialized country as "preindustrial."

Nor was the process of adaptation one-directional. Newly arrived workers at the beginning of the twentieth century confronted a factory system that was entering a new phase of development. The Amoskeag Company, along with other corporations, was being transformed into a large and more complex organization that was a far cry from the factory encountered by New England girls in the earlier stages of industrialization.

The efficiency movement and scientific management as well as a general intensification of work pace had created new pressures that threatened the informal organization in the factory. Fluctuating markets in the post–World War I period reduced employment opportunities and exposed workers – veteran workers as well as new arrivals – to a regime of insecurity. In their struggle to adapt to the workplace and to their bosses' authority, workers also had to cope with the ever-present threat of losing their jobs.

Depending on their backgrounds and when they started to work, Amoskeag workers actually experienced two different types of adaptation. The "first-generation experience" involved newly arrived immigrant workers who were encountering the factory for the first time. They had to negotiate the transition from task-oriented work habits to working within an industrial time schedule in a machine-regulated workplace. But even the first-generation experience was not simple and uniform because immigrants came from a variety of backgrounds and their responses to the discipline and scope of the giant textile mill consequently varied in intensity.

The second type of adaptation placed demands on new and old workers alike. The intensification and systemization of the pace and organization of work imposed by the factory in its transition to new modes of production and new efficiency and scientific management added strain to a process already wrought with tension. As David Montgomery points out, these patterns

> took shape in the second and third generations of industrial experience, largely among workers whose world had been fashioned from their youngest days by smoky mills, congested streets, recreation as a week-end affair and toil at the times and the pace dictated by the clock. These workers had already become habituated to industrial time schedules and work processes. They had internalized the industrial sense of time, they were highly disciplined in both individual and collective behavior and they regarded both an extensive division of labor and machine production as their natural environments [1979:10].

The two types of adaptation often overlapped because of the steady stream of new immigrant workers entering the factory.

Both old and new workers had to adapt to each other, and newly arrived workers had to be socialized into a collective group identity. As the factory was changing over time, workers' attitudes were changing as well, rendering the newcomers' adjustment doubly complex.

Transition into the factory

The Amoskeag's vast size, scale of production, and bureaucracy intensified the encounter of newcomers with the industrial system. Even those who had worked in textile mills in other places had not witnessed anything so intense. The enormous mill yard, the vast spinning and weaving rooms, and the overpowering noise of the machinery were both fascinating and intimidating. Even the size of the crowds was bewildering as workers streamed into the mill yard when the gates opened in the morning and poured back out at the end of the day.

The first step in adaptation, simply finding one's way around the enormous complex of the mill yard, with its maze of bridges, canals, and catwalks, required weeks. "Look at the way it spreads all the way up the river here. It really, it was a city in itself" (Orwell, interview). Most workers were guided to their departments for the first time by messenger boys or friends, relatives, or neighbors. Some new workers got "lost" on their journey between the employment office and their assigned department. They could not find their department and simply gave up searching for it.[4]

For workers coming into the Amoskeag from rural backgrounds, the novel experience of regimented time schedules governed by the factory bell imposed new kinds of pressures. The contrast between earlier work habits and the demands for conformity to industrial time was intensified by enclosure within a building from sunrise to sundown and the monotony of the work routines. The workrooms assaulted the senses with noises, steam, heat, dust, and noxious smells, and the risk of injury from the machinery itself was ever present.

For some workers this initial encounter was too overpowering. The noise in the weave room, in particular, prompted many workers to quit. Mary Cunion, who stayed despite these conditions, remembered those who left: "They wouldn't put the time in long enough to get used to that noise, and it would chase them out" (*Amoskeag*, p. 45). "Too much noise," "too much dirt" were often recorded in employee files as reasons for leaving (see Chapter 9). Women, in particular, were horrified by cockroaches, which often assumed giant size in their recollections.

Textile work demanded dexterity, precision, speed, and constant alertness. The operation of machinery was not only physically exacting, it was also frightening for newcomers. Jean Derome recalled her struggle with the spinning frames: "The yards would get all caught up in spinning machines and you'd have to move them. The frames were high and I was short, so I had to stretch all the time. That's about the lousiest job they had in the mill" (interview). Mary Hamilton, reminiscing fifty years later, still felt the aches in her back: "To me that was hard work. Hating it like I did, it was magnified. I did it for four days; then I came home and said 'that's it.' So then I went to night school. I worked in the weave room after that, inspecting the yarn; and that was a nice little job" (interview).

The Amoskeag's accident-claim files report mangled hands, crushed arms, and lost fingers. Workers unaccustomed to handling the machinery were often placed in added danger by poor instruction, poor supervision, and lack of advance warning, most often stemming from the language barrier. Twenty-three-year-old John Ferdelesz, for example, a newly arrived immigrant from Lithuania who did not understand English, was assigned to the picking room. After two days of instruction, he was assigned a set of pickers to run. His left arm was caught between one of the spokes and the side of the picker when he tried to pry out a piece of loose cotton while the machine was still on. His hand had to be amputated. Investigation revealed that the fellow worker who had been assigned to teach Ferdelesz was Polish. The two men had no common language. "He just used to give his head a nod; I used to explain to him what to do, but he didn't understand very well and I had to show him how to do it. When this fellow didn't understand, I took him by the coat, took him over to the picker and showed him what to do."[5]

Such cases were typical. Bosses and fellow workers were surprised when their technical instructions were not understood. Sometimes the demonstration was sloppy. Several times accidents occurred because major disasters were simply not anticipated. At other times, a new worker's own eagerness to communicate his ability to learn quickly or his effort to hide his "greenness" led to disaster. Eventually, safety warnings were posted in French, Polish, and Greek.

In addition in adapting to the physical strain new workers had to adapt to human relationships in two apparently conflicting directions. On the one hand, they had to learn how to get along with bosses without violating their own sense of integrity and self-respect. On the other hand, they had to learn how to behave as workers with the appropriate sense of comradeship and consideration for the individual and collective goals of fellow workers.

In responding to industrial conditions, like their predecessors in earlier periods, workers retained their dignity. They drew upon their own background, cultural traditions, and social ties to exercise choices and to retain some control over the conditions that threatened to engulf them. The workers' ability to do so depended to a large extent on the diversity and flexibility of the Amoskeag's work structure. At least in the pre–World War I period, the corporation's flexible hiring policies and the workers' use of their own social networks were mutually reinforcing and facilitated their adaptation.

A large number of departments and workrooms offered some flexibility and choice and enabled workers to adapt within smaller units and move around among different departments in search of better conditions. Although this diversity helped in the adaptation process, it may have delayed the emergence of a working-class consciousness by reinforcing ethnic and family clustering.

The looseness of hiring policies in the earlier period allowed workers to transfer to different jobs or departments in search of more congenial conditions. "If you left a job at one place you could go to the second floor, you find another job right away. They needed the help" (Constantine Lamoreaux, interview). And an English worker remembered a similar pattern: "One thing about the Amos-keag – they never let a man go. If he wasn't able to do his work, they'd give him another job." But what the new job would be was not always predictable: "Then of course, he might end up as a sweeper" (John Hale, interview). And yet another worker recalled: "If you get through in one part of the mill you could go up and get into another part of the mill" (William Redmond, interview). These recollections exaggerated, of course, the Amoskeag's flexibility. Workers were fired, even in the pre–World War I period. But as long as jobs were available, most workers were able to find employ-ment in another department, even if they had been dismissed for disciplinary reasons. This situation changed in the 1920s.

Second hands, overseers, and managers used this flexibility to transfer workers from one department to another to avert conflict or accommodate disgruntled workers. As their career records indicate, the majority of workers experienced transfers from department to department or from job to job, sometimes by their own choosing, sometimes by the boss's decree.

Kinship and village ties were as important as the Amoskeag's policies in facilitating workers' adaptation to the factory setting. The initial adjustment to an alien industrial environment was usu-ally cushioned by a relative or friend. As discussed earlier, few made their first foray into the mill alone, and most benefited from the initial advice as to the most suitable job to pursue. In the early 1900s when jobs were still abundant, most arriving workers were instructed by veteran workers about the availability of alternative jobs within the mill and about the best means of attaining them. In the later period, when finding a job was difficult even for local resi-dents, personal connections were critical. "I'd been putting my name in at Amoskeag for a long time," recalled Melinda Landry. "It took at least a month before I got a job; and I'd go sometimes twice a day. One of my brothers had worked at the Amoskeag store and he was known . . . I had more power because he was known" (inter-view). On the other hand, William Redmond, the son of an Amos-keag overseer, came to the employment office for his first job and found six hundred applicants waiting in line. "I went down to the head of the employment office and told him who I was and I got the job that day." Only four or five workers were hired that day (inter-view).

No matter how well connected a person was, getting a job in the post–World War I period when jobs were scarce depended on the good humor of the employment clerk. "It wasn't easy to approach

Mr. Boucher [the clerk in charge of hiring French-Canadian workers] when he wasn't in a good mood. You might as well forget about a job," recalled Alice Carignan. "I went along to see him, and he said, 'I have only this job here. You can go in to learn to spin.' I said, 'Okay. I'll try it out; if I'm not able, I'll leave it.' And I worked there four years" (interview). Some workers actually offered bribes to the employment clerk, but by the late twenties and early thirties, "you couldn't even buy a job." Michael Stamis, referring to the employment office as the "unemployment office," recalled: "I knew some people, when they want a job, they pay $10" (interview).

The most important lesson learned from experienced workers was how to bypass the bureaucracy, especially the employment office, in order to land a job in the first place and, at a later stage, how to switch to a more desirable job. Having a connection with a boss in a desired workroom, either directly or through a friend or relative, was imperative. Relatives and friends were also helpful as translators in the hiring process.

Networks for finding a job were not limited to connections inside the mill. Local grocers, lawyers, clergy, public officials, and clubs and fraternal lodges were important as well, particularly during hard times. Letters of recommendation received by the Amoskeag in 1935 reveal the diversity of patronage within the city: letters from the superintendent of the Manchester Street Railway, the secretary of the Lion's Club, the city clerk (intervening for her brother), pastors and priests, directors of local insurance agencies and the New Hampshire Finance Corporation, and a local assessor, as well as numerous recommendations from the Manchester Cotton Local of the United Textile Workers of America. A typical letter read: "This man formerly worked for Mr. Blair in No. 3 Stark giving out yarn. When the night shift stopped he was laid off and has not been able to get back. He is willing to take anything and on any shift."[6]

Even after they were hired with the help of kin or friends, new workers explored different jobs and learned various operations until they found a job they liked and a boss they could get along with. When relatives or friends felt that the job was too difficult or the boss too demanding, they sometimes advised the new worker to try again later for another. Following their advice, the new worker did not report to the assigned department, waited a few days, and then returned to the employment office to ask for another job. This type of maneuvering was possible, of course, only in the early period when jobs were still abundant.

The practice of hiring relatives was condoned by bosses because they used it to reward good and loyal workers. In the declining years of the Amoskeag, when the agent attempted to stop the time-honored custom, the bosses protested and the practice continued. An overseer in the spinning department insisted that rewarding a loyal and efficient employee by hiring a relative promoted "a feeling in the minds of the employees that the overseer was willing to help and was interested in his employees."[7]

Because new workers learned their jobs primarily by imitating veterans, association with friends and relatives was crucial from the beginning. New workers were generally sent first to the spinning room. As they learned the rudimentary procedures of handling the machinery – carding, spinning, weaving, or dyeing – they were also taught shortcuts to save time and effort. Along with instruction in work procedures, which was informal and mostly nonverbal, experienced workers also transmitted to novices important lessons about proper behavior toward bosses and fellow workers. The lessons were essential for survival in dealing with bosses, for maintaining good peer relations, and for retaining control as a collective group in the face of management. Thus, new workers learned the many unspoken codes underlying teamwork, as well as subtle lessons regarding lines of authority in the informal hierarchies among workers. After new workers had earned the trust of veterans, they were taught how to gain the collaboration of other workers, in order to control their own work pace and output, and how to exercise passive resistance to management by slowing down or stopping. The learning process was continuous; it stretched throughout many workrooms and a variety of situations. Essential both in the adaptation of new workers and in the long-term development of a group identity, peer instruction helped workers meet the demands of management without violating the codes of collective behavior.

From their initial encounter with the system, workers tried to reconcile two contradictory goals: job security and continuity in employment, on the one hand, and some freedom and control over their own schedules, on the other. Men wanted to go hunting and fishing in season. Some wanted to return to Canada to tend a farm or to assist relatives; others wished to alternate factory work with farm work in New Hampshire or with lumbering in Maine or Canada. Women also wanted to be able to withdraw temporarily after childbearing or to alternate housekeeping with factory work as family needs dictated. There was no problem when these preferences and choices coincided with the corporation's production schedules. But synchronizing schedules was not always easy. Lax periods in production sometimes hit the workers when they most needed full-time work; conversely, workers often wanted to escape when the demands in production were heaviest. From the workers' point of view, the dilemma was how to deal with the occupational world of the mill and their own needs outside the mill without jeopardizing their employment.

At the beginning of the century, workers obtained permission to leave or shared an employment pass with several family members, who took turns holding on to the same job. Sometimes they simply quit, knowing they would be rehired when they returned. Women timed their jobs in relation to the rhythms of family life. When they needed to stay at home, they dropped out. They came back when they were able to work or when family economic pressures dictated. Men at times alternated mill work with farming or construction work. Some workers shuttled back and forth according to the seasonal labor demand in agriculture and in construction. Early in the century, the Amoskeag granted time off to French-Canadian workers when family business required their presence in Canada. In 1920, when an overseer denied a worker's request for time off to return to Canada to sell some land, Superintendent Nelson reversed the decision: "We have always allowed men time off to do business of this nature and guaranteed them their jobs."[8] In the post–World War I period, however, this flexibility all but disappeared. As the union's grievance records indicate, even workers who returned after illness with suitable medical certificates were either fired or placed in lower-skilled jobs (see Chapter 11).

Workers also tried to introduce some flexibility into their schedules and production by extending their breaks and occasionally interrupting work to socialize with fellow workers. They congregated at the water fountains, took longer toilet breaks, visited other workers at their machinery, looked out the window, and wandered around. Room girls, who were on call to assist weavers when needed, were generally unpressured in their pace. They knitted, sewed, and read while waiting. When the room girls, however, went beyond acceptable limits, when they were not available when the weavers needed them, the union itself ruled against their leisure-time pursuits. In the prewar period, such practices, part of daily work routines in the mill, were known to bosses, even though the workers thought otherwise.

It was not uncommon for young workers to play games or dance while the machinery was running, with a fellow worker stationed at the door to warn of the boss's approach. When a boss came in sight his nickname ("Frog," "Giraffe," etc.) was whispered across the room and the workers returned immediately to their jobs.

> When Roberts [superintendent of burling] came in, you could hear a pin drop. Once, we didn't know he was coming. The girl on the other side across . . . was getting married and we cut up our bonus slips into confetti and threw them all, just past his face. The floor lady was called on the carpet [Anna Schmidt, *Amoskeag*, p. 216].

Occasionally, a boss joined in the fun. Second hands in particular liked to drop their earnest demeanor from time to time and take part in games or spontaneous celebrations. Overseers, however, generally maintained their stern posture even if they secretly enjoyed the activity. Boundaries had to be maintained, and young workers who misunderstood and went too far were reminded of the limits. John Daigle recalled: "The second hand, he saw me fool around. At the time I used to go into the hall and holler at the young girls. He caught me and he kicked me in the ass. That's the way they teach you" (interview). Jeanne Laplace remembered an occasion when the spinners in her room wanted to join a parade in the city. They asked for permission to go out for an hour, but the overseer refused. They all tucked up their skirts, tied scraps of cloth into fancy turbans, and started their own parade, dancing and singing through the workrooms. The boss dismissed them and told them not to return to work the following day. But next morning when they reported for work, all was forgiven, if not forgotten. Jeanne, however, was pleased with her dismissal; she used it as an excuse to transfer to weaving, which she had been planning to do anyway. Such activities would not have been dared in the post–World War I period, when job flexibility was beginning to disappear along with the workers' sense of control over their jobs. In 1920 when several women arrived twenty minutes late because a wedding they had attended ended later than scheduled, the boss sent them away for the entire day. When they protested to the union's grievance committee, the Adjustment Board handed down a no-work, no-pay ruling, and the grievance committee agreed.[9]

Workers were allowed freedom in the earlier period because it was considered conducive to smooth working relationships. Management accepted such small time losses and waste as a matter of course, just as it was prepared to ignore petty thefts of cloth. Experienced workers were well aware that as long as they did not push the company too far, they would suffer no penalties. Auguste Dulac, a doffer who worked fast so that he could meet his quota and then help his girlfriend, recalled:

> If you were a good fellow and a quick doffer, instead of taking three and a half hours, you'd go around and doff in two and a quarter hours. You had an hour and a quarter to yourself. You could even walk over to another room and come back. So I'd go and help her. But I didn't go there to talk and talk; and they knew that. They were strict people but where it deserved to be strict [interview].

Management's goal was production. So long as interruptions did not affect the quality of the product or the overall pace of work, bosses ignored the workers' attempts at pleasure and sociability. Because bosses knew what a worker was expected to do and was capable of doing, they did not push him beyond those limits. Indeed, bosses who had risen from the ranks of common workers prided themselves on their ability to set limits:

> If your boss knows all the jobs, he knows what to expect from a man and he's not pushing him . . . I knew what a man couldn't do, and I expected that he would do a full day's work. But I didn't push him over that, I didn't expect him to do anything I wouldn't do [Jean Chagnon, interview].

Not all bosses in the Amoskeag were like Chagnon, however, and relating to bosses was often complex and difficult. From the interviews three types of bosses emerge: benevolent, paternal, and tolerant, especially to young initiates; temperamental, inconsiderate, and generally difficult to satisfy; and a combination of the two extremes. Tolerant bosses left workers alone after they had developed a routine and the work was going well, but a worker could turn to them for assistance or advice in a time of crisis. The temperamental boss drove workers without letup and discriminated against certain groups. Most Amoskeag bosses belonged to the third group.

As one worker put it, the ideal formula was live and let live. "Nobody never bothered you if your work was done" (Lucille Bourque, *Amoskeag*, p. 195). "If you did your job it was all set. If you play around, well they catch you more at that time than today" (Georgine Cusson, interview). Another recalled, "The bosses were pretty fair if you put in a day's work. Old Man Drew that we used to work for – if you were a good worker, he knew what you were and he wouldn't bother you, but if you were just trying to fool the guy, he was after you and he was keeping an eye on you" (Auguste Dulac, interview).

Bosses were, nevertheless, authority figures and to survive in the corporation, a worker had to establish a modus vivendi with them. Prior to unionization, the workers' dependence on bosses was almost total. Their only recourse when abused was the agent, and few workers had the necessary courage or access. After the introduction of the union, workers did have recourse – the grievance committee.[10] But the grievance mechanism was used only to a limited extent, and the union itself lasted only a few years.

Bosses were besieged by requests for better working conditions, increases in pay, and transfers to another job. Bosses generally responded paternalistically to personal requests but were quite rigid in work relationships. For example, when Maria LaCasse told her overseer, Oscar Cram, that she was too poor to have a Christmas tree, he donated one to her family (LaCasse, *Amoskeag*, p. 262). But when the union's grievance committee accused him of arbitrarily laying off a worker, Mr. Cram adhered to his Darwinian principle: "I follow only one rule – the survival of the fittest."[11]

Despite the corporation's benevolent image, workers were basically at the mercy of their bosses. The power of the boss was almost unlimited. Even with the centralized employment office, bosses could hire and fire and, at times, even set wage rates in their individual departments. Bosses could make workers' lives miserable by assigning faulty equipment, by steering poor raw materials or difficult work in their direction, and by making them wait for materials.

Submissiveness and fear were not, however, the major ingredients in the workers' relationship to their bosses. In the early twentieth century, obedience to someone in a post of authority on a higher social level was part of the accepted order. Bosses inspired awe and respect because of their status and accomplishments. They had worked their way up. This sense of respect and feeling of awe for authority meshed with the workers' own desire for order and discipline. Anna Schmidt, a German Amoskeag weaver who worked temporarily in Lawrence, was shocked when the workers there treated their bosses disrespectfully: "They talked so awful to their bosses. We respected ours. We never talked back." When the overseer in Lawrence told her to speed up, a fellow woman worker said: "Tell him to go to hell." But Anna resisted. "Imagine, we'd never do that in the Amoskeag!" (*Amoskeag*, p. 216).

Awe and respect were reinforced by loyalty to bosses, a loyalty based on a recognition of fair treatment. Bosses who commanded such loyalty attracted some of the best workers, workers who worked overtime willingly and did extra work as well. Henry

Carignan, for example, remembered that workers were willing to bend their own rules against overtime for John Perkins: "Nobody liked overtime too much . . . At that time overtime was not paid time and a half, but for Perkins, everybody was willing to do it. Everybody was glad to work for him. One night Perkins come around and says, 'Hey boys! Who wants to give us a hand to unload this big truck?' Everybody says, 'I, I, I.' He got fifteen men to unload that one truck" (interview). Apparently, Perkins's engaging quality was his understanding of workers' needs and his ability to communicate with them. "He was a good man. He understand you. If you wanted him to do something he will listen to you, and before he make an answer he will try to make everything clear and everybody satisfied. Always everybody satisfied" (Carignan, interview). Perkins also invited all his second hands to an annual Christmas party. When Carignan became a second hand, he tried to emulate Perkins by working hard to maintain peace and fairness in his workroom and by distributing work loads evenly. "Sometimes one fellow would be jealous, and he'd say, 'this fellow got better work than me' and he'd blame that fellow for having the better work. So we tried to even it up. When the guy still feels that's wrong, we go to our overseer" (Carignan, interview).

When relating to bosses, veterans and new arrivals were confronted with the same dilemma: how to conform to the corporation's authority and power structure without sacrificing their own sense of dignity.

How workers accommodated bosses, a basic element in the adaptation process, reflects the ambivalence and complexity of the workers' relationship to authority in the mill. For some workers, submission to the bosses' authority conformed to their family and religious traditions. Bosses symbolized paternal authority to many younger workers, who treated them with awe and often turned to them for help. "We considered our overseer far above us. I was just a boy but they didn't abuse us. They were quite good" (Thomas Demers, interview). Some workers obeyed bosses because they depended on them. It was this attitude that helped them through difficult periods of adjustment and enabled them to tolerate hardship.

Veteran workers, however, drew a careful line between proper respect for the bosses' authority as part of factory discipline and mere servility. Mrs. McDullough, for example, risked dismissal when she refused to carry out an order from Superintendent Roberts because of the tone in which she claimed he had made the request.[12]

On the other hand, new workers acted submissively in the work-room and curried their bosses' favor by performing personal services, such as watering the lawn, for them. Bosses accepted gifts from workers, Christmas gifts and wedding gifts for their son or daughter, as a matter of course. Some workers gave gold watches to their bosses on their anniversary in the mill. Occasionally, bosses received gifts of money, small appliances, or freshly caught fish or game. Bribes and tips for second hands were not uncommon. Tips provided "beer money" for some second hands, given in the hope of being assigned a better machine, of having a mistake over-looked, or of keeping a job when the crunch came.

> Oh, there was plenty of that, plenty that came from the tip that was five or ten dollars . . . So they get more work, or they get better work, or sometimes when they go on a drunk over the weekend and the boss will give him a warning, and the third warning they fire him. Well, you push him ten dollars, so . . . just like today, when you go into a restaurant, if you want a good table, you got to pay for it. It's been going on and on for years, my dear [Cora Pellerin, interview].

It is not entirely surprising that immigrants from rural backgrounds where barter was still a common practice treated the boss in this manner.

Some workers resented newly arrived immigrants who embarrassed them by being lecheux (licking). Threatened by the arrival of Greek workers, French Canadians described them as more submissive than members of other ethnic groups; earlier the Irish had made similar comments about the newly arriving French Canadians. As Marie Proulx put it: "They did their work, but they'd earn their pay by licking – bringing a box of chocolates or something like that for the boss. If the boss liked to be licked, that person would be in favor" (Amoskeag, p. 69).

The submissiveness used by workers in response to bosses was part of a strategy of accommodation that often involved playacting. It entailed apparent submission to authority while internally resisting, as well as avoidance of overt conflict by transferring or quitting.[13] Although accommodation was not a collective strategy, it was nevertheless a common practice, employed by both novice and experienced workers.

Francis Landry, a form weaver, summarized his own philosophy of accommodation as follows:

> From time to time we'd have some troubles. It's just in families. Even if I'd gone elsewhere it would been worse. The bosses rep-

rimanded us and we kicked and complained, but I was obliged. Sometimes you really get mad: "that one there, if I had a chance to shoot him I'd do it." But I never said anything [interview].

Some obeyed, even when they felt that their rights had been violated, or that the procedures were wrong, because they had no choice. But behind the bosses' backs, they often continued to act as they thought fit. Others carried their repressed anger for decades. Antonia Bergeron, a slight, quiet woman, harbored anger toward her former boss for almost half a century. She remembered with indignation: "The bosses were very fresh. The boss would chase the girls and slap their behinds, give them kicks in the rear end. They'd send them away, those they didn't like, and not pay them" (*Amoskeag*, pp. 62–3). One day she ran into her former boss on the street. "I recognized him. I said, 'Get out of the way, or I'll run over you. When we worked for you, you ran after us, you'd kick us. So if you don't get out of the way I'll run you down with the car' " (*Amoskeag*, pp. 62–3). Still others, having swallowed their pride, developed an almost "split personality." "When I'm in the mill, one part of me does what the boss tells me. The other half knows that he is not right. I know who I am, and when I go home, I am myself again" (Louise Delacroix, interview).

The most effective accommodation strategy was to stay out of the bosses' way, do your job, remain as inconspicuous as possible, and avoid trouble. Workers dodged bosses who were considered difficult by transferring to another workroom. When they could not get along with the boss, they requested a transfer before the friction erupted into open conflict. When their requests for transfer were not granted, they often chose to leave temporarily and return later in order to find employment in another workroom under better conditions. "You could leave a job in the morning and have another one in the afternoon" (Ora Pelletier, *Amoskeag*, p. 186).

As the opportunities for transfer declined in the 1920s, workers became trapped in their workrooms. They could no longer afford the luxury of leaving their jobs and being rehired. Workers were now squeezed in a double bind: As the arbitrary demands of bosses and the pressures of work increased, the workers' ability to maneuver declined.

Experienced workers who knew their jobs and had a strong sense of their inner worth, along with high standards of perfection, confronted bosses directly. If they disagreed with a boss over methods of production or the quality of materials, they did not hesitate to question both the competence and the fairness of the boss. Such workers insisted that it was not their personal judgment versus that of the boss; they were protecting, rather, what they perceived as the corporation's standards of production and quality of product. Trying to hold their bosses to the very standards that the corporation had instilled in them, they considered themselves better interpreters of the corporation's work ethic and production standards than the boss.[14]

Some workers insisted that their long years of experience and familiarity with the machinery had made them experts; they "knew better" than their bosses and did not hesitate to argue. Workers who considered a procedure wrong and inefficient and refused to follow the instructions of the boss were often fired. During subsequent grievance hearings, management often found that the workers had been right. Management reinstated such workers and tried to save face for the boss at the same time. For example, William Scott, a cloth inspector, was transferred by his overseer, Mr. English, to the dyehouse for a four- to six-month period. English was "tired of having him argue each time when the overseer was bringing up a certain point: Scott is always right and the overseer is always wrong." English hoped that after a few months in the dyehouse "Mr. Scott will have been taught not to argue every point." Although management tended to agree with Scott, the transfer was upheld to allow English to save face. At the same time, management felt that Scott was not being persecuted because his job was secure. Joseph Weed, a dresser, protesting management's insistence that dressers operate with two squeeze rolls rather than one, said it almost seemed that he was "working in a flour mill." He contended that the dressers should be allowed to use their own discretion in the choice of one or two rolls. Superintendent Roberts insisted, however, that the dressers were not in a position to judge the ultimate result.[15]

Workers were sometimes faced, however, with conflicting allegiances, because family and ethnic group interests did not always conform to collective working-class goals. Family members often helped each other at the expense of other workers, thus contracting the mutually agreed upon standards. Ethnic groups' interests often obstructed working-class solidarity.

The education of new workers into working-class mores involved the transition from being *lècheux* to being firm and insistent on their rights and on fair play, from personal accommodation to collective strategies. For the majority of workers, it was a tug-and-pull process, sometimes with management, sometimes with fellow workers.

Workers' response to changes in production and personnel policies

The introduction of scientific management in the second decade of the twentieth century challenged the existing pace of work and reorganized work relations, thus requiring adaptation by both new and veteran workers. In 1911, the introduction of a task and bonus system intensified and systematized work procedures. (By 1910 most of the textile production jobs in the Amoskeag had already been put on piece rates.)[16] Finally, in the 1920s, in response to southern competition, the Amoskeag used scientific management as a justification for speedups, doubling up, and the stretch-outs in work loads. These crucial changes in the organization of work and in the speed of production compounded the pressures that had been introduced prior to the war. These new pressures, combined with frequent layoffs and an inefficient flow of raw materials, placed workers and bosses in conflict and demoralized work relationships. From 1919 on, workers in a variety of jobs, especially loomfixers and weavers, frequently protested increases in work loads, complaining that they were being "worked to death."

The corporation first attempted to introduce new efficiency measures in 1911, when time-and-motion studies were launched in several departments by Henry Gantt, Frederick Winslow Taylor's disciple and chief assistant, who was brought in as a consultant.[17] During the next five years, Fred M. Caswell, who was in charge of the Amoskeag's newly established planning office, began a systematic investigation of all work procedures in the main departments. Between 1911 and 1916, on the basis of the time-and-motion studies, Caswell recommended to the agent a variety of innovations, including a reduction in the number of workers tending certain machines, a reorganization of work routines, and the institution of bonuses for different operations.

The impact of scientific management in the Amoskeag can be fully understood only in the context of the historical development of the textile industry. In contrast to the metals industry, for example, most work in the textile industry had already been paced by machines.[18] Thus, scientific management in textiles did not assault autonomous decision making among workers; rather, it increased the pace of work and improved efficiency in different departments. As a result, it struck at traditional work routines and social ties within the Amoskeag and led to an increase in the arbitrary behavior of overseers.

In some instances the number of workers per operation were reduced and work loads and sequences were redistributed. Although such changes may have produced a more efficient operation, they undermined the network of social relations surrounding the work routines. In the spooling room, for example, the number of yarn men was cut down. Their tasks were reorganized to allow them to move back and forth between the spinning and winding rooms, delivering empty and full bobbins alternately, in accordance with the pace at which the spoolers produced them, whereas the previous practice had been for yarn men to "stroll around on the spare floor, sit on empty boxes or even sleep until more spools accumulated." The "snarler" girls, who disentangled yarn that was caught, were now separated and placed in different aisles.[19]

Workers viewed their close supervision by time-and-motion experts as an insult. Dorothy Moore recalled how women workers felt about the "spotters":

> They weren't hiring many new people when we went in, other than bringing in a lot of spotters. People like Freddy Meharg and Eddy Dunbar were time [and motion] estimators. The workers called them spotters because they sat themselves down beside a certain person who was doing a certain amount of work and timed them. They do that all the time now in factories, but then it was new. Most of the Amoskeag jobs where I worked had women employees, and it upset them terribly. Those spotters would simply plop themselves down beside the workers and make them nervous, particularly if a girl was tending a spinning frame or even a warping frame, where they would count how many threads she'd have to gather in and tie in. You can understand how she felt if she had never really had anyone stand over her before [*Amoskeag*, p. 178].

Winding, warping, weaving, and burling were put on a task-and-bonus system in 1911. By August of that year, Caswell reported progress with great optimism to Superintendent William Parker Straw. Wool was being opened up better than the wool sorter could do it themselves; an overseer who had worked in the Amoskeag for thirty years said that he "had not seen the wool coming so well since he had been in the present shop." Production had increased steadily in the warping department.[20]

H. L. Gantt described the results of placing the Amoskeag burlers in the worsted division on bonus: While the poorer workers failed on the first day, they began to earn a bonus on the last day of the experiment. Of the 161 burlers who had been put on bonus between April 15 and July 10, 21 had left the company's employment. As a result, another burling room, which was not yet under the bonus system, was put on piece rates.[21] In that room one-third of the women left as well. To Gantt, the bonus system was preferable because the separation rate for those on piece work was higher (1913:196–7). Caswell's reports to Straw of the burlers' reasons for leaving (Table 6.1) are consistent with the reasons given in Gantt's report:

> *In Mrs. Tonery's Room* – April 15–July 10.
> Grace Bolduc – June 26th Poor health – hot weather. Asked if she could return in the fall.
> *In Mrs. Dyer's Room* – April 15–July 10.
> Ella Provencher – June 6th Told if bad work continued she would be discharged. Left when next bad work was returned.
> Laura Demers – May 23rd Married.
> Heduridge Bellefeuville – May 23rd Left – Ill health.
> *In Mrs. Eckert's Room* – April 15–July 10.
> Rose Babineau – June 10th Entered Convent.
> Mary Lapoint – April 23rd Discharged for bad work.
> Rose Morin – April 23rd Discharged for bad work.
> Diana Drowin – May 21st Discharged for bad work.
> Ethel Gillespie – May 21st Discharged for bad work.
> Eva Mechon – May 6th Left – Discouraged on account of work returned.
> Mary Gunville – June 29th Home to Michigan
> Lega Deselets – June 29th Home to Michigan
> *In Miss Healey's Room* – April 15–July 10.
> Nellie Murray – June 6th Gone to New York State.
> *In Mrs. Bailey's Room* – April 30–July 10
> Kate Monahan – June 13th Wait on table at the mountains for summer.
> Jennie Cote – June 13th Discharged.
> Ruby Duff – June 11th Moved to New York City.
> Donelda Lord – May 31st Left – dissatisfied.
> Leonide Jalbert – June 2nd Gone to Canada.
> Mabel Young – June 24th Transferred from Dept. Refused to go.

To the workers, this progress in efficiency exacted a high price in fatigue and pressure. In 1911 John Golden, general president of the

Table 6.1. *Reasons women burlers terminated employment,*
September 3 through November 18, 1912

Reasons given for terminating employment	Number
Objected to associates	1
Called to Canada	1
Left because chum was discharged	1
Transferred to Harness Room	1
Left to become model, now back working	1
Discharged for dishonesty	1
Objected to working on bonus	1
Discouraged in not earning bonus each day	1
Objected to being spoken to for bad work	2
Out to care for children	2
Left to be married	2
Sickness in family	2
Called to work notices in other department	3
Left without reason or notice	3
Left on account of poor health	6
Eye troubles	4
Found better positions (bookkeeper, store clerk, housekeeper, weaver)	4
Learners, worked from 1 to 9 days	6
4-week girls, left when put on piece rate	7
Discharged for bad work	16
Total	65

Note: These terminations were monitored by the Planning Office following the introduction of task-and-bonus work in the Gray Burling Room in the Canal Building, April 15 and July 10, 1912. Caswell reported as follows: "We started the first girl on task work with a bonus on February 7, 1912. No girl got through of her own accord until May 6. Between those two dates one hundred and eighteen girls were started on this work."
Source: Amoskeag Company, Planning Office Report, November 21, 1912, Planning Office Records, Baker Library, Harvard University.

United Textile Workers of America, described the impact of the task-and-bonus system on workers in a large textile mill in Passaic, New Jersey:

> Should the operator fall below the standard which has been set a reduced price is paid, which is commonly known as the flat rate. For instance, take the weaving department. The flat rate of wages is set at $1.47 per day on four looms. If the weaver makes 251,400 picks per day he (or she) receives $2.41, but should he fall below

this number he goes back to the flat rate of $1.47, or, in other words, should he make 250,400 picks per day, he loses his bonus and goes back to the flat rate of $1.47 per day.

The workers Golden interviewed described their anguish in words similar to those of the Amoskeag workers:

> Yes, we get a little more money some days, not always, but we were pushed to the limit. The mental strain under which we work, and our anxiety and fear that we shall fall below the standard makes the job scarcely worth while [pp. 603–4].

The bonus system as well as piece rates in general drove workers to guard jealously their own output and time schedules. At the same time they learned to team up, to act collectively, to insist on maximum limits to production quotas. When bosses were pressured to meet certain quotas, the collective response of workers became more frequent.

The bonus system carried both a promise and a threat – as one former worker put it: "We were on piece work; we spinned, we had to make so many doffs and the bonus; if you didn't hurry up and piece you would lose on weight. You would keep up to make a good bonus" (Anne Beauder, interview). The system was particularly attractive to ambitious new immigrant workers, who could easily understand that working quickly put more money in their pockets. In addition, the system gave workers a sense of accomplishment, a measure of their own productivity. To Anna Schmidt, for example, who worked in the burling room, the bonus system presented a real challenge:

> You'd got a piece of cloth, and it would say one hour or two hours . . . you had to get it done in that time . . . At the end of the day, you'd add up all your coupons, and I was always way ahead. The boss used to say, 'I wish I could catch you losing'"
> (Amoskeag, p. 213).

For Alice Carignan, the trade-offs were straightforward: "The more we did, the more we got. We were a little bit ambitious and the salaries weren't high at that time. So we'd bring in a sandwich and eat while working" (interview).

At the same time, the bonus system was hard on the nerves. "Weaving in piecework; I never cared too much about that. That's the trouble, it done me nervous" (Thomas Bergeron, interview). Novice workers like Mary Hamilton had a hard time keeping up: "My father had to skip lunch one of these noontimes, so that he could fill the batteries for me" (interview). And Antoine Roberge, who rose from bobbin boy to second hand, condemned piecework as an extremely strenuous and antisocial system: "It's all piece-work. It's not like working in a shop. In a shop you make friends. But on piecework they push you all the time" (interview).

Workers who were unable to meet their quotas risked the loss of their jobs. Alice Carignan, the worker who appreciated the principle of "the more you make, the more you get," was also bitter about the push:

> We had to do a certain amount of pounds of yarn and if we didn't make enough pounds the boss wasn't happy and he'd come by and scold us: "If you can't do your amount you'll go out," and he put some out. They still demanded too much for the amount of money that we were working on. Oh that boss, I detested him! [interview].

The system pitted workers against each other – particularly when the mutually agreed upon quota was surpassed by eager workers. In 1919 two hand folders in No. 11 cloth room, Dennis Murphy and Patrick Thornton, were expelled from the union because they insisted on doing 525 to 550 pieces in an 8¾-hour day after the union had agreed with management that 450 pieces was considered a day's work for a 48-hour week. The two men insisted that they would do "as many pieces per day as they saw fit." The grievance committee requested their discharge. When Agent Straw refused to discharge them, the grievance committee hinted that trouble would result. As a precaution, Straw instructed the superintendent to lay off Murphy and Thornton for several weeks; at Straw's request, the chairman of the grievance committee promised that the men would not be "molested" when they returned to work.[22]

When bonuses for overseers and second hands were made contingent on the workers' bonuses, pressure intensified. Thomas Lloyd, a second hand in the spinning room, devised his own way of manipulating the procedures:

> They were pushing at that particular time. Those girls were getting two sets of those spindles off a five-spindle machine, and the overseer said that if I could increase it that he'd give me more money. So, being a machinist, I hopped the thing up so that they got five sets off of it.

But when his reward did not come through:

> I told him I wanted more money. Well, he was kind of sorry about it. I took the gears up and put them right back to where they was. I said, "You go ahead and find out how to get five sets off these a day," and I left [interview].

Bosses who were unnecessarily strict in enforcing discipline found their efforts to be counter productive. In a number of grievance cases brought before the corporation's Adjustment Board, the agent agreed with workers who complained of being unduly punished for absence from work and being late; the agent reminded the boss of the need for flexibility and tolerance.

The major disagreement between workers and management revolved around the question of what constitutes a fair and honest day's work.

> Talk of output restriction occurs when management observes that the conception it has of a day's work differs from that which the work group, through the medium of production, is expressing as its conception.
>
> In such situations talk of "soldiering," "goldbricking," and "loafing" on the part of management-oriented employees is matched by talk of "speed-up," "slave-driving" and "man-killing" on the part of labor-oriented employees [Collins, Dalton, and Roy 1946:2].

These changes in the speed of production, the work loads and the organization of work, and the method of pay struck at the core of earlier work relationships and codes. In this respect, the most devastating impact came from the work loads and speedups in the post war period, which intensified the impact of the efficiency measures.

Despite these pressures, the Amoskeag workers insisted on continuing to operate by the codes of behavior they had adopted. What mattered to the workers was that the job was getting done well and on time. "When we wove we were sitting down and our work ran and everything went orderly. In the earlier times we could sit down" (Jean Jalbert, interview). It was customary for a weaver or a loomfixer to sit down when his machinery was running well: "At the Amoskeag everyone was fair. When someone had a hard time, they gave him help. The loomfixer, he's got all his work running good, sits down and waits; and the weaver sits down" (Thomas Bergernon, interview). When the pace became faster, that sense of understanding was lost and sitting down at the job was labeled "loafing."

Prior to the postwar increase in work loads and speedups, Adam Laliberte recalled:

> The work was not pushing. They gave you your work and that was it. And you had time to yourself; you didn't have to rush. After a while, they gave us some extra work . . . and we were not

paid any more. And that's how they started to increase the work
load on the people" [interview].

"The pace of work," recalled James Burton, "was something you get
used to from early years. If you grew up there you got used to it.
Some people, the new workers come in and see that, they would go
out the next day" (Burton, interview).

In the earlier period, the Amoskeag had a reputation for a humane and manageable pace, idealized in retrospect by many workers who subsequently found jobs in the Chicopee mills; they felt
that the work pace in the Chicopee had driven them to the verge of
nervous breakdown. Jean Chagnon, a former card grinder who had
worked in both places, recalled:

> No comparison, mister! No comparison! I ran two cards when I
> was a kid [in the Amoskeag], and I loved the job. And in Chico-
> pee, when I went in I had to grind six cards a day. So I took the
> job, but I didn't give them what I gave the Amoskeag in 10 hours
> on two cards [interview].

Although work in the Amoskeag may have appeared more tolerable
in comparison with the pace in the Chicopee, it was still exacting.
Marie Proulx, who was committed to perfection, recalled the constant pacing of the workers with the machinery: "A person who
always wanted her work well done there never sat down, never.
You had to pick out your time to eat . . . so as not to let your work
go down. If it fell down, you couldn't get it back up again" (*Amoskeag*, p. 68).

Speedups and stretch-outs, a hardship for veteran workers and
new arrivals alike, not only dehumanized the work process and
drove workers to exhaustion, they also challenged the workers'
sense of competence and identification with the quality of the final
product. As the pressure mounted on both bosses and workers to
increase output, and as the quality of the materials and the environment declined, the earlier labor-management equilibrium was destroyed. A recurring protest concerned the time lost by piece-rate
workers who were required to perform other services. Experienced
workers continued to teach new workers – their own relatives and
friends – and they frequently helped inexperienced and slower
workers meet their quotas. Now, however, these activities interfered with their ability to meet their own quotas. They resented not
receiving compensation for the time lost in teaching other workers.
Irma Kelley, for example, refused to leave her own work to help
another worker – if helping someone meant reducing her own
wages, she would not do it. She was fired. During the subsequent

Adjustment Board hearings, the overseer claimed there had been a "misunderstanding," that he had intended to pay her for her help. Irma agreed to do it under those terms.[23] In many similar instances workers on piece rates insisted on being paid an hourly rate whenever they were required to teach new workers or finish other workers' jobs. Some piece-rate workers, however, fearing a loss of control over their own schedules, were unwilling to take on additional assignments even if they were paid overtime.

When time clocks were introduced in 1920, they provoked immediate resentment. In their efforts to punch their time cards at exactly the same moment, people were trampled in the crush. Some women emerged with broken glasses, bruised ankles, and torn dresses. The real issue, however, was not the logistics of arrival and departure but the regimentation that the time clocks imposed and the workers' loss of control over their own pace. The uniform time-clock system violated the arrangements for "flexi-time" that certain workers had negotiated. For example, a size man who was obliged to come in at 6:30 every morning to boil the size, so that the dresser tenders could start work at 7:15, had been allowed to leave at 11 without loss of pay. After the introduction of time cards, he was denied that privilege. The adjustment board did not restore his right to leave earlier but ruled instead that he be paid overtime if he worked longer hours.[24]

As shortages of materials grew in frequency and the flow of work became erratic, the issue of leaving early surfaced in a different form: Piece-rate workers in the cloth room objected to staying until closing time each day when work could not be supplied. In the past, the workers reminded management, they had been allowed to leave when their quota was met even if the workday was not over. The Adjustment Board ruled that workers could leave early when work was not available but would be required to stay when additional work beyond what they considered their "task" remained.[25] Similarly, when an overseer prohibited piece workers from leaving before closing time when there was no work to be done, the Adjustment Board ruled in favor of the workers. In 1919 the winders protested a new rule that prohibited them from reading while they were waiting for supplies. Instead of revoking the prohibition against reading, management promised them a more even flow of materials.[26]

Prior to the introduction of a formal grievance mechanism, workers took matters into their own hands. To cope with speedups and increased work loads, they devised shortcuts and slowdowns. A common shortcut involved discarding inferior materials that slowed a worker down. Instead of repairing rusty bobbins, bobbin sorters saved time by throwing them out the window into the river or sneaking them out of the mill. They were paid by the box of sorted good bobbins. Throwing away bad ones enabled them to process boxes full of good bobbins more quickly. Antoine Roberge, a former second hand, recalled an old woman's shortcuts:

> They were giving the spinners one cent for every bobbin they wound. We knew exactly who was making the bad ones. You had to take that bad one and give it to the help that made it. There was an old Dutch woman working for us and she was making the bad work. Whenever she noticed she had a bad bobbin, she used to take it out, put it in her bag and take it home. She was afraid to lose [time and pay]. That cent was a cent too. We got her one day. The watchman stopped her at the gate and she was fired [interview].

In investigating the work procedures in different departments in order to plan efficiently, Caswell found workers setting their own production quotas informally by pacing themselves. One woman, for example, who sorted and classified remnants, alternated the number of cases she completed each day. "She will do 3 cases Monday, 2 cases Tuesday, and 3 cases Wednesday. By so doing the operative earns $1.74 one day and $2.61 the next day, adding up to $13.05 a week." Caswell concluded that "it appears that some diplomacy is used by the operative in regulating her wages."[27]

In the upper canal spinning room, Caswell found that the yarn men who marked the boxes of yarn "completed and delivered" had punched twelve completed boxes on the spoolers' cards. Seventeen boxes were considered a "big day's work," but the day in question was Saturday, a half day. Caswell could not understand how twelve boxes could have been completed in a half day's work.[28] He concluded that the spooler girls had accomplished this feat by throwing away bad yarn that could not be fixed easily. Spool heads that were partly or entirely broken were not repaired and the yarn from those spools was cut off and thrown away. The union representative himself disclosed this practice to management: "Those girls do this with the idea of getting a big day's pay." In an effort to prove good faith, the union representative promised to end this practice.[29]

By increasing supervision in the rooms, raising fines for substandard work, and tightening the squeeze on inspectors, section hands, forewomen (in the burling room), second hands, and bosses, management hoped to stop these infractions. They adopted a carrot-and-stick policy toward bosses, rewarding them with a bonus based on the earnings of their workers and penalizing them when their workers produced substandard work.[30] Although discipline and quality control improved, the problem of shortcuts and wastage nevertheless escalated. Job control was the workers' answer. In the early 1920s when winders were slowed down by frequent breakages in the yarn and unacceptable materials, they took matters into their own hands and removed boxes of yarn that were unsuitable. Arguing that they were slowed down by the faulty materials supplied by the corporation, they insisted on their rights to determine their own speed.[31]

Speedups and work pressures were most effectively handled by collective group action. Collective slowdowns in specific operations became a common practice. "We all knew what to do," Lucille Bourque recalled, "If there was a warp out we'd all run in and help one another. We'd hurry up and get it done. The minute it got done we'd all sit down and go slowly" (interview).

Workers agreed on an acceptable pace and production quota and defended it. As a newly appointed foreman, Jean Chagnon made sure that the grinders checked their settings before they started their cards.

> A guy could get killed, but nobody wanted to check their settings. They were all old grinders; they didn't do half of what they were supposed to do. They always got away with it. They didn't after that. I don't cover up for nobody . . . One of them said, "Get away from here. I'm gonna kick your ass!" I said, "You try it." [The employment office had warned Chagnon before he accepted the job that] "You known what it is – Polish, Greek, French, all nationalities is working in here! Are you afraid?" [interview].

Workers responded to speedups and stretch-outs through both individual manipulation of production processes and job control – a collective group action by a production unit or an entire workroom.[32] Clustering along kinship and ethnic lines in the workrooms facilitated job control. Workers expressed their collective identity when sacrificing higher quotas for the sake of control over the work pace, when filing protests with the grievance committee, and when slowing the machinery. In acting together to protect their rights, they also held the corporation to the earlier standards of the workplace and the product.

The collective identity, however, did not necessarily generate an overall working-class solidarity that transcended ethnic, class, sex, and skill divisions. Conflicts among individuals or among various interest groups persisted. At times, union activity even tended to accentuate these conflicts. In addition to personal animosity among individuals, workers of certain occupations were antagonistic toward laborers in other occupations. At times loomfixers pressured weavers by refusing to fix their looms or by stalling, thus making it impossible for the weavers to meet their quotas. To protest the increase in work loads and the elimination of spare fixers, loomfixers slowed down or stopped fixing looms altogether. Thus the weavers were punished along with management.[33]

In the burling room, the perchers exercised power over the burlers by spotting "bad work" as they picked up rolls of mended cloth from the burler. Although the grievance committee praised the perchers for their refusal to accept "bad work," the committee also pointed out that "many of the men on perching were cheating the girls, and that if the girls were not cheated out of time they would be receiving more money than the men in many cases." Most of the perchers were married men, whereas the women burlers were in their teens and early twenties.[34]

Ethnic conflicts were the most divisive force among the workers. Although ethnic clustering united groups of laborers, ethnic solidarity sometimes counteracted working-class unity. On one occasion when two Greek weavers were dismissed, only Greek workers went on strike (Creamer and Coulter 1939: 182). Discrimination or job segregation along ethnic lines as practiced by bosses and minor supervisors found its counterpart in ethnic conflicts among the workers. Jean Chagnon recalled breaking up frequent fights among members of different ethnic groups when he was second hand in the card room. "One Polish fellow, they used to call him Hot Dog, and a German fellow, they used to call him Kaiser – he had a big long mustache. I had to break up those fights. They were really swinging. Oh, I broke up a lot of fights" (interview).

The emergence of workers' collective action

This discussion has considered two types of worker adaptation: The "historic" adaptation of workers from rural backgrounds to the pressures of industrial time and work schedules and the adaptation of workers to changes in the work pace instituted in the cause of efficiency and scientific management. Any effort to discern an overall pattern in workers' responses must consider the complexities and great variety in these responses at any given time. Nevertheless, the following generalizations seem valid.

Challenges to workers' adaptability came in two major areas, corresponding to the newness of the labor force and the stage the corporation had reached in its own development. Workers were first challenged by the demands to conform to industrial time schedules and the intricacies and strain of handling machinery. They were next challenged by changes in the factory system, in the modes of production and in the organization of work. Both new and old workers had to adapt to the efficiency measures introduced by scientific management – to speedups, to increased work loads, and to the reorganization of earlier work patterns. Workers had to adjust to new rules and standards; eventually they had to adjust to the decline in the quality of raw materials and of the final product, a decline they found demoralizing. Although developments burdened all workers, the pressure was doubled for new ones. In earlier times, the demands on new arrivals were blunted by the Amoskeag's flexible regime; now workers had to operate under more demanding conditions. At the same time, older workers, who had been socialized to collective group responses, were less willing than they might have been in the past to tolerate the kinds of accommodations made by new workers.

To some extent the changes in worker adaptation follow a generational sequence, which also corresponds to historical changes in the corporation. First-generation newcomers from rural backgrounds were in awe of the bosses and the system and tended to act more submissively than more experienced workers. They were more inclined to individual interaction with bosses, either directly or through relatives, than toward group action. Second-generation or veteran workers, who were less awed by the system and had learned to exercise shortcuts to control their work pace, displayed a stronger group identity. Rather than being *lècheux*, they confronted bosses directly; if their requests were not granted, they found their own informal routes for exercising some controls within the limits of the system. These two styles of behavior also varied somewhat among ethnic groups, depending on their time of arrival. French Canadians, who had penetrated the mills in larger numbers, were less likely to be submissive than such recent arrivals as the Greek workers, who entered the Amoskeag at a period of diminishing flexibility and who themselves had no prior industrial experience and little in the way of support networks within the mills. New immigrants who had greater language difficulties and less access to translators within the mills were also less likely to exercise initiative and develop collective action.

These two different models of worker response were also related to the time period of their employment in the Amoskeag's history. As the corporation declined in the post–World War I period, workers moved away from passive acquiescence and individual accommodation and toward collective group protest. This transition over the corporation's history resulted from changes within the composition of the labor force as well as from the changes introduced by scientific management.

The proportion of immigrants entering the Amoskeag declined progressively in the post–World War I period, both because of new immigration laws and because fewer workers were needed through the 1920s. Changes in the composition of the labor force also coincided with post–World War I developments within the corporation, which drove even the more docile workers into protest. The entrance of the union into the Amoskeag, and union activities between 1918 and 1922, provided an important rallying point for collective action, one that was not available earlier. Thus, whereas new immigrant workers were struggling to survive in a new work environment, the veteran workers were resisting speedups and stretch-outs, the reduction of wages, and the increase in hours. They did so in an organized fashion, especially in the later period. The corporation's children were coming of age, and distinctive working-class attitudes were beginning to emerge. How widespread such attitudes were among the Amoskeag's workers in the pre-strike period is questionable, however.

The overall patterns in the Amoskeag are consistent with changes in workers' behavior and responses to scientific management in other industries during this time. In his discussion of workers' control of industrial processes in the twentieth century, Montgomery (1979) emphasizes the differences between two generations of workers. The workers who exercised controls over their work process and who insisted on their own standards in defining the quality and pace of production were not green immigrants. They were second-generation immigrants who had developed working-class mores and a collective group identity.

Although this model generally fits the Amoskeag experience, it is necessary to distinguish among the many layers of worker consciousness among the workers. To describe workers' behavior in the Amoskeag as a linear transition from a *lècheux* attitude to a working-class identity would oversimplify a complex development. Acquiescence on the surface may have covered up more organized protest. Conversely, it is difficult to ascertain the exact extent of workers' collective protests and controls in the later period. Patterns of response were decidedly more visible after 1918 when the union provided a formal protest mechanism through its grievance system. But the question remains: Did collective group protest actually increase in the postwar period, or did it become more organized and visible because the union provided a new vehicle for protest? Also, the dichotomy between submissive workers and self-conscious second-generation protesters may be a false one. Not all new immigrant workers were submissive, nor were all veteran and second-generation immigrant workers committed to working-class solidarity. Some workers fluctuated from one type of behavior to the other, depending on their level of dissatisfaction, the risks involved, and other circumstances. Sometimes members of the same families differed in the style of their responses and in their commitment to collective action. Those divergences came to the foreground especially during the strike of 1922 when some families were split between strikers and nonstrikers.

The lines of conflict were not always sharply drawn, even between workers and bosses. There were times when workers were at each other's throats because of personal or ethnic conflicts or because of rivalry over better materials or better machinery. In some instances workers called on bosses to intervene in their quarrels. However, the increasing pressures from management and the deterioration of working conditions in various departments in the later period drove workers to joint action as the paternalistic balance was upset in the post–World War I years. There was not a neat chronological division of the style of worker resistance: Some workers displayed a conscious working-class ideology before World War I, others continued to act submissively after the war. The difference in those periods lies in the tones that respectively dominated them. Collective group action and efforts to exercise workers' controls, both informally and through the union, began to predominate in the immediate postwar period. The defeat of the union following the strike of 1922 led to a disillusionment of many workers with collective action and to a return to informal group action, as well as individual maneuvering, in handling difficult working conditions.

The diversity in worker behavior certainly removes any doubt about a single process of assimilation to industrial life. Whereas Gutman emphasizes continuity and recurrence in the adaptation of new workers to the factory system, one must also recognize subsequent changes in behavior beyond the initial adaptation to new work schedules and complicated technology. The transfer of preindustrial work habits into the factory setting, which Gutman stresses and which is also evident in the Amoskeag, represented only one part of the story. Subsequently, workers addressed the factory on its own terms by their own means of resisting scientific management and speedups. In so doing, they drew not merely on their premigration traditions but, most important, on their own experience and expertise as industrial workers, especially their knowledge of how to manipulate technological processes and production schedules.

Although the Amoskeag tried through its efficiency program to transform a fluid, immigrant labor force into a stable, disciplined, and obedient industrial unit, in some respects, its policies inadvertently encouraged the transformation of individual accommodationist workers into collectively active groups prepared to manipulate the system to meet their own standards and needs. Hence, particularly in the postwar period, the Amoskeag saw the emergence of an urban, industrial working class, now able to address management on its own terms.

Whether that transformation was actually completed is difficult to establish because the process was hindered by declining employment opportunities in the Amoskeag during the 1920s and the loss of flexibility in the corporation's own hiring policies. These developments rendered protesters and maneuverers more vulnerable and therefore more cautious, except in the last two years prior to the shutdown when there was little left to lose. The outright denial of union solidarity on the part of many interviewees is a reflection of their sense of defeat, which, in their memories, resulted from the traumatic events of the strikes and the shutdown.

7 Household organization and the timing of life transitions

An important aspect of family life in the past was the synchronization of individual life patterns with the organization of the family as a collective unit. The movement of individuals through a variety of family roles and household configurations is anchored into the family as a collective unit. Just as individuals make their transitions in and out of a variety of family and work roles over their lives, their families too are constantly reorganized and restructured as they gain and lose members and as the age configurations within them undergo constant change. Although such changes in Manchester were most evident within the nuclear household, which was the predominant form of familial residence, they also involved changing patterns of coresidence with extended kin and strangers.

The household itself is, therefore, an important unit of analysis, which allows the determination of the domestic boundaries of the family as a unit and the patterns of change in age configurations as well as an examination of the decision-making process within the family. It is important to realize that a profile of a household at a specific point in time obscures the constant movement of family members in and out of different household patterns over their life courses. People went through a series of life transitions which impinged not only on their own lives but also on the structure and membership of their families and households. Leaving home, getting married, setting up independent households, all such individual transitions were related to collective family decisions and affected the family and household structure directly and indirectly. Households were like a revolving stage on which different members appeared and disappeared, under their own momentum or under the impact of external conditions. It is important, therefore, to understand how individual life transitions and the movement of different family members in and out of the household were synchronized with the family as a collective unit.

Households were the basic organizational unit of the family, the cells that together made up neighborhoods and entire communities, throughout European and American society during the period under study. In American cities only about 3% of the population lived alone.[1] Almost all men and women expected to live out their

154

lives in familial or surrogate familial settings. An examination of the household, therefore, is virtually a study of the entire population.

Much historical debate over the impact of industrialization on family structure has centered on the question of whether the household was nuclear or extended. Laslett and Wall (1972) have established the predominance of the nuclear family during the preindustrial era. Three generations of the same family rarely coresided in the same household. At the same time, the difference between *family* and *household* must not be overlooked. Households were predominantly nuclear, but extended family ties outside the household were pervasive. In the majority of cases, although extended kin lived in separate households, those households were located in the same building or at least in the same neighborhood. Nuclear households, on the other hand, were strictly limited to a family unit consisting of a couple or one parent and children. At times they included nonrelatives, such as servants, boarders, or lodgers.[2]

Because most analyses of urban households in the second half of the nineteenth century are based upon household units as enumerated in the population census, they capture only snapshots of family and household structure at one point in time or at several decade intervals if more than one census was involved. Such cross-sectional views overlook the variety of changes in the structure of the household over the lifetime of its members. The absence of longitudinal data tracing lifetime changes in household membership complicates the task of reconstructing a sequence of change in household configurations and structures over the life course. In reality, a household that is nuclear at one point in time can be extended shortly thereafter and resume a nuclear form at a later date (Hareven 1974; Berkner 1972). If the household is viewed as a process over time rather than as a static unit at a single point in time, changes in the structure and membership of the household can be inferred by looking at age structure as a proxy for longitudinal patterns (Hareven 1978b). Households expanded and contracted as individual members and families moved over the life course, either by choice or under the pressures of social and economic conditions. This fluidity in the organization of the household is related to its role in society as the basic organizational unit of residence.

Inherent in the dynamic process of the household was a contradiction in its functions: It served as a source of order, stability, and continuity, and at the same time it encouraged a certain instability. As the locus for new family formation and childrearing, the household also provided a continuity in the lives of older people. It was the place to which young people returned in times of need; the place where migrants and older people without families found a familial setting. Yet at the same time, the household also dislodged members from its midst – thus generating instability in the population. Families launched children into the outside world when they reached adulthood, sent out members they were unable to support, or dissolved if their heads or crucial members were stricken by illness or death or became too old to maintain their independence.

The paradox lies in the way changes within households both promoted and stabilized population movement. In a sense, households were engaged in indirect exchanges across neighborhoods and wide geographic regions. As some members went out into the world, newcomers moved in. Those whose lives were disrupted by migration or death were absorbed into other families. Young people could move to new communities, confident that they could co-reside with relatives or strangers. Similarly, working mothers were able to place young children in the homes of relatives or strangers, and dependent older people moved into other people's households. Such exchanges among relatives, neighbors, or complete strangers were laced throughout the entire society.

The predominance of the nuclear household

This chapter examines patterns of household structure and the timing of life transitions in Manchester. Unlike the chapters on work patterns and kinship, which focus specifically on Amoskeag workers and their families, this analysis is based on a cross section of the Manchester population, as derived from a sample of households from the 1900 census.[3] This allows an examination of the familial and household patterns of the textile workers in the larger population context.

In Manchester, as in other communities, familial residence was the dominant pattern. The majority of children and young teenagers lived with their parents (Figures 7.1 and 7.2). Most men older than 19 were heads of households; close to half the women older than 19 were wives of household heads. The proportion of female-headed households without husbands present was very low and most women household heads were widows. Solitary residence was rare. Some women listed by the census taker as living alone were actually residing in one-room units in large boardinghouses.

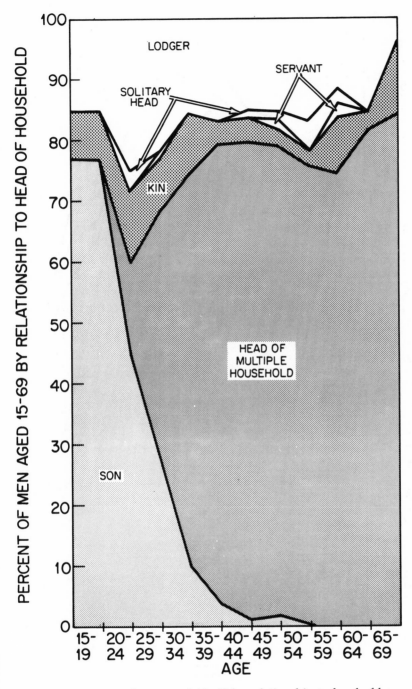

Figure 7.1. Percent of men aged 15–69 by relationship to head of household, Manchester 1900. (Figure by Louise Tilly.)

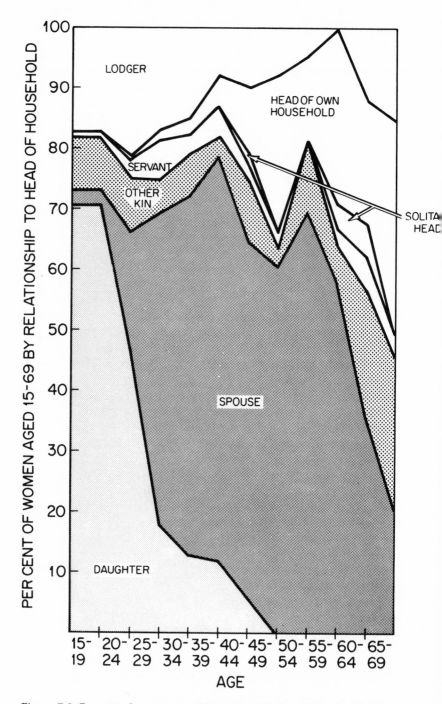

Figure 7.2. Percent of women aged 15–69 by relationship to head of household, Manchester 1900. (Figure by Louise Tilly.)

Each tenant had a separate room, but the kitchen and bath were shared.

> "We used to have three regular floors in the tenements, but they used the attics, too, in those days . . . You had to carry up water if you wanted it. If you wanted a hot bath, you had to start the fire in the stoves and warm it, just a pail of water at a time . . . But it took a lot of coal to get a bath" [Mary Cunion, *Amoskeag*, p. 48].

Proportionately few people lived in extended households (namely, those containing relatives other than members of the nuclear family); of those who did, most were older people, primarily widows. Young men and women who left home before getting married lived in a transitional household arrangement, either with relatives or as a boarder or lodger in another person's household. Boarders and lodgers constituted 12% of all males and 11% of all females, including a quarter of all people in their twenties (Figures 7.1 and 7.2).[4]

In their earlier years, few men and women lived alone. Such arrangements were considered exceptions, particularly where young women were involved. Cora Pellerin, for example, once she was of age, left the family boardinghouse and moved into an apartment of her own. She was proud of being such an exception:

> When I was seventeen I got my own room. I lived there for four years, and then I got an apartment all by myself . . . I used to pay $5.00 a week for everything. In the corporations it was much cheaper, but you couldn't get an apartment in the corporations if you weren't married. It was family housing. Not too many women were living alone in their own apartments. I was a wildcat [laughs] . . . Some mothers of my girlfriends, after they knew that I was in an apartment, they didn't want their daughters to chum around with me any more [*Amoskeag*, p. 205].

For the majority of young people on their own, particularly immigrants, boarding and lodging provided the most important household arrangement in most American industrial cities at the beginning of the century. Boarding and lodging took two forms: residence of one or several boarders with a family in a surrogate family arrangement (Modell and Hareven 1973) and residence in a commercial boardinghouse, which was usually run by a widow or a married woman whose husband was working. Commercial boardinghouses usually had ten to fifteen boarders, sometimes each boarder had his or her own room, other times two or more boarders shared a room. Boardinghouse dining rooms were open to both residents and nonresidents. Boarders who lived with families also had separate rooms or shared a room with several boarders or with

160   Family time and industrial time

Table 7.1. *Population by household structure and sex,*
Manchester 1900 (in percent)

Household structure	Male (N = 1,400)	Female (N = 1,548)	Total (N = 2,948)
Nuclear	48.9	46.2	47.5
Augmented/nuclear	27.4	28.8	28.1
Extended	16.0	17.4	16.7
Augmented/extended	6.6	6.1	6.3
Single	0.6	0.4	0.5
Augmented/single	0.5	1.0	0.8
Total	100.0	100.0	100.0

another family member. Sometimes they ate with the family, sometimes they prepared their own food and ate before or after the family, and sometimes they ate in commercial boardinghouses. Although commercial boardinghouses abounded in Manchester, this discussion is limited to boarding with families.

More than three-quarters of the population in the Manchester sample lived in nuclear households. Although less than one-quarter lived in extended households, the proportion of individuals in extended households was still higher than in comparable communities during the same period.[5] About 28% of the people lived in nuclear households that included boarders (nuclear augmented) and about 6% lived in extended households that included boarders (extended augmented). There were no significant differences between men and women regarding their types of residence (Table 7.1).

A classification of households (rather than of individuals) renders a similar pattern of nuclear household predominance, which is consistent with the overall pattern in the late nineteenth century and the early twentieth. More than three-quarters of the households were nuclear, although the percentage of extended households (about one in five) was higher (Table 7.2) than in other American cities. In reality, however, because this pattern records the situation only at one point in time, a higher proportion of the population at one point or another most likely lived in extended households or headed such households. Households in the sample were simple in structure and relatively small in size. The mean household size was 5.1 and the mean family size was 4.2.

Augmented households, which included unrelated individuals, were more prevalent. About 27% of households were augmented,

Table 7.2. *Household structure by sex of head,*
Manchester 1900 (in percent)

Household structure	Male heads (N = 480)	Female heads (N = 100)	Total (N = 580)
Nuclear	80.2	70.0	78.4
Extended	18.3	20.0	18.6
Single	1.4	10.0	2.9
Total	100.0	100.0	100.0
Augmented	25.4	33.0	26.7
Nonaugmented	74.6	67.0	73.3
Total	100.0	100.0	100.0

whereas only 24% were extended (Table 7.2).[6] In comparable communities the proportion of augmented households was higher than that of extended households, and taking in boarders was by far the more common practice than coresidence with kin.[7] This was also true for Manchester, especially if one examines the distribution of individuals rather than of households. Whereas 23% of the population in the sample lived in extended households, 35% lived in augmented households (Table 7.1).

Extension and augmentation were generally alternative, although not mutually exclusive, practices. Few households took in both extended kin and boarders. Nuclear households were much more likely to be augmented by taking in nonrelatives than were extended ones. Given limited space, most households had to select one alternative over the other.

Although considered alternative strategies, both household extension and augmentation reflect the flexibility of households as regulators of migration and as the locus of the lives of unattached individuals as well as of the nuclear family. At the same time, boarding with unrelated individuals and living with extended kin were not identical processes, as Katz (1975) seems to suggest. Although boarding was a form of "surrogate family arrangement" in its overall social function, boarders were not generally considered to be family members.

An examination of the characteristics of household heads provides a fuller understanding of the social and economic functions of these various households. Although both men and women were likely to head extended households, men were more likely to head nuclear households, and women were more likely than men to head

Table 7.3. *Household structure by sex and age of head, Manchester 1900 (in percent)*

Household structure	Age of head						
	20–29	30–39	40–49	50–59	60–69	70–79	80+
Males	(N = 73)	(N = 143)	(N = 124)	(N = 82)	(N = 48)	(N = 7)	(N = 3)
Nuclear	79.5	79.0	79.8	82.9	83.3	85.7	33.3
Extended	16.4	21.0	19.4	14.6	16.7	14.3	33.3
Single	4.1	0.0	0.8	2.4	0.0	0.0	33.3
Total	100.0	100.0	100.0	100.0	100.0	100.0	100.0
Augmented	23.3	23.8	25.8	26.8	31.3	14.3	33.3
Nonaugmented	76.7	76.2	74.2	73.2	68.8	85.7	66.7
Total	100.0	100.0	100.0	100.0	100.0	100.0	100.0
Females	(N = 4)	(N = 10)	(N = 29)	(N = 24)	(N = 17)	(N = 10)	(N = 6)
Nuclear	100.0	80.0	65.5	70.8	70.6	70.0	50.0
Extended	0.0	20.0	27.6	16.7	11.8	20.0	33.3
Single	0.0	0.0	6.9	12.5	17.6	10.0	16.7
Total	100.0	100.0	100.0	100.0	100.0	100.0	100.0
Augmented	0.0	60.0	41.4	29.2	23.5	30.0	16.7
Nonaugmented	100.0	40.0	58.6	70.8	76.5	70.0	83.3
Total	100.0	100.0	100.0	100.0	100.0	100.0	100.0

Table 7.4. *Household heads employed in textile or nontextile industry by household structure and ethnicity, Manchester 1900 (in percent)*

Household structure	Ethnicity				
	Native	Canadian	Irish	Other foreign	Total
Textile	(N = 22)	(N = 34)	(N = 16)	(N = 26)	(N = 98)
Nuclear	86.4	88.2	87.5	80.8	85.7
Extended	13.6	11.8	6.3	19.2	13.3
Single	0.0	0.0	6.3	0.0	1.0
Nonaugmented	77.3	64.7	68.8	84.6	73.5
Augmented	22.7	35.3	31.3	15.4	26.5
Nontextile	(N = 186)	(N = 133)	(N = 31)	(N = 36)	(N = 386)
Nuclear	76.3	78.9	74.2	80.6	77.5
Extended	19.9	18.8	25.8	13.9	19.4
Single	3.8	2.3	0.0	5.6	3.1
Nonaugmented	72.0	72.2	77.4	88.9	74.1
Augmented	28.0	27.8	22.6	11.1	25.9

augmented households and single-member ones, few as the latter were. Women's higher tendency to head single and augmented households reflects their vulnerability to isolation. Heading augmented households allowed a small number of widows and older single women to avoid solitary residence and at the same time retain their autonomy (Table 7.3).

In the Manchester sample, the ethnicity of the household head was not, in itself, a factor in whether a household was nuclear or extended. The occupation of the head, however, was a crucial variable. Textile workers were more likely to head nuclear households, whereas nontextile workers were more likely to head extended households (Table 7.4). Employment in the textile industry made little difference, however, in the case of household augmentation.

Ethnicity was a factor among textile workers in the case of augmentation, however. Canadian households were more likely to be augmented than those of other ethnic groups (Table 7.4), and Canadian textile workers were more likely to head augmented households than heads in other occupations. As recent migrants to Manchester, with fewer kin present in the city, they were more likely to take in boarders.[8] Ethnic origin and textile employment were mutually reinforcing in determining household organization. In contrast

Table 7.5. *Persons employed in textile and nontextile industries by ethnicity, Manchester 1900 (in percent)*

Ethnicity	Textile (N = 490)	Nontextile (N = 921)
Native	27.4	49.8
Canadian	47.1	36.0
Irish	12.2	7.5
Other foreign	13.2	6.6
Total	100.0	100.0

to other occupational groups in the city, textile workers tended to have both larger families and households, reflecting both higher fertility and a greater propensity to take in boarders.[9] The family and household patterns of textile workers, particularly French-Canadian workers, reveal the characteristics of a migrant population attracted to Manchester by opportunities for employment. It was a population that included larger numbers of children and a greater tendency to maximize employment for the entire family unit (see Chapter 8). Textile workers were predominantly of immigrant origin, and French Canadians constituted the highest concentration of any ethnic group among textile workers (Table 7.5). The migrant character of textile workers was particularly reflected in the higher proportions of boarders and lodgers, as well as recent arrivals and young people, among them.

When the patterns of household structure of the overall sample in the city's population are compared with those of the residents of the neighborhood surrounding the Amoskeag mill yard, the majority of whom were, indeed, textile workers, the distinct characteristics of textile workers are even more evident. There was a smaller proportion of nuclear households in the mill-yard neighborhoods, a larger proportion of single-member and extended households, and an increased tendency toward augmentation.[10]

In summary, household structure was related to the age, sex, ethnicity, and occupation of the household head. These differences in characteristics of the heads of nuclear, extended, and augmented households, as well as the low proportion of single-member households, point to the important role of the household in the adaptation process. Because the proportion of extended households was almost equal to that of augmented households, the taking in of extended kin or strangers would seem to be two alternative routes to the same goal of individual and household adaptation over the life course and during periods of migration.

Why did the majority of the population live in nuclear households, and when nuclear families did open their homes to others, why did they tend to admit strangers rather than kin? The answer does not lie in the unavailability of kin. The chain migration of French Canadians along kinship lines allowed them coresidence with kin for short periods upon arrival. The Irish, who were earlier immigrants to Manchester, would have had kin already present in the city by 1900.

The predominance of nuclear residence reflects an overall commitment in American society to the separation of the family of orientation from the family of procreation. Newlyweds set up independent households, if not immediately, at least within a few years of marriage. Married children rarely resided with their parents. Mary Dancause, who first lived with her mother-in-law, made up her mind to move out at any cost:

> For five years after I was married, I used to have a room on the top floor in my mother-in-law's boardinghouse. As long as I was single and I worked there, I didn't mind living there; but after I got married, I didn't want to live there. We stayed because my husband paid the rent; but after the third child was born, I said, "If you don't want to leave, I'm leaving." So we moved out and went and lived in the same tenement my sister lived in. We were four couples living in that tenement. I suppose my husband still paid the rent for his mother's boardinghouse after we moved out [*Amoskeag*, pp. 54–55].

Neither was it customary for two or more sets of married siblings to share households. A census sample of three Quebec communities, the communities of origin for many of Manchester's French Canadians, suggests the dominance of the nuclear household in Quebec as well.[11] In rural Quebec 70% of all households were nuclear without any boarders, compared with about 50% in urban Manchester, where household extension and augmentation was much more a feature of urban, industrial life than of rural conditions.

Exceptions to the nuclear household occurred throughout people's lives. Under crisis conditions, individuals and sometimes entire families moved in with their kin. "I remember during the strike my oldest sister had just got married, and my father and mother told her 'come back home with your husband.' We had to pile up four in the bed instead of two so they could have a bed to themselves" (Ora Pelletier, *Amoskeag*, p. 242). Coresidence with extended kin also occurred when a nuclear family dissolved by death and during such other crises as illness or illegitimate birth. When they were unable to care for their children, mothers often placed them with their own mothers or with older sisters or aunts.

In the absence of public welfare, the household assumed such caring responsibilities, just as it had in preindustrial society. Now, however, these functions were performed voluntarily and informally, whereas in the colonial period certain households, often designated by the authorities, took care of dependent people for the community (Demos 1970, Rothman 1971). In Manchester, retarded children and orphans were often placed in other people's households; sick or disabled relatives were cared for in one's own household, as were elderly people. The predominant pattern was one where the nuclear family maintained its boundaries but was engaged in mutual assistance with kin outside the household.

The tendency of households to take in boarders rather than kin and the large numbers of individuals who lived with strangers may reflect cultural and economic preferences. Boarders, unlike kin, allowed a certain freedom. They were less likely to interfere in one's family life. Financial terms and time limits were arranged more definitively.

The timing of life transitions

Although research to identify the basic familial transition patterns and link them with changing social and economic conditions has begun only recently (Modell, Furstenberg, and Hershberg 1976, Hareven 1978b, Chudacoff and Hareven, 1978, 1979, and Modell and Hareven 1978), it is clear that the timing of the movement of individual family members in and out of the family configuration affected both the individual and the family as a collective unit. The synchronization of all the various "time clocks" that govern the scheduling of individual and family events – starting and leaving work, leaving home, getting married, setting up an independent household, becoming parents, and launching children from the home – involved the coordination of individual time schedules with those of the family as a group under circumstances shaped by institutional constraints. For example, the determination of when a child was to begin work was dependent on family needs, employment opportunities, and child labor laws governing the age of commencement of work.

Timing was often a source of major conflict and pressure within the family because "individual time" and "family time" were not always in harmony. Decisions were not made exclusively on the basis of individual preferences; they depended, rather, on the choices and needs of the family as a collective unit and on available institutional supports (Hareven 1977).[12] Life transitions, therefore, were closely interconnected. For example, the timing of a young person's departure from home was contingent on the needs of parents in their transition to old age.

In their study of transitions to adulthood in late nineteenth-century Philadelphia, Modell, Furstenberg, and Hershberg (1976) argued that such basic moves as entry into the labor force and marriage and the setting up of an independent household were slowly paced, required a long time for a specific age group to accomplish, and did not follow an established sequence. Modell and his associates attribute the more orderly and compressed pattern of life transitions in contemporary society to the dominance of age norms over familial considerations. Currently, they argue, the timing of transitions is normatively defined, whereas in the past, familial needs took precedence over age norms: "Transitions are today more constrained by a set of formal institutions. Timely action to nineteenth-century families consisted of helpful response in times of trouble; in the twentieth century, timeliness connotes adherence to a schedule" (p. 30).

In Manchester, as in Philadelphia, transitions to adulthood were slow and erratic. In contrast to the patterns prevalent today, most people started work early in life but left home, married, and set up independent households later.

Early life transitions were largely the same for men and women. In their teens and early twenties they followed similar life paths: The majority lived with their parents. As Figures 7.1 and 7.2 indicate, slightly less than half the men and women in their early twenties were still living as sons and daughters in their parents' households. About one-quarter of the population resided as extended kin or boarders in other people's households for a period after leaving home, usually until their late twenties or early thirties.[13]

Although leaving home and getting married overlapped to some extent, the two transitions did not necessarily coincide. For most young people, in fact, leaving home preceded marriage. Boarding and lodging represented a transitional stage between leaving home

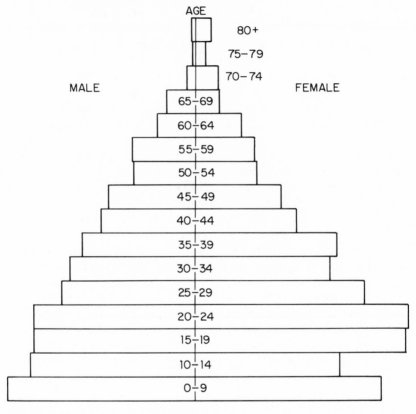

Figure 7.3. Population of Manchester by age and sex, 1900. (*Source:* Sample of 1900 U.S. Census Manuscript Schedules.)

and setting up separate households. Women were likely to become boarders at younger ages than men. Almost one-fifth of female boarders but only one-tenth of male boarders were between the ages of 15 and 19, a difference that reflects the higher concentration of female migrants in this age group. As Figure 7.3 suggests, there was a high concentration of people in the 15–24 age group, particularly women. This bulge in the age pyramid resulted primarily from the high proportion of young French-Canadian women migrants in Manchester (Figure 7.4).[14] Even though only one-quarter of the entire sample was boarders, about 37% of the boarders were concentrated in the age group 20–29; the next highest concentration (18%) included the ages 30–39 (Table 7.6). Within the

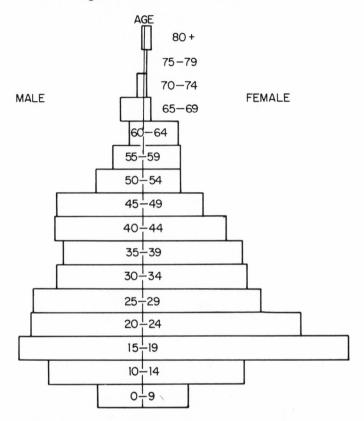

Figure 7.4. Canadian population of Manchester by age and sex, 1900. (*Source:* Sample of 1900 U.S. Census Manuscript Schedules.)

age group 20–39, boarders were most heavily concentrated in the age group 20–24. After that, their proportion in the population declined.

Typically, in Manchester as in other American industrial communities at the time, young men and women boarded with families whose own children had left home recently or in households without children. In Irene Taueber's terms, it was "a social equalization of the family" – a young adult and a portion of his income replaced another young adult and a portion of his income (1969:5). The young adult moved from his family of orientation to what might be called his family of reorientation, reorientation to the city, to a job, to a new neighborhood, to an independent household. Boarders

Table 7.6. *Age of boarders and lodgers by sex, Manchester 1900 (in percent)*

Age	Male (N = 172)	Female (N = 172)
0–9	6.4	9.9
10–14	1.7	1.7
15–19	9.9	18.0
20–24	21.5	22.7
25–29	15.1	14.5
30–34	10.5	10.5
35–39	9.9	5.2
40–44	5.2	5.2
45–49	7.0	4.1
50–54	4.7	1.7
55–59	3.5	0.0
60–64	2.9	2.9
65–69	0.6	1.7
70–74	1.2	0.6
75–79	0.0	0.6
80+	0.0	0.6

usually came from a rural family with an excess of sons and daughters or an insufficient economic base to an urban family with excess room and present or anticipated economic need often occasioned by the departure from the household of a son or daughter (Modell and Hareven 1973:177).[15] The tendency to board declined fairly regularly for men and women after their mid-twenties but increased substantially for men and women in their sixties.[16] Boarding and lodging served older people as well by providing them with the opportunity to move in with other people when they became unable to head their own households.

The large population of boarders in their twenties also reflects the the timing of marriage, which, particularly for women, was often delayed until their thirties. A comparison of boarders with sons and daughters living in their parents' households confirms the role of boarding and lodging as a transitional stage between leaving home and getting married: Boarders were slightly older than sons and daughters who were still living in the parental household. About three-quarters of the male boarders were older than 20, whereas about three-quarters of the sons were younger. Similarly daughters living at home tended to be younger than female

Table 7.7. *Boarders and lodgers by ethnicity and sex,*
Manchester 1900 (in percent)

Ethnicity	Males (N = 172)	Females (N = 171)	Total (N = 343)
New Hampshire	22.7	24.0	23.3
Rest of Northeast	13.4	9.9	11.7
Rest of United States	4.7	5.3	5.0
Canadian	40.1	44.4	42.3
Irish	12.2	10.5	11.4
Other foreign	7.0	5.8	6.4
Total	100.0	100.0	100.0

boarders, and female boarders, in turn, were younger than male boarders.[17]

In addition to serving rural–urban migrants, boarding aided young immigrants as well. Of the boarders in Manchester, 60% were foreign immigrants, whereas a little less than a quarter were New Hampshire natives and 12% were natives of neighboring New England states (Table 7.7).[18]

Rural families, both native and foreign, considered the availability of boarding facilities an essential condition for allowing their young daughters to live "alone" in Manchester. When her family decided to return to Quebec after a three-year work period in Manchester, 13-year-old Cora Pellerin wanted to stay behind:

> So I begged my mother to leave me. My mother said, "If I can find a good boardinghouse, I'll let you stay." So she found a family-style boardinghouse that would take me, my sister, and my brother. My sister was eighteen and my brother was sixteen. The woman who kept the boardinghouse said to my mother, "As long as they mind me, you don't have to worry. If they don't mind me, I'll write you and let you know." So my mother went back to Canada and we stayed here, but I'm the only one in my family who has always lived in Manchester [*Amoskeag*, p. 202–3].

Mary Dancause preferred living and working in a boardinghouse to taking care of her younger siblings at home:

> When I was fourteen years old I started working in a boardinghouse, and I went to live there. They had a law in the mill, they wouldn't let you work that young. It was good, though, working in the boardinghouse. My future mother-in-law ran it. She had fourteen children! You don't see that any more. She brought up

fourteen children. Anyway, she had good, good food. She always used butter.

She was in the kitchen at five o'clock every morning. The people who ate in the boardinghouse, most of them worked in the mill. It was on Stark Street. You eat and then go down the road, and there's your job. The mill workers came for breakfast at five thirty. I had to wake up at five o'clock to get ready. It was pitch black and cold in the winter. At noontime, they had quite a few come that worked in the stores: a barber, a meat cutter, one worked in an office.

I met my husband in that boardinghouse. He had two brothers that lived there. My husband was four years older than me. He started work in the Amoskeag before my time. He used to clean the floor. Later he became a loom fixer. I was twenty-two when we were married. Before we were married, when I lived in the boardinghouse, I was just a worker. They were good to me, very good to me. They were paying me $3.00 a week as a waitress, and I used to clean the rooms upstairs, too, after the night meal was all done. Everything was cheap then. You paid 5 cents for a pair stockings. Only 5 cents. And a blouse was a dollar. My room and meals were free [*Amoskeag*, pp. 53–4].

Although young people began to establish individual households in their early twenties, the proportion was small, with less than one-fifth of the men in this age group making the transition. More than one-quarter of all males and about one-fifth of all females in their early twenties were boarders (about 3% of the women were servants). By combining all these categories, it is evident that more than four out of every five males and females in their early twenties were still living with their parents or in surrogate family households. By their late twenties, however, about two out of five men were household heads and about half the women were wives. The proportion of this age group still living at home declined to about one-fourth of all males and less than one-fifth of all females (Figures 7.1 and 7.2).

Marriage was delayed to allow young people time to accumulate sufficient resources to set up separate households and to make proper provisions for the support of other family members, including aging parents. Later marriage also postponed the commencement of childbearing. Because later marriage signaled for most women a withdrawal from the labor force, a delay of marriage enabled women to work longer and to postpone childbearing.

The transition to marriage was a slow process, although women were expected to marry young. Late-marrying women were often dubbed "old maids." But as Marie Anne Senechal points out there was some distance between expectation and reality:

> When we were young we used to hear people say, "Oh, she's going to be an old maid. Isn't that awful?" At age twenty, if you're not married, you become an old maid. You couldn't get a fellow. Actually it's easy to get a fellow. But they thought you couldn't get one to like you [*Amoskeag*, p. 280].

About 28% of the men and 34% of the women married between the ages of 20 and 24. By the age of 30, half the men and more than three-fifths of the women were married, and by age 35, the transition into marriage for both men and women was almost complete (Figures 7.5 and 7.6). Thus men and women differed much less in the timing of marriage than in the timing of work lives.

Transition to household headship continued slowly. Three-quarters of the men aged 35 to 45 were household heads, and slightly less than two-thirds of all women were wives living with their husbands (Figures 7.1 and 7.2). The proportion of wives within this age group remained stable until their late forties when widowhood became increasingly common.[19]

Later life transitions

Widowhood, the most critical transition in middle and later life, occurred far more frequently for women than men. Among women who survived beyond age 50, widowhood was the most common experience, often signaling the beginning of "old age."[20] Beginning in their middle to late forties, widowhood reached the dramatically high level of more than one-third of all women in their late fifties and sixties. There were about two-and-a-half times as many widows as widowers among people in their sixties. By their late seventies, three out of five women were widowed. In contrast, the proportion of widowers under 55 did not reach one in ten, and even among men older than 60 the rates remained well below the corresponding rates for women (Figures 7.3 and 7.4). The data for widowhood reflect the younger ages and longevity of wives and the higher propensity of men to remarry.

The loss of household headship, commonly attributed to "old age," was not as dramatic a transition in the Manchester population. The majority of men in their sixties were still employed and married (or had remarried) and were still heading their own households. Rates of household headship did not decline for men until their mid-seventies, whereas the proportion of women living as

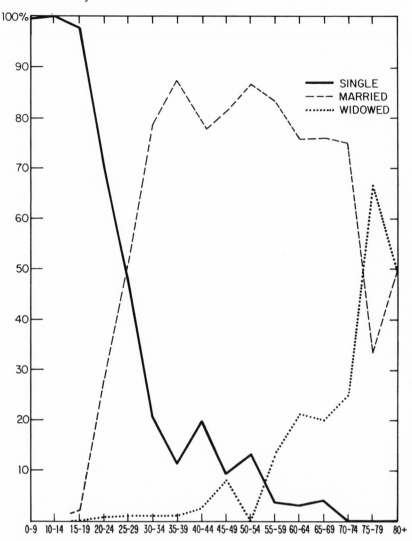

Figure 7.5. Males' marital status by age, Manchester 1900.

wives of household heads dropped in their sixties. In reality, however, the important transition in women's lives had already begun
in their mid-forties, with the onset of widowhood.

Widowhood in middle age usually placed women in positions of
household headship. About one-quarter of women in their late forties and one-third of women in their late fifties were household

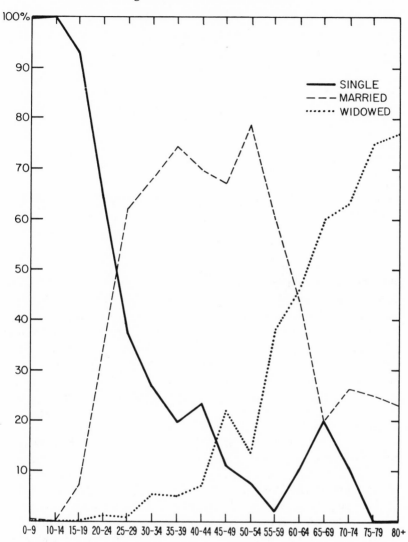

Figure 7.6. Females' marital status by age, Manchester 1900.

heads. As widows advanced beyond the age of 50, however, it became increasingly difficult for them to continue as household heads.

Older men and women naturally tried to continue heading their own households as long as possible, for to move into another person's household was usually regarded as a loss of independence. In

Table 7.8. *Relation to head of persons 45 years of age or older by age and sex, Manchester 1900 (in percent)*

	Aged 45–64		Aged 65+	
Relation to head	Males (N = 215)	Females (N = 214)	Males (N = 40)	Females (N = 60)
Solitary head	1.9	1.9	2.5	1.7
Head with other members present	76.7	22.9	75.0	36.7
Spouse	0.9	57.5	0.0	16.7
Son or daugher	0.5		0.0	
Other kin	4.7	8.9	15.0	33.3
B/L, servant	15.3	8.9	7.5	11.7
Total	100.0	100.0	100.0	100.0

the absence of data on income, it is impossible to determine to what extent older people heading their own households were actually autonomous. Household headship in itself, of course, does not automatically indicate autonomy, although it was considered a form of independence, particularly when it involved control over household space. Under some conditions, particularly a shortage of housing, control over housing space may have enabled older people to enter into arrangements with their adult children, who may have provided services or financial aid in exchange for housing space (Chudacoff and Hareven 1978).

For those unable to continue as household heads, few alternatives were available. They moved in with children or other kin or boarded with strangers (Figures 7.1 and 7.2),[21] for residence in an old-age home was considered degrading, a fate that befell paupers, the chronically ill, and those without kin. Older men were more likely than older women to live in other people's households as boarders and lodgers (Table 7.8). Only 5% of widows 55 and older boarded in other people's households and close to one-third lived in households headed by one of their children (Table 7.9).

The greater propensity of older women to live with kin reflects an overall tendency in the society to shelter women in family arrangements rather than have them live with strangers. Young women stayed longer at home than did young men, and older women were more likely to be placed in families than were older men. This practice was both protective and utilitarian – young or old, unattached women often contributed to housekeeping and child care.

Table 7.9. *Relation of widows aged 55 years or more to head,*
Manchester 1900 (in percent)

	Widows aged:		
Relation to head	55–64 (N = 37)	65+ (N = 40)	Total 55+ (N = 77)
Solitary head	8.1	2.5	5.2
Regular head	54.1	52.5	53.2
Parent	24.3	35.0	29.9
Other kin	0.0	2.5	1.3
Servant	8.1	2.5	5.2
Boarder/lodger	5.4	5.0	5.2
Total	100.0	100.0	100.0

To retain the headship of their households, widows had to work, as well as seek support from their children. Whereas the majority of married women living with their husbands were generally not employed, nine out of ten widows who continued to head their own households were in the labor force.[22] About two-thirds of the widows older than 50 who were household heads had at least one child at home (Table 7.10). Of widows 70 or older, two-fifths of those heading their own households had at least one child at home.

Thus the transition into the later years of life was marked not by the departure of all children from the household but rather by parents' efforts to maintain the integrity of the household unit. The presence of at least one adult child in the household was a pervasive pattern both for married couples and for widows in the later years of life. Household headship in old age hinged on some form of support from one or more working children in the household or the presence of boarders.

Viewed as the major family transition into middle age today, the "empty nest" was a rarity at the turn of the century. Of women married twenty years or longer (comparable in age to contemporary women in the empty-nest state today), only about one in five had *no* child in the household (Table 7.11). Similarly, close to two-thirds of married male heads of household aged 60 or more had at least one child at home (Table 7.10). Recent demographic studies have stressed the increasing prevalence of an empty-nest stage in the lives of contemporary couples in America. Uhlenberg's comparison of successive cohorts of white American women from 1880 to 1920 showed a consistent increase in the proportion of couples who ex-

Table 7.10. *Age of married male and widowed female heads by number of own children in household, Manchester 1900 (in percent)*

Number of own children in household	Age of head					
	30–39	40–49	50–59	60–69	70–79	80+
Married male heads	(N = 142)	(N = 115)	(N = 78)	(N = 41)	(N = 6)	(N = 21)
0 children	12.7	15.7	17.9	29.3	50.0	100.0
1+ children	87.3	84.3	82.1	70.7	50.0	0.0
Total	100.0	100.0	100.0	100.0	100.0	100.0
Widowed female heads	(N = 6)	(N = 21)	(N = 20)	(N = 15)	(N = 10)	(N = 5)
0 children	16.7	14.3	15.0	40.0	50.0	80.0
1+ children	83.3	85.7	85.0	60.0	50.0	20.0
Total	100.0	100.0	100.0	100.0	100.0	100.0

Table 7.11. *Children absent or present in household by number of years woman married, Manchester 1900 (in percent)*

	Number of years woman married						
	0–1 (N = 156)	2–5 (N = 70)	6–9 (N = 69)	10–14 (N = 69)	15–19 (N = 66)	20+ (N = 152)
Children absent	50.6	28.6	8.7	13.0	9.1	19.1
Children present	49.3	71.4	91.2	86.7	90.8	81.0

perienced an empty nest. Even more dramatic has been the increase in the duration of the empty-nest period in a woman's life beyond age 60 (Uhlenberg 1978). Among two-parent families, on the average, the last child leaves home when the parents are in their forties, thus leaving the nest empty for two or more decades. The empty nest has resulted from earlier marriage, earlier childbearing, and the decline in fertility and mortality since the late nineteenth century (Glick and Parke 1965, Glick and Norton 1977). Higher fertility, as well as the wider span of childbearing in the nineteenth century (women often bore their last child when they were in their late thirties or early forties), meant that at least one child was still at home when parents were in their late fifties and early sixties (Chudacoff and Hareven 1978, Uhlenberg 1978).

Demographic factors, however, only partly explain the absence of an empty nest. The correlation of children's ages with that of household heads indicates that children were present in the households of their aging parents not simply because they were too young to move out (Table 7.12). The empty nest was rare in this population not because of demographic reasons but rather because it was customary for at least one adult child to remain at home to care for aging parents.[23]

Among the foreign-born, the likelihood of an empty nest was even lower then among the native-born. The proportion of empty nesters among native-born heads of household increased after age 50, but among the foreign-born the proportion of older people with empty nests remained steady into their sixties (Table 7.13). Foreign-born couples may have been more dependent on their children's assistance in old age because they possessed fewer resources and had less opportunity to accumulate savings. In addition, children of the foreign-born were more likely to stay on in the parental household because of the strong sense of familial solidarity that stemmed from premigration traditions. The higher fertility of foreign-born families does not explain their greater tendency to keep an adult child in the household because generally only one child remained at home regardless of the number of children in the family.[24]

The transitions of the later years – the empty nest, widowhood, and loss of household headship – followed no ordered sequence, were not closely synchronized, and took a relatively long time to complete. Most men who survived to old age continued working and retained their earlier status in the family. Only at very advanced ages, when their capabilities were no doubt impaired by

Table 7.12. *Age of household heads with at least one own child by age of oldest child, Manchester 1900 (in percent)*

Head's age	Age of oldest child									
	0–9	10–14	15–19	20–24	25–29	30–34	35–39	40–44	45–49	50–54
20–29 (N = 43)	93.0	7.0								
30–39 (N = 133)	57.9	24.8	15.0	2.3						
40–49 (N = 117)	16.2	13.7	33.3	29.9	3.4	1.7	1.7			
50–59 (N = 84)	1.2	8.3	15.5	33.3	32.1	7.1	2.4			
60+ (N = 55)	5.5	3.6	5.5	20.0	18.2	16.4	16.4	10.9	1.8	1.8

Table 7.13. *Heads 40 years of age or older with 0, 1, or 2 or more own children in household by head's age, sex, and nativity, Manchester 1900 (in percent)*

Number of own children in household	Age of head		
	40–49	50–59	60+
Native-born male head	(N = 45)	(N = 39)	(N = 25)
0 children	35.6	38.5	56.0
1 child	20.0	25.6	24.0
2+ children	44.4	35.9	20.0
Total	100.0	100.0	100.0
Foreign-born male head	(N = 79)	(N = 43)	(N = 33)
0 children	12.7	7.0	15.2
1 child	7.6	25.6	24.2
2+ children	79.7	67.4	60.6
Total	100.0	100.0	100.0
Native-born female head	(N = 17)	(N = 9)	(N = 16)
0 children	47.1	22.2	75.0
1 child	23.5	66.7	25.0
2+ children	29.4	11.1	0.0
Total	100.0	100.0	100.0
Foreign-born female head	(N = 12)	(N = 15)	(N = 17)
0 children	16.7	13.3	29.4
1 child	16.7	33.3	11.8
2+ children	66.7	53.3	58.8
Total	100.0	100.0	100.0

infirmity, did a substantial number experience definite changes in their household status. However, these men represented a minor fraction of their age peers. Because widowhood was such a common experience in their lives, older women underwent more marked transitions than men. But the continuing presence of adult children in the household meant that widowhood was not directly associated with a dramatic transition into the empty nest.

Here once again, the relationship between the household as an organizational unit and the timing of life transitions is critical. The household fulfilled a major role in people's adaptation to the later years of life.[25] Household membership among older people involved coresidence with extended kin and strangers as well as with nuclear kin. Childless older couples and those whose children had left home took in boarders and lodgers as surrogate kin. Widowed

Table 7.14. *Percentage of married-male-headed households by age of head and presence or absence of children and others, Manchester 1900*

Age of head	Children present	Children absent	N
30–39	87.3	12.7	142
No others	61.3	72.2	
Others	38.7	27.8	
40–49	84.3	15.7	115
No others	58.8	61.1	
Others	41.2	38.9	
50–59	82.1	17.9	78
No others	65.6	71.4	
Others	34.4	28.6	
60–69	70.7	29.3	41
No others	72.4	66.7	
Others	27.6	33.3	
70+	37.5	62.5	8
No others	100.0	80.0	
Others	0.0	20.0	

Note: "Others" includes kin, except for children, boarders or servants, and any other nonrelatives.

women unable to maintain independent households moved in either with their own children, extended kin, or strangers.

Older people thus lived in one of four basic household types: with children present only; with children and others (such as extended kin or strangers); with no children and no others; and with no children but with others present. Such residential clusterings differed according to the age of the individual and the older person's marital status. The most prevalent pattern of accommodation was that of coresidence with one or more children. Approximately three-fourths of the married couples and two-thirds of the widowed heads of household 50 and older lived with children.[26]

This was true for women even if they had only one living child. As Daniel Scott Smith has claimed for a nationwide sample in 1900, there was no direct correlation between the number of living children and the probability of the mother's coresiding with at least one child (1979: 294). This flies in the face of the theory that high fertility was a form of old-age insurance.[27]

Coresidence with extended kin or with strangers was less common among older people than residence with their own children (Tables 7.14 and 7.15), although boarding and lodging were widely

Table 7.15. *Percentage of households headed by widows by age of head and presence or absence of children and others, Manchester 1900*

Age of head	Children present	Children absent	N
30–39	83.3	16.7	6
No others	20.0	0.0	
Others	80.0	100.0	
40–49	85.7	14.3	21
No others	33.3	0.0	
Others	66.7	100.0	
50–59	85.0	15.0	20
No others	70.6	100.0	
Others	29.4	0.0	
60–69	60.0	40.0	15
No others	77.8	50.0	
Others	22.2	50.0	
70+	40.0	60.0	15
No others	83.3	55.6	
Others	16.7	44.4	

Note: "Others" includes kin, except for children, boarders, servants, and any other nonrelatives.

practiced among the population at large. Except in the case of widows, even older people without children present were not more likely to live with others than those with children present. Living with extended kin or as boarders and lodgers was clearly less crucial for married couples than for widows in their adjustment to the empty nest.

A comparison of married male heads and widowed female heads older than 50 reveals the latter's vulnerability to isolation and dependence. Generally, female heads age 60 to 80 were less likely than married male heads to have a child in the household. Widowed heads over 80, however, were more likely to have children present (Table 7.10). This suggests either that the children of widows were likely to reside longer with their aging mothers than children in a dual-parent home or that children returned home at the point in their mothers' lives when they were most needed.

In their attempts to achieve an equilibrium whereby at least one child remained at home, older people and their adult children were caught in the triple bind imposed by their personal needs and preferences, economic insecurity, and the cultural norms of independence and autonomy. Children reaching adulthood were confronted with the dilemma of having to help their parents just at the point when they were struggling to form careers, marry, and set up independent households. Parents were confronted with the dilemma of holding on to the headship of their households as they were aging and the family head's ability to work was waning. The timing of most transitions in and out of the household revolved around these interlocking – and often conflicting – expectations of autonomy both from the young and the old within the confines of a general adherence to nuclear residence.

The principle of the nuclear household included a commitment to the residential separation of the family of procreation from the family of orientation. Both adult children and aging parents adhered to this expectation of autonomy. Children expected to marry and set up independent households, and aging parents expected to maintain their independence by continuing to head their own households. It was a dilemma of considerable proportions that often generated conflicts of interest within the family.

Implications of patterns of timing

The seemingly erratic and disorderly patterns of the timing of individual life transitions discussed above were largely shaped by family obligations and needs. Because the functions of family members were defined like those of a corporate body, the timing of early and later life transitions were interconnected in a continuum of familial needs and obligations.

In modern society most family roles and work careers are thought of as individual. Historically, most apparently individual transitions were treated as family moves and had to be synchronized with family needs. In addition to the ties they retained with their family of origin, individuals took on obligations toward their families of procreation and the families of their spouses. The complexity of obligations cast individuals into various overlapping, and at times conflicting, functions over the course of their lives. A son became a father and later, when his aging parents needed assistance, he became a son again, sometimes taking on even more filial responsibilities. Although one role might gradually come to dominate and another recede in importance, the alteration was not always smooth.

The different patterns of timing converge around the issue of interdependence and mutual familial responsibilities compounded by economic insecurity. The timing of life transitions was governed not so much by age norms as by family economic strategies and interdependence. It was also influenced by the economic opportunity structure in the community and was limited by institutional constraints, such as compulsory school attendance and the enforcement of child labor legislation. The absence of such institutional supports as welfare agencies, unemployment compensation, and social security was an additional source of pressure. Given these internal and external constraints, flexibility in the timing of transitions was essential.

Against this backdrop of multiple obligations, the differences in the patterns of timing between people at the turn of the century and contemporary individuals are now understandable. At the turn of the century, children left home at a later age because their labor was needed by their families of origin for a longer period. The timing of leaving home also hinged on opportunities for both employment and housing. Manchester offered employment to both young adult migrants and the native born. Young adults lived with other families or in boardinghouses or with their parents. Both parents and young adults benefited when they continued to coreside. The parents received money and the young adult room and board as well as other family services such as laundry. It is important to remember that even young boarders sent money back to their parents. Whether they lived with their parents or boarded with others, young people continued to function as part of the economic system of their family of origin.

Delayed departure from the parental home was also connected to late marriage and late household formation. Marriage was contingent on getting a job and being able to afford a separate household. Although newlyweds lived temporarily with their parents, the majority moved out, thus endorsing the principle of the separation of the family of origin from the family of procreation. By delaying marriage, young couples also postponed parenthood. As Modell (1978) points out, the decline in the age of marriage over this century occurred when household headship, economic independence, and immediate parenthood were no longer factors.

In the industrial community at the turn of the century, late marriage provided a special advantage for women: It allowed them to work in the mills for a longer period of time. In fact, most women interviewees said they preferred to marry later.[28] They could accumulate a dowry as well as contribute to the support of their families of orientation. The delay also postponed the arduous task of rearing children while working. Cora Pellerin recalls her own decision to put off getting married: "He was supporting his mother. And I was satisfied the way I was. I had plenty of time to raise a family" (*Amoskeag*, p. 210). At the same time, however, they resented family pressures to postpone marriage indefinitely or to give up the opportunity to marry altogether because of obligations to support aging parents. Anna Douville, for example, was embittered when her sisters tried to prevent her marriage because they wanted her to support their aging parents.

> I got married the oldest, in September, thirteen days after I turned twenty-five. My husband turned twenty-six in April. I hated to leave my folks alone. I was the only one working, and I was the only one left single. All the others were married. The boys left home after the Amoskeag shut down and scattered all over to places like Wisconsin and Connecticut [*Amoskeag*, p. 289].

Because of the contradictions of independent adulthood and obligations to the family of origin, individuals adopted a diversity of timing strategies. Many worked and continued in school at the same time; some worked and lived at home; others worked and boarded; some married early but continued to live as boarders along with their spouses; others married and lived temporarily with parents.

The transitional period prior to marriage, when young adults lived in parental households or as boarders or servants in other people's households, has been defined by Joseph Kett (1977) as semidependence and by Michael Katz (1975) as semiautonomy. In either case, young adults were placed in an ambiguous situation. Writing about transitions to adulthood in the early nineteenth century, Kett concluded: "No clear and distinct barrier divided semidependence from independence; no consensus existed as to the moment when a boy became a man" (p. 29). Neither were clear transition points evident in Manchester. The same mixture of freedom and subordination that Kett sees as characteristic of "semidependence" was experienced by the young men and women in Manchester. Although they contributed to the familial economy, they were expected to behave as "obedient children" in their parents' households.

In some respects then, life in an industrial community offered a greater opportunity for familial interdependence. It was possible for the entire family unit to work in the same community, and for children to remain at home later into their teens or even into their twenties, allowing for a greater overlap among generations within the family. Young people were tied to their families by both residence and obligations. Industrial work did not override these obligations – in fact, it tended to reinforce them.

The patterns of timing discussed here encouraged interdependence among family members, flexibility in the household unit, and the function of the family as a source of social security, along with a certain sense of reliability: Family members could count on each other. At the same time familial priorities in the timing of transitions could be a source of pressure, conflict, and strain for young people wishing to become independent.

Young men, more so than young women, harbored a resentment toward the ambiguity in their status – of being full-fledged workers in the factory while still being a "son" at home. A 20-year-old who held a skilled or semiskilled responsible job similar to that of a 40-year-old did not enjoy the same independence as the 40-year-old as long as he was still living as a son in his father's household. Young sons and daughters found themselves in a generational squeeze, having to stay at home and support aging parents at a point in their lives when they were ready to move in search of jobs elsewhere or leave home and get married and form independent families. Although the diversity in timing described as "flexible" may have been flexible regarding age norms, it occurred within a framework that imposed considerable rigidity on individual preferences.

8 Family work strategies and the household economy

The interdependence of members of the nuclear family and their extended kin developed in a regime of economic insecurity. Most working-class families lived in poverty or near poverty. Family economic survival depended on the contributions of individual members and the marshaling of collective family resources. Even though families had ceased to be production units, they continued to function as work units and thought of themselves as such, regardless of whether the entire family worked in the same place or whether all members were employed simultaneously. Thus, work careers were not viewed strictly as individual pursuits but as part of a collective family enterprise. "There was no question . . . It stands to reason that the father expected, when there was nine or ten children, that they're all gonna start working and pitch in" (Richard Laroche, interview). "When we worked, we all gave our pay at home except one of my sisters. She gave it at the beginning. Then, when she thought she wanted to get married, she'd give $7 and keep the rest" (Ora Pelletier, *Amoskeag*, p. 239).

The custom for working children to contribute most of their wages to their families was an unwritten law. Several investigations of New England textile towns, including Manchester, revealed that this was the pervasive pattern throughout the industry. The size of the contribution of sons and daughters differed, however. Whereas sons contributed only 83% of their income to their parents, daughters delivered 95% (U.S. Department of Labor, Women's Bureau, 1923, pp. 137–40).

The work of women and children was considered essential to family survival and economic advancement. Although American culture censored work outside the home for married women, working-class and immigrant families did not entirely subscribe to that mos. Nevertheless, as sons and daughters entered the labor force, mothers gradually withdrew. As younger siblings came of age, older children left home to start independent lives. Because interdependence and collective effort was the key to survival, family economic strategies took precedence over individual choices and priorities.

189

When Marie Proulx arrived with her family from Canada, her father made it clear that her labor was needed:

> Papa said: "Well, now, my little girl, we'll no longer be around the house. We'll have to look out so that we'll work." I told him, "I'm going today with my cousin to the mills."
>
> My father was never able to support a family of eight children on $1.10 per day. It was miserable at first. Oh, were we miserable! Our old parents worked till their foreheads were sweating to try to have what we get for nothing today. So I had to go work somewhere, and all there was were the mills, there was only Amoskeag. We had to help our father; I was the oldest one. Four dollars and twenty cents per week – I couldn't go far with that. [*Amoskeag*, pp. 67–8].

Given this need for a collective family effort, what were the family's labor-force configurations? How did they change over the life course? What kind of trade-offs did families make? Was the work of children a substitute for that of mothers? Similarly, did the income contributed by boarders alleviate the need to send other family members into the labor force?

Although for the majority of men at the beginning of the century a work career was a lifelong affair, for most women it encompassed only one segment of life. Women's work outside the home often stopped with marriage or shortly thereafter. In the Manchester population sample, the largest concentration of employed women was between the ages of 15 and 24. About three-quarters of the women in the age groups 15–19 and 20–24 were employed (Figure 8.1). Labor-force participation rates increased almost five times between the early and late teens when most young men and women started to work (Figure 8.3).

The proportion of teen-age women in the labor force in Manchester was much higher than in comparable communities. In Essex County, Massachusetts, for example, the proportion of teen-age daughters in the labor force in 1880 was considerably lower than it was for sons (Mason, Vinovskis, and Hareven 1978), and the same was true in Philadelphia in the late nineteenth century (Goldin 1978). The high employment rate of teen-age women, both local and migrant, in Manchester reflects not only family needs but also the drawing power of the textile industry. As an alternative to the only other massive employer of women – domestic service – the textile industry was particularly attractive.

Not all young women, however, were enthusiastic about starting

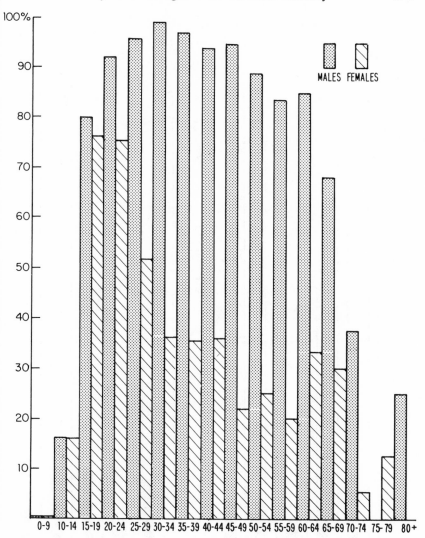

Figure 8.1. Labor-force participation rates by age and sex, Manchester 1900.

to work. Lucille Bourque, like many others, did not want to leave school:

> At first, I didn't want to go to work. I was only sixteen when my mother sent me down to the mill. I wanted to continue with high school, but she wouldn't send me. She'd say, "You don't need an

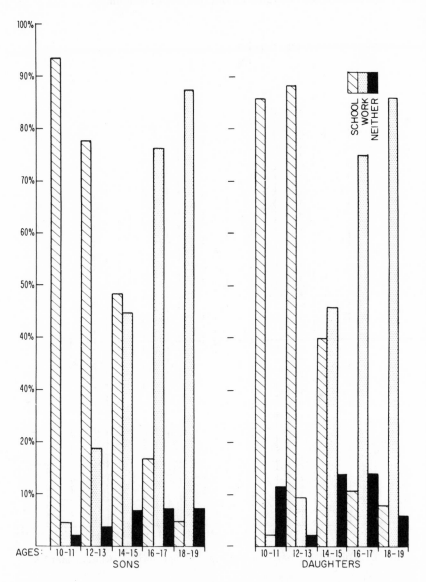

Figure 8.2. School/work status of sons and daughters aged 10–19 by age and sex, Manchester 1900.

education. You're going to get married and wash diapers." I thought if I didn't find a job, maybe she'd let me go back to school. So in the morning, I'd leave and walk uptown the minute the stores were open. I'd go from one store to another just looking. Then at noontime, I'd come home. I did that for three or four days. My mother asked, "Did you find a job?" and I said I hadn't. I didn't go to the employment office either. I was afraid I'd get a job, and I didn't want one. When my sister Flora came home for dinner, my mother said, "Why don't you take her with you?" Flora brought me to the employment office, and they sent me to the rayon plant [*Amoskeag*, pp. 192–3].

And Yvonne Dionne, who excelled as a student, was bitter about being pulled out of the convent school and sent to work:

I always enjoyed the work at the Amoskeag when I was there, though if I could have done without, I would have stayed home. But when everything is hard to get, and you want to have a few extra things, you have to help out the family. We were brought up in a large family – my father was a weaver and a loomfixer – and as soon as one girl was old enough, she went to work. That was the way. The oldest one started, and the rest of the family had to follow suit. We didn't feel bad about not going to school because nobody could afford to. Our parents were too poor. None of us even finished grammar school. I think I got through the eighth grade.

It did bother me at one time when I was at Sacred Heart School, because I had good marks. As soon as somebody got sick, I was supposed to go and help out; schooling came next.

One day, Alice, my sister-in-law, took sick, and Mom told me that I had to go help my aunt, Mrs. Girard. "She's very tired, and she's old and very sick," she said, "so you leave school and go and help her for a few days." That was during the middle of June. We were just going to have our graduation, and they used to have a prize for not missing school. I had gone to mass every morning the whole year, and I had my good conduct and everything. It was all *Très Bien*.

The nun called up my mother and said, "Where's Claudia?" (My name was Claudia at the time.) My mother said, "She's helping another family that needed help." "Have her come back right away," the nun said. "She has a surprise, a gift coming to her. If she's not here by the afternoon, she loses it." So my mother called me right up. When I got into class, the sister told me,

"You almost missed it." I got a nice big book. On it was a leaf, which had a banner inside that read: *Prix d'honneur*. That means honor prize. I managed to get good grades when I was there, but that was the end of my education. It would have been a wonderful thing to be able to speak English, to meet with people.

I used to ask my mother, "Why is it always me?" The nuns were very lenient with me at that time because they knew the family needed help. My mother used to say, "Why don't you come back right after school?" I had to do my share of the cleaning up, sweep the floors and clean the blackboards. I had to be in the choir even though I had no voice at all. So my mother had a talk with the sister superior. "I wish you could send her home right after school because I need her" [*Amoskeag*, pp. 196–7].

Marriage definitely represented the most crucial transition in women's work lives. Approximately two-thirds of all single men and women 10 years of age and older were in the labor force (Figure 8.3). The labor-force participation rates of men rose in their early twenties to approach 100% by age 30, where they remained until they dropped to 86% for men in their fifties and declined slightly more as they moved into their sixties. Men continued to be gainfully employed into old age: More than two-thirds of all men in their late sixties were still working and more than one-third in their early seventies. Among women, on the other hand, participation rates declined to just over one in two for the age group 25–29 and to just over one in three for the age group 30–34 (Figure 8.1). This dramatic drop in labor-force participation for women in their early twenties was linked to marriage. Only 23% of the married women in the sample were listed in the census as gainfully employed, in contrast to nine of ten married males (Figure 8.4). Women's rates continued to decline until their sixties, at which point they began to increase, reflecting the need of widows to work (Figures 8.1 and 8.5). Because marriage placed the major responsibility for family support on men, the majority of women retired from the work force after marriage.

The national labor-force participation rates for married women were even lower. The 1900 census reported that only 5.6% of all married women in the United States were gainfully employed. Although these figures may have understated social reality, because women's work outside the home was commonly underenumerated by census takers, the rates for Manchester are nonetheless strikingly high. The low proportion of married women employed in Man-

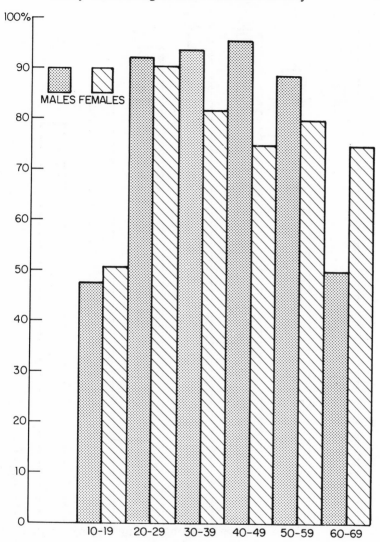

Figure 8.3. Labor-force participation rates of single persons by age and sex, Manchester 1900.

chester (23%) was more than double that for the state of New Hampshire as a whole and more than four times that for the United States. This was a result, to a large extent, of the attractiveness of the textile industry to both married and single women.[1] In addition, the work itself was female intensive (Table 8.1).

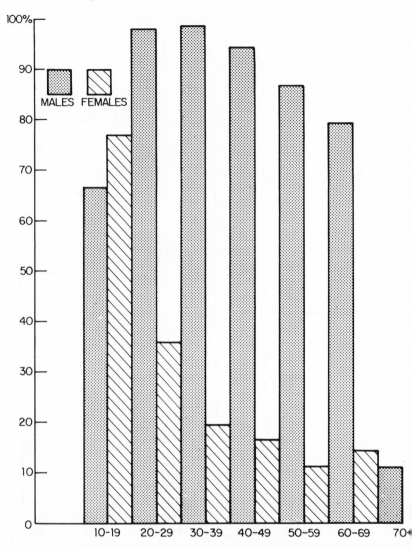

Figure 8.4. Labor-force participation rates of married persons by age and sex, Manchester 1900. (No employed females older than 70.)

Women listed in the census as unemployed may have worked prior to the time the census was taken or may have entered gainful employment shortly thereafter. The limitations of cross-sectional data prevent the clarification of these fluctuations and variations from census data alone; it is impossible, therefore, to determine how many of the women who dropped out of the labor force after

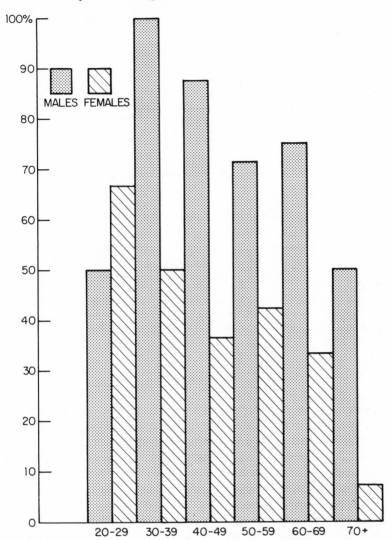

Figure 8.5. Labor-force participation rates of married persons by age and sex, Manchester 1900.

getting married actually reentered after the completion of child-rearing. That women's employment rates by age did not rise again until their sixties suggests that they did not customarily reenter gainful employment in large numbers after their children had reached adulthood.

Women who continued to work after marriage generally did not

Table 8.1. *Occupation of persons aged 19–45 by sex and marital status, Manchester 1900 (in percent)*

	Males		Females	
Occupation of persons aged 19–45	Single ($N = 213$)	Married ($N = 336$)	Single ($N = 244$)	Married ($N = 106$)
Nontextile	74.2	77.1	49.2	47.2
Textile	25.8	22.9	50.8	52.8
Total	100.0	100.0	100.0	100.0

Table 8.2. *Work status of married women by relation to head, Manchester 1900 (in percent)*

	Relation to head		
Work status of married women	Spouse ($N = 444$)	Other ($N = 103$)	Total ($N = 547$)
Working	12.6	68.9	23.2
Not working	87.4	31.1	76.8
Total	100.0	100.0	100.0

experience a smooth, unbroken work career. As long as there were jobs available in the Amoskeag (prior to the 1920s), many married women shuttled back and forth between the workplace and the home. These comings and goings, which are not recorded in the census, differ from the career patterns of today's women, who experience more defined gaps in their work lives that extend over most of the childrearing period.[2]

The crucial factor in keeping women out of the labor force was not marriage itself but coresidence with their husbands. As would be expected, the majority of married women (81%) lived with their husbands; of this group, only 12.6% were in the labor force. The remaining married women, who lived in other household arrangements, such as married daughters who lived in the households of their parents or extended kin, or as married boarders, were more likely to work than the wives of household heads (Table 8.2). In itself an important factor in keeping women out of the labor force, marital status was reinforced by household status.

Table 8.3. *Work status of wives with husband heading household and working by number of years married, Manchester 1900 (in percent)*

| | Number of years married | | | | | | |
Work status of wife	0–1 (N = 17)	2–5 (N = 70)	6–9 (N = 68)	10–14 (N = 66)	15–19 (N = 64)	20+ (N = 131)	Total (N = 416)
Working	23.5	21.4	13.2	15.2	10.9	4.6	12.3
Not working	76.5	78.6	86.8	84.8	89.1	95.4	87.7
Total	100.0	100.0	100.0	100.0	100.0	100.0	100.0

Table 8.4. *Percentage of wives working with husband heading household and working by age and number of own children 0–4 years old, Manchester 1900*

Age of working wife	Number of own children 0–4 years old				
	0	1	2	3	4
15–19	0.0	50.0			
	(N = 2)	(N = 2)	(N = 0)	(N = 0)	(N = 0)
20–24	46.7	9.1	60.0	0.0	0.0
	(N = 15)	(N = 11)	(N = 5)	(N = 1)	(N = 2)
25–29	41.7	10.5	0.0	18.2	0.0
	(N = 24)	(N = 19)	(N = 16)	(N = 11)	(N = 3)
30–34	5.0	8.3	15.4	9.1	
	(N = 20)	(N = 24)	(N = 13)	(N = 11)	(N = 0)
35–39	5.4	14.8	18.2	0.0	0.0
	(N = 37)	(N = 27)	(N = 11)	(N = 3)	(N = 1)

Many women who did not drop out immediately after marriage did stop working within the first five years of matrimony (Table 8.3), probably for childbearing and childrearing purposes. The labor-force participation rates of wives in their twenties were much higher when their youngest child was 4 or older (Table 8.4). Thus, motherhood, rather than marriage itself, may have been the major reason for women's withdrawal from the labor force.[3] Many interviews suggest, indeed, that conflict concerning the work of married women focused on child care rather than on domestic duties or the family's life-style.

The occupations of husbands were also a factor in the labor-force participation of their wives. Wives of blue-collar or service workers were more likely to work than wives of husbands in other occupations. Within the blue-collar category itself, the husband's level of skill had little impact, except that the wives of husbands in skilled jobs were slightly more likely to work than the wives of men in unskilled or semiskilled jobs. (As will be shown later, however, the children of men at lower levels of skill were more likely to work than the children of men who were more highly skilled.) The greater tendency of the wives of skilled workers to be employed suggests that more than economics was involved (Table 8.5). Their husbands' access to manual and service occupations may have facilitated their employment, whereas men at lower levels of skill may

Table 8.5. *Work status of wives with husband heading household and working by occupation of husband, Manchester 1900 (in percent)*

	Occupation of husband							
Work status of wife	Professional (N = 7)	Semiprofessional (N = 41)	Clerical (N = 37)	Skilled (N = 151)	Semiskilled (N = 98)	Unskilled (N = 76)	Farmer (N = 5)
Working	0.0	4.9	2.7	18.5	13.3	9.2	0.0
Not working	100.0	95.1	97.3	81.5	86.7	90.8	100.0
Total	100.0	100.0	100.0	100.0	100.0	100.0	100.0

Table 8.6. *Work status of foreign-born and native-born wives and daughters aged 15 – 65, Manchester 1900 (in percent)*

Work status	Foreign-born	First generation native-born	Other native-born
Wives	(N = 270)	(N = 46)	(N = 118)
Working	20.4	10.9	9.3
Not working	79.6	89.1	90.7
Total	100.0	100.0	100.0
Daughters	(N = 143)	(N = 86)	(N = 48)
Working	86.7	79.1	50.0
Not working	13.3	20.9	50.0
Total	100.0	100.0	100.0

Note: These figures refer to the twelve-month period immediately preceding the taking of the 1900 census.

have had less access to jobs not only for their spouses but for themselves as well.

The middle- and upper-class ideology that censored the work of wives and mothers outside the home had not yet greatly affected working-class families, particularly first-generation immigrant families. Married immigrant women were twice as likely to work as second-generation or native-born women (Table 8.6). Among immigrant workers, Canadian women were more likely to be in the labor force than Eastern European or Irish women. The Canadian families had migrated to Manchester to find work for as many family members as possible. But by the second generation, American values of domesticity had become dominant over the desire for maximum employment of the family (Table 8.7).

In working-class families, wives' work outside the home was still viewed as an important contribution and even as an integral aspect of the family's economy. As Françoise Bissel put it: "I myself believe that if a girl gets married and if you have no children, they should help work and help the husband. Course, when the children come . . . then you have somebody take care of them or you board them out" (interview).

Most couples interviewed perceived no conflict caused by the wife's work outside the home. Most husbands had recognized the economic necessity of having their wives work. The additional income often made the difference between eating eggs or bare bread

Table 8.7. *Work status of women, foreign-born, native-born of foreign-born parents, or native-born of native-born parents, by place of birth, Manchester 1900 (in percent)*

				Place of birth			
Work status	Canada	Poland/ E. Europe	Ireland	Other foreign	New Hampshire	Rest of Northeast	Rest of United States
Foreign-born women	(N = 387)	(N = 9)	(N = 79)	(N = 83)			
Working	40.3	22.2	34.2	25.3			
Not working	59.7	77.8	65.8	74.7			
Total	100.0	100.0	100.0	100.0			
Native-born women of foreign-born parents					(N = 303)	(N = 51)	(N = 17)
Working					21.5	33.3	11.8
Not working					78.5	66.7	88.2
Total					100.0	100.0	100.0
Native-born women of native-born parents					(N = 190)	(N = 60)	(N = 30)
Working					18.9	20.0	16.7
Not working					81.1	80.0	83.3
Total					100.0	100.0	100.0

Note: These figures refer to the twelve-month period immediately preceding the taking of the 1900 census.

for supper, and men admitted that a second income was essential for the purchase of a home, a car, or even smaller amenities. Angelique Laplante's description of her husband's attitude is an accurate summary: "He was for my working because my mother kept the kids for a little while. When there's just one working, you can't very well save. So we wanted a car like anybody else" (interview). Some husbands viewed their wives' employment in the factory as auxiliary, even when the wives were working full time. They did not urge their wives to work, nor did they discourage them. But, at the same time, they were not ready to care for the children.

Antoine Roberge, a highly skilled worker who eventually rose to a managerial position, described his wife's attitude toward work: "She wanted to work. She loved to work . . . I could afford a lot of things which only with my pay we couldn't afford. I liked to help her wash the floors, and she was a good housekeeper and she loved her work. She found time to take the kids to a show and we bought a car in 1935" (interview).

Husbands accepted their wives' work as a necessity: "My husband didn't like the idea of my working too much," reminisced Amelia Gazaille, a French-Canadian who had worked in the mills all her life. "I did the housework, and I let him help me. We both did it together. And when the children were too young, I worked, and my mother took care of my children" (interview).

Husband-and-wife teams shared responsibilities both in the mill and at home. Some men, especially those who worked with their wives in the same workroom, appreciated their wives' desire to work. As Omer Proulx put it:

> Well, she wanted to work to advance herself. First of all, if she hadn't worked, we'd never have been able to build a house. She worked many years weaving. When she had babies she went a while not working . . . Then one of her sisters built a house and she wanted to do as much as her. It was her mother who saw to our baby and I was in the house as much as my wife. We washed dishes together. We worked together [interview].

Women who worked outside the home viewed their factory labor and their domestic tasks as complementary, if not interchangeable. It was all part of their collective family enterprise. Their domestic responsibility – the care of children, the clothing of family members, the feeding of the family and often boarders as well – was itself a form of production. At the beginning of the twentieth century, most food was still produced and canned at home; clothing was often made and remade in the household. Ora Pelletier recalled:

> My mother would make all our clothes, except for coats or a
> Sunday dress. She even used to make our stockings. My aunt
> had a big family, and they were all working. She used to give my
> mother big bags of stockings that were ripped at the foot or
> something. My mother would cut the foot off and make a new
> one. She used to make us house slippers from old men's coats
> [*Amoskeag*, p. 241].

To augment the family budget, women often took in boarders
and provided child care for working mothers. Maria Lacasse helped
to provide for her twelve children by working in the mills intermittently, taking in boarders, and performing a variety of other tasks.
She recalled:

> My husband never stopped me going to work when we need-
> ed the money. I also had to make all the clothes, even the pants
> for the little boys. I used to sell sandwiches to the girls in the mill
> if they didn't bring their lunch. My husband was just across the
> street . . . and he used to whistle from the mill yard and tell me
> how many sandwiches he wanted. [*Amoskeag*, p. 261].

Maria's daughter remembered, however, the domestic conflict
provoked by the multiplicity of her mother's work roles:

> My father didn't really want her to work. That was a big issue
> because she always wanted to go in and earn a little money. But
> the minute she said she wanted to work, there would be a big
> fight. He'd say, "No, you're not going to work. You're going to
> stay home." And that's why she did other things. She'd make
> clothes for him, take in boarders, rent rooms. She used to rent
> one or two rooms for $12 a week to people who worked in the
> mills. Sometimes she'd also work little stretches at night in the
> mills, from six to nine because we lived right in front of the mills.
> When there were big orders, the mills were always looking for
> people to work. But my father didn't want to keep the children.
> That was women's work; his work was outside [Alice Olivier,
> *Amoskeag*, p. 255].

Maria herself recalled the strain involved in juggling the care of her
infant and work in the mill:

> But I'd had a baby during the summer, so I didn't want to work
> all day Saturday. I said to the boss, "You're a married man, so
> I'm going to tell you – I had a baby, and I'm nursing it." He said
> they had a big order to fill, so I said I'd stay until four [*Amoskeag*,
> p. 261].

Women like Maria Lacasse viewed themselves as standbys who
stepped in to work in the mill during times of economic crisis, thus

assuring some continuity in the family's income. Preparedness of this sort was built into the lives of those families who were constantly struggling to survive in a regime of insecurity.

Although men retained the belief that women carried the major responsibility at home, they often contributed to domestic work when their wives were employed. In addition to helping with cleaning, men cut wood and carried coal for long distances, purchased food, and repaired their dwellings. During the spring and summer some men also cultivated small farm plots outside the city. Frequently men and young boys cut hay on their farm after a day in the mill. "I used to work in the mill eight hours and run home as fast as I could, take shortcuts through the fields," one man recalled. "It was time to go haying. We used to cut a big field of hay with my four brothers. They helped me put that hay in the barn" (James Burton, interview).

Richard Laroche's mother was able to work outside the home because his sisters helped carry the burden of child care: "The girls as soon as they were old enough to help out at home, they were taught to cook, they were taught to help out with the washing. They didn't grumble." Both Laroche and his wife worked when their children were old enough to be on their own: "When the children were smaller she stayed at home, but once they were old enough to shift for themselves she went to work and we started pooling our resources for the children's education" (interview). Paul Cutler's mother worked as a maid in the fancy homes of the North End. To enable her to hold this job, an older child stayed home to care for the younger children (interview).

Couples like the Lalibertes felt that there was "no sense of hiring somebody to take care of the kids" (interview). It was preferable for the wife to stay at home. But most families felt that a wife's income could not be sacrificed, even though child care imposed a heavy burden on working women, especially when no relatives were available to assist them. Some working women entrusted supervision of their young children to their teen-age daughters. Mary Dancause's parents brought her back from Canada at age 12 to look after the younger children to allow her mother to work in the mill. Such arrangements were not, however, without hazard, as Yvonne Dionne recalled:

> My mother said she always had "one in the crib and one in the oven," so it was pretty rough on her. When I was little, she worked in the Amoskeag. She'd leave one of my sisters, who was twelve or thirteen, in charge of us; but my sister wouldn't stay in

the house. She'd go outside to be with her friends. One day I tried to reach the kettle to take it off the stove, and I dropped it and burned myself and one of the babies. My mother never went back to the mills after that [*Amoskeag*, p. 197].

The more common pattern was to leave young children in the care of older relatives – mothers, mothers-in-law, and aunts. Some mothers hired housekeepers to care for their children in their own homes; others left their children in another woman's house on their way to work and picked them up at the end of the day. Still others "loaned" their children for the entire week and took them home on weekends. Women who could not afford such arrangements left their children in the orphanage or placed them in the Villa Augustina, a Catholic boarding school outside Manchester.

Some insight into the economic conditions of working-class families in Manchester can be gained from an examination of the budgets of a sample of workers' families (from a survey by the U.S. Bureau of Labor Statistics[4] of a number of American cities, including Manchester).

A cotton bleacher, aged 27, and his wife, aged 30, who worked as a doffer, earned $1,066 annually, of which $102 was contributed by the wife, who worked only six weeks. This couple with two children, aged 5 and 4, spent:

Food – $457.79
Clothing – $219.84
Housing – $114.00
Fuel and light – $53.46
Furniture – $145.13
Miscellaneous – $212.78

The family was $137 in debt at the end of the year – $137 for a doctor's bill.

In another family, the husband, 47, was a dyer in a cotton mill and his wife, 29, was at home caring for seven children, who ranged in age from 9 months to 11 years. Some of the children were possibly from the husband's first marriage. As the only breadwinner, the husband earned $1,205. The family supplemented this income with $46.60 earned from the family garden and $105.60 received in gifts of food and clothing. Food was the biggest expenditure, and by the end of the year, the family had an outstanding $20 grocery bill and a $6 doctor's bill.

On the other hand, a family with only one child and both husband and wife working enjoyed a surplus. The husband, 56, earned $918 a year as a dresser; his wife, 42, earned $672 as a quiller; and their lodger contributed $30. Their child, 13, was in school. Additional income in the amount of $15.38 came from their garden and chickens. With their surplus they bought Liberty Bonds for $143 and deposited $197 in their savings.

In another family, all three members – husband, wife, and daughter – worked. The father, a truck driver, earned $800, the wife earned $144 as a seamstress, and the 23-year-old daughter earned $732 as a bookkeeper in a cotton mill. This family purchased high-quality food (expensive cuts of meat and high-grade flour and sugar), and the daughter spent $30 for her vacation and $30 for silk dresses. The family invested half its $190 surplus in Liberty Bonds and half in savings.

The most solvent families were those in which the husband, wife, and at least one child worked. The most vulnerable families were those with small children and only one major source of income. A 38-year-old mechanic in a cotton mill provided the only support for his wife and three children, who ranged in age from 3 months to 11 years. He earned $1,236 and covered a $24 deficit with savings.

Despite the margin of insecurity within which families operated, the typical family labor-force configuration in the population sample was one in which the major portion of the income was provided by the head and supplemental income was provided by teen-age children rather than the wife. Approximately half the male-headed households relied on the work of the head only, and in 38% one or more family members other than the head and the wife worked. Most additional workers were teen-age children. The critical supplement to the family's income came from the work of family members other than the wife (Table 8.8); wives worked in only 12.8% of male-headed households. Assuming these figures reflect choices, children or other relatives were sent to work rather than the wives. Only when additional income was still needed did the wife go to work.

From a collective family economy perspective, these patterns reflect certain trade-offs that shaped the family's labor-force configuration. Children's labor was not a substitute for that of their mothers except when three or more children worked, in male- as well as female-headed households (Table 8.9). The labor of one or two children would not provide the necessary supplement. Children were most likely to work in households where the parents were older and the head's occupational status was relatively low. Regardless of oth-

Table 8.8. *Work status of members of male-headed households with wife present, Manchester 1900*

Work status	Number	Percentage
No one works	9	2.0
Only husband works	225	50.8
Only wife works	4	0.9
Only husband and wife work	36	8.1
Only other family member(s)[a] works	13	2.9
Only husband and other family member(s) work	139	31.4
Only wife and other family member(s) work	2	0.5
Husband, wife, and other family member(s) work	15	3.4
Total	443	100.0

[a]Family members other than head and spouse.

Table 8.9. *Work status of wife of household head or female household head by number in family working other than head, Manchester 1900 (in percent)*

| Work status | Number in family working other than head | | | |
	0	1	2	3+
Wife	(N = 275)	(N = 77)	(N = 32)	(N = 60)
Working	14.5	11.7	15.6	5.0
Not working	85.5	88.3	84.4	95.0
Total	100.0	100.0	100.0	100.0
Female head	(N = 33)	(N = 30)	(N = 16)	(N = 21)
Working	48.5	40.0	43.8	14.3
Not working	51.5	60.0	56.2	85.7
Total	100.0	100.0	100.0	100.0

er characteristics, immigrant children were especially likely to work. In households where one or two children worked, mothers also tended to work. In households where children under 15 were working, mothers were also more likely to work. Of married women with both husband *and* children under 15 working, 16.3% worked. By contrast, only 11.8% of women with husbands working and no children under 15 working were in the labor force. The

Table 8.10. *Work status of wives and female heads
by presence or absence of boarders and lodgers,
Manchester 1900 (in percent)*

Work status	Boarder-lodger absent	Boarder-lodger present
Wives	(N = 351)	(N = 92)
Working	11.7	17.4
Not working	88.3	82.6
Total	100.0	100.0
Female heads	(N = 71)	(N = 29)
Working	35.2	44.8
Not working	64.8	55.2
Total	100.0	100.0

mother–child work pattern was complementary rather than mutually exclusive.[5]

Nor was the presence of boarders and lodgers in the household a substitute for the work of wives and children. Those households that depended on the wages of wives and children also needed additional income from boarders. (There was no statistically significant correlation between the presence of boarders in the household and the labor-force participation of other family members.) In fact, wives in male-headed households with boarders were more likely to work outside the home than wives in households without boarders (Table 8.10). Some women took in boarders and also worked in the mill. Women who ran large boardinghouses, however, took in boarders as an alternative to mill work.

Balbina Skrzyszowski, for example, set up a boardinghouse shortly after she and her husband arrived from Poland. Her son Mitchell recalled that she alternated the operation of the boardinghouse with mill work: "My mother used to run that big red block that was torn down . . . She was running it for a while and made meals. She was doing it temporarily because most of the time she spent in the mills" (interview). Amy Franklin's mother also ran a boardinghouse as an alternative to mill work. Most of the boarders were cigar makers:

> She went bankrupt too . . . they were getting too much good food for what they were paying . . . strawberry shortcake and cream pies! She was giving them all her profits. The cigar makers

never paid the full amount. They were always behind. They'd miss a meal, the next time the'd bring a friend to take the place of that meal. That's how cheap they were. She lost. She was a widow. She had saved a little bit of money – $800–$900. She had been weaving all her life. She wanted to get out of the mill and she thought that would be a break for her . . . She went back to weaving [interview].

The complementarity of the family economy, especially the propensity of additional family members to work, correlated to both the head's occupational status and migration status. In households where the head was in a lower skilled occupation, additional family members worked to supplement their low income (Table 8.11). The oldest child of a household head in the textile industry was more likely to work than children whose fathers were in other occupations.[6] Households headed by textile workers were also more likely to rely on the work of additional family members. In such households, 58% of the members were also employed in textiles. Other family members were more likely to work, in addition to the head and his wife, when the head was employed in textiles rather than in other occupations, a consequence also of the larger number of children in households headed by textile workers.[7]

Immigrant households, especially more recent arrivals, were more likely than natives to depend on the work of family members other than the head and wife. In approximately half the immigrant families, additional members worked, whereas additional members worked in only one-quarter of the native households. When only one additional family member worked there was little difference between households, but the difference was dramatic when two or more additional members worked (Table 8.12). The tendency of immigrant families to send their children to work is clearly seen in the employment of daughters. Whereas 86.7% of the foreign-born daughters aged 15 to 65 worked, only 50% of the daughters of natives were in the labor force (Table 8.6). Unless family economic need dictated otherwise, native-born families tended to keep their daughters in their teens or twenties at home without regular employment. Anticipating marriage, daughters stayed in school longer or helped to care for younger siblings or to do housework.

These differences between immigrant and native-born families parallel the situation in other New England communities in the same period (Mason, Vinovskis, and Hareven 1978). The propensity of families to maximize the employment of their teen-age children was characteristic of the textile industry, which acted as a

Table 8.11. *Number of family members working other than head and wife in male-headed households by occupation of head, Manchester 1900 (in percent)*

Number in family working	Occupation of head							
	Professional (N = 7)	Semiprofessional (N = 41)	Clerical (N = 37)	Skilled (N = 155)	Semiskilled (N = 100)	Unskilled (N = 78)	Farmer (N = 5)
0	71.4	65.9	70.3	69.0	62.0	43.6	60.0
1+	28.6	34.1	29.7	31.0	38.0	56.4	40.0
Total	100.0	100.0	100.0	100.0	100.0	100.0	100.0

Table 8.12. *Number of family members working*
other than head and wife in male-headed households
by head's nativity, Manchester 1900 (in percent)

	Nativity of head	
Number in family working	Immigrant (N = 278)	Native (N = 177)
0	51.8	75.7
1	17.3	17.5
2+	31.0	6.8
Total	100.0	100.0

magnet for both teen-agers who migrated alone and families with teen-age children, who depended more heavily on the labor of their children than native-born families.

Women without husbands usually worked or were dependent on the labor of their children. As suggested earlier, single women worked most of their lives. Married women who had dropped out of the labor force sometimes returned to permanent work when they were widowed. A higher proportion of widows, especially household heads, tended to be in the labor force than wives. Widows with working children in the household were less likely to hold jobs. Of those female household heads with one or more children employed, only a little less than one-third worked, whereas half the female heads without working children were in the labor force (Table 8.9).

Older household heads, both male and female, were particularly dependent on the family as a collective work unit. Male heads in their fifties or older were more likely than younger household heads to have children working in addition to themselves and their wives. One additional family member worked in 23.1% of all households headed by men aged 50 to 59, and two additional members worked in 38.5% of the households headed by men in this age group (Table 8.13).[8]

At the turn of the century, E. S. Rowntree (1901) defined the economic dilemma faced by working-class families in England by identifying two stages in the family cycle when poverty was most likely to strike: first, at the beginning of the cycle, when the children of the couple were still too young to work, and again, near the end, after the children of the aging couple had left home. Although

Table 8.13. *Number of family members working other than head and wife in male-headed households by head's age, Manchester 1900 (in percent)*

Number in family working	Age of head				
	30–39 (N = 141)	40–49 (N = 114)	50–59 (N = 78)	60–69 (N = 45)	70+ (N = 10)
0	76.6	50.0	38.5	44.4	60.0
1	14.9	20.2	23.1	17.8	30.0
2+	8.5	29.8	38.5	37.8	10.0
Total	100.0	100.0	100.0	100.0	100.0

the situation was similar in Manchester and other New England industrial communities at the turn of the century, the squeeze experienced during the childrearing years was alleviated when the children reached the legal working age of 14, for they remained working members of the household for a longer period. Some children even falsified their ages so they could begin working earlier. And in Manchester, unlike Britain, at least one child was still at home and working as parents entered old age. The parents expected the child to contribute his or her earnings to them, an arrangement that often made a wage-earning child dependent on parents: "In the old days we had to give our pay at home," recalled Thomas Bergeron. "If I had to have something I'd just ask him [the father]. He always kept the $40 I gave him. He wouldn't give it to me. The old days it was that way . . . Once in a while he'd give us a couple of dollars. The old people were keeping you to one job" (interview).

Immigrant families relied on the wages of wives and children to supplement the male head's income and viewed all these earnings as essential to the family's collective effort. "In our culture the oldest children always went to work" (Alice Olivier, *Amoskeag*, p. 262). The high proportion of working male and female youngsters suggests both the availability of teen-age employment opportunities in the textile industry and the family's economic needs and cultural values. The high correlation between immigrant status and the textile employment of teen-agers shows the extent of family reliance on the earnings of teen-agers. The number of working children younger than 15 was probably even higher than the figure recorded in the census. Child laborers were underreported and ages were falsified. Most families expected children to begin working just as soon as they were able or permitted to enter the labor force. Although employers claimed a reluctance to hire younger children, many former workers said that the enforcement of the requirement that children submit age certificates was a sham. "When I was eleven, my father had a birth certificate made for me in the name of my sister Cora, who died as a baby, because you couldn't go to work unless you were 14," Cora Pellerin recalled (*Amoskeag*, p. 202).

Children in their teens or early twenties who lived at home contributed most, if not all, of their earnings to their families, a custom followed by most interviewees. Amelia Gazaille, who worked as a doffer in the Amoskeag, gave her entire pay to her mother and received a dollar for her own spending money (interview). Jean Jalbert and his brother started to work at ages 14 and 11, respectively, before the New Hampshire child labor law was passed. As Jalbert recalled:

> It was necessary for him [his brother] to work to help out our family . . . It always brought in a few dollars at home and it always helped. We always got along with what we had. We were enough young ones working. I worked and I gave my pay up until age 20 . . . I had another brother that was younger. It had been a long time that he wanted to pay his board; so my mother made him pay his board, and he didn't do any better than I did [interview].

And Richard Laroche recalled:

> You either paid board, or in some cases you'd turn around and take a week's pay and give it to mother, and mother turned around and gave you a couple of dollars for your expenses, depending on how much you made a week . . . Very few households were getting where they'd tell you "you're gonna pay me $6 a week, or $10 a week" and so on. The boy got the work, the girl got the work, when you'd come home you'd give mother $5, $10, whatever [interview].

Mary Hamilton identified the contribution of children's earnings to the family economy as a French-Canadian custom: "My mother and father were real French [Canadian] people, and I would bring my envelope home, then my mother would buy me whatever I needed" (interview). But the custom was prevalent among other ethnic groups as well. Even Yankees who did not need income from their children collected a certain amount from them for board in order to instill a sense of responsibility. "I had to pay my board," recalled Thomas Orwell, a native of New Hampshire who lived with his aunt. "My aunt didn't really need the money in those days, but she said, 'Pay your board.' I paid $3 or $4 a week for $50 worth of food" (interview).

Some children continued to contribute even when they were no longer members of the household. Ethel Stemkowski, a Polish woman who came to Manchester as a young girl, worked as a maid in a private house in Massachusetts after the mills shut down. She sent her pay to her parents in Manchester: "I kept a dollar and sent back five. It wasn't very much, but at least it was something" (interview).

By contrast, William Redmond, the son of an Amoskeag overseer, was privileged enough to be able to hold on to his earnings:

> My father was working. There were two or three in the family working at that time, so we were pretty well off. We owned our own home and everything. While most people were paying on their property, our property was all taken care of. My father worked in the mill quite a while and we had a sister who worked in the mill and then I had a brother who worked in the shoe shop. So I kept the money I earned. They never bothered me [interview].

But Anna Hall took on additional work in the mill to earn a little extra for herself because all her regular pay went to her family: "Then my sister got married and the boss gave me her work. There were six sides at $6.27 a week and I could keep the 27 cents. That was my pay . . . I saved my money for a pair of shoes" (interview).

The work lives of both men and women were shaped by family economic needs, available employment opportunities in the community, and cultural values regarding labor. The continuity of men's work over their entire life course reflects the basic dependence of the family unit on the labor of its male head. That only almost one-quarter of all wives were employed, despite the availability of textile employment for women, reflects how pervasive the norms of the larger society had become, although their effect on immigrant families was less. Despite the apparent preference to keep wives at home, it is also clear that the work of children was not a substitute for their mothers' employment. The family's labor-force configuration was complementary. In families with working children, wives also worked and some even took in boarders as well.

The most obvious response to insecurity, the interdependence of family members, often provided the only means of coping with unemployment, job difficulties, and death. The economic survival of the family depended on the active participation of all family members. Women made vital economic contributions to the household economy even when their work outside the home was intermittent. As in household structure and the timing of life transitions, so in the family's organization as a work unit, flexibility and the subordination of individual preferences to collective family needs were at the base of family survival.

9   *Work lives*

In contemporary society the very concept of a work career implies an orderly sequence of jobs. It connotes regularity and continuity. Although a career does not necessarily entail upward mobility, it is considered a continuous process in which individuals accumulate experience and skills and move in a progression from simpler to more complicated tasks. "A career," writes Wilensky, "is a succession of related jobs, arranged in a hierarchy of prestige, through which persons move in an ordered (more or less predictable) sequence" (1961: 523).

The historical experience of the careers in Manchester was significantly different. Workers moved from job to job and experienced frequent interruptions. The high mobility of the population and frequent unemployment resulting from erratic production schedules rendered orderly and stable careers the exception rather than the norm. Consequently, the careers of the Amoskeag workers must be understood within their own context. Most important, the patterns of orderliness and continuity in those apparent "disorderly" careers must be identified, and the extent to which they were shaped by individual choices and by the vagaries of the industrial system must be understood. To accomplish this, it is necessary to identify the shape of work careers from both the workers' and the corporation's point of view.

Careers and historical changes in the corporation

Throughout the first decade of the twentieth century, the Amoskeag, like many of its contemporaries, identified labor turnover as its most severe problem. Labor turnover seriously preoccupied American industrialists, economists, and labor reformers during the 1920s as well. The U.S. Bureau of Labor Statistics,[1] the U.S. Department of Labor, Women's Bureau (1926), and private industry conducted numerous studies of the situation. Some studies made specific recommendations for curbing turnover, including the establishment of employment offices such as the Amoskeag's, that would centralize hiring and firing practices. Rates of labor turnover

218

were dizzying throughout various industries. One study concluded that one-third of all the men hired by factories remained for less than one year (Slichter 1919). A systematic analysis conducted under the auspices of the U.S. Bureau of Labor revealed that in order to maintain an annual labor force of 13,700, the Amoskeag company needed to hire at least 24,000 workers (Brissenden and Frankel 1922). As the Ford Automobile Company had to hire 60,000 workers per year in order to maintain a labor force of 12,000, the Amoskeag's turnover was not as dramatic as it might appear (Nevins 1954). Nonetheless, from the corporation's perspective, turnover imposed a continuous need to recruit new labor and undermined the efficiency of workrooms. The Amoskeag's yearly turnover rates were considerably higher than those for the textile industry as a whole during the first decade of the twentieth century. Turnover rates leveled off after reaching a peak in 1914 but began to climb again in 1924 (Creamer and Coulter 1939). As calculated by business, labor turnover rates are measured only by voluntary separations. If involuntary separations resulting from layoffs had been included, turnover rates would have doubled (Table 9.1 and Figure 9.1).

In the pre–World War I period and through the war itself, labor turnover in the Amoskeag was predominantly initiated by workers, particularly for reasons of job mobility or working conditions. The employment office instituted a record-keeping system designed to centralize hiring and firing. It was also instructed to calculate labor-force turnover rates for each department in the hope of uncovering the causes of turnover, whether such factors as ethnicity, for example, influenced job stability.[2] As shown in Chapter 2, the welfare program launched by the Amoskeag between 1911 and 1912 was also addressed – at least in part – to the problem of turnover. Whether these measures had a direct impact on career continuity is difficult to assess; the program was probably more effective in attracting workers to the mill than in keeping them there.

In one of the most comprehensive contemporary analyses of turnover, Slichter (1919) singled out common laborers and low-skilled workers, young boys and girls, and young men and newly married workers as those most prone to leave their jobs. Slichter concluded that the longer workers were affiliated with a company, the better the working conditions, and the more skilled the jobs, the less likely workers were to leave. He drew most of his data from the metals industry, clothing manufacture, and other small concerns. Perhaps for that reason, the patterns he outlined do not entirely coincide with the Amoskeag's, although there are some similari-

Table 9.1. *Labor turnover rates for Amoskeag and cotton-textile industry, 1914–34*

	Amoskeag rate					Bureau of Labor Statistics rate for cotton textiles[c]
	Based on actual periods of employment and no employment[a]				Based on accessions and separations[b]	
Year and type of rate	Cotton section		Worsted section			
	Men	Women	Men	Women		
1914						
Accessions	n.a.	n.a.	n.a.	n.a.	117.5	n.a.
Separations	n.a.	n.a.	n.a.	n.a.	123.0	n.a.
1923						
Accessions	256.6	295.2	176.8	224.9	n.a.	n.a.
Separations	245.7	282.7	167.4	221.5	n.a.	n.a.
1924						
Accessions	n.a.	n.a.	n.a.	n.a.	29.5	n.a.
Separations	n.a.	n.a.	n.a.	n.a.	40.9	n.a.
1925						
Accessions	n.a.	n.a.	n.a.	n.a.	42.1	n.a.
Separations	n.a.	n.a.	n.a.	n.a.	52.8	n.a.
1926						
Accessions	n.a.	n.a.	n.a.	n.a.	59.6	n.a.
Separations	n.a.	n.a.	n.a.	n.a.	55.5	n.a.
1927						
Accessions	n.a.	n.a.	n.a.	n.a.	42.9	n.a.
Separations	n.a.	n.a.	n.a.	n.a.	46.8	n.a.
1928						
Accessions	168.2	218.5	183.3	220.5	76.9	n.a.
Separations	167.6	212.3	156.3	207.7	67.2	n.a.
1929						
Accessions	n.a.	n.a.	n.a.	n.a.	99.9	n.a.
Separations	n.a.	n.a.	n.a.	n.a.	110.2	n.a.
1930						
Accessions	178.9	245.3	187.8	226.6	79.2	42.0
Separations	186.1	252.6	210.3	237.5	88.6	58.3
1931						
Accessions	216.3	273.5	173.3	223.9	77.0	47.4
Separations	218.6	286.2	175.2	225.0	82.2	53.5

Table 9.1. (cont.)

	Amoskeag rate					Bureau of Labor Statistics rate for cotton textiles[c]
	Based on actual periods of employment and no employment[a]				Based on accessions and separations[b]	
	Cotton section		Worsted section			
Year and type of rate	Men	Women	Men	Women		
1932						
Accessions	288.3	315.0	331.1	440.8	78.7	67.5
Separations	264.3	300.8	237.9	417.9	43.8	62.6
1933						
Accessions	225.2	163.6	216.3	281.3	110.1	83.6
Separations	287.5	363.0	288.4	361.2	73.9	56.5
1934						
Accessions	201.5	268.9	264.8	387.8	91.0	53.7
Separations	193.7	255.3	241.4	364.8	72.8	57.4

[a]Based on a tabulation of a sample of Amoskeag Company income-tax records.
[b]Figures for 1914 are based on Paul F. Brissenden and Emil Frankel, *Labor Turnover in Industry* (New York: Macmillan, 1922), pp. 176–7. Figures for remaining years are based on an NRP tabulation of company personnel records. Accessions and separations resulting from temporary layoffs were not counted.
[c]Adapted from *Handbook of Labor Statistics: 1931 Edition* (U.S. Department of Labor, Bureau of Labor Statistics, Bulletin No. 541, September 1931), p. 669, and *Handbook of Labor Statistics: 1936 Edition* (Bulletin No. 616, 1936), p. 808.
n.a.: Data not available.
Source: Daniel Creamer and Charles W. Coulter, *Labor and the Shutdown of the Amoskeag Textile Mills* (Philadelphia: Work Projects Administration, 1939), p. 270.

ties. Slichter's most important contribution to an understanding of the causes of labor turnover is the attention he gave to the interaction between workers' personal characteristics and the organization, schedules, and policies of the workplace.

The workers and management did not view labor turnover in quite the same way. Consequently, the ensuing analysis of the

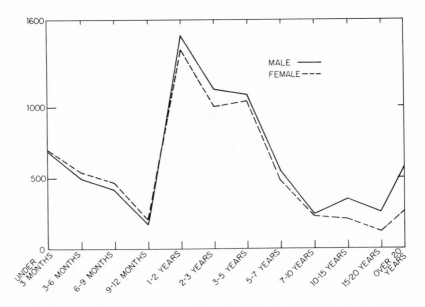

Figure 9.1. Length of service of employees in the Amoskeag Manufacturing Company on October 1, 1915. (*Source:* Amoskeag Co., *Turnover of Employees*, BLH.)

Amoskeag's employee files will differentiate between workers' choices or needs, on the one hand, and the organization of production and personnel policies in the factory, on the other, as causes of career fluidity. Given the shift in the Amoskeag's own history from labor shortage in the pre–World War I period to labor surplus in the 1920s and 1930s, it will be possible to examine both voluntary and involuntary labor turnover. To what extent did the workers view the mill as a resource, as a place where they could come and go, depending on their needs and preferences and their success or failure with other job opportunities? On the other hand, to what extent were the workers victims of production schedules, depression cycles in the textile industry, and arbitrary decisions on the part of management?

Individual careers are the product of personal attributes, choices, skills, and luck and are affected by the timing of the first job, age, experience, and the availability of employment opportunities. But in the time period studied here, careers were also shaped to a large extent by the age configurations and economic situation of the family. The age at which children or young adults entered the labor force was closely related to family needs, as was the decision as to whether wives or mothers should hold jobs. Similarly, in the absence of compulsory retirement legislation, the age at which older people withdrew from the labor force depended on whether they had children of working age living at home who could support them in later life. The decision as to when children should start work or leave home depended on the number of other siblings in the household who were too young to work and on the ability of aging parents to continue to hold jobs. Even when career decisions were not arrived at collectively, the common expectation was that individuals would conform to the family's needs. The interaction between individual time, family time, and industrial time shaped career patterns of individuals and families. Adaptation to changing economic and structural conditions in industry significantly determined the timing and flow of career patterns. For instance, under conditions of labor shortage, workers had the flexibility to choose jobs, plan for the future, and decide whether to keep a son in school or send a daughter to work. Under conditions of labor surplus, on the other hand, families were less able to chart careers and stick to them and to balance long-term careers for different family members against each other.

The point in their lives at which men and women encounter changes in industrial time is also significant in shaping a career. Technological changes affecting workers' control over their jobs or curtailments in employment, such as strikes and shutdowns, affect people differently, depending on whether such events are encountered at the beginning, the peak, or the end of their work lives.

Because most existing historical studies of work careers have been limited to cross-sectional data, it has been impossible for historians to reconstruct longitudinal patterns.[3] This study, however, uses longitudinal data in the form of employee records, which allows the charting of the rhythms of careers over workers' entire lives and under the impact of changing industrial and economic conditions. Ideally, this discussion would be extended to include a person's entire work life, inside and outside the mills. Unfortunately, the Amoskeag data are not matched by comparable career information outside the mills. By necessity, therefore, the discussion that follows is limited to the careers within the corporation.

The period of this study saw the labor market shift from a condition of shortage to one of labor surplus and the replacement of the Amoskeag's earlier system of informal hiring by a centralized personnel policy enforced by a new employment office. During the war, the strike of 1922, and the thirteen-year decline that led to the final shutdown of the mills, the flexibilities that characterized the prewar period of corporate expansion gradually disappeared, and job insecurity emerged as the overriding theme in the lives of the corporation's workers.

To examine the effect of these changes, the labor force in this sample was divided into several groups, in accordance with the years in which individuals first started to work in the Amoskeag. The first group entered the mill between 1912 and the outbreak of the Amoskeag's first major strike in 1922, a period that, except for the immediate postwar years, represented a peak of prosperity in the Amoskeag's history. It began with the annexation of several other mills in the city and the contruction of the Amoskeag's last large mill, the Coolidge Mill. These developments coincided with an increase in production, the rationalization of personnel policies, and the introduction of efficiency measures. It was also a period of labor shortage, a problem that the corporation's employment office tried to address by encouraging greater career stability among the employees.

The second group in the sample consists of individuals who started work during the period 1922–30, following the strike. During this period, management struggled to maintain the pre–World War I paternalistic balance in labor relations, but because of the pressure of southern competition, which forced intermittent curtailments of production, workers were frequently laid off. At times whole workrooms were closed. The chances of being rehired declined consistently during this period, and workers were uncertain of being reemployed once they had left.

The third group in the sample experienced job insecurity at its worst. Starting work in the 1930s, they endured the Amoskeag's final decline (following a temporary recovery in 1931), which ended with the shutdown of the mills in 1936.

Thus the historical factors affecting career continuity and stability were different for each of the three groups, given the Amoskeag's struggle with contracting markets and postwar fluctuations in the textile industry.

Because of the uncertainties of an unstable market and changing styles, management after 1922 considered it too risky to manufacture for inventory and switched to manufacturing for orders. Customers did not place large advance orders; rather, they bought for the short term. As a result, the Amoskeag bunched orders for immediate delivery, causing periods of intensive production followed by slack periods. In 1923, the cotton industry experienced a slump, and in 1928 and 1930 both the worsted and cotton divisions within the Amoskeag curtailed production because of a depressed textile market.[4] At times, entire sections were shut down, especially in the 1930s.

The employment office also fulfilled an important role in the shaping of work careers. After a change in company policy in 1911, every worker applying for a job or a transfer was expected to present himself to the employment office. Overseers were expected to file their requests for workers to fill certain vacancies with the office, where clerks would then distribute the jobs to suitable applicants. However, a worker's likelihood of being hired, transferred, or returned to a job after he or she had left still depended a great deal on chance, on the arbitrary choices of the overseer and the employment clerk, and on personal, family, or neighborhood connections, as well as on his or her formal work record.

A former employment office clerk, reminiscing in 1975, summarized the process:

> It was up to me whether a person was hired or not. If an overseer requested a particular person for a job, I would check his records, find out if he was qualified and if he had been around in the past looking for employment. I had people there coming in day in, day out, looking for employment. I would consider them before I would the request of an overseer or a second hand, except on special occasions. On certain jobs it wouldn't matter who you'd hire because there were always openings; but when there were no openings, you'd have to take them according to their qualifications, because even after we hired them, the overseer had the final say on whether he'd put them to work or not [Joseph Debski, *Amoskeag*, p. 129].

Because an overseer could put in a request for a specific worker – someone who had worked for him previously or someone he knew through other contacts – workers standing in line in front of the employment windows were often bitterly disappointed to find themselves turned down in favor of someone who had "jumped the queue." In the prewar period and during the war, labor shortages made for good job prospects, and the employment clerks were not very selective about the type of worker they hired. Many assignments were arbitrary, and because so many textile jobs could be learned within a short time period, workers in unskilled or semiskilled jobs often floated from job to job. Nor did the employment clerk always examine the file carefully, or if he did, he often failed

to take seriously earlier dismissals for rule violations, poor performance, or instability. Often such workers were rehired because their
files were never checked.

Initiation to work

Because more than half the workers started their mill careers as
teen-agers, the role of the Amoskeag in the initiation of young people to work was considerable. Most teen-agers in Manchester expected to start their work careers in the Amoskeag.

They started work during school holidays from about age 14 and
shifted toward full-time factory employment as they reached age 16,
in conformity with the 1911 New Hampshire Child Labor Law.[5]
Some started earlier if they were successful in persuading their
bosses that they were of age.

Whether they themselves chose to drop out of school early or
were urged to do so by their parents, the Amoskeag was the most
logical place for them to seek their first job. Elizabeth Miller, for
example, a young Scottish girl, started work in the Amoskeag at age
12: "My father knew the boss. That was the only place to go" (interview). Elizabeth and her sister both worked in the Amoskeag as
burlers for their entire lives. Fed up with being "bossed around" by
her mother, 14-year-old Anna Schmidt was determined to find a job
in the Amoskeag. She told her mother, "I'm gonna get a job." Her
mother said, "Go ahead. I know you won't get a job." Anna went
into the burling room with her cousin and asked, "Do you have a
job?" The boss said, "Go and get your papers from the employment
office." She was hired right away and was taught burling by the
same cousin who took her to the employment office. As a worker,
Anna felt confident – "I could do things just the way I wanted"
(interview).

Once the child labor law was in effect, the Amoskeag tried to
enforce the age limit by requiring age certificates from young boys
and girls. It was, however, fairly easy to bypass this regulation.
Often, the employment clerk simply asked the age and accepted the
answer at face value. Some children did not even stop at the employment office but went directly to the workrooms. If the overseer
asked for their age, they simply lied.

Marie Proulx was 12 years old when she arrived in Manchester
with her family. She went to her cousin in the Amoskeag and the
cousin pointed out the boss. "He saw that I was a Canuck." He

showed Marie with his fingers the number 14. "I said, 'Yes.' So he said, 'Ok, you'll start tomorrow'" (*Amoskeag*, p. 67).

Other children who continued on to high school worked in the Amoskeag during summers, generally in the same workrooms as their relatives, who taught them their first jobs. After they graduated from high school at age 16, they entered regular employment in the Amoskeag. Others went to school in the morning and to work at 1 P.M.

First full-time jobs for young people were also secured through relatives and friends, who introduced them to the overseer in a specific workroom or to the employment office. Relatives made sure that the overseer knew about the new employee and that a job was available for him or her in the same workroom where the friend or relative worked.

When Alice Carignan was not busy on her own job, she visited her sister. "That's where I learned to wind. When I wasn't working, I'd go see my sister and she would teach me. And at that time we could transfer, so, after I knew how to wind, I asked the boss for a transfer" (interview).

Emily Renoir, who learned how to weave at age 13, worked with her brother: "We got along well, but when things didn't go right, sometimes we'd fight. We'd tell the boss. The boss found that funny. We were just little things. Children of 12 years old were not treated badly" (interview).

For young people, the first job in the Amoskeag represented something of an investment. It was an opportunity to learn the basic operations of a certain job, and, in their spare time, also to check out other jobs and to acquire additional skills. The first job provided an excellent opportunity for testing work processes and relationships. For those working temporarily during the summer or part-time while in school, it provided the opportunity to make a good impression on a boss and thus establish contact for future employment.

Adolescents were generally first taught spinning and doffing. In their first two years they worked at different jobs that were easy to learn. Although some continued to work as sweepers, oilers, and truck boys, the more ambitious used this opportunity to study the entire textile production process. By watching older workers, they acquired specific skills in other jobs and were able to prove to the boss that they knew other jobs as well, thus laying the groundwork for eventual advancement.

James Burton, who started out as a sweeper, recalled:

> I used to have a lot of spare time during summer vacations while still in high school. When I was done cleaning my work there, instead of sitting down for half an hour, I'd go by the doffers and take some bobbins and learn how to doff. After awhile, I would beat all the doffers that were doffing there. The boss seen me and he said, "You can doff pretty good. Next week I'm going to put you on the doff" (interview).

Not all who went to the mill for their first job expected to stay on or even to return if they left. Many young boys and girls were sent there to learn work habits, somewhat like being sent to a finishing school. Even the sons of textile managers were sent first to the mills to learn the rudiments of textile work before being sent on for advanced training. F. C. Dumaine sent his own sons to apprentice in the Amoskeag to learn the textile business before they were sent on to bigger and better jobs. After the initial period of apprenticeship, workers from affluent families were sent on to other jobs. Thus, the commencement of work in the Amoskeag was a time of learning and selection, a time to decide whether to stay or leave, a time to decide which job would be sought after initial training.

Career rhythms

The following analysis is based on a 2.5% random sample of the 73,640 individual employee files maintained by the Amoskeag beginning in 1911.[6] Of the workers in the sample, 43% started and completed their careers in the Amoskeag between 1912 and 1921; 16.7% between 1922 and 1930; and 9.6% after 1930. The remaining 30.7% overlapped through different periods. The files recorded each hiring, separation, and transfer over an employee's entire career, including the reason given by the workers for each separation. The overseer usually recorded the reason on a duplicate dismissal slip; one copy was given to the worker, the other copy was filed in the employment office.

The group of Amoskeag workers in this sample consisted of 829 men and 609 women (Table 9.2). About 40% were French-Canadian immigrants; Greek and Polish immigrants constituted 12% each; and immigrants from the British Isles about 11%. United States natives (including American-born children of immigrant parents) constituted 14%. There was little change over time in the proportion of various ethnic groups in the sample, except for the proportion of Greek workers, which diminished, and the proportion of

Table 9.2. *Characteristics of labor force in
Amoskeag Mills*

	Number	Percentage
Sex		
Male[a]	829	57.6
Female[a]	609	42.4
Total	1,438	100.0
Ethnicity		
U.S.	194	13.6
French Canada	579	40.5
British Isles	160	11.2
Poland and		
E. Europe	174	12.2
Greece	178	12.4
Other	139	9.7
Unknown	7	0.5
Total	1,431	100.0
Years worked		
0–1	859	60.0
2–5	343	24.0
6–9	107	7.5
10+	123	8.6
Total	1,432	100.0

Note: Includes only persons who started work in 1912 or
later.
[a] Mill sample.

French Canadians, which increased. The proportion of French Canadians in this sample rose from approximately 34% in 1912 to
close to 41% in 1916, to 50% in 1920, and finally peaked at 60% in
1928. The numerical prominence of the French Canadians was not
matched, however, by advances in status. With few exceptions,
they never achieved supervisory or managerial positions.

Despite the city's dependence on the Amoskeag as its chief employer, approximately 60% of the people in the sample worked
there for less than one year, although because of frequent interruptions in employment in even these cases the time elapsed between
initial hiring and final separation was often much longer (Table
9.2). These figures are comparable to Creamer and Coulter's (1939)
reconstruction of the work patterns of the Amoskeag's labor force,
which reported that about 36% of the men and 26% of the women

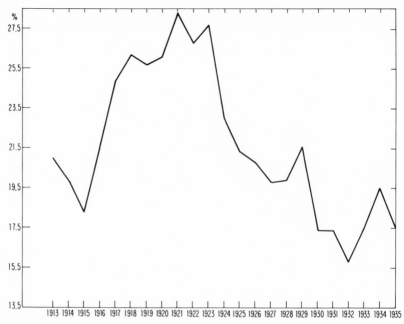

Figure 9.2. Labor-force participation rates in the Amoskeag Mills of the sample, 1912–35.

who left the Amoskeag between 1911 and 1935 had worked there no more than six months. Clearly, textile work attracted floaters as well as more stable workers.

Because of the intermittent character of textile production, as well as individual workers' personal preferences or handicaps, multiple hirings and separations were the pervasive pattern in the mill. More than half the workers in the sample were employed in the Amoskeag more than once, and almost two out of five were employed ten times or more.

Relating individual career patterns of workers in the Amoskeag to historical changes in the corporation, the following analysis examines the factors affecting continuity and discontinuity in work careers. Beginning with individual and group attributes (sex, ethnicity, level of skill, and family background), the analysis then proceeds to examine the encounter between individuals at a given stage and during specific phases in the life of the corporation.

An examination of the Amoskeag's labor-force participation rates (i.e., the number of workers each year) in the sample reveals a high

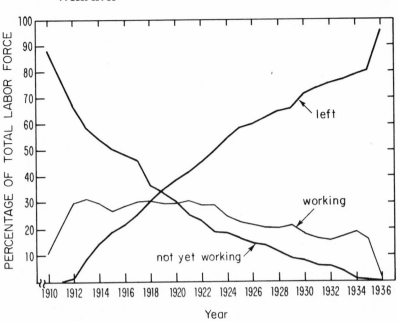

Figure 9.3. Employment status of the labor force by year from 1910 to 1936.

proportion of workers concentrated in the period 1917 to 1924, re-flecting the increase in hiring during World War I. In the period 1923–7 the rates fell as rapidly as they had risen and after 1929 de-creased dramatically, except for a slight increase prior to the Amoskeag's last gasp (Figures 9.2 and 9.3).[7]

Both the age and sex structure of the labor-force sample changed over time. The proportion of males dropped from 63% in 1912 to 56% in 1916, to 52% in 1920, and to 51% in 1928. Sex ratios re-mained fairly steady in the 1920s but rose again in the 1930s. A chronological examination of the age distribution of the workers indicates an overall aging of the labor force over time (Figure 9.4). The proportion of teen-agers declined steadily from 1912 to 1936, particularly the age group 15 to 19, which was reduced by almost half between 1912 and the 1930s. The proportion of those 20 to 24 also declined with the big postwar drop in production. On the oth-er hand, the age group 25 to 29 remained relatively stable, except for the period immediately following the strike. The relative decline of this age group after 1922 may reflect the failure of workers to return after the strike or a reduction in the hiring of teen-age workers in

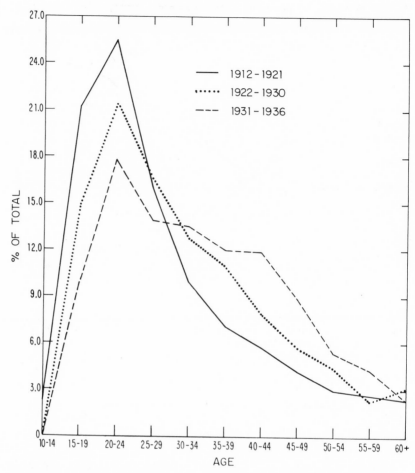

Figure 9.4. Age distributions of people working in the Amoskeag Mills, 1912–36.

the post-strike period. By contrast, the proportion of workers in their forties increased.

Age characteristics of workers who left the mill also changed over this time period. Examination of separation rates by age shows these rates differed significantly over the course of the Amoskeag's history. (Final separation rates were calculated as the proportion of each age group leaving the mill for the last time, thus taking into account the age structure of the labor force.) During the 1915 and 1918 upswing, workers younger than 40 were less likely to leave

Table 9.3. *Rates for last departure from the mill by age,*
1912–36 (in percent)

Age each year[a]	1912–14	1915–18	1919–21	1922	1923–29	1930–35	1936
10–14	3.4	0.0	0.0	—[b]	0.0	—[b]	—[b]
15–19	17.9	8.7	13.1	13.8	19.4	19.2	—[b]
20–24	39.7	22.2	14.3	21.6	19.6	29.8	100.0
25–29	39.0	21.8	16.0	26.8	15.4	26.8	100.0
30–34	29.2	16.1	17.7	13.6	13.2	19.8	100.0
35–39	34.9	19.6	13.5	6.1	14.6	22.7	100.0
40–44	13.8	24.7	17.1	30.4	10.5	22.1	100.0
45–49	27.3	19.3	7.4	8.3	9.2	30.4	100.0
50–54	9.5	19.5	28.1	0.0	13.9	22.2	—[b]
55–59	0.0	7.9	22.2	10.0	14.3	25.9	100.0
60+	40.0	13.8	27.9	18.2	20.5	38.9	—[b]
Total	28.2	17.8	15.5	17.8	15.8	24.9	100.0

[a]Mill sample.
[b]No people in the labor force available to separate.

than previously. The immediate post–World War I period was
characterized by a dramatic reduction of workers older than 50, reflecting the layoffs and firings of older workers who had been part
of the war effort. This period also saw an increase in the separation
of workers in their twenties and mid-forties, particularly immediately after the 1922 strike (Table 9.3).

During the 1920s, young workers and workers in their prime (less
than 44 years old) were less likely to leave than in the earlier periods. In the 1930s prior to the shutdown, the age group showing the
greatest tendency to leave was 60 and over. As the shutdown approached, young workers and those in their prime were less likely
to leave, whereas older workers were the most likely to do so, a
result of declining employment opportunities both inside and outside the Amoskeag. Basically, before 1922, young workers would
leave in search of better opportunities; during the twenties and early thirties, they were less willing to take the risk. At the same time,
older workers found themselves most vulnerable to layoffs as the
labor force was reduced.

The careers of most workers in the sample were relatively brief.
Almost half the individuals worked in the Amoskeag less than 10%

Table 9.4. *Percentage of time an individual worked of the total time he/she could have worked in the Amoskeag by sex*

Percentage of time worked	Male[a]		Female[a]		Total
	Percent	Number	Percent	Number	
0–9	49.1	(395)	40.1	(239)	45.3	(634)
10–19	17.3	(139)	20.1	(120)	18.5	(259)
20–29	5.2	(42)	8.2	(49)	6.5	(91)
30–39	4.4	(35)	5.0	(30)	4.6	(65)
40–49	1.6	(13)	2.2	(13)	1.9	(26)
50–59	7.1	(57)	5.4	(32)	6.4	(89)
60–69	3.1	(25)	3.4	(20)	3.2	(45)
70–79	1.6	(13)	1.3	(8)	1.5	(21)
80–89	3.6	(29)	5.7	(34)	4.5	(63)
90–99	4.5	(36)	8.6	(51)	6.2	(87)
100	2.5	(20)	0.0	(0)	1.4	(20)
Total	100.0	(804)	100.0	(596)	100.0	(1,400)

Note: Forty-four observations are missing.
[a]Mill sample.

Table 9.5. *Duration of work interruptions by sex (in percent)*

Duration of work interruptions	Male[a] (N = 804)	Female[a] (N = 596)	Total (N = 1,400)
Less than 1 year	71.1	66.3	69.1
1 year	7.1	9.9	8.3
2–5 years	12.2	13.7	12.8
6 or more years	9.7	10.1	9.8
Total	100.0	100.0	100.0

[a]Mill sample.

of their potential work lives (Table 9.4). Only a small number spent more than 80% of their potential work lives in the mill.[8] The typical career was short and punctuated by frequent interruptions. About two-thirds of the workers experienced uninterrupted careers, but most of this group were employed only once and did not return after their first separation.[9] Those who stayed or returned after their first hiring experienced numerous separations and rehirings, although some separations were initiated by the workers themselves in order to be transferred to a preferred department (Tables 9.5 and

Table 9.6. *Average length of work interruption*

Length of work interruption (in months)	For all individuals[a]		For all individuals with work interruptions of known length[a]	
	Number of workers[a]	Percentage	Number of workers	Percentage
0	970	67.2		
6 or less	142	9.8	142	32.9
7 to 12	135	9.3	135	31.3
13 to 18	47	3.3	47	10.9
19 to 24	42	2.9	42	9.7
24+	65	4.5	65	15.1
Unknown	43	3.0		
Total	1,444	100.0	431	100.0

[a]Mill sample.

9.6). Transfers are not counted as separations and rehirings except when they actually involved a formal separation and a return.

The reasons for leaving shed light on the career rhythms of workers and distinguish personal departures from those inspired by industrial conditions, that is, voluntary departures from compulsory ones. They allow an examination of the extent to which workers viewed the mill as a resource, a place where they could come and go, depending on their needs and preferences and on their success or failure with other job opportunities; and the extent to which the workers were at the mercy of the system. The reasons for final leaving must be viewed cautiously, because they were recorded by the overseer or the foremen rather than the workers themselves. However, the inclusion in the records of accounts of conflict between workers and overseers, complaints by workers about their bosses, and even severe criticisms of working conditions indicate that even if a worker's statement was not always recorded accurately, there was not too overt an attempt to censor it.

We have classified reasons for leaving into the following categories: authority conflict, rule violation, work performance, working conditions, career advancement, job mobility, involuntary conditions (death, illness, infirmity), family responsibilities, and structural conditions resulting from layoffs and shutdowns. Authority conflicts include dismissals resulting from violations of the boss's instructions: "argued with the boss," "refused to work," "doesn't like to be bossed," or "caused trouble in the workroom." Misunderstood instructions sometimes caused authority conflicts; others resulted when workers questioned the validity or fairness of an order. "Unfair" orders included those that slowed a worker down, such as an order to clean up the mess left behind by the evening shift, or an order to fill another worker's quota at the expense of one's own work.

Rule violations included smoking in the mill, drinking on the job, interfering with the routines of other workers, engaging in fights, and stealing cloth.

Inadequate work performance accounted for those who "produced bad yarn" or "poor cloth," who were too slow, who never properly learned to handle machinery, who were unable to adjust to the pace or unable or unwilling to conform to rigid time schedules, as well as those who "stayed out," who took long breaks, who arrived late or left early.

Working conditions included difficult conditions in the workplace and the workers' inability to carry out assignments. Workers complained about "too much noise," "too much dust," "not enough pay," faulty machinery, intolerable heat in the spinning and weave rooms, damaging chemicals, and backbreaking work in the yard. Some women were just too slightly built to handle looms or spinning frames or were unable to keep up with the machinery. Mary Dancause, for example, could not handle the spinning frame:

> I quit one day. About ten rollers had fallen on the floor, one here and one there. I was going crazy. I got my pay and I threw my apron into the garbage, I was so mad. I never went back again to spinning. I couldn't stand it any more [*Amoskeag*, p. 56].

Only a fine line separated those who left voluntarily because they could not stand the conditions and those who were dismissed because of poor work performance. Some workers, especially those who entered the mill as children, deliberately tried to get themselves fired. Richard Laroche, who could not tolerate the spinning room when he was sent there to work at age 14, started to smoke to get himself fired. Lucille Bourque tried to trick the boss into firing her:

> If I do enough bad work, they'll kick me out. I saw a man coming, and I figured he must be some big shot, so I got my scissors and made like I was cutting a skein of yarn. I saw him looking dazed. "Stop her! What is she doing?" I thought, oh boy! I'm going to get fired. I'm glad. But my boss showed the man some trucks loaded with yarn where the skeins were bad. After he left,

Table 9.7. *Reasons for final leaving*[a]

	Number	Percentage
Authority conflict	11	0.8
Rule violation	5	0.3
Work performance	258	17.9
Work relations	4	0.3
Work conditions	67	4.6
Career advancement	15	1.0
Job mobility	338	23.4
Family	28	1.9
Involuntary	75	5.2
Structural	337	23.3
Transfer	3	0.2
Unknown	303	21.0
Total	1,444	100.0

[a]Mill sample.

my boss said, "We cover for you, you cover for us" . . . We got a lot of bad skeins because they were dyed different colors . . . "Maybe there was too much dye," he said . . . "But don't ever do that . . . Don't ever do anything like that! Jesus!" [*Amoskeag*, p. 193].

Reasons for job mobility included: "looking for a better job," "leaving town to work somewhere else," "going to work in a shoe shop." Almost a third left for reasons that did not specifically entail occupational advancement: "going back to school," "going back to Canada," "wanted to change jobs in the mill (but was turned down)," "left without notice," "leaving town." Only a few people actually cited finding a better job elsewhere as their final reason for leaving. Of those who left involuntarily, a small number quit because of illness, old age, or feebleness. Some died. Very few, mostly women, left for family reasons.

Structural reasons included layoffs resulting from temporary or permanent work stoppages, and strikes.

Few workers left because of authority conflict and rule violation (Table 9.7). A larger proportion left because they could not tolerate the working conditions. A major portion of those who left voluntarily did so for reasons of job mobility. Of those who left involuntarily, structural reasons were the major cause.

Men and women differed somewhat in their reasons for final sep-

Table 9.8. *Reasons for final leaving by age at start of work* (*in percent*)

Reasons for final leaving	Age at start of work[a]				
	12–15 (N = 89)	16–25 (N = 614)	26–35 (N = 215)	36–45 (N = 133)	46–73 (N = 83)
Work related	16.9	32.2	31.6	30.8	27.7
Structural	48.3	31.1	39.5	39.8	43.4
Family	0.0	2.8	3.3	1.5	2.4
Job mobility	34.8	33.9	25.6	27.8	26.5
Total	100.0	100.0	100.0	100.0	100.0
Total number leaving = 1,134					

[a] Mill sample.

aration. It is not entirely surprising that men tended to leave more frequently because of working conditions, whereas women did so for family reasons. The typical pattern of Amoskeag women differed from that of other cotton-mill workers. *Lost Time and Labor Turnover in Cotton Mills* (U. S., Bureau of Labor, Women's Bureau, 1926) makes it clear that women textile workers in general tended to leave more frequently for reasons of illness than Amoskeag women. The Amoskeag women seem to have developed a strong identity as textile workers and were attached to their work as a trade. They left as often as men for mobility reasons but were less likely than men to leave because of difficult working conditions.

The age at which workers started and the reason for leaving were closely related. Workers who began when they were 12 to 15 years old were less likely to leave for work-related reasons and more likely to leave for structural or mobility reasons, whereas workers who started when they were 16 to 25 were the least likely to leave for structural reasons and the most likely to leave for work-related reasons.[10] The youngest starters were more likely to leave shortly after being hired, involuntarily or voluntarily: those who did not fit were laid off or fired, others quickly decided to search for other jobs, and still others came to the Amoskeag only to learn, planning in advance to move on.

The older the workers were when they started, the less likely they were to leave in search of career advancement. Among those starting at age 26 or older, structural reasons for leaving were more important than either work-related reasons or job mobility (Table 9.8). During curtailment in the 1920s, management dispensed with the

Table 9.9. *Reasons for final leaving by age at start of work and time period of start (in percent)*

Reasons for final leaving[a]	Time period of start of work		
	1912–21	1922–30	1931–36
Aged 12–15 at start	(N = 69)	(N = 16)	(N = 3)
Work related	15.9	18.8	0.0
Structural	42.0	68.8	100.0
Family	0.0	0.0	0.0
Job mobility	42.0	12.5	0.0
Total	100.0	100.0	100.0
Aged 16–25 at start	(N = 384)	(N = 160)	(N = 69)
Work related	38.5	25.0	14.5
Structural	20.3	36.9	76.8
Family	3.1	3.1	0.0
Job mobility	38.0	35.0	8.7
Total	100.0	100.0	100.0
Aged 26–35 at start	(N = 150)	(N = 44)	(N = 20)
Work related	38.0	22.7	5.0
Structural	32.0	54.5	60.0
Family	4.0	0.0	5.0
Job mobility	26.0	22.7	30.0
Total	100.0	100.0	100.0
Aged 36–45 at start	(N = 84)	(N = 27)	(N = 20)
Work related	29.8	37.0	25.0
Structural	33.3	40.7	65.0
Family	1.2	3.7	0.0
Job mobility	35.7	18.5	10.0
Total	100.0	100.0	100.0
Aged 46–73 at start	(N = 56)	(N = 14)	(N = 13)
Work related	26.8	14.3	46.2
Structural	35.7	71.4	46.2
Family	3.6	0.0	0.0
Job mobility	33.9	14.3	7.7
Total	100.0	100.0	100.0

[a]Mill sample.

very young (Table 9.9) and the very old and held on to workers in their prime despite Agent Straw's repeated assertions that performance and suitability for the job took precedence over age in all matters of rehiring or layoffs (Chapter 11).

The historical changes affecting the corporation were equally sig-

Table 9.10. *Reasons for final leaving by first year employed (in percent)*

Reasons for final leaving[a]	First year employed		
	1912–21 (N = 745)	1922–30 (N = 262)	1931–36 (N = 125)
Work related	34.4	24.8	17.6
Structural	27.5	44.3	69.6
Family	2.8	2.3	0.8
Job mobility	35.3	28.6	12.0
Total	100.0	100.0	100.0

[a]Mill sample.

nificant in determining the reasons for separation. The proportion of people leaving for reasons of job mobility declined over time for each age cohort. As the shutdown approached, the group most likely to leave for job mobility reasons became steadily older (Table 9.9). Significantly, the trend toward separation for compulsory reasons increased in the last decade of the Amoskeag's existence. From the post–World War I period to the shutdown, workers left increasingly for structural reasons, namely, firings or layoffs, rather than voluntarily (Table 9.10). The opportunity structure was narrowing around them and their chances to exercise choice dwindled with it.

A comparison of the workers' reasons for final leaving fails to reveal any pattern consistent with the reasons offered for earlier separations. Of those workers whose final as well as earlier reasons are known, only a few gave final reasons that were consistent with some of the intervening reasons, and in more than three out of four cases none of the earlier reasons were consistent with the final one.[11] A discrepancy between the final reason and reasons affecting periodic separations is expected. Of all the categories, job mobility, structural pressures, and work performance were the most frequently cited, though the majority of workers rarely gave the same reason more than once, especially those who quit several times.

Determinants of career continuity

In the historical context of the textile mill, few workers actually experienced "permanence" as it is defined today – namely, staying with the same employer for an extended period. Production cycles and personnel policies affected even stable workers, and even long-term workers left temporarily, either in search of a better job or for personal and family reasons. Many such interruptions were brief, either because the worker failed to find a better job or because the personal or family problem was resolved. The frequency with which "repeaters" returned indicates both their dependency on the mill as the city's major employer and their use of the mill as a resource. Some workers who came and left voluntarily viewed the Amoskeag as a kind of home base: They left in search of better opportunities, knowing that they would be readmitted if and when they decided to return. Those who worked during the twenties and thirties did not enjoy that flexibility. Once they quit their jobs in the Amoskeag, it was quite unlikely they would be readmitted. Workers rarely left voluntarily during this period, and the cases of those employed more than once were very few.

To examine career rhythms as they changed over time, the workers in the sample were classified into four career types: temporaries, fluctuators, repeaters, and persisters. *Temporaries* worked for one year or less and were employed only once; *fluctuators* worked for one year or less but were employed more than once during this time period; *repeaters* worked longer than one year and during that time were employed more than once; and *persisters* worked more than one year without career interruptions (Table 9.11).

These typologies are based on both the length of time a person worked in the mill and the number of career interruptions experienced. Because career interruptions were part of the organization of work itself, the length of a worker's employment did not necessarily mean greater career stability. Thus, in this setting, career continuity does not mean an absence of interruptions. The longer a career, the more likely it was to be punctuated by interruptions.

The temporaries and fluctuators, the most transient groups in the work force, encompassed 60% of the sample, with the repeaters and the persisters making up the remaining 40%.

Temporaries included floaters who left the Amoskeag after their first encounter. This group includes workers who could not stand textile work after their first try, those who were dismissed because they did not fit, and those who came to work temporarily to earn a specific amount of money or to help out a family member. Raymond Dubois exemplifies one kind of temporary. The son of millworkers who had migrated to Manchester when hard times hit Lowell in 1926, Raymond left school to become a winder. But he did not like the job – each workday was like being "in jail for eight

Table 9.11. *Career typology by number of years worked and number of times employed*

Number of years worked	Number of times employed[a]			
	1	2–5	6–9	10 or more
0–1	571 T	276 F	11 F	1 F
	(39.9%)	(19.3%)	(0.8%)	(0.08%)
2–5	74 P	191 R	60 R	18 R
	(5.2%)	(13.3%)	(4.2%)	(1.2%)
6–9	14 P	48 R	20 R	25 R
	(1.0%)	(3.3%)	(1.4%)	(1.7%)
10 or more	8 P	40 R	45 R	30 R
	(0.5%)	(2.8%)	(3.1%)	(2.0%)

Note: T = temporaries, F = fluctuators, R = repeaters, P = persisters. The labor force was divided into those who worked less than one year and more than one year in order to retain a larger sample size. To ascertain the reliability of lumping those who worked two years with those who worked ten, all the variables in the following tables were cross tabulated with a more detailed breakdown of number of years worked: 0–1, 2–5, 6–9, and 10 or more. Correlations similar to the compressed categories and on the same level of significance were derived. One year or less was definitely the break-off point.
[a]Mill sample. $N = 1,432$.

hours, and you knew there was just no escaping" (*Amoskeag*, p. 153). He left the mill for another job as soon as he could.

Fluctuators, who worked one year or less but were employed more than once, included those who "tried again and again" within a short span of time, those who went back and forth from the Amoskeag to other jobs, at times working in other towns, and those who were fired or left voluntarily after failing to adjust in several departments.

Marie Anne Senechal recalled her father's work history, which provides a good example of a fluctuator:

My father got fired once . . . He made a mistake in the cloth, and [he] said to the boss, "the hell with you," and walked out on him. The next day the boss said to me, "Tell your father to come back in" . . . My father would go away to cut wood. Then he'd come back and work in the mills. When they'd send for him, I'd write to him and tell him . . . "Be down for Monday" . . . They would tell [him at the mill,] "If you want to work when we need you, we'll send somebody for you" . . . But he couldn't earn his own bread" [*Amoskeag*, pp. 277–8].

Repeaters worked longer than one year and were employed more than once. Some workers were repeaters throughout their entire work lives in the Amoskeag. Repeaters viewed their jobs as permanent, even though interruptions, voluntary or involuntary were common. Women who left periodically for childbirth are included in this group.

Ora Pelletier's career demonstrates a repeater pattern. She began working during summer vacations when she was 15. At 16, she left school for a steady job as a spinner. She discovered, however, that spinning was not to her liking:

> I really hated spinning because you have to run around so much . . . When I had a hard time, I'd just sit there and cry . . . I decided that there were enough other kinds of jobs in the mill that you didn't have to do one that you didn't like. You could leave a job in the morning and have another one in the afternoon [*Amoskeag*, p. 186].

Ora went on to successive jobs as a doffer and a warper. When she first began as a warper, she found she was being paid less than the others. She told her boss, "When you can pay me the price you're paying them, then I'll come back." That afternoon she was rehired at the standard wage. Ultimately she grew sick of the mills and "quit the Amoskeag dungeon" to work in a shoe shop, "but I couldn't take it on account of the cement glue and the ether . . . I liked working in the mill better, so I went back to the Amoskeag as a warper" (*Amoskeag*, pp. 187–9). Ora worked at the Amoskeag until it closed.

Repeaters were individuals whose work lives were interrupted either by the Amoskeag's production schedules or by their own decisions to use the mill as a resource while experimenting with other jobs or rearing children. The repeaters also included part of the Amoskeag's reserve labor force. Because of the cyclical pattern of production, the Amoskeag, like many other textile mills, kept a "spare" labor force on the employee list.[12] The names of these workers were kept on the payroll, and they were called in when needed. On the average, the Amoskeag called in 85% of these workers, and during periods of high production, the proportion reached 95%.

The persisters were the "old reliables," although repeaters also carried on a continuing relationship with the Amoskeag. Beginning in 1915, an "old reliable," John Jacobson, the son of Swedish immigrants, worked as a runner boy (errand boy) for a couple of years. In the process he skipped several rungs on the ladder by apprenticing directly to become a loomfixer. He held that job for about five years and was then promoted to second hand, a position he occupied (although he was transferred) for three years. He was promoted a year later to overseer of weaving and after three years he finally became assistant superintendent of weaving. Although not all persisters rose quite as rapidly as Jacobson, many persisted nonetheless for far lesser rewards.

During periods of depressed activity, 15% to 25% of the labor force was on reserve. To employ a certain weekly average of textile workers over a given year, therefore, the Amoskeag had to employ as many as twice that number, which partly explains why slightly more than half the workers in the sample worked for less than one year. To cope with immediate need, "spare workers" were sometimes actually present in a workroom; most of the time, however, they were called in.

Even though their work was not constant, the reserve labor force experienced the same continuity in its long-term relations with the corporation as did the permanent labor force. Repeaters Yvonne Dionne and Emelia Carignan were members of the reserve labor force. Yvonne's work career was erratic, punctuated by curtailments in the 1920s and 1930s. She used the shoe shop as a backup resource: "If the mill was slack, I'd go to the shoe shop. I always had a job waiting for me there" (*Amoskeag*, p. 199). Emelia's work career was influenced by a personal situation: "I didn't work for many years, but from time to time, when I had a small chance I'd work because the times were hard. Amoskeag would stop two or three days, two or three weeks without working. Often it was at night. When we had children it was at night that I'd go to work, and I finished the year that my son was born" (interview).

Several different career types can be found in the same family. The Anger siblings provide such an example. Florida Anger was involved with the Amoskeag for eighteen years, during which time she held thirty-five jobs and worked a total of fourteen years. Continuous from 1917 to 1924, her career was limited thereafter by industrial curtailment and childbearing. Her brother Henry started working in the mills at age 14 and learned a variety of jobs over the next five years. He worked elsewhere for the next twelve years but returned in 1933 and worked for six months until the mill closed. Leo, another brother, quickly learned that the mills "were not for him." A temporary, he worked there for only a week.

Table 9.12. *Career typology by reason for leaving and sex (in percent)*

Reason for final leaving	Temporaries	Fluctuators[b]	Repeaters[b]	Persisters
Male[a]	(N = 273)	(N = 424)	(N = 919)	(N = 38)
Work related	40.7	50.7	32.8	13.2
Structural	19.8	18.2	34.4	50.0
Family	0.7	0.0	0.4	0.0
Job mobility	38.8	31.1	32.4	36.8
Total	100.0	100.0	100.0	100.0
Female[a]	(N = 152)	(N = 174)	(N = 966)	(N = 43)
Work related	42.1	40.2	29.7	4.7
Structural	22.4	21.3	35.1	55.8
Family	5.3	6.3	7.6	7.0
Job mobility	30.3	32.2	27.6	32.6
Total	100.0	100.0	100.0	100.0

[a] Mill sample.
[b] Note that fluctuators and repeaters normally have a reason cited for each instance of leaving, so that the totals of the reasons for leaving in the table are higher than the total number of workers.

Within each career typology there were significant differences between men and women. Male temporaries, fluctuators, and persisters were more likely to leave for job mobility reasons than women in the same categories. Male fluctuators and persisters were likely to leave for work-related reasons. Women in all categories were much more likely to leave for family reasons and to some extent for structural reasons. Once again, this suggests the greater propensity of women to tolerate more difficult working conditions and lesser opportunities for advancement and to cling to their mill jobs until they had to leave because of family obligations or layoffs, whereas men were more likely to leave in search of better working conditions and opportunities for advancement (Table 9.12).

A persistent pattern that emerges from this analysis is that women had more continuous careers in the mill than did men. Women were more often repeaters or persisters, whereas men tended to be temporaries or fluctuators (Table 9.13). Both single men and single women had less continuous careers than did married men and women. Single workers were more likely than married workers to be temporaries, and married women, who are usually assumed to have had unstable careers, actually tended to be repeaters much

Table 9.13. *Career typology by sex (in percent)*

Typology	Male[a] (N = 829)	Female[a] (N = 609)
Temporaries	42.5	36.3
Fluctuators	23.9	14.9
Repeaters	28.2	40.3
Persisters	5.4	8.5
Total	100.0	100.0

[a]Mill sample.

Table 9.14. *Career typology by marital status at end of work and sex (in percent)*

	Marital status at end of work	
Typology	Single	Married
Male[a]	(N = 316)	(N = 297)
Temporaries	44.6	32.0
Fluctuators	27.5	22.9
Repeaters	23.4	40.1
Persisters	4.4	5.1
Total	100.0	100.0
Female[a]	(N = 219)	(N = 242)
Temporaries	41.6	27.3
Fluctuators	15.5	14.9
Repeaters	32.4	50.4
Persisters	10.5	7.4
Total	100.0	100.0

[a]Mill sample.

more than either married men or single men and women. Both single and married women were more frequently persisters than were men (Table 9.14).

There are several possible explanations for these behaviors. Married women may have experienced greater career continuity because they had already achieved a certain level of skill in their jobs before marriage. Such women often viewed their work in the mill as their life's career. They continued working to maintain the status they had achieved. As Chapter 8 suggests, a wife's income was in many cases also needed in order to balance the family budget. Within the culture of work that developed in the mill, working married women were not looked down upon because so many women had to do it at some point in their lives. Although childbearing imposed strains on a woman's ability to work and caused interruptions in her career, even women with infants continued to work. The availability of support networks among extended kin and in the neighborhood made child care for working mothers possible (see Chapter 8). In addition, married women exhibited greater career continuity because family responsibilities rendered them less mobile, and therefore less able to search for jobs in other communities, than single men and women. But married women also continued to work because they formed attachments to their jobs and enjoyed the sociability at the workplace.

The greater career continuity among married women should not be misconstrued as meaning that women experienced more intensive employment than did men. Creamer and Coulter (1939) found that after 1923 a greater percentage of married women than single women experienced twenty-seven or more weeks of unemployment. The difference between single and married men was not as striking. These findings of Creamer and Coulter for the later years of the Amoskeag provide some insight into what being a repeater meant; the fact that married women in the sample tended to be repeaters does not suggest that they were steadily employed for a major portion of the year. The employment of repeaters varied considerably; for married women it involved shorter periods of employment and greater gaps than it did for single women, which results in the greater tendency of married women, as compared to single women or men, to form part of the reserve labor force.

The age at which workers started also had a significant impact on career continuity, especially for those starting very young and those starting in the middle or later years. Those who started very young or very old were most likely to persist in the mill. Of those starting work between ages 10 and 14, 40% worked five years or longer. This pattern is emphasized by the fact that for those who worked ten years or more, the highest proportion had started at ages 10 to

Table 9.15. *Number of years worked by age at start of work (in percent)*

Number of years worked[a]	Age at start of work				
	10–14 ($N = 61$)	15–19 ($N = 432$)	20–24 ($N = 341$)	25–29 ($N = 167$)	30–34 ($N = 120$)
0–1	39.3	50.5	70.7	65.9	61.7
2–5	29.5	31.9	20.8	19.8	17.5
6–9	11.5	10.9	2.1	4.8	8.3
10+	19.7	6.7	6.5	9.6	12.5
Total	100.0	100.0	100.0	100.0	100.0

[a] Mill sample.

14 (Table 9.15). Boys and girls between ages 12 and 15 were least likely to be temporaries and most likely to be repeaters. Among these teen-agers, more than half the males and almost three-quarters of the females tended to be repeaters. In these younger age groups, women had significantly more continuous careers than men. The differences among those starting in the later years of life were less pronounced (Table 9.16).

Teen-agers (12–15 years old) were more likely to develop long careers, especially young women. Young men were more prone to alternate mill work with other jobs in the city or to juggle two jobs simultaneously. Thus, even though young men starting in their teens had greater career continuity than those starting in their twenties and thirties, they too tried to experiment with jobs outside the mill.

Slichter's (1919) analysis of turnover in different industries contends that young starters, especially boys, were typically more mobile than other workers. In addition to their actual search for other jobs, they were also more restless and felt less of a sense of urgency to embark on semi-permanent careers. Many interviewees recalled similar feelings. Nevertheless, Amoskeag teen-agers demonstrated greater career continuity than those in the national sample. This was so not only because fewer alternative employment opportunities were available to them but because their work was governed by a strong sense of family and community discipline. A boy who had reached the age of 14 without working was considered an exception (see Chapter 8).

Table 9.15. *(cont.)*

		Age at start of work			
35–39 (N = 102)	40–44 (N = 79)	45–49 (N = 51)	50–54 (N = 34)	55–59 (N = 20)	60+ (N = 22)
71.6	57.0	62.7	55.9	40.0	63.6
12.7	21.5	23.5	20.6	55.0	4.5
5.9	5.1	7.8	17.6	5.0	31.8
9.8	16.5	5.9	5.9	0.0	0.0
100.0	100.0	100.0	100.0	100.0	100.0

Table 9.16. *Career typology by sex and age at start of work (in percent)*

	Age at start of work				
Typology	12–15	16–25	26–35	36–45	46–73
Males[a]	(N = 61)	(N = 425)	(N = 149)	(N = 109)	(N = 83)
Temporaries	19.7	43.5	45.0	53.2	34.9
Fluctuators	24.6	25.9	23.5	17.4	22.9
Repeaters	54.1	25.9	26.8	21.1	32.5
Persisters	1.6	4.7	4.7	8.3	9.6
Total	100.0	100.0	100.0	100.0	100.0
Females[a]	(N = 47)	(N = 351)	(N = 120)	(N = 60)	(N = 24)
Temporaries	10.6	38.5	37.5	41.7	37.5
Fluctuators	14.9	12.8	22.5	15.0	8.3
Repeaters	72.3	39.9	30.8	38.3	33.3
Persisters	2.1	8.8	9.2	5.0	20.8
Total	100.0	100.0	100.0	100.0	100.0

[a]Mill sample.

Slichter also found that young boys and girls demonstrated greater stability in communities where a mill was the exclusive employer. Although this generalization holds true primarily for southern mill villages, it is also partly true for Manchester, because of the Amoskeag's domination of the city's economy. However, those who were unable or unwilling to adapt to work in the Amoskeag sought other employment in the city, as well as in neighboring New England communities.

More than any other age group, those who started employment between age 15 and their mid-twenties used the mill as a launching pad or as a temporary backup that would allow them to search for alternative jobs. As these young workers (fluctuators) explored their opportunities inside and outside the mill, the bosses sorted through labor pools of young novices to determine, from their initial training period, their potential as steady workers. Young starters tended to be repeaters unless they left voluntarily – or were weeded out by management.

Like the very young workers, those starting in their mid-forties or later also demonstrated career continuity (Table 9.16). For men and particularly women in this age range, the older they were when they started, the more likely they were to have fairly continuous careers. This group included women who returned to work after the completion of childrearing and men and women who entered textile work after employment in other jobs.

The mill was the final working place for older men and women. Some of these late starters were, in fact, newly arrived immigrants from Quebec, Poland, and Greece and native-born workers from neighboring New England communities. Some may have also been returning home to Manchester after having migrated to other communities during their twenties and thirties. By the time they found a place in the Amoskeag, they were generally weary of job experimentation, and unless they were laid off or fired, they tended to stick to their jobs.

Those who started work in the Amoskeag in the intervening age group (16–45) were more likely to have temporary careers, although women were more likely than men to be repeaters. This age group experienced the most varied and checkered careers. Once again, the reasons given for the final separation shed some light on these patterns. Those starting work between ages 26 and 45 were less likely to leave for reasons of career mobility than were younger starters and more likely to leave because of working conditions. Men in this group often alternated mill work with other jobs in the city. To avoid the confinement of the mill, they worked outdoors on construction or road work and returned to the mill at the end of the season, as long as the Amoskeag was flexible enough to permit such a pattern.

Women during these years had more disrupted careers because of childbearing and childrearing. Thus, among the reasons for final

Table 9.17. *Career typology of French Canadians by presence of other relatives working in the mill (in percent)*[a]

Typology	No relatives (N = 400)	Relatives not coinciding (N = 23)	Relatives coinciding (N = 156)
Temporaries	40.8	39.1	12.8
Fluctuators	23.3	17.4	16.7
Repeaters	30.8	30.4	63.5
Persisters	5.3	13.0	7.1

[a]Mill sample.

separations cited by women, family reasons ranked higher for this age group than for any other age group. However, women depended more consistently on the mill throughout their work lives, which may have been a conscious family strategy. Whereas brothers, sons, and husbands were encouraged to search for better and higher paying jobs, sisters, daughters, and wives were expected to keep the family budget on an even keel by working in the mill. However, women's greater career stability in the "good" years of the Amoskeag's history did not work to their advantage in the declining years before the shutdown. Once the mill was in its final throes, women's careers became as precarious as those of men, and often even more so.

The presence of kin in the mill was another important factor in career continuity (see Chapter 5).[13] French-Canadian workers who had kin in the mill tended to start work at a younger age and experienced greater career continuity than those without kin. Even when their kin no longer worked in the Amoskeag, they still had a better chance of getting a job, especially a preferred place. The impact of kin was particularly evident in the difference between repeaters and temporaries. Although women generally showed greater career continuity than men, the presence or absence of kin was an even more powerful determinant than sex (Table 9.17), because the support that relatives offered in the mill enabled workers to find more desirable jobs and adjust better to them. Most important, the more kin present in the mill, the greater a family's investment in staying there.

The relationship between career continuity and initial or final level of skill is less clear. For both men and women, no linear relationship between job at start and career continuity seems to exist,

Table 9.18. *Career typology by level of skill at end of work and sex (in percent)*

Typology	Level of skill at end of work			
	White collar	Skilled	Semiskilled	Unskilled
Males[a]	(N = 14)	(N = 190)	(N = 235)	(N = 376)
Temporaries	28.6	43.2	40.0	43.6
Fluctuators	21.4	23.7	21.7	25.8
Repeaters	35.7	28.9	32.3	25.8
Persisters	14.3	4.2	6.0	4.8
Total	100.0	100.0	100.0	100.0
Females[a]	(N = 29)	(N = 158)	(N = 305)	(N = 99)
Temporaries	37.9	27.8	39.7	39.8
Fluctuators	17.2	13.9	14.8	15.3
Repeaters	17.2	48.1	40.7	35.7
Persisters	27.6	10.1	4.9	9.2
Total	100.0	100.0	100.0	100.0

[a] Mill sample.

with the exception of white-collar employees.[14] This is particularly true for men. On the other hand, women who started in skilled or semiskilled occupations had fewer career interruptions than did men. Career continuity for women was related to the level of skill attained by the end of their work lives, whereas final occupation did not have a strong relationship to career continuity among men. Women who ended their careers in skilled jobs more often tended to be repeaters (Table 9.18). This is puzzling in view of the fact that the majority of women were employed in semiskilled jobs, the most numerous job category in the mill. It is possible that women tended to end up in skilled jobs because they were repeaters. Being a repeater may have eventually rewarded women with higher skilled jobs.

These findings also contradict the assertion of labor-turnover analyses in the first two decades of the twentieth century, which claimed that skilled workers experienced greater career continuity than the unskilled. An analysis of occupational mobility patterns (upward and downward mobility between first and last jobs) showed no correlation between career continuity and occupational advancement (Chapter 10). However, because the status and skill hierarchy in the textile industry was not as clearly defined as in

Table 9.19. *Career typology by ethnicity and sex (in percent)*

	Ethnicity[a]				
Typology	United States	French Canada	British Isles	Poland/ E. Europe	Greece
Male and female	(N = 194)	(N = 579)	(N = 159)	(N = 174)	(N = 179)
Temporaries	47.9	33.2	40.3	44.3	45.8
Fluctuators	20.1	21.2	22.0	10.9	24.6
Repeaters	20.1	39.6	33.3	37.4	24.0
Persisters	11.9	6.0	4.4	7.5	5.6
Total	100.0	100.0	100.0	100.0	100.0
Males	(N = 115)	(N = 295)	(N = 93)	(N = 91)	(N = 132)
Temporaries	49.6	35.6	39.8	51.6	46.2
Fluctuators	23.5	24.7	25.8	12.1	29.5
Repeaters	19.1	34.2	31.2	29.7	18.9
Persisters	7.8	5.4	3.2	6.6	5.3
Total	100.0	100.0	100.0	100.0	100.0
Females	(N = 79)	(N = 284)	(N = 66)	(N = 83)	(N = 47)
Temporaries	45.6	30.6	40.9	36.1	44.7
Fluctuators	15.2	17.6	16.7	9.6	10.6
Repeaters	21.5	45.1	36.4	45.8	38.3
Persisters	17.7	6.7	6.1	8.4	6.4
Total	100.0	100.0	100.0	100.0	100.0

[a]Mill sample.

other industries, it is possible that level of skill is not as good a measure as the type of job in which a person was employed. Labor analysts at that time found that spinning rooms tended to have the highest turnover, weave rooms less, and burling rooms the least. It is possible, therefore, that the quality of a job (in terms of the actual work process involved) was more significant in determining career stability than occupational status.

Ethnicity, on the other hand, was closely correlated with career continuity. Polish and French-Canadian workers were the most likely to be repeaters – French-Canadian men more than men in any other ethnic group and French-Canadian women even more than French-Canadian men (Table 9.19). Polish women tended to be re-peaters as much as French-Canadian women.

These patterns confirm the Amoskeag's own conclusion that French Canadians could provide a promising continuous labor force, as is evident by management's conscious systematic recruitment of them in 1900. As early as 1885, as other companies decried the transient nature of French-Canadian workers, the Amoskeag defended them as the base of the industry. Polish workers also tended to be reliable as repeaters and persisters, especially the women. Although they arrived later than the French Canadians, their immigration to Manchester was with the specific intention of working in the Amoskeag, and they tended to stay there.

The greater propensity of both French-Canadian and Polish women toward career continuity reflects their premigration traditions, which viewed the entire family as a work unit, with all family members, including women and children, expected to make a continuing contribution to the family economy. Among both these ethnic groups, as well as the Greeks, women contributed to keeping the family income stable by working in the mills. The Greek situation, however, was considerably different from that of the French-Canadian and Polish workers. As the most recent arrivals, Greek men encountered difficulties primarily because of ethnic discrimination and because they had fewer kin support networks. They generally solved this dilemma by working in shoe shops and service industries. Nor did many Greek women persist in the mill, although they did have a greater tendency than Greek men to be repeaters.

Clerical jobs were most often performed by native-born and second- or third-generation Irish and English women. Native-born women had the highest rate of job permanence, a reflection of their concentration in the clerical category. Most of these women were "persisters" in the sense that they worked there uninterruptedly, until they found a better job or a husband. On the other hand, unless they were in managerial, clerical, or highly specialized positions, native-born men worked in the Amoskeag only temporarily until they found other jobs; they rarely returned. Overseers and second hands, most of whom were native-born, were the most permanent.

Most striking in this analysis of ethnic and sex differences is the consistent tendency of women to experience greater career continuity than men, regardless of ethnic group. Within each ethnic group, women were more likely than men to be repeaters and persisters.

Industrial time, namely, the historical events relating to the structure and the organization of the corporation itself, affected career continuity more than any other factor, particularly during the period of the Amoskeag's decline. The year during which a person began work had an impact on career continuity. With the exception of

Table 9.20. *Career typology by year first employed and sex (in percent)*

Typology	Year first employed		
	1912–21	1922–30	1931–36
Males[a]	(N = 559)	(N = 179)	(N = 88)
Temporaries	40.1	44.7	53.4
Fluctuators	24.0	22.3	26.1
Repeaters	30.4	29.1	12.5
Persisters	5.5	3.9	8.0
Total	100.0	100.0	100.0
Females[a]	(N = 404)	(N = 148)	(N = 48)
Temporaries	32.2	43.2	52.1
Fluctuators	15.3	14.9	12.5
Repeaters	45.2	31.1	18.8
Persisters	6.7	10.8	16.7
Total	100.0	100.0	100.0

[a]Mill sample.

those who started work in their early teens, those workers who were first employed in the later history of the mill were more likely to be employed only once and for a brief period. During the final period of the Amoskeag's existence, the proportion of fluctuators and repeaters declined, and the proportion of temporaries and persisters increased, although the persisters worked for only brief periods. Few workers first hired during this period even thought of leaving. With the job opportunities in the Amoskeag shrinking rapidly, this was not a time to experiment with career mobility. Most workers who did leave were fired or laid off, and the chances of reemployment were quite slim (Tables 9.20 and 9.21). The career patterns of men and women differed little, and women, who had shown greater career continuity than men in earlier periods, were now even more vulnerable than men to layoffs and dismissals. Although the mill's decline affected all age groups, the impact was greater on the career continuity of older workers (Table 9.21).

Careers thus varied in accordance with sex, marital status, ethnicity, type of job, the structural organization of work in the mill, and the years workers were first employed. For many Amoskeag workers, as well as for textile workers in general, labor turnover represented the reluctance of people from rural backgrounds to con-

Table 9.21. *Career typology by age at start and period of work commencement (in percent)*

	Period of work commencement		
Typology[a]	1912–21	1922–30	1931–36
Age 12–15	(N = 85)	(N = 19)	(N = 3)
Temporaries	14.1	26.3	0.0
Fluctuators	23.5	5.3	33.3
Repeaters	61.2	63.2	66.7
Persisters	1.2	5.3	0.0
Total	100.0	100.0	100.0
Age 16–25	(N = 501)	(N = 199)	(N = 74)
Temporaries	39.7	41.7	50.0
Fluctuators	20.6	19.6	17.6
Repeaters	34.5	32.2	16.2
Persisters	5.2	6.5	16.2
Total	100.0	100.0	100.0
Age 26–35	(N = 189)	(N = 56)	(N = 22)
Temporaries	39.7	48.2	45.5
Fluctuators	21.2	23.2	36.4
Repeaters	34.4	16.1	9.1
Persisters	4.8	12.5	9.1
Total	100.0	100.0	100.0
Age 36–45	(N = 111)	(N = 34)	(N = 23)
Temporaries	41.4	64.7	65.2
Fluctuators	15.3	20.6	17.4
Repeaters	33.3	14.7	13.0
Persisters	9.9	0.0	4.3
Total	100.0	100.0	100.0
Age 46–73	(N = 75)	(N = 18)	(N = 14)
Temporaries	29.3	33.3	71.4
Fluctuators	21.3	11.1	21.4
Repeaters	34.7	44.4	7.1
Persisters	14.7	11.1	0.0
Total	100.0	100.0	100.0

[a]Mill sample.

form to industrial schedules, especially their tendency to move in and out of factories during harvest, hunting, and fishing seasons. This was possible, of course, only during periods of labor shortages. A whole series of subjective issues that cannot be measured properly might have played a role: an inability to adjust to industrial work; a chronic restlessness, which one person expressed as "I just move to move"; and a whole variety of personal problems. How so many varied individual attributes, preferences, and problems interacted with external factors to create the career patterns that have been observed cannot be fully analyzed. That the decisions that may be reflected in these careers were not strictly individual but part of a larger configuration of several work careers within a family unit, each with its own fluctuations and variations, further complicates the situation. How individuals synchronized their entry into and exit from the labor force with those of other family members in the context of common family needs involved a good deal of collective planning. Families planned their resources and their labor-force strategies in relation to childbearing, children's entry into the labor force, and future support in old age.

Career patterns were affected by the season of the year, business cycles, production policies, management's arbitrary decisions regarding personal conflicts, as well as an individual's own satisfaction or dissatisfaction with the workplace. In planning their careers, workers were constantly challenged by changing conditions in the workplace and the labor market. Although their careers may seem disorderly, they nevertheless reflect a life plan, if only a modest one, and its fulfillment or its frustration and revision in the face of new conditions.

Some erratic careers were chosen; others were the product of external factors, such as the vagaries of the factory and the market, particularly in the later history of the Amoskeag when career interruptions or final separations were initiated by the corporation rather than by individuals.

The decline in opportunity and flexibility in the Amoskeag affected both those who preferred continuous careers and those who had previously enjoyed the freedom to interrupt their careers. Those who had been attracted to the Amoskeag because of the promise of stable employment faced a sudden sharp increase in job insecurity; those who preferred textile work because of its flexibility were trapped in a pattern of intermittent employment. Thus, the fluctuating and transient careers of many workers in this study were responses to, rather than merely consequences of, the fluctuation and insecurity of the labor market.

Workers felt integrated into the Amoskeag, despite their brief and intermittent careers, which in most cases represented only a segment of their work lives. Such transiency, however, was typical not only of large portions of the working population in that period but also of an entire society in motion. In their analysis of population turnover in the United States in the late nineteenth century, Stephan Thernstrom and Peter Knights (1971) raised the central question: If the population was constantly on the move, what provided American society with continuity and cohesion? In the case of Amoskeag workers, continuity was provided by the factory as an institution. Even interviewees who had worked only briefly in the Amoskeag expressed a deep sense of place and identification with the "old Amoskeag," and those who had bitter and angry memories still viewed their Amoskeag careers as occupying an important place in their work lives. The all-encompassing character of the Amoskeag enveloped their lives. Workers had a sense that, for better or worse, they would always be part of it. They were associated with the Amoskeag as children, even before they were old enough to work; they were still associated with it in old age, after they were too old to work. In addition to their ties to the Amoskeag, their sense of continuity was fortified by the work ethic and the ethnic and kinship networks that extended beyond the factory walls and the nearby neighborhood to encompass the entire industrial region of New England.

10 Career advancement

Historical studies of occupational mobility over the past two decades have graphically illustrated the distance between the promise of mobility and the narrowness of the opportunity structure in American cities in the nineteenth and early twentieth centuries. Stephan Thernstrom's study of nineteenth-century Newburyport, Massachusetts, concluded that "relatively few of these laborers or their children enacted the success story envisioned by their contemporary Horatio Alger, though many made small social gains that must have been significant to them – moving a notch or two upward within the working class" (1964:4). Thernstrom's subsequent study of social mobility in late-nineteenth- and twentieth-century Boston revealed that "about a quarter of all the men who first entered the labor market as manual workers ended their careers in a middle-class calling; approximately 1 in 6 of those who first worked in a white-collar job later skidded to a blue-collar post" (1973:232–3).

Although Thernstrom's and other historical mobility studies have analyzed citywide occupational structures, the study of the Amoskeag affords the rare opportunity of exploring in depth the patterns of advancement within one industrial establishment.[1] Because the context of the occupations and their meaning within the framework of one establishment is known, the determinants of career advancement can be examined – how it was achieved in certain cases and why it failed in others. In this analysis of occupational mobility it would be impossible to avoid the problem of the existing studies, namely, the definition and imposition of categories for mobility. However, because some contextual information is available, categories of career advancement in relation to the perceptions of both the workers and management can be formulated.

Most mobility studies measure people's movement vertically, up and down the occupational structure. Although vertical mobility existed to some extent within the Amoskeag, the pervasive pattern was horizontal – the movement within each rough category of skill among a large number of interchangeable jobs differed from that of the larger society.[2] In a textile mill, a worker could move around

259

among different jobs and still remain within the same status ranking. This was especially true in the Amoskeag, because of its enormous size and versatility.

Thus, textile mills in general, and the Amoskeag in particular,
afforded workers the opportunity for a great variety of internal job
changes. Many new jobs did not necessarily involve a move up or
down, but rather a change in the nature of the job and the surrounding work relationships. Still, some job changes actually involved advancement. Cameron Stewart, who escaped to college after a brief stint in the Amoskeag, observed: "Some people worked
themselves up into the overseer and second-hand positions. But
they were so few in relation to the total number working in the mill
that there really was very little opportunity" (Amoskeag, p. 313).

The sharpest distinction in the Amoskeag's occupational structure was between the managerial and blue-collar levels. At the top
of the ladder were the superintendents and below them were the
overseers. Within the blue-collar category the differences in status
and pay of various jobs were smaller. The second hands, at the top
of the blue-collar jobs, had blue-collar status, although their responsibilities were supervisory. Below this small managerial crust,
jobs fell within the skilled, semiskilled, and unskilled categories.
Each group contained a considerable number of jobs that were not
distinct in status but differed in their attractiveness or significance
to the workers. Although it was fairly easy to identify skilled jobs
on the top, such as loomfixer, weaver, and card tender, and unskilled jobs on the other extreme, such as cleaner, oiler, and yarn
boy, the intermediate category of semiskilled jobs was less clearly
defined.

The gap in status and wage rates between skilled and semiskilled
jobs was wider than that between semiskilled and unskilled jobs.
For example, carding-room wages for grinders (skilled workers)
were $26.72 in 1921, whereas card strippers (semiskilled) received
$17.99 and sweepers (the lowest among the unskilled) received
$12.01. Among the major skilled jobs, loomfixers received the high-
est wages and weavers the lowest. Clerks' wages in various departments were similar to those for semiskilled jobs.[3] But even within
each category the status of certain jobs tended to change in response to technological developments. For example, weaving on
automatic looms was considered a less skilled job than semiauto-
matic weaving; and ring spinning was considered less skilled than
mule spinning. Many textile jobs could be learned in a relatively
short time, and the distinctions in pay rates between certain kinds
of jobs were not always that precise. In the workers' minds, status

depended on a job's overall difficulty, dirtiness or cleanliness, and the type of machinery or type of operation involved. Among the skilled jobs, for example, weaving was preferable to carding. Despite its noise, workers preferred weaving because it required more skill and did not tie them to the machinery as much as carding.

An examination of the opportunities for occupational advancement within the mill must therefore take into account two main layers of the job structure: managerial and blue collar. Managerial positions, such as overseer and superintendent, which few workers could actually achieve, required a move out of the blue-collar ranks. The major opportunities for advancement in blue-collar jobs were from the unskilled to the semiskilled and skilled ranks, although, with the exception of several specific jobs, differences in status and pay between blue-collar job categories were small. The second hand, who was in a somewhat ambiguous position between the managerial and blue-collar levels, was usually a blue-collar worker who had advanced from the skilled-worker rank. As a supervisor, he was in charge of production and discipline in a specific workroom and, in a way, acted as an intermediary between the overseer and the workers. In 1919 Agent Straw and the union reached an agreement whereby second hands were designated as supervisors and, therefore, excluded from union membership. This principle was reaffirmed in regard to the mechanical departments, when the grievance committee voted almost unanimously to withdraw all second hands from the union. Straw reaffirmed the principle in regard to the electrical department: "A man who takes a position, the distinctive duties of which are supervision, in the exercise of which he represents the employer, should while holding it cease to be a member of the union."[4]

For most workers, advancement meant at best a move from an unskilled to a semiskilled job or from a semiskilled to a skilled job. Very few workers were successful in jumping from an unskilled to a skilled job. The majority, if they advanced at all, moved to the middle and upper levels of skill.

Within the blue-collar category, only advancement to loomfixer (men) and room girl represented any real change in status. Both jobs ranked higher than other skilled jobs and carried some supervisory power. Loom fixing was recognized as the most skilled job both in the mill and the community. The job required mechanical skills that exceeded the routine manipulation of machinery typical of other textile jobs. Because loomfixers were responsible for maintaining and repairing the machinery, they held considerable power over weavers, who depended on their assistance when looms were malfunctioning or broken. Loomfixers could (and many did) exercise favoritism toward certain weavers and slow down or sabotage others. To cause weavers on piece rates severe losses, they had only to procrastinate in repairing their looms. The corresponding category for women, room girls (later called smash piecers), carried some supervisory prestige. They helped weavers whose yarn was stuck or broken and displayed an expertise in handling machinery that surpassed that of weavers. They also instructed new weavers.

Occupational opportunities for men and women differed because certain higher-paying jobs were closed to women. The jobs of card tender, framefixer, and loomfixer were restricted to men; others, such as burling, were explicitly limited to women. In jobs held by both men and women, such as spinning, drawing in, and weaving, there was no wage differentiation along sex lines. The average wages of women, in fact, in one Amoskeag weave room in 1928 were at times higher than those of men.[5]

Expectations for advancement

Aided and abetted by management, the ethos of the self-made man pervaded the Amoskeag despite the limited opportunities it offered. F. C. Dumaine, the treasurer, was a prime example. Thought of as the man who "owned" the corporation by many workers, Dumaine had been a poor orphan in Hadley, Massachusetts, when the then treasurer, T. Jefferson Coolidge, "adopted" him into the Boston office, giving him the position of messenger boy. Although the career histories of overseers were less dramatic, they were nevertheless self-made men (except those who were sons of overseers) who had advanced through the system from the ranks of unskilled workers. Agent Straw and his son, whose family was rooted in the New England patrician tradition, were the exceptions.

The *Amoskeag Bulletin* promised advancement and offered lessons for its attainment: "Don't be content with the job you are in, that is to say to stay there. Keep your nerve and push on . . . Don't follow the old ruts and cowpaths, imagining they will lead to success."[6] Intended to convey images of success to tempt the Amoskeag's rank and file, a biographical sketch of an overseer was published in each issue. The lessons accompanying the biographies stressed the personal virtues of the overseers and implicitly promised the same reward to those who emulated them. For example, Dennis F. Harrington was described as one who "has a fine record in the department and has reaped the reward of long and faithful service. His connection with wet finishing has been so continuous and steady that it is no more than natural that he should rise to the highest position there." Assuring readers that an overseer's promotion had resulted from "constant attention to work," the *Bulletin* ignored the equally, if not more, significant factors of ethnic origin and patronage networks.[7] Because readers of the *Bulletin* were limited to workers who spoke English and were also members of the Amoskeag Textile Club, it is doubtful that the majority of workers were influenced by its stories of achievement. They encountered the bosses in their daily work, nevertheless, and their personal examples inspired the hope of someday becoming bosses themselves.

Climbing the ladder

An analysis of the career patterns and personal background of the overseers whose profiles were published in the *Bulletin* offers some insight into the origins of success leading to the Amoskeag's upper ranks. The profiles included men who had become overseers sometime before 1918. Unlike the labor force they supervised, of the 118 overseers whose biographies were published in the *Bulletin*, 83 were born in the United States, almost half coming from New Hampshire and the rest from other New England states and New York. Among those who were foreign-born, 11 came from Canada (6 from Quebec), 11 from England and Scotland, and 2 from Ireland. The remainder came from Germany, Austria, Denmark, Sweden, and Alsace-Lorraine. Whereas most of the New Englanders had come from rural backgrounds, most of the British immigrants came from towns such as Nottingham and Manchester, England, and Paisley, Scotland, which were already known for their active textile production. Some of these men had been recruited to Manchester to teach their expertise to Amoskeag workers and to introduce new techniques or machinery.

The origins of second hands were similar to those of the overseers in many respects. Like the overseers, more than half of the second hands were native-born, although their ranks also included a larger number of French Canadians, an ethnic group almost entirely absent from the ranks of overseers.

Overseers started their first job in the Amoskeag at an average age of just over 20, although about half had started by age 18 and many others even earlier in their teens. The six who were older than 30 when they entered the Amoskeag had already worked in textile jobs elsewhere. Most of the overseers had had only a grade-school education, although several had attended high school. The entire group included only one Lowell Textile Institute graduate and two college graduates.

The majority of the overseers who started in their teens entered the Amoskeag at the bottom rungs of the ladder as yard boys, filling boys, bobbin boys, or sweepers. They advanced to more skilled jobs, eventually becoming loomfixers and then second hands or third hands before they were appointed overseers, on the average about twenty years after beginning their first job in the Amoskeag. Of the 118 overseers described, 65 had worked thirty-five or thirty-eight years in the Amoskeag before reaching the desired rank, and another 20 had worked between twenty and thirty years; 47 had taken less than twenty years to reach this level and had become overseers by the time they were 40. C. Pierce, who became an overseer at age 34 after nineteen years of work in the Amoskeag and was also recognized as an inventor, jumped from sweeper to second hand – he worked so well that "all obstacles were quickly swept away and he forged rapidly ahead." Similarly, G. L. Pierce, who was also recognized for his important inventions, started at age 11 as a sweeper and became an overseer at age 26. Edwin A. Graf, who "was brought up to be a mill man," started as a filling boy at age 20, progressed to loomfixer and then became second hand and eventually overseer. His father, H. A. Graf, had started at age 17 and followed the usual progression – from loomfixer to spare second hand to second hand to overseer.

In comparison to the career patterns typical of most workers in the mill, it is remarkable how relatively few job changes the overseers experienced between their first initiation and their elevation to second hand and eventually overseer. (It is possible, of course, that this difference is exaggerated; the *Bulletin* may not have had access to information on all their jobs or may not have listed all of them. In contrast, the career patterns reconstructed for the other workers were culled from the individual employee files, which listed all their job changes.)

The *Bulletin* liked to stress the quick rise of some young workers to positions as second hands. E. A. Dean, for example, who became a second hand at age 29, had started out as a filling boy and subsequently became a spare loomfixer, a loomfixer, and then a second hand. Dean had "drifted into a weave room just as naturally as duck takes to water . . . [because he] was brought up in the atmosphere of the mills." L. E. Erskine became a second hand at age 22 after having started as a card grinder. The *Bulletin* noted his youth with surprise. A. H. Vose, who had become a second hand at age 23, was described three years later as being "among the younger men who are fast coming to the front."

In addition to their long periods of service in the Amoskeag and their mastery of mechanical skills, many overseers had family ties in the Amoskeag that kept them in good stead. Eight of the overseers were sons of overseers. Of those, three had actually worked with their fathers in the same room. Four of them had had an overseer brother and many of them had other relatives working in the mill as well, who either preceded them or overlapped with them. Two of the overseers had sons and three had brothers working as second hands. Many had an Amoskeag pedigree going back several generations. Arthur Ward was the grandson of James Reid, overseer in the Fancy Dye House, and Dick Sanborn boasted that his grandmother had once worked as a weaver in the Amoskeag. The three sons and one daughter of William Alger were the fourth generation of the family to work in the mill.

Some men who rose quickly to the rank of second hands were also from Amoskeag families. A. J. Hople, a second hand at age 23 who started as an apprentice wool sorter, took "to the wool business as a duck does to water, for not only his father, but also his father's father followed the same line of business." Five of the second hands were sons of overseers. One was the son of a foreman who worked in the same shop. Donald Biron, a second hand, was the son of Théophile Biron, the first French-Canadian overseer in the Amoskeag.

Beyond family ties, membership in fraternal lodges was an important factor in advancement. It has often been observed that in the late nineteenth century the United States was a nation of joiners. But the Amoskeag bosses exemplified the ultimate in joining: Rather than sticking to one fraternity or lodge, most of them listed multiple memberships. In addition to different Masonic lodges, the Elks, the Odd Fellows, and the Improved Order of Red Men, they also belonged to their respective ethnic associations and fraternities – the Knights of Columbus and Knights of Phythias, the Scottish clans, and the Association Canado-Américaine. Théophile Biron was among the founders and the first president of the Association Canado-Américaine.

The testimony of former workers, some of whom had advanced to higher levels, bears out the significance of fraternal ties in facilitating advancement. Antoine Pelletier, for example, who had risen to

the position of assistant overseer, was emphatic about the importance of being a Mason:

> You advanced by loyalty [to an organization]. To be a boss, you
> had to be a Mason. I seen many persons rummaging around to
> get a job as boss. They'd give up their religion to become a boss.
> I knew Canadians that changed their religion. They never went
> to church because they were afraid to be seen with Catholics.
> They were afraid for their jobs. I know one man who turned a
> Mason to be a boss. And after the Amoskeag shut down he was
> one of the best Catholics we ever seen at St. Mary's [interview].

Thus the backgrounds of overseers and the rank and file were
quite different. First, overseers were predominantly native-born
rather than foreign-born, and of those who were foreign-born,
most were from English-speaking countries; the few German and
Swedish overseers had been recruited as experts. Second, overseers
generally had much longer and more stable careers than the rank
and file. Third, they were Protestant and Masons, whereas the majority of workers were Catholic, and they belonged to numerous
orders, clubs, and fraternities in addition to the Amoskeag Textile
Club. The only career pattern they held in common with other
workers was their use of family ties as a means for advancement in
the mill. The status of their relatives facilitated both their training
and advancement to a level beyond the connections of the average
worker. An outstanding example is Charles Whitten, whose brothers were agents of the Amory Mills and the Stark Mills (formerly
independent, these mills were later annexed by the Amoskeag).

The kin, friendship, and fraternal-lodge networks were reinforced by a degree of meritocracy in the workrooms. Established
overseers in prestige positions hand-picked promising young men
and groomed them for their positions. The *Bulletin* biographies expressed great pride in the overseers who had selected and prepared
the potential overseer for advancement. Many young men worked
under the supervision of close to a dozen overseers in the course of
their training. Having the right boss at the beginning of one's career was an important key to advancement not only in terms of ac-
quiring skills but also in terms of the prestige gained through such
an association and the value of continued access to such a boss.

All interviewees agreed that, no matter how hard one tried, the
chances for advancement were slim without recommendation by
the boss or access to the right connections. The entire hiring and
placement system also taught the workers that personal connections

– family, neighborhood, or ethnic ties and club membership – were vital to advancement. Patronage and favoritism were not alien to the Amoskeag workers: To most workers and bosses, the issue was not whether they should be used, but how best to do so. The model of patronage, favoritism, and exchange of services was at the base of hiring, placement, transfer, and advancement. As discussed earlier, these informal ties and patronage practices persisted even after the Amoskeag tried to systematize personnel relations by establishing the employment office. Management tolerated patronage and encouraged it implicitly. Managers and workers alike maneuvered their careers within the mill through personal connections. What workers and bosses alike did not accept, however, was the abuse of patronage – the advancement through family or friendship ties of unqualified individuals into positions of responsibility.

For the rank-and-file workers, occupational advancement did not follow an orderly, predictable progression. The decision to promote or transfer a worker to a better job was the overseer's responsibility, although second hands, who were closer to the workers, could influence the overseer or direct his attention to a particular person. Nor was work performance the only criterion in such decisions: Kinship ties, friendship, ethnic background, reciprocity, and indebtedness for favors played an important part. For example, in certain cases, unqualified individuals were advanced by the superintendent, the agent, F. C. Dumaine, or one of his "boys" in the Boston office. Overseers and second hands sometimes complained about unqualified workers who were in the mill only because of their Boston connections. (Antoine Pelletier, interview).

When an evening textile school for Amoskeag workers was established in 1912 as part of the new Textile Club, the corporation's rhetoric took a somewhat different direction. Although the biographies and the accompanying editorials continued to stress personal qualities, the Amoskeag now extolled the Textile School as an important new mode for achieving the goal of advancement:

> Until this organization was effected, the employee in the mills as well as in other occupations, was compelled to acquire slowly day by day knowledge of his occupation. If he was keen of perception, applied himself assiduously to his task, or was favored by extraordinary circumstances, he was advanced from time to time, until he was at the head of some department. But the majority were forced to keep along without reaching the higher goal.

Under the new order of things this has been changed. While as of yore, all cannot gain the height, if they wished, the knowledge to make his work clearer, easier and more successful has been given him [sic] [Browne, p. 169].

The Textile School, management promised, would facilitate advancement and would provide workers with a more systematic preparation through the acquisition of specific skills. But, like the Textile Club and the other self-improvement programs, the Textile School was used primarily by workers who had a command of English and whose minds were already set on advancing to the upper ranks.

For example, John Jacobson, reminiscing about his advancement to superintendent, stressed his early ambition to climb the ladder and was proud of having become an overseer at such a young age. "I happened to be appointed as a young man. In those days people didn't reach the level of overseer . . . until they were in their fifties [or] sixties" (Amoskeag, p. 137).

Jacobson attributed his high achievement at such a young age to hard work and dedication. He attended the Amoskeag's Textile School and also took courses with the Scranton Correspondence School for Business, which the Amoskeag had arranged. Similarly, Tommy Smith, who started as a dye mixer in the Amoskeag's Scottish dyehouse and was determined to advance, diligently learned techniques from his bosses and attended the Amoskeag's Textile School in the evenings. Subsequently, he commuted to Boston several evenings a week after work in order to study. His training, along with his family connections to the Scottish bosses of the dyehouse, helped him advance to overseer and eventually assistant superintendent of the dyehouse. Bill Alger, who was praised in the *Bulletin* for his ambition to rise, "made up his mind that a fellow had a better chance for advancement in one of the weave rooms . . . He got in with Augustus Canis, the man whose duty seems to have been to produce a line of weave room men with qualifications for advancement to an overseer's berth in the fast growing mills of the company."[8]

To be qualified for a higher-level job when an opening occurred, ambitious young workers used their spare time to acquire new skills. Beginning at age 15 as a sweeper, Auguste Dulac used the opportunity to learn other jobs: "Every time we swept we had about an hour leeway for doing nothing. Then we could do what we wanted. I learned how to do the other jobs. It didn't take too long" (interview). Similarly Jean Chagnon started out as a sweeper in 1923 in the card room. Seven or eight months later he advanced to card boy: "And I like that job very much. So about a year later I got a job as a card tender." He worked in that job for four or five years. At age 19 he enlisted in the navy. When he returned to the Amoskeag, he resumed his old job as a card tender. He was then promoted to a card winder (fixer), and after a year he became assistant foreman: "If you got in good with the old men, they would teach you. If you're smart enough you can pick a lot up on your own. They taught me what they knew, especially Martin Martell. I'll never forget him." When Chagnon became a boss, he found himself in charge of Martell: "I was kind of ashamed of being his boss. He knew so much more than I did. But he was proud that he taught me the job" (interview). Some advanced by playing "roulette" with jobs, moving from job to job until they eventually landed a higher-level job in the right department.

For others, the climb was not so premeditated and systematically structured. Some skilled workers were promoted to second hand and some second hands were promoted to overseer without going through an orderly occupational sequence. When an opening for a supervisory position occurred suddenly, the overseer chose a worker he had known for some time whose loyalty had been proven. Being in the right place at the right time was an important factor in advancement. Ferdinand Huard, one of the few French-Canadian overseers, recalled:

> My first job as a boy was a sweeper, then I was a band boy, and oiler and a starter [at age 14]. I worked up to be a second hand in the spinning room. The overseer had kind of taken to me a little bit. He knew a boss in the dress room and heard that they needed a second hand there. That was one of the biggest paying jobs. So I was second hand there for three years, and then I was appointed overseer. And I stayed overseer as long as the Amoskeag lasted till the flood [great flood in 1936, which immediately preceded the shutdown] [interview].

Because establishing good relationships with bosses was conducive to future advancement, boys and girls working during school vacations were under pressure to perform well. A bad first impression not only hurt their chances for permanent jobs but also their future chances for advancement. In such a close-knit community, where many members were related to each other, a bad start reverberated beyond the confines of a specific workroom. Rumors circulated quickly through kinship, friendship, and neighborhood networks. Successful weavers and spinners, particularly the young men who became third or second hands, achieved their promotions because they ingratiated themselves with bosses during their first jobs, learned their own assignments quickly, and in their spare time acquired the basic knowledge of other operations. They felt that they were promoted because of their reliability and because they were in the right place at the right moment.

Even workers at lower-level jobs viewed minor career advancement as a reward for performance – if they worked well, got along with fellow workers and superiors, and stayed long enough in the Amoskeag, they were bound to succeed. The world of the mill was considered a world of opportunity, at least to the level of loomfixer or second hand. Becoming an overseer did not lie within the range of ambition of most workers.

Recognizing that opportunities for advancement were limited, most workers were resigned to minimal advancement if any. They retained the belief, however, that a steady work performance would be rewarded with better, if not higher-level, jobs. "If you don't ask for a better job, you don't get it," concluded Adam Laliberte, "but if you asked and if you were a good worker and did your work, even if it wasn't a good job, you had a better chance. That's how I got mine" (interview). Repeating the formula she had no doubt learned from her bosses, Blanche Duval claimed: "Promotion depends on the individual. One is promoted when one does a good job." She was promoted from weaver to room girl, the job she really wanted, she said, "because they thought I was a good weaver and they needed room girls" (interview).

Henry Carignan, who made his way up from card boy to card fixer, also insisted that talent was the key: "As long as they wanted to work they advanced. Naturally, they had to have the talent. As long as a worker was able to make his way, and the boss saw that he was able to do it, he'd pass him" (interview). Although Carignan claimed that ethnic background was no barrier to advancement, he did admit that language was an obstacle in many workers' careers, including his own. His wife, Emelia, concurred: "He was a very good fixer . . . but it's the English that he didn't have. He never went to English school. He came up to the United States when he was 18 years old" (interview). The Amoskeag shut down just as Henry was about to test the system: "I advanced a bit. If I had continued, I don't know how it would have turned out. But I had care of all the cards in the department in 1935, when it closed" (interview).

Although some men may have hoped to advance eventually to second hands, the lowest supervisory position, they nevertheless understood the limits in the system as well as the personal factors that impeded their advance: "We always had the hope of getting to earn more than we were earning. But the ambition to look for a higher position wasn't there. I knew I didn't have the education for it because I left school in my eighth grade" (Etienne Saucier, interview).

Most workers placed decent working conditions, job security, and the freedom to change jobs higher in priority than advancement to higher status. In the workers' own minds, job status was determined by working conditions as well as higher pay. For women, in particular, whether a job was a dead end or a stepping-stone to a higher level was not as important as its level of difficulty, its pace, and their ability to control the machinery. Women preferred clean, quiet jobs – burling, for example, even though it did not necessarily lead to advancement, because it was more pleasant, and required a hand tool rather than machinery. Thus, to most interviewees, advancement was equated with the achievement of decent working conditions, adequate pay, and job security, rather than a higher level in the hierarchy. Among the newer immigrants, especially, any job initially and a secure job subsequently were more important than status, whereas the more established workers, especially members of the earlier immigrant groups, the Irish, British, Scots, Swedes, and Germans, were more concerned with status and prestige.

Because some workers could make more money on piece rates, they preferred their lower-skilled but higher-paying job to a higher-status but lower-paying position. Jean Chagnon, for example, who had worked hard to achieve a supervisory position, was ambivalent when the opportunity for promotion finally came. He was working twelve to sixteen hours overtime a week when his boss asked him if he would like to become a shift foreman, after having worked as a card grinder for five years. He wondered what he should do: "Well I wasn't too interested then. I worked a lot of overtime. I wanted to buy a home. I was making about as much as the general foreman." When the boss continued to pressure him, he consulted his wife: "Do you think I ought to take a job as a foreman? I might lose some money." But finally he decided in favor of status. "It was beginning to show on me, the hours I was putting in. I said I'm not going to be a young guy all my life, so I might as well take it" (interview).

Determinants of occupational advancement

To determine the corporation's and the workers' attitudes toward advancement in accord with reality,[9] the impact of several factors on career advancement must be weighed: a worker's first job, career continuity, the coincidence between the age at which a worker started and historical time (i.e., whether young starters had a greater opportunity for advancement at one point in the mill's history than another), and the role of personal and group attributes – sex, ethnicity, and family connections.

As in other occupational mobility studies, upward and downward mobility is measured by comparing a worker's first and last jobs in the mill. However, in the Amoskeag, such a comparison tends to oversimplify career patterns. The picture is further complicated by the checkered nature of many careers and the movement of workers in and out of the mill almost at will. Nevertheless, of the 585 workers who started after 1912 and worked longer than one year, 104 had the same occupational status at the start and the end and experienced no intervening changes, whereas 353 had several intervening ups and downs. Of those who had a different occupational status at the end of their careers, 6 experienced no intervening status changes, whereas 86 changed status a number of times.[10]

Of those persons who had intervening changes in job status between their first and last job, only 93 moved up occupationally, whereas 341 moved down and 41 moved up and down.

Career variables

The career mobility patterns within the mill show the severe limitations of the opportunity structure. Most careers advanced from one ladder rung to the next, with those who started at the lowest unskilled levels more likely to advance to the next step than those starting in the semiskilled ranks. Skilled workers had little opportunity for upward mobility, which is to be expected, because at the highest level of skill, workers could go higher only by attaining managerial rank. They could, of course, go down. Thus, 73% of the skilled workers experienced no change in their careers, the remaining 27% went down, and no one experienced upward

Table 10.1. *Job mobility by occupation at start of work (in percent)*

	Occupation at start of work[a]			
Job mobility	White collar (N = 22)	Skilled (N = 192)	Semiskilled (N = 355)	Unskilled (N = 283)
Down	9.1	27.1	23.1	0.0
No change	90.9	72.9	63.1	59.0
Up	0.0	0.0	13.8	41.0

[a]Mill sample, excludes temporaries.

mobility. Among those starting in unskilled occupations, 59% remained stationary, as did 63% of those starting in semiskilled occupations. Only about 14% of the semiskilled workers managed to move up. Although 41% of those starting in unskilled occupations improved their status, their advancement was no higher than the next level of skill (Table 10.1).

Although opportunities for mobility were limited for both men and women, for men the most prevalent upward move was from unskilled to semiskilled jobs, whereas among women the most typical upward move was from semiskilled to skilled (Table 10.2). This difference in mobility patterns reflects the tendency of women to enter the mill at the semiskilled job level, whereas men were more likely to start in unskilled jobs (Table 10.10).[11]

Were the rewards promised by the Amoskeag for stable and continuous careers rhetoric or reality? Were longer and more continuous careers rewarded with occupational advancement? Among men, there was no relationship between length of service and the final level of skill. Women, on the other hand, showed an increase in their level of skill when they worked longer, with the most crucial difference among those women who worked ten years or longer, a group that included the "old reliables."

The length of time a person worked, however, is not necessarily an indicator of career continuity. As Chapter 9 suggests, the more reliable measure for career continuity is the combination of length of career and number of career interruptions. There was no direct relationship between career continuity and career advancement, except among repeaters (those employed over longer time periods with frequent interruptions).[12] A larger proportion of repeaters than fluctuators experienced upward mobility. Persisters, who had

Table 10.2. *Job mobility by sex*

	Males		Females	
	N	%	N	%
Upward mobility[a]				
Semiskilled				
to white collar	2	1.8	2	2.8
to skilled	19	17.3	36	50.7
Unskilled				
to white collar	4	3.6	1	1.4
to skilled	29	26.4	10	14.1
to semiskilled	56	50.9	22	31.0
Total	110	100.0	71	100.0
Downward mobility[a]				
White collar				
to semiskilled	1	1.1		
to unskilled	2	2.2		
Skilled				
to semiskilled	9	9.9	24	41.4
to unskilled	15	16.5	8	13.8
Semiskilled				
to unskilled	64	70.3	26	44.8
Total	91	100.0	58	100.0

[a]Mill sample, excludes temporaries.

the longest and least interrupted careers, did not experience greater upward mobility.

The age at which repeaters started had an effect on their career advancement. Repeaters who started at a younger age were more likely to move up than older starters (Table 10.3). Overall, upward mobility decreased with age, except for the oldest age groups, for whom upward mobility increased somewhat. This may reflect those older skilled workers who were brought in from Lawrence and Lowell after the strike of 1922. Thus, repeaters were rewarded for their stability with a greater opportunity to advance and often used their career interruptions as a means for advancement. When they found themselves stuck in one position, they quit and tried to get rehired in a better job. Although this method worked in many cases, it also backfired. There was no guarantee, of course, that leavers would actually find a better job when they returned. Partic-

Table 10.3. *Job mobility of repeaters by age at start of work*
(*in percent*)

	Age at start of work[a]				
Job mobility	12–15 (N = 66)	16–25 (N = 246)	26–35 (N = 76)	36–45 (N = 45)	46–73 (N = 35)
Down	19.7	15.9	19.7	28.9	17.1
No change	43.9	58.1	67.1	62.2	65.7
Up	36.4	26.0	13.2	8.9	17.1
Total	100.0	100.0	100.0	100.0	100.0

Note: Repeaters were the only workers for whom there was a correlation between career continuity and occupational advancement.
[a]Mill sample.

ularly in the later period, as job availability lessened, workers who left temporarily had to accept inferior jobs on their return.

The variables of timing

Occupational advancement and the level of job at the end of his or her career were affected by the worker's age at the point in the mill's history when he or she started. Between the ages of 12 and 25, workers starting at an older age were less likely than those starting younger to advance occupationally. For men, occupational advancement declined with age until the age of 46 or older. For women, upward mobility declined consistently with age. The patterns of mobility of older workers may partly reflect the concentration of women in this age group.

Workers starting between the ages of 12 and 15 showed the greatest upward mobility. This pattern is to be expected; as the lowest-skilled workers, or learners, they could move to a different job at the same level of skill, advance to a better job, or leave the mill altogether. That 59.5% of the women and 43.8% of the men in this group of unskilled beginners experienced no change over their careers illustrates the limited opportunities for advancement within the textile mill. Workers starting between ages 16 and 25 tended to advance less than those in the younger age group but more than those who were older than 26 when they started. However, even though the age group 16 to 25 experienced a lower rate of career advancement than the younger group, their advancement may represent a more substantial accomplishment, because it occurred after their assumption of regular work responsibilities rather than during an initial learning period (Table 10.4).

Age at start also indirectly affected career advancement; workers' subsequent mobility patterns were affected by the level of skill at which they entered, which, in turn, was affected by their age at start. With the exception of women beginning at ages 36 to 45, workers starting when they were at least 26 years old were more likely to begin in skilled jobs than workers starting at younger ages. Workers entering the mill at age 46 or older tended more to start in unskilled jobs (Table 10.5). Workers starting in their mid-twenties may well have brought some skills and experience with them; they also may have been more determined to acquire new skills and to advance quickly. On the other hand, those starting in their mid-forties or later, except for workers in highly skilled trades, were generally either new immigrants or less skilled workers who entered as a temporary labor force. Women were more likely to start in semiskilled jobs and less likely to start in unskilled jobs than men in each age group, but the proportion of women starting in semiskilled jobs decreased with advancing age.

The same trends are evident at the end of mill careers. The final jobs of workers entering at age 26 or older were more likely to be skilled, whereas those of workers starting younger than 26 were most likely to be semiskilled; the final jobs of those starting at age 46 or older were the most likely to be unskilled (Table 10.6).[13] Thus, because their final position was the result of both the age and the skill level at which they started, advancement was more likely when a worker started at a higher level of skill. Unskilled workers who started at an older age remained stuck in lower-level jobs.

Although the age at which workers started was an important factor in determining advancement, it was not as significant as the level of skill at which they entered the mill. The relative importance of these factors was not the same for men and women, however. For men, the level of skill and the age at which they started were more strongly correlated. The younger the age at which the man entered, the lower the level of skill of his first job. Among women, the relationship between age at start and the level of skill was not so direct, although women starting at a younger age were more likely to land semiskilled jobs (Table 10.6).

Although age at start and skill at start were major variables affecting career advancement, a more significant factor was that point in the mill's history at which the worker started. The timing of the

Table 10.4. *Job mobility by age at start of work and sex (in percent)*

			Age at start of work[a]			
Job mobility	12–15	16–25	26–35	36–45	46–73	Total
Males	(N = 48)	(N = 238)	(N = 80)	(N = 50)	(N = 56)	(N = 472)
Down	16.7	16.0	20.0	24.0	12.5	17.2
No change	43.8	58.0	70.0	68.0	73.2	61.4
Up	39.6	26.1	10.0	8.0	14.3	21.4
Total	100.0	100.0	100.0	100.0	100.0	100.0
Females	(N = 42)	(N = 212)	(N = 75)	(N = 36)	(N = 13)	(N = 378)
Down	11.9	14.2	14.7	22.2	7.7	14.6
No change	59.5	68.4	70.7	69.4	84.6	68.5
Up	28.6	17.5	14.7	8.3	7.7	16.9
Total	100.0	100.0	100.0	100.0	100.0	100.0

[a]Mill sample, excludes temporaries.

Table 10.5. *Occupation at start of work by age at start of work and sex (in percent)*

Occupation at start of work	Age at start of work					
	12–15	16–25	26–35	36–45	46+	Total
Males[a]	(N = 60)	(N = 422)	(N = 148)	(N = 107)	(N = 85)	(N = 822)
White collar	0.0	0.9	2.7	2.8	0.0	1.3
Skilled	1.7	14.9	31.1	31.8	30.6	20.7
Semiskilled	30.0	34.6	29.7	29.0	17.6	30.9
Unskilled	68.3	49.5	36.5	36.4	51.8	47.1
Total	100.0	100.0	100.0	100.0	100.0	100.0
Females[a]	(N = 47)	(N = 347)	(N = 120)	(N = 62)	(N = 22)	(N = 598)
White collar	0.0	4.3	8.3	1.6	0.0	4.3
Skilled	10.6	21.3	36.7	30.6	18.2	24.4
Semiskilled	78.7	59.1	42.5	40.3	36.4	54.5
Unskilled	10.6	15.3	12.5	27.4	45.5	16.7
Total	100.0	100.0	100.0	100.0	100.0	100.0

[a]Mill sample.

278

Table 10.6. *Occupation at end of work by age at start of work and sex*

Occupation at end of work	Age at start of work					
	12–15	16–25	26–35	36–45	46–73	Total
Males[a]	(N = 61)	(N = 419)	(N = 145)	(N = 106)	(N = 85)	(N = 816)
White collar	1.6	1.4	1.4	0.9	2.4	1.5
Skilled	9.8	19.8	30.1	31.1	31.8	23.7
Semiskilled	34.4	33.7	24.7	22.4	15.3	28.8
Unskilled	54.1	45.1	43.2	44.9	50.6	46.1
Total	100.0	100.0	100.0	100.0	100.0	100.0
Females[a]	(N = 47)	(N = 345)	(N = 119)	(N = 61)	(N = 22)	(N = 594)
White collar	4.3	4.6	8.4	1.6	0.0	4.9
Skilled	19.1	24.1	37.8	26.2	22.7	26.6
Semiskilled	70.2	55.7	41.2	42.6	31.8	51.7
Unskilled	16.4	15.7	12.6	29.5	45.5	16.8
Total	100.0	100.0	100.0	100.0	100.0	100.0

[a]Mill sample.

Table 10.7. *Job mobility by year first employed and sex (in percent)*

Job mobility	Year first employed		
	1912–21	1922–30	1931–36
Males[a]	(N = 331)	(N = 99)	(N = 39)
Down	16.9	12.1	33.3
No change	60.1	65.7	59.0
Up	23.0	22.2	7.7
Total	100.0	100.0	100.0
Females[a]	(N = 272)	(N = 81)	(N = 23)
Down	16.9	9.9	4.3
No change	64.0	76.5	91.3
Up	19.1	13.6	4.3
Total	100.0	100.0	100.0

[a]Mill sample, excludes temporaries.

commencement of work affected job mobility as well as career continuity. Both upward and downward mobility tended to decrease as the shutdown approached, although men hired between 1931 and 1936 experienced relatively high downward mobility (Table 10.7). This was not true for women, who experienced less career change throughout the history of the Amoskeag.

Career advancement occurred less often in the last period, partly because there was no time to advance. More significant, however, was the decline in opportunities for advancement in the last period of the Amoskeag's history along with the overall deterioration in occupational stability. Jobs were less steady and the continuity of workers' careers was disrupted. In this last period workers moved from job to job. Holding on to a job became more important than advancing. Opportunities for rising to higher levels of skill became especially limited after the recruitment of "trusted" skilled workers from Lowell and Lawrence, who filled many of the positions that could have provided promotion for local workers.

Although the period of the corporation's history in which workers started affected all age groups, its impact was greatest on people who started work between the ages of 16 and 25. In this age group people starting between 1912 and 1921 were more likely to move upward than those starting in subsequent periods. After 1930, however, in the last period of the mill's history, young starters shared the same fate as the rest of the workers (Table 10.8). Caught

Table 10.8. *Job mobility of workers aged 16–25 by year first employed (in percent)*

Job mobility	Year first employed[a,b]		
	1912–21 (N = 298)	1922–30 (N = 115)	1931–36 (N = 36)
Down	16.1	10.4	22.2
No change	59.1	69.6	72.2
Up	24.8	20.0	5.6
Total	100.0	100.0	100.0

[a]Only workers aged 16–25 were affected by the time period when they were first hired.
[b]Mill sample, excludes temporaries.

Table 10.9. *Age at start of work by sex (in percent)*

Age at start of work	Males[a] (N = 832)	Females[a] (N = 608)
12–15	7.3	7.9
16–25	51.1	58.1
26–35	18.0	19.9
36–45	13.3	10.2
46–73	10.2	3.9
Total	100.0	100.0

[a]Mill sample.

in the squeeze of the mill's decline, they were actually more affected by the loss of opportunity than were the other age groups.

Personal and group variables

Sex and ethnicity, the personal and group variables that usually affect occupational mobility, had little impact on the Amoskeag workers' patterns of advancement. Sex in itself was not a determinant of advancement within the mill (Table 10.4). The mobility patterns of men and women differed because women started work at younger ages than men and were more likely than men to start in semiskilled jobs (Tables 10.9 and 10.10). Women advanced

Table 10.10. *Occupation at start of work by sex* (*in percent*)

Occupation at start of work	Males[a] (N = 824)	Females[a] (N = 599)
White collar	1.3	4.3
Skilled	20.6	24.4
Semiskilled	30.8	54.6
Unskilled	47.2	16.7
Total	100.0	100.0

[a]Mill sample.

to higher-skilled jobs because of their higher level of skill at start, and because of their younger age at start.

Thus, the contrasts between men and women in job mobility patterns are not so much a function of sex differences in the opportunity structure within the mill as they are a consequence of a different pace in the launching of their respective mill careers. Textile work offered significant employment opportunities for women without wage discrimination.

Similarly, ethnicity in itself had surprisingly little effect on career advancement within the mill, considering that newcomers usually entered in the less skilled jobs and that language barriers and lack of experience made their adaptation and progression more difficult. In Boston, Thernstrom (1973) concluded that immigrants fared far worse than the native-born in their opportunities for advancement within the city's occupational structure. He also discovered significant differences among ethnic groups: Irish and Italians climbed the occupational ladder more slowly than Jews and British immigrants. In comparing the proportion of each ethnic group in the lower occupational ranks, he found that Irish and Italians were overrepresented in jobs at the bottom of the ladder, whereas Poles and French Canadians were less heavily represented in such jobs. Although most jobs in the Amoskeag corresponded to the lower rungs of a city's overall occupational ladder, comparison with Thernstrom's results is nevertheless revealing. In the Amoskeag, as in Boston's occupational structure, native-born and British workers were underrepresented in the lower occupational levels. Most of the few British left in the Amoskeag were concentrated in the managerial ranks. The situation of French Canadians was different, how-

Table 10.11. *Level of skill at start of work by ethnicity (in percent)*

Skill level at start of work	United States (N = 188)	French Canada (N = 579)	British Isles (N = 160)	Poland/ E. Europe (N = 172)	Greece (N = 179)
			Ethnicity[a]		
White collar	8.5	1.7	4.4	0.6	0.0
Skilled	16.0	22.6	16.9	34.9	13.4
Semiskilled	31.9	45.3	31.9	39.0	49.2
Unskilled	43.6	30.4	46.9	25.6	37.4
Total	100.0	100.0	100.0	100.0	100.0

[a]Mill sample.

ever.[14] Unlike in Boston, where French-Canadian workers were heavily represented in the lower-skilled jobs, in the Amoskeag they had advanced into semiskilled and skilled jobs, and most French Canadians had actually started at these higher levels of skill (Table 10.11).

The absence of a correlation between ethnicity and occupational advancement among French Canadians, Poles, and Greeks in the Amoskeag suggests that modest opportunities for rising from an unskilled to a semiskilled job were not closed to members of recently arrived ethnic groups. More important than ethnic origin as such in facilitating workers' advancement were the age and level of skill at which workers started and their access to kin networks within the mill. Because age and skill level at start were not a function of ethnicity, declining opportunities for advancement in the 1930s did not affect ethnic groups differently. In addition, few new immigrants entered the mill in the twenties and thirties. The Greeks and Poles, who were the latest arrivals, entered before 1920 and were not caught in a tighter mobility squeeze than the other workers (Table 10.12).

In their discussion of ethnic differences within industrial establishments in Poughkeepsie, Griffen and Griffen concluded that "factories promoted a leveling between ethnic groups within the world of manual work. Immigrant children shared the skilled as well as the unskilled work with men of native parentage and seem to have benefitted as much from it" (1978:206). Although manual work in the Amoskeag, as in Poughkeepsie, may have had a level-

Table 10.12. *Year first employed by ethnicity (in percent)*

Year first employed	United States (N = 239)	French Canada (N = 729)	British Isles (N = 242)	Poland/ E. Europe (N = 209)	Greece (N = 227)
	Ethnicity[a]				
Up to 1911	18.8	20.6	34.3	17.2	20.7
1912–21	49.8	46.0	44.6	60.8	74.9
1922–30	22.6	24.7	14.0	14.4	3.5
1931–36	8.8	8.8	7.0	7.7	0.9
Total	100.0	100.0	100.0	100.0	100.0

[a]Mill sample.

ing effect among immigrants, a similar effect was not evident for immigrants and natives.

That sex and ethnicity did not affect career advancement was true only for the mass of lower-skilled and semiskilled jobs. The upper level of overseer was closed to both women and members of most ethnic groups. Of the later arriving ethnic groups, only the French Canadians had even a slight chance of becoming overseers. Even then, few made it to this rank. There were no Polish or Greek overseers, and few Polish and Greek second hands, although a relatively large proportion of French Canadians made it to the rank of second hand. Women were completely excluded from both categories.

Family and kinship ties were more significant in career advancement than ethnicity per se. Among French Canadians, for whom kinship networks have been detailed in Chapter 5, those workers who had other kin in the mill were more likely to move up than those without kin,[15] and the employment of relatives affected the career advancement of kin even when their careers in the mill did not coincide (Table 10.13).[16] In some respects, being preceded by kin was more useful than coinciding with them. Members of the same kinship group often followed chains of employment in the same job or workroom, thus paving the way for incoming relatives. Kin facilitated occupational advancement by helping to find better jobs, by hiring their relatives, by monitoring opportunities in the mill, and by interceding with bosses (see Chapter 5).

The point in the corporation's history at which workers entered

Table 10.13. *Job mobility of French Canadians by presence of other relatives working in the mill (in percent)*

Job mobility	No relatives (N = 234)	Relatives present at some time (N = 148)
Down	17.9	14.2
No change	67.5	62.2
Up	14.5	23.6

and their level of skill at the beginning of their careers appear to have been the most significant determinants of occupational advancement. Thus, the type of workers most likely to advance (in most cases from one level of skill to the next) were: women who started at a young age in semiskilled positions; men who started at a young age in unskilled positions; men and women who had relatives present in the mill; and men and women who started work in the earlier period of the Amoskeag's history.

The occupational structure of the city did provide some escape from the Amoskeag's limited opportunity structure. Some young men who left the Amoskeag entered small businesses and became successful shopkeepers. Some even went on to college or professional schools and landed managerial jobs in insurance companies, utility companies, and government offices. Conscription for service in World War I was particularly effective in prying some young men away from the mill and exposing them to the educational and employment opportunities of the world outside. Young women left the mill to become clerks on Elm Street, Manchester's main business street. Others left to become nurses' aides, beauticians, and salesladies. Although most outside jobs, including clerical employment, paid less than the Amoskeag, they commanded higher status in the community and were considered, therefore, better. They also offered women greater hope of finding a husband of higher status. The search for higher status was often curtailed, however, when the low pay of outside employment forced them to return to the mill. The high rates of labor turnover do not mean that those who left actually landed better jobs. Most outside jobs were on a comparable or lower level. As Chapter 9 shows, most Amoskeag leavers went to explore other opportunities, only to return to the mill again and again.

Workers in the sample whose careers were traced after they left the mill did not experience exceptional career advancement. Of those who left, 23% worked in the shoe factories in Manchester. The work in the shoe factories did not command a higher status, however. Most jobs in the textile and shoe industries were interchangeable. Again, workers moved back and forth – those tired of being "mill rats" went to work as "shoe skunks" and vice versa. Approximately 8.5% of the Amoskeag leavers succeeded in entering professional and semiprofessional occupations, 17.5% entered clerical jobs, 18% entered skilled jobs, 34.5% found semiskilled jobs, and 21% found unskilled jobs.[17]

The majority of leavers whose subsequent jobs are known entered jobs that were comparable, or lower, in status and pay to those of the textile mill. Of the low-skilled and skilled trades that Amoskeag leavers entered – in the shoe factories, the building trades, or small industry or services – most provided no major advancement in status over mill work and no major increase in pay; on the contrary, many of the jobs outside the mill were lower paying. Except for shoe work, however, they were "cleaner" and, consequently, more prestigious.

Both the quantitative evidence of mobility patterns and the workers' own perceptions suggest that, given the Amoskeag's truncated occupational ladder, opportunities for advancement within the mill were limited. By their movement in and out of the mill, workers expressed their frustration with the limited opportunity structure, as well as their dissatisfaction with working conditions. That chronic repeaters returned to the Amoskeag reflects their preferences for job security and higher pay over status advancement. For the majority of workers – inside or outside the mill – circumstances dictated that working conditions and security of employment took priority.

11 The struggle to maintain the balance

Agent Herman Straw, the chief architect of the Amoskeag's paternalistic order, was speaking to the second hands, the overseers, and his son William Parker Straw, the chief superintendent and agent-designate, in 1918: "The union is kind of like a flood," Straw said. "If a flood is coming into the mill and you get a broom to try to push the water out, it won't do any good. It's the same thing with the union. You might want to sweep them out. Don't. You won't clean up the whole thing that way" (Henry Carignan, interview).[1] Straw still hoped that paternalism would stem the tide. During the next three years, however, which were also Herman Straw's last years in office, union activity increased, labor relations deteriorated, and the paternalistic dam burst. Straw's son, William Parker, had to do battle with the "flood" – the strike of 1922 – without the experience or the charisma of his father.

Although the Amoskeag had not been free of labor troubles in the pre–World War I period, neither had it experienced a plant-wide strike since the 1880s, and the company was proud of its success in labor relations. Attributed by management to the effectiveness of the corporate welfare program and employee loyalty, its "success" may have also been the result of the watchdogging of the Amoskeag's own detectives and the Manchester police force. "Agitators" were identified and run out of town as soon as they arrived at the railway station, and prospective union activists were intimidated by the threat of blacklisting.

Although Manchester continued to be known as a strikeless city, union activity in various industries was progressing rapidly prior to the war, especially in the cigar and shoe industries. Union meetings and Labor Day parades and picnics, most often sponsored by the Central Labor Union, were frequently reported in the press between 1901 and 1905. Following the Labor Day parade in 1902, the *Manchester Mirror* editorialized: "The strength of labor in Manchester opened many eyes. A frequently heard remark was 'Why I had no idea that the unions were so strong here.' Individually and collectively, the local unions made a splendid showing" (September 2, 1902). In 1903 the *Mirror* reported that labor had been rapidly organizing for the preceding two years. The beer bottlers, the beer truck drivers, and the sheet and metal workers were actively organizing. The textile workers, however, did not organize until 1918.

Officially, the strike of 1922 was fought over hours and wages. In addition, it expressed an intensification of the workers' own sense of loss of control over the work process. Its outbreak actually represented the deterioration of the traditional balance in labor relations that the Amoskeag had tried to maintain in the immediate postwar years. The strike, as well as the tensions leading up to it, was a manifestation of a growing crisis in corporate authority and work relations.

Although the major crisis emerged in the postwar years, it was rooted in problems of the immediate prewar years – the staggering curtailments in production that resulted in job insecurity, changes in the organization and pace of work, and the entrance of the union. Following the boom of the war years, job opportunities, along with production, began to wane as the struggle between the New England textile industry and southern competition began in earnest. The shift from labor shortage to labor surplus was a primary cause of the deterioration of the prewar balance.

The corporation's inability to cope with its own giant size, inefficiency, and antiquated machinery, intensified the labor problems. In the effort to modernize and rationalize, and to increase efficiency, the tensions in the mill escalated. The union's demands – uniform rules in wages, production schedules, and personnel policies – favored the abandonment of the old paternalistic system. Although the Amoskeag survived until 1936, the internal pressures that began to gain momentum in the immediate postwar period and culminated in the strike, coupled with the declining textile market, marked the beginning of the end. The changes in labor relations and the daily negotiations and conflicts between management and the United Textile Workers during this period illuminate union strategy in a paternalistic setting and the workers' attitudes toward changes in the organization of work and the pressures for efficiency. They suggest just how precarious the balance between corporate paternalism, trade unionism, and the workers' traditions was.

The uneasy tug and pull between labor and management, which escalated into open conflict on the eve of the strike, was expressed most clearly in the grievance mechanism instituted in 1919. The Amoskeag grievance records allow not only a reconstruction of the official relations between capital and labor but also an exploration of the texture of daily relations within the workrooms.

During World War I and in the period immediately following, paternalistic practices were attacked by two protagonists, the proponents of scientific management and the union. The prewar paternalism had been instituted to prevent unionization. Essential to the prewar balance was a view of the corporation as not merely a producer of goods but also an institution, an institution that instilled pride and loyalty in its workers. The workers' familiar orientation was balanced by the corporation's paternalistic attitude, a balance that was initially disturbed by the partial curtailment of production in the prewar years and the corporation's first efforts to introduce scientific management. It was further shaken following massive curtailments of production in the postwar years, by increases in work loads, successive reductions in wages, and a general deterioration of working conditions and materials. Even though the Amoskeag had introduced scientific management prior to the war, the full impact of speedups and stretch-outs was not felt until after the war.

During the war, because mobilization increased production, the Amoskeag experienced an even greater labor shortage than it had earlier in the twentieth century. The pressure of wartime production required a continuous recruitment of workers and led to further speedups and increases in work loads, which necessitated a redefinition and realignment of work relationships.

The crisis of the Amoskeag did not merely concern production and wages – it was an institutional crisis, in which both workers and management had to revise their behavior to meet new demands and adjust to new pressures. Speedups did not merely mean more work for less money; they threatened the quality of work and the sociability that made even dull work tolerable. The attitudes of bosses toward workers changed too. The demands for increased production combined with the reduction in personnel pressured the overseers and shook their earlier confidence. As a result, their previously flexible attitudes were abandoned.

Workers no longer enjoyed the freedom to move in and out of the mill or change jobs within the mill. After 1919 a worker who stayed home because of serious illness, even after injury in a mill accident, could not count on finding a job when he or she returned. Several women who returned to work with doctors' certificates attesting to their illness nonetheless lost their jobs. One woman who had been on the critical list for two weeks, according to the doctor's testimony, had to file a complaint with the grievance committee before she could get her job back.

To the corporation, the presence of the union complicated relations between workers and management and threatened to disturb the traditional balance. To many workers, the union represented an unknown agent in their interaction with the corporation – most workers neither were certain how to deal with it nor knew what to expect from it. Union members seemed to be in conflict with both the policies of paternalism and the workers' traditional means of manipulating labor relations through their kin and ethnic groups. Introduction of the union thus placed both management and workers in ambivalent positions that required a reexamination of traditional relationships.

Entrance of the union

The United Textile Workers gained membership in the Amoskeag for the first time during World War I. Outside UTW organizers came to Manchester early in 1918, as part of a campaign to organize a number of New England plants. They began recruiting workers under cover when the Amoskeag gave its workers a 7.5% pay increase, whereas the Lawrence and Lowell mills were raising wages by 10%. In April 1918 the Amoskeag matched the regional increase of 10%; and on May 14, 1918, the dyehouse workers struck, demanding a 25% increase, the first Amoskeag strike since the end of the nineteenth century. Strikes broke out simultaneously in Lowell, Massachusetts, and several Rhode Island communities. Temporarily settled, the dispute was renewed in June 1918 when wages were increased 12.5% compared to only 10% in Lawrence. When six other New England mills granted increases of 15%, however, the UTW struck the Amoskeag, as well as other mills in the region, during the first week in July. Although union membership was limited, their numbers were sufficient in various departments to shut down operations. The strike was settled within five days with a 15% increase, following the intervention of an arbiter sent by the secretary of war. The union added five thousand members and organized ten locals, each affiliated with the Manchester Textile Council (loomfixers, doffer tenders, ring spinners, weavers, cloth finishers, wool sorters, carders, winders, twisters, and dyers and bleachers).

Industrial demobilization after the war, along with a fluctuating textile market and stiff competition from southern industry, prompted a gradual curtailment of production schedules. Cotton production declined from 188.7 million square yards in 1917 to 125.4 and 110.2 million square yards in 1923 and 1924, respectively.

The decline in the worsted section from wartime levels was even more severe: from 14.1 million square yards in 1917 to 6.2 million square yards in 1923, with a slight increase to 7.2 million square yards in 1924 (Creamer and Coulter 1939).

In response to union demands, the 48-hour week replaced the 54-hour week in February 1919, but because piece rates were not changed, the new workweek was equivalent to a reduction of almost 7.7% of full-time weekly earnings. The Amoskeag compensated for this decline by granting a 15% increase on May 14, 1919, to become effective on June 2, which was in conformity with other New England textile mills. This increase was followed by a 12.5% increase in December 1919. The last wage increase in this period occurred near the end of May 1920. On January 3, 1921, following a reduction in the workweek in the entire cotton section to only three days, wages were reduced by 22.5%.

The shrinkage in operations and the increase in losses began to shake the stability and security of the labor force. On June 2, 1920, the wool-sorting and top-making departments in the worsted section were put on a five-day schedule; the spinning, drawing, twisting, dressing, weaving, and baling departments were to operate three and a half days per week, the dyeing and finishing departments four days. At the end of July, the worsted section was shut down indefinitely because of "business conditions" and the uncertainty of the wool supply. It remained closed until July 1921, when operations were resumed on a part-time basis. By late October 1920, the cotton section was also affected. Three weaving departments were on a three-day schedule, and one spinning department was shut down completely (Creamer and Coulter 1939). Wage cuts were preceded and followed by what the union called a "scientific method to reduce wages" – the introduction of the stretch-out and speedup without the accompanying essential adjustment in the flow of materials, methods, and working conditions.[2]

Work loads were increasing steadily between 1919 and 1921, and the number of warp frames per warper and looms per weaver escalated. In 1921 management discontinued an earlier agreement with loomfixers and announced that they would be required to perform a reasonable day's work, "no limit being put on the number of warps being put in by any fixer in any given length of time." When asked by a union representative if the loomfixers would receive more pay for the additional work, management answered "not a cent."[3] In 1921 the doffers in a spinning room were asked to run more work for less wages. They had been running 50 sides (spinning frames) and were receiving $18.21. Under the new schedule, they were paid a weekly wage of $17.40 for 56 sides.[4]

The union's first period in the Amoskeag lasted from 1918 until the end of the strike of 1922. The union never commanded a large membership and did not prove particularly effective in handling labor relations in the mill. Only the skilled and some semiskilled workers understood what the union offered. A former weaver discussed the new uncertainties introduced by the union:

> Before the strike, the union wasn't too strong. There were a lot of people that didn't believe in it. The stewards asked you to join the union. They'd come after you with a paper to sign your name and pay your dues; and if you wanted to go in, all right. If you didn't, well, you didn't have to. But there was a catch. If you had a second hand or a boss that was for the union, he wouldn't declare himself because he didn't have to, so you would have no way of knowing it. If you didn't like the union, he could make it hard for you. On the other hand, if you liked the union and he didn't like it, he could also make it hard for you [Cora Pellerin, *Amoskeag*, p. 207].

During the union's short life, management tolerated its presence and cooperated in maintaining the grievance mechanisms and meeting the workers' demands for adjustments. Whenever possible, it tried to use the union as a disciplining agent, but it was not prepared to accept a closed shop. At the same time, management tried to assert traditional methods of control and reaffirm its existing principles in the face of union demands. The agent prohibited union organizers from recruiting and collecting union dues during working hours and warned them that they would not be paid for hours lost in this manner; he also threatened to fire union members who refused to work with non-union workers.[5]

When union members tried to pressure non-union workers to join the union, the corporation insisted on the open-shop principle. When 305 men in the Land and Water Power division refused to work until non-union members were excluded, and the union requested that the corporation give preference to union members applying for jobs, management responded: "Our conclusion is that no such discrimination can be made, and that our present policy cannot be changed, which is to give everyone, regardless of their affiliation, the same opportunity to work and so to support themselves and their dependents."[6] Some workers were convinced that management was actually trying to undermine the union when union members from certain workrooms were fired and night-shift work-ers, who were not unionized, were encouraged to work in the day-time.

Protesting such actions, day-shift workers continued to claim first priority in all matters of hiring and firing. In 1919 one hundred women, worsted winders and twisters, stopped work to protest the staggered schedule in which the day shift worked mornings and the night shift worked afternoons. They wanted the night shift dis-charged and the day shift reinstated to full-time work. The union's grievance committee claimed that "day workers should be given preference inasmuch as they do all the classes of work and are obliged to run all the bad work in the department." They could not understand why some of them should be replaced during their regular working hours by night-shift workers who were con-sidered temporary. Superintendent Arthur Roberts explained that night-shift workers were vital to the organization and that their interests were as important as those of the day shift. When a union member insisted that the day-shift workers be given preference because the night-shift workers were not unionized, management pointed out "that the Amoskeag did not recognize the union in-asmuch as the union was not considered when dealing with help in a matter of this kind." The grievance committee left in pro-test. As they filed out of the meeting room, one committee mem-ber, Emma Lauttenberg, remarked: "We can receive no satisfac-tion here."[7]

The grievance mechanism

Prior to the introduction of the union, various aspects of labor rela-tions, production schedules, and personnel were handled informal-ly by the overseer within the broader framework of management rules. Superintendents and overseers had a great deal of discretion in interpreting wage rates, scheduling jobs, promoting workers, shifting workers from job to job, and laying off and hiring. The union demanded: hourly compensation for piece workers whose performance was impaired by an inefficient flow of materials; a fair allocation of work loads; standardized wage rates across different divisions in the mill; promotion, layoffs, and rehiring based on seniority; specific rules governing changes and transfers; and the protection of individual workers from arbitrary dismissals or other mistreatment. Because management showed no inclination to meet these demands, the union systematically set out to establish precedents through the use of the grievance mechanism, the one demand to which management had agreed.

The grievance system allowed individual workers as well as entire groups to file complaints with an elected grievance committee in their particular local. Each committee consisted of three or four union members, one of whom was from the workroom where the alleged violation had taken place. Sometimes, though not generally, a committee member himself filed the complaint. The committee usually heard the complaint, investigated the case, recorded the details, and then forwarded the complaint to the Adjustment Board. The Adjustment Board included representatives of management, usually one or two superintendents, the agent, and the Amoskeag's efficiency expert, Fred Meharg. Most negotiations initiated by the Adjustment Board involved the board and the overseers or the superintendent in the department in question. If they failed to reach an agreement, they turned to the agent. The agent intervened immediately in serious cases, especially those involving a danger of work stoppage. In an agreement between the union and management it was ruled that

> in the event that a Grievance Committee, the Executive Board or any branch of the Textile Workers fails to make a satisfactory settlement with F. T. Meharg, acting as the Adjustment Board for the Amoskeag Manufacturing Company, and they wish to take the matter up with Mr. W. P. Straw, Agent, it will be necessary for them to have Mr. T. J. Reagan representing the UTW of America present at this meeting.[8]

Although the grievance mechanism was intended to channel the complaints of individual workers or entire groups, the union also used it to test corporation policy on wages, methods of pay, and work loads and as a negotiating mechanism.

Between October 1919 and February 1922, the Adjustment Board heard approximately 270 grievances. In addition to their value in indicating the escalating crisis in labor relations, the grievance reports, through the workers' own narratives and the testimony of grievance committee members, provide insight into the activities in different workrooms and the texture of work relationships. A careful reading of the grievance records allows a distinction to be made, in some situations, between the union's concerns and the issues that were important to the workers.

Grievances fall into several categories: pay adjustments, including collective demands for pay increases as well as individual complaints of discrimination in such matters as premiums and fines; the miscounting of cloth and the miscalculation of piece rates; the work process and the pace of work, such as speeding up, doubling up, increased work loads, unclear instructions, blame for other people's errors; interference with workers' judgment about method and procedure; unhealthy or difficult working conditions, and low-quality materials; union rights, such as the collection of dues, the recruitment of new members, and discrimination because of union membership; and individual rights, such as discrimination against workers by overseers – favoritism shown by overseers in matters of transfer and promotion, demotion by overseers for revenge, and denial of the right of workers to return to their jobs after illness or vacation.[9]

Few individual wage adjustment grievances were filed. Those pertaining to union rights and the work process were more numerous, but the majority involved complaints about pay rates and work relationships, particularly treatment by overseers. The grievance committee did not investigate complaints thoroughly. It rarely pursued contradictory evidence and did not resolve ambiguous testimony from different workers, which when exposed or obtained by the Adjustment Board considerably weakened the credibility of the individual worker or the committee. The committee also made itself vulnerable to counterattacks and arbitrary rulings by management by failing to honor previous agreements between the union and management. When confronted with such contradictions, the grievance committee was usually helpless to defend its case, and the Adjustment Board or the agent took advantage of the situation to reject the grievance and "consider the matter closed." No matter what type of grievance was at issue, the agent had the final word. If the grievance committee or the individuals filing the grievance were dissatisfied with the decision, they could appeal to the agent and ultimately to Treasurer F. C. Dumaine in Boston. Although cases were rarely brought to the attention of Dumaine, they were frequently taken to the agent, particularly in cases of conflict between an individual and an overseer when the Adjustment Board was convinced of the validity of the grievance but reluctant to antagonize the overseer. The agent then stepped in and tried to appease both sides.

Top officials of the labor union, such as the regional or the international president, were rarely involved. During a deadlocked hearing, the grievance committee members threatened to resort to the Textile Council. Agent W. P. Straw revealed his lack of familiarity with the procedures and the Textile Council itself when he asked "just what body the Textile Council came up from." Denis Fleming, secretary of the union, explained that the council was "made up of four members of each of the local unions, and endeavors to make settlements which cannot be made through the grievance committees of the local unions."[10] The Textile Council was called in only to resolve situations involving the violation of a previous agreement between management and the union and in cases of threatened or actual work stoppage.

In handling grievances, the corporation was more favorably inclined toward individual complaints than those involving an entire workroom or skill group. Even trivial individual grievances were investigated and followed up – they meshed better with the corporation's paternalistic traditions and were not as threatening as collective complaints from an entire division. Most individual grievances, except those that seriously challenged the authority of an overseer, were resolved in favor of the workers or a compromise was effected, whereas most collective grievances were denied. Most group requests for pay increases or changes from day work to piece work to avoid being penalized by company inefficiency were rejected. Requests for pay raises, in particular, were generally rejected after comparisons with the wage scales of other textile mills or those of equivalent occupations within the Amoskeag. The corporation was more objective in reviewing grievances protesting inefficient management, poor materials, and faulty machinery.

In the last year before the strike, the Adjustment Board increasingly settled grievances in favor of management. Of the 32 grievances pertaining to union rights, only 3 were resolved in favor of the union; the Adjustment Board turned down 19 other requests and compromised on 10 others. Similarly, the majority of wage cases were decided in favor of management. In cases of individual rights, the Adjustment Board still tended to rule in favor of the workers. Of the 58 individual cases heard, 13 were settled in favor of management, 23 in favor of the workers, and the remainder were compromised.[11] Workers threatened to stop work and actually did stop work several times when grievances did not receive immediate attention. Under such circumstances, the corporation reminded the union of their agreement that no work stoppage would take place while grievances were being heard and investigated. When the union itself threatened work stoppage, management acted more expeditiously but did not necessarily make greater concessions.

Although management conceded as little as possible, it went to great lengths to play up the significance of the concessions it did make. At one point Straw said to the grievance committee that "there would always be grievances among men" but that he would "try to smooth out the difficulty as much as possible." Thomas Mc-Mahon, president of the UTW, acknowledging Straw's conciliatory approach, said that he "experienced more trouble with second hands than he did with agents and . . . in case of conflict he thought it better to destroy the acorn before it grew to an oak."[12]

The grievance committee was handicapped by its inability to investigate charges systematically on site during working hours, particularly when the grievance involved the condition of the machinery, the distances in the workroom, the sizes of section, and work relationships. In addition, after a long workday, workers were too tired to follow up a complaint. An early request that committee members be permitted to handle grievances during working hours was immediately rejected. The agent ruled that grievances would be handled during working hours only at the request of the Adjustment Board or when a work stoppage was imminent. The corporation's representative on the Adjustment Board, charged with deciding whether the situation was urgent enough to allow the grievance committee to act during working hours, ruled that such a decision rested with himself and the agent alone. Grievance committee members had to report to him; if he deemed it essential, they would be permitted to investigate during working hours but under no circumstances were committee members to be compensated for their time.

Management also took advantage of every possible opportunity to curtail the functions of the grievance committee, particularly when it could prove that the union was not keeping its part of the bargain. On one occasion, the carders' local was in conflict with management because the union's business agent had alienated the company's representatives as well as fellow union members by handing out union cards in the workrooms instead of doing his job, which was to "go among the units and adjust peacefully little grievances, such as are occurring day by day." The union fired the offending official, but its request that the position itself be retained was turned down by Straw: "We have a good system of handling complaints and differences, and it is easy at all times to get Mr. Meharg at his office to settle any complaints." The matter was considered closed.[13]

Management insisted that workers had the right to present grievances directly to the overseers and those farther up in the hierarchy,

rather than through the grievance committee. Union representatives frequently complained that this situation opened the door to
exploitation. For example, a worker returning to his job after a
stomach operation was thought to be physically incapable of handling his job by his overseer. The Adjustment Board offered him a
choice: a job paying $17.76 a week or one paying $18.27. The worker accepted the first offer, claiming that he was perfectly satisfied.
When the grievance committee protested that the worker should
have been allowed to return to his original job and that his complaint should have been settled through the grievance-committee
mechanism, rather than directly with management, the Adjustment
Board insisted that "the company would at all times maintain the
right to talk with any of its employees whether or not they were
affiliated with any union, and that operatives registering a grievance who did not belong to the union would receive the same courteous treatment as those affiliated with the union."[14]

In handling grievances, the agent, as well as most superintendents, tried to walk the tightrope between corporate control and discipline, on the one hand, and a paternalistic attitude allowing some
flexibility, on the other. The maintenance of smooth relations with
the union, high morale in the workroom, and efficient control of
production without antagonizing the workers was especially difficult to achieve when the workers' rights had been visibly violated
by stubborn overseers. Similarly, the agent had to defend workers
against arbitrary layoffs without undermining the traditional authority of overseers. It was particularly important to contain conflicts before they flared up and spread into other workrooms. In a
plant where close to one-half the labor force had relatives in the
same workroom or in other departments, the danger that discontent
in one department might spread like wildfire through others was
always present.

The size of the corporation and the multiplicity of workrooms
often served as a safety valve. In most instances of conflict between
two workers or worker conflict with an overseer, management simply transferred the worker to another room, even when the grievance had been ruled valid. With the gradual diminishing of opportunities and the massive layoff after the war, however, such
compromise solutions became less feasible. When a grievance was
settled with the recommendation that a worker be transferred to
another division, the worker often had to wait for a space to open
up. Thus, workers were subjected to the penalty of layoffs, even

when they were within their rights, because other openings were not available.

The conciliatory approach often entailed long conversations between the agent and the overseer, in which the agent tried to persuade the overseer that he would not be humiliated if he readmitted a complaining worker into his department. At the same time, management tried to stop ruthless behavior by overseers who acted like the "czars."[15] However, the reinstatement of a worker did not provide immunity from subsequent attacks by the overseer. Workers who returned to their original departments were vulnerable targets for layoffs and demotions when the next opportunity arose. One worker who filed a grievance recalled the overseer's threat that "his time would come," and, indeed, it did.[16]

Whereas the agent and the superintendent were careful to cooperate with the union and to maintain a semblance of neutrality, overseers often caused "bad blood" between the union and management by assuring workers that their rights would be protected without union intervention and threatening workers with the loss of their jobs if they resorted to the grievance procedure. One overseer told non-union workers that "it was not necessary for them to join the union, that their jobs were secure, and that the company would stand behind them at all times."[17]

The numbers of grievances increased as the workers' sense of insecurity and helplessness and their loss of control over their jobs increased. The resort to such informal procedures as transfers was becoming much less viable. The winding down of production and the shutting down of entire sections of workrooms made workers vulnerable to layoffs. Under these circumstances, workers risked their jobs even by simply asking for a transfer. Also, the advantages accruing from transfers were disappearing, because the problem a worker faced in one room could easily be repeated in another room.

In the absence of a grievance mechanism in the prewar period, it is difficult to judge whether the content and nature of workers' complaints changed after World War I. That no formal complaints were filed does not mean, of course, that grievances did not exist; but the oral-history accounts suggest that the level of discontent in the prewar period was generally lower and that workers were more likely to express their protest and insist on their rights by manipulating the system.

The corporation's policies and attitudes in the 1920s began to erode the workers' confidence in the security of their jobs, a prime attraction in prewar times. Whereas job permanence for steady workers had been a major promise of the corporation in the prewar period, after the war, the objectives were switched; permanence on the job became the worker's goal rather than the corporation's. Lay-offs were a daily threat and therefore an important instrument of punishment as well.

There was a definite change in mood, too. In 1920 when new loomfixers were hired to fill positions as they opened up, "spare" fixers (in the labor reserve) complained about being passed over in favor of outsiders. Embittered by this treatment, they reminded Superintendent Roberts that they could leave town. The superintendent replied that they were free to do so. Gone were the days when management would go out of its way to keep from losing an expert loomfixer. Amoskeag workers began to feel superfluous.

Overtime and work pace continued to irritate. Management offered to pay time-and-a-half for overtime, but workers were opposed to overtime in principle, because they feared that temporary overtime might evolve into a permanent practice. In October 1921 the dresser tenders claimed that time-and-a-half was not the issue; overtime was. The grievance committee was "positively . . . adverse to any scheme that would tend to lengthen the hours permanently even though the extra hours be paid for at the rate of time and a half." Although management assured the grievance committee that the company did not intend to lengthen the hours of work or force anyone to work overtime,[18] the issue remained volatile. On another occasion, the weavers protested the extra forty minutes that the weave rooms were running each day. The weavers were apprehensive of the offered overtime because they felt that "sooner or later, the working week will be increased and they want it definitely understood how long this overtime will be necessary, and if it is absolutely compulsory." The UTW executive board signed an agreement with Straw that the extra time would continue until March 6, when the issue would be reconsidered.[19]

Workers also felt it was unfair to be forced to work overtime because of company inefficiency. When the department was ordered to run until 5:40 P.M., the warper tenders refused to work later than 5. They asked why it was necessary for them to work late when they had had to wait for beams during the day, sometimes as long as seven hours. Although no one ever said who was responsible for the delay, the workers felt that they should not be forced to work overtime when they were strictly on piece rate. When asked why they had not complained to the overseer, they said it was useless to complain to the overseer "because he will simply shout at you, 'Go sit down!' "[20]

Although most complaints about changes in pace were accompanied by requests for adjustments in pay, workers also protested because the new pace hampered their ability to produce good work and participate effectively in jobs that required a team effort. Speedups clashed with their pride and motivation to produce good cloth or good yarn and keep machinery functioning smoothly. In most instances they did not object to piece rates as such but rather to the obstacles that prevented them from meeting their quotas and thereby earning a living wage. Workers on piece rates naturally became more reluctant to teach newcomers, even their own relatives, without compensation on an hourly basis.

The corporation's "scientific" method of saving money by increasing work loads, which the workers saw as a device for cutting wages, was a major source of conflict. In December 1921 when some of the worsted weavers were required to run six loom sets, they complained. A weaver who was unable to handle the work was transferred to another department, although the overseer claimed that the transfer was temporary and that the woman would be returned to her own department by the end of the day. The weavers were nevertheless concerned that sooner or later all of them would be asked to run six looms. They warned management that they were going to use any means at hand to offset such a move. Denis Fleming, a UTW representative, suggested that the problem could be solved by telling management "to go to hell."[21] Weavers had complained earlier that "a scientific method of decreasing the wages has been instituted by increasing the length of the cuts, from 130 to 150 yards, and that the only remedy is to increase the wages of the various operations." Straw concluded, however, that the company had already gone "sled length" in meeting their demands and that the question of a 6% increase could not be entertained.[22]

Because of the interdependence of different operations in textile production, increased work loads in one occupation affected related operations. When two-harness work was changed to three-harness work, the loomfixers protested that such time-consuming activity would keep weavers waiting longer. Given their increased work loads, the loomfixers said they would like to be relieved of any responsibility if the weavers complained about the long waiting time.[23] Because the machines were running at different speeds, the worsted shearmen voted not to accept the piece-rate plan proposed by management. Insisting that their tasks required "skilled labor" and considerable responsibility, they said that "they must be very attentive to imperfections at all times, and a failure to do so, by being negligent or otherwise in the performance of their work, means a loss in production to the company."[24] The workers were proud of producing strong yarn and good cloth, of blending the most subtle colors of yarn and weaving the most intricate patterns in cloth. Their self-respect depended on receiving recognition for the quality of their work, not only from their bosses, but also from their peers.

It is no surprise that about one-third of the collective grievances during this period protested inefficient machinery, poor materials, and erratic schedules. Although the workers disliked being timed by an efficiency expert and resented being transformed into machines, they did not object to efficiency as such. Efficiency was their goal too; but efficiency could not be attained with defective machinery and unreasonable work loads. Union representatives were even willing to sacrifice some of the privileges of the earlier era. For example, room girls who mended threads in the weave rooms would give up their easy chairs and stop sewing and reading while waiting for assignments; in turn, management would not make them move across the room to another section of looms. When Miss Gariepy disobeyed the overseer's instructions to help another room girl, she was dismissed. She had refused to help because the other girl's section was smaller than her own and because she would have had to cross another section of 80 looms to get to the other girl's section. The union used her refusal as a test case. Denis Reagan of the UTW reminded Straw that management had agreed that room girls were required to service only those looms immediately to the right and the left of their sections. He also pointed out that the easy chairs had been removed and that the girls were no longer knitting or sewing while waiting for assignments. In response, the Adjustment Board and the agent ruled that, except in emergencies, room girls would not be forced to work beyond their immediate areas. Miss Gariepy was reinstated.[25]

Warper girls complained that the colored yarn was running so badly that it was "impossible for us to make a fair day's pay." One warper said it was the worst she had seen in her twenty-six years in the Amoskeag. The increase in the pay rates, they said, would not remedy the situation – it was impossible to make a living with such yarn. Straw promised to make the colored yarn heavier and guaranteed a 40-cent-per-hour rate until the quality of the yarn could be improved, when they would return to piece work.[26]

When twenty-two winders and doublers complained that the "yarn was running entirely too light and that it was breaking badly," the overseer tried to solve the problem by giving the defective yarn to new workers who were working on hourly rates. The learning process was consequently retarded, and the new workers continued to produce samples of defective yarn even after six weeks of training. After trying to discuss the problem with the second hand, the winders and doublers concluded that "one might as well talk to oneself as to talk to Harold Snow about conditions." When some of the women complained to the overseer, he threatened that the "old girls would get through" if the work did not improve. Superintendent Roberts reported that he would try to have the spindles improved.[27]

When worsted-doubling workers complained about "bad work" the union representatives accused the Amoskeag of failing to keep its promise to improve the quality of materials and eliminate short bobbins. "There were times when the work ran good for a week at a time, and then it would appear that the doublers were making too much money and the work would immediately come bad again." William Parker Straw denied that the company supplied bad bobbins because "bad work in one department meant bad work in all departments and eventually bad goods." The workers insisted that the poor quality of the work was evident in the amount of waste. The union representative said: "We are making more waste now than has ever been made in the eleven years I have worked in this department. We do not any longer use waste cans, but we use a larger receptacle." Rather than pay serious attention to their complaint, Superintendent Roberts remarked: "If the winders used more intelligence, their work would run better."[28]

The attitudes of individual workers sometimes differed from those of the union. Whereas the union concentrated on general policy issues pertaining to rights and status, seniority, wage rates, and the pace of production, individual workers were concerned about job security, their right to be rehired if they went on leave, adequate compensation, and fair treatment by bosses. Their grievances reveal also a concern with the *quality* of work relations, procedures, materials, and the product itself. Transcending strictly individual needs, those concerns express the workers' own dedication to the standards set earlier by the corporation. Even unskilled and semiskilled workers took pride in their work. Their grievances thus reflect not only their protest against unreasonable speed and inadequate wages but also their determination to maintain the high standards that made Amoskeag products top quality.

The crisis of the old order

The disputes between the workers and management went beyond wages, hours, and working conditions. The paternalistic balance itself was threatened by two key issues: the authority of the overseer versus the rights of workers and the principle of seniority. In cases of the overseer's authority, management at times sided with workers when the overseers were too ruthless or arbitrary. Management was less agreeable to accepting the principle of seniority, threatening the informal system of patronage that both overseers and workers advocated. Whereas grievances pertaining to wages and working conditions were important to the workers, seniority was more of an issue for the union leadership than for the rank-and-file workers. Some workers felt threatened by the principle of seniority because it clashed with their traditional networks of patronage.

Overseers perceived the principle of seniority and the grievance mechanism as direct assaults on their autonomy and authority. Whereas authority previously had flowed directly from management through the bosses to the workers, now the bosses faced union interference in their own departments. They were surprised when superintendents and the agent occasionally sided with the union and offered a settlement.

The traditional system of paternalism in the Amoskeag did not endorse an overseer's ruthless handling of employees. Overseers were expected to act as benevolent despots. Discipline usually escalated from an initial warning for the first offense to firing or layoff for repeated offenses. Most of the interviewees maintained that they had enjoyed good relations with bosses, especially in the earlier period.

From the grievance files, however, the overseers emerge as men with little tolerance for the workers, men who harbored grudges and played favorites. They appear as tyrants, whose decisions in hiring, firing, and the assignment of work quotas or machinery sections did not always reflect the rational and just system under which the corporation claimed to be operating. The grievances protest the overseer's arbitrary use of power in ways that made work more difficult and less efficient without serving any visible purpose: Why force a room girl to tend two sections of looms, one at each end of the room, wasting both the time and the energy expended in running back and forth, when she could just as easily be assigned to the adjacent sections? Why make weavers wait for warps half a day when a surplus of warps exists in another division? Why fire a loomfixer with eight years of experience and replace him with a runner boy, who has never fixed looms in his life?

Theoretically, workers could take their complaints about over-seers to superintendents as well as to the agent. They were reluctant to do this because a personal complaint might have jeopardized their subsequent relations with the overseers. Overseers were more immune than ever to workers' complaints after the war, because jobs were scarce and few workers would risk dismissal. Overseers often laid off "difficult workers" under the guise of a shortage of work in the department. In such cases, it was not always easy to call the bosses' bluff. The grievance committee had to prove that another worker with less experience or skill had been hired as a replace-ment. The cumulative personnel files recorded each worker's entire career history – workers could no longer "live down past sins" or assume the identity of another worker. In 1920, for example, the grievance committee protested that three men could not get jobs "since the time of the trouble in the Finish Burling Department." Herman Straw promised to find jobs for these men somewhere else in the mills.[29] But even workers returning after illness found it diffi-cult to reclaim their jobs; and blackballed workers found it impos-sible.

The overseers insisted on their prerogative to decide when to punish and when to forgive a worker. As grievance hearings esca-lated in intensity, overseers struck back, placing their personal pride before harmony in the workroom, workers' rights, or efficient production, even when the agent ruled against them. Over and over, they insisted that no one could dictate to them whom to hire and whom to fire and that the union was not going to tell them how to run their workrooms.

The grievances directed against overseers placed superintendents and the agent in a bind – the men who were expected to channel corporate benevolence to the workers were not as tactful and as ac-commodating as management had expected them to be. Mr. Ward, an overseer in No. 9 weave room, put a weaver on a loomfixer's job when unemployed and experienced loomfixers were waiting for work. When questioned about this he said that he "knew nothing about grievance committees" and that he would run his room as he saw fit. He said that he "could make fixers out of weavers" if he wanted to, but he "did not make a fixer out of this man." Resenting the interference, he claimed that he "was working for the interest of the corporation and himself and not for the loomfixers."[30] The Adjustment Board sent the weaver back to weaving, and Superintendent Baker promised to instruct Ward to receive grievance committees courteously.

Management reinstated workers who had been fired arbitrarily and instructed overseers to repair faulty equipment that prevented workers from meeting their quotas. Whenever possible, however, the superintendent and the agent upheld the overseer's decisions in hiring and firing. When they did overrule an overseer and reinstate a worker, they tried to appease the overseer. Sometimes the worker was sent to another department as punishment before he was allowed to return to his own. Sometimes a worker was ordered to obey the overseer without question, but, at the same time, the overseer was prohibited from subjecting the worker to the unreasonable conditions that had led to conflict. More than the mistreatment of workers by overseers was at issue in these disputes: Industrial paternalism itself was at stake.

The issue of seniority was a crucial dividing line between management and the union. The union insisted that management follow an exclusive seniority rule regarding promotions, layoffs, and rehiring. The Amoskeag had encouraged long-term, continuous service by rewarding longtime workers with a modest pension, corporation housing, and the opportunity to purchase housing plots, but the principle of seniority itself had not been a tenet of the Amoskeag's policy. Management was willing to encourage seniority when it was in the corporation's interest, but it was not willing to recognize it as a *right* of the workers. Prior to the new policy introduced in 1928, older workers were kept on even after they began to show signs of slowness and inefficiency, especially if they were useful in transmitting skills to young workers. There was an implicit assumption in the Amoskeag's policy that a worker who had served the company for many years deserved some consideration and recognition. After World War I, the Adjustment Board often reinstated older workers despite overseers' objections. When an overseer insisted that he laid off a drawing-in girl because she was "not very good," the Adjustment Board reinstated her because she had worked for the Amoskeag for twenty years. When 74-year-old Henry Provencher was fired, the grievance committee protested. Superintendent Thompson said that a young man could do a better job than Provencher, who, unlike most older workers, had been with the company only six years. Management and the grievance committee reached a compromise: Provencher was transferred to an easier job.[31] Continued employment for older workers was a major bone of contention between William Parker Straw and the Boston office in the late 1920s. Some interviewees claimed that W. P. Straw's refusal to succumb to F. C. Dumaine's pressure to get rid of the older workers was one of the disagreements that led to Straw's resignation. When Henry Rauch became agent in 1928, he moved immediately to fire older workers (Debski, interview).

In the immediate postwar years management refused to be bound by seniority as an automatic right, particularly when it interfered with an overseer's right to judge the efficiency of his own workers. The union, however, insisted that seniority protected a worker's individual rights, particularly when workers were threatened arbitrarily. Between 1919 and 1922, the grievance committee was concerned with such cases as the replacement of an older worker who had been with the Amoskeag since 1892 with a younger man, who shopped for an overseer on a regular basis and watered his garden. George Reid, who was discharged for "inattention to work," had also been replaced by a younger man. The grievance committee suspected that his dismissal might have been prompted by his membership on the grievance committee. Reid had overheard William Swallow, head of the employment office, say to the effect that he "knew all about Mr. Reid."[32] The last-hired first-fired principle was defended by the drawing-in girls when they refused to teach new girls until the principle was established. The agent ruled, however, that "each overseer is responsible for the quality and quantity of the output in his own room . . . and in order that he *can* be held responsible, the right of the selection of his own employees must be allowed him."[33]

The agent continued to stress the importance of individual initiative and merit. "We thoroughly recognize the desirability from the humanitarian standpoint of retaining our old and faithful employees, as is evidenced throughout the mills, but one cannot agree to the demand that seniority of service is the only consideration," said William Parker Straw to the union representative. Straw felt that younger workers might be discouraged by strict adherence to a policy of seniority. Management determined wage levels on the basis of accomplishment as well. When the back tenders, who were predominately older workers, requested a pay increase, Straw replied that it would be granted only if they did 25% more work. The grievance committee advised management "that the back tenders were mostly old men, who could not do anything else." But Superintendent Walsh insisted that if they could not do more, they should not be paid more.[34]

In 1919 worsted loomfixers who had been with the Amoskeag since 1892 complained that they had worked only three and a half days in eight months, whereas younger men had worked more frequently. The union suggested a compromise that would allow workers to rotate in times of job scarcity so that younger employees could continue to work as well. The older men felt that they were being discriminated against because of old grudges harbored against them by overseers. They agreed, nevertheless, to rotation, rather than seniority, to give the younger men a chance. Superintendent Roberts, however, objected to rotation because it would "make a football of his sections for everybody to kick," and the Adjustment Board consequently ruled that the union should draw up a list of loomfixers by order of seniority, thus affirming seniority as a principle, "all other things being equal."[35]

The principle of seniority was tested again when fifteen finish burlers who had worked anywhere from six to fifteen years were laid off while a woman with only five months' experience was hired. Agent Straw replied to the complaint that "the longer he lived, the more he thought there were advantages in youth and that it would not always follow that the older operative from the point of view of service was the best operative."[36] Straw also referred to a company policy that his father had presented to the union the preceding year:

> The matter in hand involves a principle which is basic, and upon which depends the successful operation of any corporation – namely, the right of an overseer to lay off, when the lessening work seems to demand it, the person who in his opinion may be most advantageously spared. We approve of the idea that the last person hired should be the first to be laid off, all other things being equal, but there are obviously certain other factors which may enter into the consideration when, if the rule of seniority service is strictly adhered to, neither the interests of the company nor the employees are served.[37]

The corporation did not accept seniority until the 1930s and even then did not adhere to it consistently. Unlike grievances pertaining to working conditions and wages, the union's campaign for seniority seemed more an expression of the union leaders' own principles than the workers' preferences. The workers saw seniority as a threat to their own informal patronage channels, without any assurance that the new principle would work.

The rift between management and workers became increasingly irreparable in the last year before the strike. Grievances were generally resolved in favor of management or ignored altogether, and none of the fundamental disagreements were settled. Toward the end of the period, management even refused to grant concessions that required no sacrifice for the corporation. In 1921 when fifty workers in the tentering department complained of "unbearable" heat and humidity, the superintendent who investigated the situation found the conditions "very favorable." He saw no reason "to install fans at this time" and added that he was planning to reduce the labor force in that room by 25%. The agent endorsed the decision.[38]

Work discipline was also beginning to fall apart. A warper complained that her workroom was run in a "slipshod manner." The French Canadian who was distributing work sometimes did what he was asked and sometimes did not. "He is inclined to be sweet to one of the tie-over girls," she noted, which was why the girl got the best work (the best quality yarn). The room was in a "state of confusion, and he will howl from one end of the room to the other." Although the Frenchman was transferred, the workers found the new overseer also difficult to work with, and he too was transferred subsequently to another workroom.[39]

The old order was falling apart. The workers' sense of betrayal by the corporation and feelings of despair were exacerbated by the deterioration of materials and the decline in quality. Their faith in the paternalism of the Amoskeag was no longer justified. Even though the strike would be fought over wages and particularly hours, the insecurity, the discontent, and the gradual loss of family control over the work process help to explain why workers without a strike tradition, workers who had little familiarity with the union and little identification with it, went out on strike in 1922. But the events of the crucial years between World War I and the strike mean much more: They represent the collapse of the equilibrium between management and workers that had rested on mutual codes of behavior since the beginning of the century.

12   *The collapse of the balance*

> February 13th, my God! There was nothing! The gates were
> opened; no one entered and they had what they called pickets.
> No one went in on the 13th of February because of the pickets.
> No one!
>
> Henry Carignan, interview

For Amoskeag workers, the strike marked the end of the world they
had known. It meant the end of an era of confidence and good work
relations and the beginning of an era of insecurity and mistrust.
Decades later, many former workers identified events as having occurred either before or after the strike, as if referring to a natural
disaster: "Things just were not the same after the strike."

It came without warning. On February 2, 1922, the following notice was posted in all workrooms:

> Commencing Monday, February 13, 1922, a reduction of 20 per-
> cent will be made in all hour and piece rates in all departments of
> the Amoskeag. At the same time the running time of the mills
> will be increased from 48 to 54 hours per week, in accordance
> with the schedule posted herewith.
>
> —W. P. Straw, Agent[1]

One month earlier, fifteen thousand workers in Rhode Island had
struck to protest a similar 20% wage reduction and the increase in
the workweek to 54 hours. Workers in Nashua, Dover, Newmarket,
and Somersworth, New Hampshire, also struck. Regionwide, the
strike involved 56 mills employing 55,927 workers; an additional 9
mills employing 10,012 workers were indirectly involved. By March
the strike had spread to Lawrence and Lowell, Massachusetts. In
Rhode Island the strike was sponsored by the United Textile Workers and the Amalgamated Textile Workers of America; in Lowell, by
the UTW and the One Big Union; and in New Hampshire by the
UTW (Tilden 1923). Not all the strikers were union members. Even
though the union led the strike, only one-fourth of the Massachusetts and New Hampshire strikers and less than one-half of the
strikers in Rhode Island belonged to the union, according to the
calculations of the Bureau of Labor Statistics (Tilden 1923).

In Massachusetts, where the legal workweek was 48 hours, the major issue was wages, but in New Hampshire and Rhode Island both hours and wages were at issue. To the UTW, the 48-hour week was the crucial issue at the Amoskeag. Neither labor nor management was willing to compromise.

Following the posting of the February 2 notice, the UTW dispatched its vice president, James Starr, to Manchester. Of the 12,150 strike votes cast, Starr reported 99% in favor of striking, although management accused him of padding the votes, claiming that in reality only about 3,000 workers voted to strike.

A UTW committee, accompanied by Starr and Horace Rivière, the French-Canadian organizer for the UTW, announced to the agent that "the organized employees of the Amoskeag and Stark mills could not report for work the following Monday under the new scale."[2] Straw responded:

> There can be no compromise in the reduction of wages and in the increase of hours posted. Regardless of the decision of the Unions, we shall open the mill gates next Monday morning with the idea of giving work to those who care to accept the new conditions and who recognize the futility of delay with its consequent loss of wages [*History of the Amoskeag Strike*, pp. 3–4].[3]

The strike began on Monday, February 13. As pickets marched in columns of two opposite each gate, hundreds of workers stood in the neighborhood to watch the outcome. When the gates were closed at 6:45 A.M., after the arrival of the workers, management discovered that too few workers had reported to operate the plant. The agent issued the following notice to the newspapers: "The Amoskeag Mills are now closed until further notice. Advance notice of their reopening will be duly given."[4] Maintenance work continued and jobs in progress were completed. The overseers, second hands, and office workers filled orders and salvaged materials.

Few workers were entirely surprised by this dramatic sequence of events. Adam Laliberte claimed that his father had anticipated the conflict several months earlier: "Everything was going so bad. They could tell in advance just like today when you see a depression coming along" (interview). The strikes in the other New Hampshire communities, especially in nearby Nashua and Suncook, where relatives of Amoskeag workers were employed, had offered a preview.

Because strikes more often succeed when factories are in full production, the mid-February strike occurred at a poor time strategically for the workers. Not only was it the depth of winter, which further strained their resources, but production at the mill was at low ebb. It may actually have been convenient for the corporation to provoke a strike.[5]

Manchester became strike city. Police Chief Healey issued warnings to strike leaders; Mayor George E. Trudel appointed an Aldermen's Committee to handle problems arising from the strike. The first mass meeting for workers in Manchester's history convened on Sunday, February 20, at the Palace and Park theaters. The UTW's Tag Day Committee collected $4,848 and sent delegations of women strikers to other New England cities to raise funds by selling tags and to mobilize the sympathy of other unions in the Northeast. On February 28, Thomas McMahon, president of the UTW, made his first official visit to Manchester. "We stand to arbitrate the matter of wages," he said in a union meeting, but "we will never arbitrate the hours of labor." But neither the corporation nor the strikers would compromise on either score (*History of the Amoskeag Strike*, p. 9).

During the first two months of the strike, as picketing continued along the mill yard, union leaders and the strike committee organized mass meetings, rallies, and parades to boost strikers' morale. Strikers sold tags and roses in the streets to raise funds for the strike. On March 13, Samuel Gompers, president of the American Federation of Labor, addressed a mass meeting, urging the strikers "to fight to the end no matter what the consequences may be." Although no financial assistance was offered, Gompers announced that credentials would be issued to strike leaders, allowing them to address union locals throughout the country for fund raising. Boston philanthropist Elizabeth Glendower Evans came to Manchester to offer her support to the strikers and subsequently raised funds for them in Brookline and Boston.

McMahon encouraged the strikers, dismissing any hope for arbitration: "We're ready now to fight until Labor Day." In the first months of the strike, union leaders not only tried to rally workers' support by promising victory but held out the hope of achieving additional gains. Not only did they want the 20% wage cut reversed; they wanted an additional 20% as well.

But by April, in response to rumors in the city that desertion was noticeable in the strikers' ranks, the union organized a mass parade in which thousands of workers marched, shouting slogans and carrying banners emblazoned with the figure "8" for eight hours. Although the union claimed that 10,000 workers participated in the parade, the newspaper reporters counted 4,200. "Eight hours" became the battlecry. It was written on banners and pasted on hats. It became the official greeting among the workers. Shortly thereafter, Straw dispelled a rumor that the Amoskeag might resume operations after May 1: "There are rumors that Amoskeag would reopen May 1st. Even if workers wished to return the mills could not possibly start up owing to a lack of orders caused by the general worldwide business depression and the present strike" (*History of the Amoskeag Strike*, p. 49).

From the beginning of the strike and until almost the end, both management and the union resisted the efforts of various organizations and public figures to effect a compromise. The first such attempt was made by the Manchester Ministerial Association, a committee of the local clergy. It was followed by a committee of the mayors of the strike-affected towns, the New Hampshire State Commissioner of Labor, Governor Albert O. Brown of New Hampshire, and finally a citizens' committee appointed by Mayor Trudel. All these proposals for compromise failed, as did a last effort by Bishop Albert Guertin.

In the first month of the strike, Governor Brown blocked a move to enact a 48-hour week legislatively. Citing the opposition of the Grangers, who felt the 48-hour law would have a restrictive impact on agricultural labor, the governor refused to convene a special session of the legislature. He also cited the expense involved in convening the legislature, even though the Manchester delegation had agreed to serve without compensation. On May 29, however, the governor invited the workers, manufacturers, and mayors of the struck mill towns to attend a conference at the State House to discuss his compromise proposal for a 51-hour week and a 10% wage reduction. It was a foregone conclusion that both management and workers would reject the compromise, as indeed they did.

Labor leaders in Manchester and elsewhere suspected that the meeting had been called by the governor not to seek a compromise but to provide the corporation with an excuse to resume partial operations, for following the failure of the compromise, the governor recommended that the mills open one of their units "to afford employment to former employees who are out on account of the strike and who are needy, in some instances subsisting on charity, and desiring to work" (*History of the Amoskeag Strike*, p. 75). This announcement followed shortly upon the Nashua Manufacturing Company's decision to reopen its mills after being granted an injunction "restraining its striking operatives from picketing, influencing and terrorizing workers and those who may become workers."

The Amoskeag Company responded favorably to the governor's invitation, and on June 1 the Amoskeag announced the opening of the Coolidge Mill: "Preferences will be given within reason to former employees of this mill, but vacancies will be filled from applicants who have already registered at the employment department in order of the dates of their application or from other experienced operatives who may present themselves at the opening hour." The Amoskeag also promised that additional mills would be opened if a sufficient number of people expressed a desire to work (*History of the Amoskeag Strike*, p. 78).

Neither municipal, state, nor federal agencies supported the strikers. Shortly after the strike began, a delegation of the strikers traveled to Washington to enlist the support of Senator George H. Moses in introducing a resolution calling for a congressional investigation of the strike. Moses declined on the grounds that the issue was local, not federal; it was simply a dispute between New Hampshire workers and a New Hampshire corporation. Moses took the opportunity, however, to point out that the workers had brought this problem upon themselves. As far as he had been able to find out "not a labor man or union in New Hampshire had made one feeble gesture" in support of the 48-hour labor law which he had introduced in the Senate some time ago (*History of the Amoskeag Strike*, p. 20).

Within the city itself, Police Chief Healey exceeded his authority to prevent picketing and openly urged the police force to protect the corporation and demoralize the strikers. Healey's stance was consistent with his earlier ties with the Amoskeag: "Dad and Chief Healey were like that (showing interlocking fingers), remarked F. C. Dumaine, Jr. (*Amoskeag*, p. 337). There is also evidence that the Amoskeag passed considerable sums of money to the police during the strike. In the semiannual accounts in the treasurer's office for the period ending May 20, 1922, the Division of Contingent Account recorded "Manchester Police Department $2,262.50." In the six-month period ending December 2, 1922, the payment amounted to $691.55 (Creamer and Coulter 1939:200).

Mayor Trudel paid lip service to the need to settle the strike but did little to bring about a compromise or to aid the strikers. Although he accepted the invitation, he did not attend the special meeting for mayors convened by the governor in Dover, because, he explained, Manchester had been slighted by not being chosen as the site for the meeting. Starr accused him of being an agent for the Amoskeag, as City Hall was being used as an "employment agency" for strikebreakers. William Swallow, director of the Amoskeag's employment office, had been in regular communication with City Hall by telephone, apparently recruiting strikebreakers, who were being hired by the city to work on a "golf course." The mayor denied the accusation.

The mayor's position is not surprising. Several of the aldermen were Amoskeag overseers and superintendents. The Aldermen's Committee, which the mayor had appointed at the outset, engaged in little action during the nine months of the strike. On June 5, 1922, the mayor prohibited the strikers from holding their fourteenth tag day on the grounds that businesses were objecting to it.

The churches, in efforts to end the strike as soon as possible, acted as intermediaries between management and the strikers. With one exception, however, the clergy did not publicly endorse the strike and provided no outright support to the strikers (*Manchester Mirror*, March 11, 1922). The exception, the Reverend Herbert R. Whitelock, said in a public assembly: "If there is to be a cut anywhere and someone must take a loss, why not begin with the agent, president, treasurer and cut them to about $100 a week and split the difference with the laborers." Bishop Guertin, within whose dioceses most of the strikers lived, expressed his "deepest feelings of sympathy and . . . praise for the thousands of men and women" involved in the strike and suggested "mutual understanding" (*Manchester Mirror*, March 18, 1922). Early in the strike, parishioners of St. Anne's Church expressed their disappointment that the priest had delivered an entire Sunday sermon without any mention of the strike.

Some of the clergy viewed the strikers as rebellious children who were offending the churches' hierarchical view of order and submission to authority. Also, some of the churches had received endowments of land and financial support from the Amoskeag earlier in the century. When reflecting on the clergy's stance during the strike, some former workers felt that the clergy who had tried to act as mediators demanded impossible compromises: "They had an archbishop . . . He had big shares in the Amoskeag and he came up and gave the people the impression that it was better to have half a loaf than not to have any. Coming from a Bishop!" (Dorothy Moore, interview).

Finally, there were the newspapers. The workers could not even count on the ethnic newspaper. Two days before the strike *L'Avenir National*, published in Manchester, warned workers of impending disaster: "We do not contest the workers' right to stop work if they are not satisfied with the conditions," conceded the paper, but it questioned whether the time for the strike was well chosen. "Is it opportune? We are not speaking about the cost of living . . . We ought to speak of the quality of life rather than the cost." The paper then proceeded to question the truthfulness in the number of votes – twelve thousand votes in support of the strike – that the union had reported. It criticized the union's secret balloting and insisted that a citizens' committee should have had an opportunity to count the votes. It doubted, therefore, that the vote actually expressed the preference of the majority of the workers. The paper pointed out that if factories could not keep their costs down, they would close up completely for an indefinite period and would reopen only when enough employees were willing to return to work. Finally, the paper urged workers to return to their jobs:

> We genuinely believe that a serious examination of the situa-
> tion from all sides will inevitably lead the employees of the
> Amoskeag and Stark mills to the conclusion that they would be
> better off returning to work Monday morning. If they take this
> course, they will do themselves a service and the city of Man-
> chester as well [*L'Avenir National*, February 11, 1922].

Angry French-Canadian strikers referred to the newspaper as *tête de cochon* (pig's head). The iron fist wielded by the Amoskeag over the community, and its indirect, if not direct, influence on munici-pal government was evident to the workers throughout the strike. Because the Amoskeag controlled about two-thirds of the city's jobs, most of the workers could not hope to find other employment. Nor were they prepared for such a long strike. A few workers found employment in factories, some found temporary construction jobs, and others just "loafed and ate beans." The year 1922 was a preview of the year 1936.

Coping with the strike

Beans became a symbol of the strike. The union's commissary dis-tributed food to strikers free of charge on the basis of need. The supplies were distributed every three days in quarter-pound lots for a family of two persons, with a quarter-pound more for each additional person, according to the U.S. Bureau of Labor. A loaf of bread was allotted daily; on Mondays half a pound of sausage, salt pork, and salt cod was furnished; spare ribs and cabbage or other vegetables were distributed on Wednesdays; Fridays, codfish. In addition to the seventeen thousand strikers and family members aided by the commissary, the union provided a free restaurant for single workers, where two meals were served each day (Tilden 1923: 918–19). The commissary continued to function temporarily even after the strike was over, so great was the workers' need.

The interviewees, unfortunately, cannot recall such a variety of foods; but they do remember flour and dried beans. Perhaps, as the strike progressed, fewer and fewer supplies were available and perhaps the distribution was not equitable. Several interviewees agreed with Antoine Roberge, who felt that strikers who had joined the union earlier had received preferential treatment (interview).

Determined to fight to the finish, workers sought alternative employment. McMahon encouraged strikers to take farm jobs until an agreement was reached. A "back to the land movement" organized by the Canadian government convinced 360 families to return to Canada and take up farming in the western provinces (*Manchester Leader*, March 3 and March 25, 1922). In March, workers began to return to Greece and Poland as well. Others migrated to nearby mill towns. Françoise Bissel, for example, went to work in Laconia, New Hampshire, while her husband remained in Manchester, keeping watch over the strike situation: "My brother was living up there at that time; and I worked there for nine months. My husband stayed with our little child and I sent the money home. He didn't do nothing. All he did was sit home" (interview).

Some women worked as maids in New Hampshire resorts; others found similar jobs in Boston. After all her savings were spent, Angelique Laplante went to Boston for a brief stint as a maid:

> It was board and room and five dollars doing housework. My husband worked for some contractors. I didn't stay after two or three days. I was too lonely and my kids stayed alone in the house . . . I came back and worked for my mother in the boardinghouse . . . Amoskeag didn't push us out for the rent. We went to the Amoskeag lawyer and we paid so much a week from what we had [interview].

Henry Carignan recalled: "We worked outside the city. I went to work in Epping [New Hampshire] for a while in the brickyard, and different places like that . . . One of my brothers went to work in the Manchester plumbing supply and another one worked in Lowell" (interview). Marguerite Renaud's brother found a job for her husband in Lowell. They stayed with her brother until their baby was born and then returned to Manchester (interview).

Some families lived on their savings until they ran out. Albina Laliberte recalled:

> My mother was a very thrifty woman and we never suffered from the strike, hunger or anything. But we had to go through a lot because they had just bought that house. And they paid $7,000 for the house, so they had it pretty rough being a large family. My mother happened to save a little bit from what my sisters worked earlier, and that carried us through. No one was working for nine months [interview].

Some workers had stocked up with supplies. Adam Laliberte recalled his father's preparation:

> He said to me, "I don't want you to go in there as a scab." He ordered 100 pounds of flour, 100 pounds of peas, 100 pounds of beans, anything that could keep. When people asked him why he was buying so much, he said that the mill is going to close down on strike. My mother was so glad to see 100 pound bags here and 100 pound bags there. She used to make a head cheese and we used to have pea soup [interview].

Although some families who lived in corporation housing paid no rent during the strike, the Amoskeag did not evict them. Many who lived in private housing were being evicted and had to move in with relatives or leave the city. The strikers did not set up tents in the vacant lots north of the city that local businessmen made available.

For most strikers, the long months of enforced idleness stripped away the few resources they had. Help from the city's welfare department was minimal. The church did not organize relief activities; only individual assistance was given on a casual basis. But neither were Amoskeag workers accustomed to turning to churches for charity in normal times. Relatives helped each other, but when their resources ran out, the only effective help had to come from relatives in other communities.

As desperation increased, the crowds lining up outside the union's commissary became unwieldy. Paul Morin, an Amoskeag worker who had actually objected to the strike, volunteered to keep the crowds in order: "You'd put your arm out in front of the door, and they'd break it. They were hungry. That's why I took the job, because I was in shape then from playing baseball" (*Amoskeag*, p. 308). Alexandre Bolvin, who had been in favor of the strike, recalled the crowds fighting for leftovers:

> It was terrible in 1922. I'll never forget it. There was a store on the corner of Merrimack and Maine . . . Someone threw a little piece of lard out, and there were maybe 1,500 of us in the street waiting for that little piece of lard to catch it. There was no food [interview].

Prior to the opening of the Coolidge Mill, Police Chief Healey warned Starr, Rivière, and other strike leaders that picketing and demonstrations would not be tolerated. After conferences with the governor and the mayor, Healey issued a statement assuring the workers that they could enter the mills without fear. When the mill gates opened on June 5, six thousand striking textile workers and sympathizers paraded in the surrounding streets. They had begun to congregate around 4 A.M. Healey had suspended all leaves and called in his reserves, but the police could do little more than keep the large crowd moving slowly up and down the streets. The two pickets assigned by the union to face the entrance gate disappeared in the overwhelming crowd of pickets. From time to time their banners were spotted opposite the gate. At 6 A.M., as the gates were about to open, a male worker approached followed by others in pairs, and within a short time one hundred workers had entered. "It was quite apparent to the neutral observer that a number of the operatives in the mass came with the intentions of working. They were evidently scared by the thousands lined up outside the gates and remained away from the looms," observed the eyewitness who subsequently wrote *The History of the Amoskeag Strike* (p. 81). "We arrived to work in the morning," recalled Elizabeth Miller, a former weaver, "and no one wanted to go in. People were picketing. When they opened the gates for a while the people started to go in slowly. 'Rats!' the pickets shouted. 'Don't be a rat,' they'd say" (interview).

The mass demonstration on the first morning was remarkably peaceful – only two electricians were arrested. The scene at the closing of the mills at the end of the day was more turbulent. Two thousand workers assembled on the south side of West Bridge Street to await workers who were leaving the mill. The author of *The History of the Amoskeag Strike* described the events:

> As the closing hour drew near people began to hurry across the bridge to be present when the workers left the mill. They were

met at the foot of West Bridge Street by policemen who cau-
tioned them to keep moving. The line increased in numbers until
at 5:15 o'clock one side of the highway was banked solid with
humanity.

At 5:30 o'clock the buzz of machinery stopped. The main gate
was thrown open and as if by signal the paraders faced the mill.
Vainly the officers tried to start the procession moving. They
were unable to budge the crowd. The first worker came out of the
building and started for the gate. A roar went up and he hurried
down the street accompained by the jeers of the strikers.

It took but a few minutes to clear the mill and the crowd then
dispersed. Some of the strikers continued to parade the streets
but the majority left the vicinity when the iron gates were closed
and quiet prevailed soon after 6 o'clock.

The next morning the police had a more difficult time. Howls and
jeers increased in intensity whenever a worker approached the
gate. At the close of the second day, the Amoskeag announced that
the number of looms in operation had increased by 25%. Union
leaders claimed, however, that management was deliberately exaggerating the figures. On the afternoon of June 6, at the closing hour
of the Coolidge Mill, an open conflict erupted between the police
and the strikers. Horace Rivière, George F. Mooney, Ralph H.
Morse, and Edward Trottier, members of the union strategy board,
and another fourteen strikers were arrested. On June 7, 1922, the
New York Times headlined: "Police Disperse Thousands of Disorderly Textile Strikers of the Coolidge Mill."

Throughout this period the local press and strike opponents blew
reports on union clashes out of proportion, exaggerating rumors of
intimidation by pickets. The clashes between the demonstrators
and the police were triggered by the arrest of a striker, Victoria
Ciechon, who was caught just when she was about to throw a paper
bag full of sand over the side of the bridge into the mill yard as the
strikebreakers were leaving the mill. Protesting the arrest, the pickets who were patrolling the upper end of the road ran to the scene
and began to jeer the police. The police arrested thirteen workers on
charges of inciting to riot. The police chief's son, Captain Charles R.
Healey, arrested a Greek worker who allegedly had followed a
strikebreaker to his home and assaulted him. As news of the arrests
circulated, protesters gathered along the Merrimack Common and
the surrounding streets, near the police station, and a police captain
and an inspector were hit on the head as they tried to make several
arrests. When Rivière and three members of the union strategy

board went to the police station to inquire about the arrest of the demonstrators, they themselves were arrested but later released on $1,000 bail.

The following day, in a session at police headquarters that continued till after midnight, union officials assured the police that they would cooperate in every possible way to prevent further disturbances. The next day Starr and Rivière ordered the pickets to march in silent processions. When shouting erupted at one point in the line, the union leaders immediately calmed the crowd. Alexandre Bolvin, one of the pickets, recalled the silent procession: "We were supposed to go in the picket line two at a time and walk back and forth in front of the gate, but we couldn't talk to anyone going by" (interview).

On June 7 the Superior Court of the State of New Hampshire granted the Amoskeag Company a temporary injunction prohibiting even peaceful picketing. Chief Healey declared that the injunction would be strictly enforced and that no picketing of any description would be tolerated. The strikers did not attempt to violate the injunction when the workers entered the plant, but protest erupted once again at noon and night as the workers went home.

Following closely on the court's action and in response to Chief Healey's request came the decision of the Manchester Parks and Playgrounds Commission to ban all speakers at the strikers' gatherings on the Commons. But the commission, faced with community pressure, particularly the intervention of the Reverend Herbert A. Jump, pastor of the First Congregational Church, modified its prohibition and agreed to allow local speakers to address the gatherings.

Writing for a national readership, Jump, who referred to Manchester as the "City of Michael Healy," described his encounter with the president of the Park Commission:

> As president of the Ministerial Union I asked Chief Healy to soften his request. He declined. I pointed out that the one message of the sixteen strikers' meetings held thus far had been to obey law, keep order, be good citizens. And the further fact bulked large in my mind that by a grim coincidence the president of the Park Commission which would have to act upon this request was the one director of the Amoskeag who lived in Manchester. Learning that a hearing upon Chief Healy's request was to be held the next morning, I put in an appearance as a protesting citizen. I modestly quoted the first amendment of our national constitution with its assertions concerning free speech, free

press and free assemblage. Imagine my amusement to hear the chairman, the aforesaid director of the Amoskeag, interrupt me as I finished reading the Constitution by saying, "Oh, Mr. Jump, that is very old. That document was written a long time age."[6]

When the Amoskeag decided to reopen the Coolidge Mill, in the fourth month of the strike, many workers had to make a serious decision. Those who had struck against their will could return, but those who were committed to the strike had to choose between principle and starvation. The savings of most had been depleted; those on the margin of subsistence even before the outbreak of the strike were now completely destitute, and a resolution of the conflict in the near future was unlikely. Whether to remain on strike or return to work divided workers as well as families. "One French woman named H. went in to work," recalled Bolvin, "and when she came out her brother spit in her face. Poor woman, what could she do?" (interview). Blanche Duval recalled:

> At the time of the strike, everyone made enemies . . . They called us all sorts of names if we went in. I loafed a long time before returning, but we had property, and we were going to lose it if we didn't go to work, despite the fact that it made enemies. I'd tell them, "We're not going to lose our property on account of that strike. As long as they're offering us work, we'll work. If you don't like us, then don't look at us. That's all" [*Amoskeag*, p. 317].

For some time after the strike Blanche and her sister-in-law did not speak to each other. She felt that her sister-in-law could afford to loaf because she was an "old maid," and those whose parents supported them had nothing to lose. But Blanche knew what had to be done:

> There were plenty that went in during the strike. They were like us – they needed the money, they had big families, they couldn't afford to stay out any longer. There were as many people going in as there were staying out. Those that stayed out had their parents to back them up, so they stuck it out. We belonged to the union, but we had to go in to work [*Amoskeag*, p. 319].

Some families held out as long as they could but finally gave in: "Just before the strike, the big strike that we had, my husband had loafed about six months. No one in my family worked. My daughter was married, and her husband didn't work. We were twelve in the house to eat. I said, 'I guess I'll go in and weave' " (Antonia Bergeron, *Amoskeag*, p. 63).

Joseph Debski, former employment clerk, claimed in retrospect that most workers who returned to the Coolidge Mill were "family people." Many interviewees drew similar distinctions between those who returned to work and those who persisted: Those who had families to support eventually went back in; those who were single, and younger, could afford to stay out. Although some cited the desperation of their families in justification, others did not re-enter despite their family responsibilities but tried instead to find work outside Manchester.

On July 21 the Superior Court made its temporary injunction permanent but modified it to permit two pickets at each mill gate. At the same time the court turned down a petition by the strike leaders for an injunction to restrain the Manchester Police Department from ordering West Side residents to remain indoors while Coolidge Mill workers returned home at the end of the workday.

It is difficult to assess what role intimidation by pickets actually played in discouraging workers from returning to the Coolidge Mill and the other mills that reopened one by one during the strike. Even though the demonstrations were orderly and little mass violence took place, many former workers recalled considerable anxiety over the possibility of being attacked on entering the mill. Pickets not only threatened workers at the mill gates, they followed them in the streets and actually menaced their homes. Threats that "scabs" would be killed or thrown into the river circulated among the strikers. Like many workers, Henry Carignan simply shrugged off the threats and entered: "They never threw me in the river [laughs]. They called me a scab or something like that, but I didn't pay any attention as long as they didn't hurt me. I kept quiet [laughs]. You have to eat, so you say nothing" (*Amoskeag*, pp. 330–1).

During the first few days after the Coolidge Mill reopened, workers were brought in by covered trucks. Management also brought in food for them, so they would not have to face the crowds at lunchtime. Alexandre Bolvin recalled:

> We had people working in the mills when the big strike was going on, and people were bringing food in to them, because they couldn't come out. When they would come out of the mill to go home at night, they were taking a chance of getting killed . . . There was a fellow and he had a lunch car on the corner of Maine and Amory. He was making good money. We didn't see it, but we found out that at night he went into the mill to feed the people. We used to call them rats [interview].

Another former worker actually remembered that the man who took food into the mills was beaten.

Women felt less threatened than men by the pickets. Maria Lacasse recalled that the women felt the pickets would be less likely to
harm them:

> It was the men who didn't want to go back during the strike,
> because there were pickets. They were afraid they were going to
> get killed. There was another woman on the block who said,
> "How about us women going to work? If we go to work, they're
> not going to attack us because we're women." So I decided I was
> going to go back because fall was coming, and we didn't have
> any money. We didn't know how we were going to live. That's
> what the strike was all about: they didn't give the workers
> enough money. But I knew they were not going to win; so when
> that woman asked me, I had the children kept, and I went in to
> work. I told my husband to stay home; I was afraid he would be
> hurt by the pickets [*Amoskeag*, pp. 260–1].

Despite the bitterness, crowd behavior was remarkably orderly.
The Rhode Island strikes, in contrast, were riddled with violence –
clashes between crowds and the police, shootings, explosions, ar-
son, and murder.

In the period following the opening of the Coolidge Mill, the corporation and the strike leaders were engaged in a recurring contest
over their respective readings of the number of workers who had
returned. The union leaders claimed that the Amoskeag was padding the figures to demoralize the strikers. When the police corroborated the numbers reported by the Amoskeag, the strikers accused
the police of acting as press agent for the company. News reporters
who were allowed into the Coolidge Mill to ascertain the true number of workers counted 223 people at work, not including overseers
and second hands. Strike leaders contested this number, claiming
that the Amoskeag had planted workers in different rooms in order
to exaggerate their numbers, a common practice by management in
various strikes (Hiller 1928). But regardless of the figures, the number of returning workers, along with imported strikebreakers, was
increasing at a steady pace, and new departments were gradually
opening up.

On July 20 Straw announced that 1,325 workers were on hand and
that 1,890 looms were in operation, including 1,586 looms in the
Coolidge Mill, 140 looms in No. 3, Southern Division, and 164
looms in the mill on Granite Street. Straw said:

> Since the strike began, we have finished and shipped several
> thousand cases of cotton goods, and several thousand pieces of
> worsted goods, and are now finishing in our cloth rooms regu-

larly the product of our looms. This cloth is coming through in a most satisfactory way, and in fact there has never been anything to criticize about it [History of the Amoskeag Strike, p. 140].

Straw invited additional workers to apply for jobs by telephone, letter, or in person. "Within a very short time, if enquiries continue to come in, as we have no doubt they will, we shall doubtless open some of the other mills, probably one of the mills in the Stark division" (History of the Amoskeag Strike, p. 140). On August 17, Straw announced that the work force had increased to 2,375 and that 4,001 looms were in operation. The Amoskeag proceeded to open departments No. 1 and 2 of the Langdon Mill, followed by the Amory and No. 11 mills. The strike leaders claimed that many of these workers were contract labor from Canada. "A large percentage of these people never worked in the textile mills before and many of them are children," said Starr. Strikebreakers were in fact imported from other communities as well as from Canada.

On Monday, September 5, despite a downpour, about 4,300 workers according to the union, or 2,000 according to the police, marched in the celebration of Labor Day. The parade included representatives from every union in the city. The textile division, headed by Starr, Rivière, White, and Dennis Fleming, carried various banners and wore costumes. They were preceded by a satirical performance depicting labor and corporation leaders and the strike staged by the strikers. Special songs about the strike and its leaders were sung. "They invented songs to create hatred between the ones who worked and the ones who didn't work. There was one about Mr. Straw and Mr. Starr. I can sing it in French, but it's bad. It goes, 'Starr mange la bullshite et Straw mange la . . .' [laughs]. That was the song they used to sing around the gates of the mill" (Blanche Duval, Amoskeag, pp. 318–19).

As the workers gradually gave in, the Amoskeag, too, came under pressure. In August the Pacific Mills in Lawrence, where the only issue was wages, settled with the restoration of the old wage scale. Nine mills in Maine did the same. With the reopening of other mills, the Amoskeag began to experience difficulty in attracting sufficient numbers of strikebreakers from New England. On September 10 Straw announced:

> The Amoskeag Company , in accordance with the policy of paying a wage equal to that paid in communities comparable with Manchester, follows at once the recently-announced action of the mills in Maine, operating on a 54-hour basis, by advancing its wage scale effective Monday, September 11. The running time of

the mills will remain unchanged, 54 hours per week [*History of the Amoskeag Strike*, p. 150].

The Manchester Leader, giving the corporation's announcement prominent coverage and presuming to speak on behalf of the Manchester community, urged the strikers to return to work: "*The Leader* hopes that you will go back to work at the restored wage, working extra six hours and being paid for them, and then leave the question of the length of the working week to the . . . government" (*History of the Amoskeag Strike*, pp. 152–3).

The strike leaders continued to insist on the 48-hour week. Horace Rivière immediately warned the workers that "it is a scheme on the part of the company to destroy trade unionism" (*History of the Amoskeag Strike*, p. 151). The workers remained firm. The electricians' local was the first to vote against returning to work. At an open straw vote at the Strand Theater on September 12, almost all of the two thousand people present voted in favor of remaining on strike. They also insisted that there should be no discrimination against former strikers when the mills reopened. Their eight-hour slogan was amended to "Eight hours and no discrimination," and Rivière described the mills as "silent cemeteries."

With the opening of the Bag Mill at the beginning of the thirty-eighth week of the strike, however, more workers returned. Nearly forty-five hundred workers were reportedly on the job, and rumors of a break in the strikers' ranks circulated on the streets of Manchester. Despite the union's unanimous vote to continue the strike, the Amoskeag's wage increase encouraged many workers to return – they saw in the wage restoration an indication of the Amoskeag's willingness to compromise.

On October 17, at the request of a special committee appointed by the mayor to seek a compromise, Straw designated as participants several officials of the company, members of the overseers organization, the president of the second hands association, and three representatives of the employees who had returned to work. Strike representatives refused to meet with current employees, however, and the conference was canceled.

On October 28 the workers accepted Bishop Guertin's compromise proposal: a restoration of wages to the level that existed prior to the reduction of February 10, 1922; a 51-hour workweek until February 1, 1923, at which time officials of the company and representatives of the workers would determine whether the 48-hour week was warranted by economic conditions or other circumstances; no discrimination either by the company against striking

employees or by the striking employees against fellow workers who
had returned to work earlier. The Amoskeag, however, rejected the
bishop's proposal. In a long, polite letter dated October 31, Treasurer F. C. Dumaine wrote that the trustees would not consider any
compromises and that the mills were open to anyone who wanted
to return; that, indeed, many workers had already done so.

The Amoskeag then opened four new departments, making the
greatest gains in returned workers since the opening of the
Coolidge Mill. On November 3 the Amoskeag reported 8,300 looms
in operation in 17 of its 20 main mills. On November 10, 1,600
looms were added and several days later three more departments
were opened. One thousand job applications were received. Many
of the "returnees" were strikebreakers. Early in November the
Amoskeag had begun to hire skilled workers who had been discharged from the Lawrence mills after the strike (*Boston American*,
November 21, 1922). Strikebreakers were imported from Canada,
and the United States Immigration Service began to investigate the
illegal practices of smuggling in strikebreakers (*Boston American*,
November 24, 1922). A reporter for the *Boston American* calculated
that about one-third, or two thousand of the Amoskeag's workers
were imported strikebreakers from Canada, Massachusetts, and
Maine. "Those strangers have been coming in truck loads and temporarily quartered in a big boardinghouse on the West Side. After a
few days in the mills they have been distributed throughout its
neighborhoods, but they have been foregathering nights at the
boardinghouse" (*Boston American*, November 23, 1922).

On November 14 the Amoskeag reported that twenty mills were
in operation, and the following day, the company announced the
conditions under which striking workers could return to the mills:
acceptance of the 54-hour week and the present wage schedule
(rates raised to those prevailing before February 13). Currently employed workers would not be replaced by returning strikers. All
employees would be allowed to return except those who "may have
been guilty of violence or intimidation or of inciting violence and
intimidation, and those whose conduct during the strike has been
such as to destroy the possibility of maintaining the relation of employer and employee with mutual respect" (*History of the Amoskeag
Strike*, p. 175).

Starr advised the various locals to reject the company's terms, and
on November 21 the union representatives informed management
that 99% of its members had voted agianst the proposition. When
Straw announced that 60% of the plant was in operation and that

management would not modify its terms, Starr and the other leaders encouraged the strikers to persist and outlined plans to carry the 48-hour-week fight to the legislature. In addition to the controversy over hours, the strikers were concerned that the corporation would discriminate against returning strikers and would refuse employment to those who had been prominently involved with the strike. But the unanimous vote to reject the corporation's proposal only temporarily bridged the divisions that had begun to appear among the strikers. On November 15 the *Boston American* noted:

> Real news about the strike situation in this city is not coming from the leaders . . . it is coming from the many little groups who are meeting on the streets and from those who come around on the quiet to observers of the trend to ask what they think about it . . . Unity of opinion does not prevail. No matter how much the leaders may deny it or disguise the situation, diverging lines of opinion are evident in the camp of the strikers.

The basic division, reported the paper, was between those who wanted to continue the strike, fighting for the 48-hour week, and those who were prepared to return to work and at the same time carry the fight to the legislature.

A few days after Starr had urged the strikers to continue their fight, he met in Manchester with the officers of the International Metal Trades Unions, which were affiliated with UTW and the American Federation of Labor. Although he admitted to the press that his "mind [was] practically made up as to what action is advisable," he sought the advice of the metal tradesmen and promised that their advice would be "the law and the gospel," thus hoping to set the stage for his subsequent announcement:

> I am anxious to do what is right without fear of criticism or desire for commendations. More than anything else, I am concerned about the welfare of the thousands of strikers who have shown a loyalty to their cause and a devotion to their leaders unexcelled in the annals of strike history . . . Of course, this strike could go on, but with the winter coming on and little children to consider . . . with the forty-eight-hour week given into the hands of the legislative representatives of the people, I am not sure that it is the part of wisdom or humanity to mark time" [*Manchester Leader*, November 25, 1922].

To the officers of the metal trades unions, Starr said that "the real and permanent victory for the 48-hour week is not to be won in the offices of the textile corporations, but in the legislative halls of the state house" (*Manchester Leader*, November 25, 1922).

The following day the UTW executive board voted to end the strike. To the strikers assembled at the Eagle Theater and Sweeney Post, the vote was a surprise. Only a few days earlier Starr had urged them to reject the corporation's proposal and persist in their battle. Starr now reminded them of the gains they had made during the past nine months and assured them that the union chiefs would carry on the 48-hour fight in the New Hampshire legislature. The Amoskeag immediately announced its plans to open the remainder of the mills. The 48-hour bill was passed in the House of the New Hampshire legislature in 1923 but defeated in the senate. After the legislative defeat of the 48-hour law, Starr and Rivière decided to resort once again to economic tactics. "If we can't secure the 48 hours through the legislature, we will secure it by economic strength"[7] (*The Textile Worker* 10, No. 12:730). This unexpected and dramatic reversal of Starr's position left the strikers with the feeling that they had been used as pawns in the union's larger game.

Profiles of strike participants

To what extent was the strike an expression of working-class consciousness? Can those who went on strike out of conviction be distinguished from those who stayed out because they had no choice and who reentered just as soon as it was possible? An analysis of the career histories of workers in the sample whose records indicate that they participated in the strike reveals some major differences between the strike participants and the overall labor force. As expected, there was little difference in skill levels at the start of their careers, but at the time of the strike there was a higher concentration of skilled workers among the strike participants. More than 37% of the participants were in skilled occupations, more than 22% were in semiskilled occupations, and 17% were in unskilled occupations, whereas in the overall sample, the proportion of skilled workers was much lower and that of unskilled workers was much higher.

The greater tendency of skilled workers to strike may reflect a more serious personal investment in working conditions and work relations. It is also possible that skilled workers were more likely to be union members: The first and most important locals to be organized within the Amoskeag were those in skilled trades – electrical workers, weavers, loomfixers, and slasher tenders. The length of careers was also significant: Strike participants had generally worked longer in the Amoskeag and thus had a greater stake in their jobs than the overall sample of the labor force. And those who had worked nine years or longer were the most likely to have participated in the strike.

Ethnic differences between strikers and the overall labor force sample were also significant: American-born workers and British immigrants were less likely to have participated in the strike. Proportionally, Polish workers participated more than French Canadians, and Greek workers participated the least. These differences reflect the historical entry of ethnic groups into the Amoskeag. By 1922, British-born and American workers had assumed managerial positions and, to a large extent, identified with the corporation. The French Canadians, who at that point constituted the core of the labor force, had reached maturity as workers and thus had a stake in good working conditions and fair labor relations. They had also been exposed to systematic unionizing by French-Canadian organizers. That Polish workers were more likely to participate in the strike than French-Canadian workers even though they were recent arrivals may have been a result of their socialization to working-class behavior in textile mills in Poland. The lower participation of Greek workers should not obscure the fact that some of the strike activists were Greeks.

An analysis of the career profiles of strike activists described below renders a somewhat different picture from that of the participants discussed above. The activists included those whom the Amoskeag listed as "agitators" and those who were arrested and indicted for leading demonstrations and for inciting to riot. Their names appeared often in the newspapers. Activities that gained workers a place on the Amoskeag's list also included strike committee membership. A total of 75 individuals among the activists were identified as "strikers and sympathizers" and specifically labelled "agitators."[8]

The sex imbalance of the activist group is immediately obvious: 88 were men and 15 were women. Unlike the majority of the labor force in the sample, a major portion of the activists had been employed more than five years: About two-thirds of the activists had been in the Amoskeag's employ six years or longer prior to the strike, and of those, 45 had been employed for ten years or longer. By comparison to the overall sample, the activists clearly belonged to the "old reliables" group.

The ethnic composition of the activists also differs from that of the overall labor force: The Irish, native-born, and Scottish workers were overrepresented in comparison to their proportion in the labor force, whereas the French Canadians were underrepresented.[9] The activists were "old-timers" in the Amoskeag: For the 101 for whom this information was available, 59 had started work in the Amoskeag before 1912. For those for whom information was available the age distribution at the time of the strike matches that of the overall labor force: 25 of the activists were in their twenties, 24 in their thirties, 15 in their forties, and 17 in their fifties. Only 8 were younger than 20 and only 5 were in their sixties. Despite their being typed "agitators," more than two-thirds returned to work after the strike, and most remained in the Amoskeag's employ for at least ten years; of the others, some were not readmitted, and others went to work elsewhere or left town.[10]

Career histories of some of the "fiercest agitators" on the Amoskeag's list suggest that, by and large, they were characterized by a long-term commitment to the corporation and fairly stable careers in middling or higher-skilled jobs. John Jay Sherry, whose letters of recommendation from his bosses indicate that he was a respected employee, was also a prominent member of the strike committee and a delegate to various negotiation sessions during the strike. The Irish-born Sherry began work in the Amoskeag as a weaver in 1874 at age 14. He transferred to become a molder and worked in the foundry for thirty-five years. Following a neck injury resulting from a burn he received on the job, he became a member of the safety committee. He returned to the foundry after the strike and was recommended for a $20 pension in 1924. Sherry retired and received his pension but died within the year.

Another prominent member of the strike committee, Max Morgenstern, a German immigrant who was also on the union's tag day and finance committees, was decribed by management as an "agitator and disturber" and was one of the 32 workers served with injunction papers. He began working in the mill in 1910 at age 31 as a cloth stamper. After two years he became a section hand, a position he had held for ten years when the strike started. He returned to the mill after the strike but worked only in such unskilled positions as bobbin cleaner, counter man, and freight checker, continuing at the Amoskeag until his death in 1923.

George Mooney, of Irish origin, who was arrested during the strike for "inciting a riot," began working in the mill at age 24 in 1916 as an apprentice in the wool sorting department. He left the Amoskeag to serve for a time in the National Guard and was once fired because he "wanted to have his own way." He returned shortly thereafter, however, and continued to work as a wool sorter until 1922. Although blacklisted after the strike – "not to hire again" – he was rehired in 1925; he left in 1927 without stating a specific reason.

William V. Coverett began working in the Amoskeag at age 42 in 1914 as a pickerman. He was transferred from one department to another five times, working in a variety of low-skilled jobs, such as scrubber, pickerhand, card tender, waste hand, and card stripper. He returned to work after the strike and was employed as chief card stripper until 1935, when his services were "no longer needed." He was the president of the Carders Local 1147 in 1923. In a letter to the editor of *The Textile Worker* in 1923, Coverett wrote that "the strike in New Hampshire was one of the best things that ever happened for the uplifting of humanity. It showed the mill barons and the state politicians that there is only one American plan and that is the United Textile Workers plan."[11]

Lorenz Drescher, an Austrian, started his long career as a temporary loomfixer in 1907. He was a striker and a sympathizer who filed complaints, along with the union leaders, against the police chief and other police officers for ordering strikers to stay in their homes after work hours in order not to interfere with workers returning home from the Coolidge Mill. After the strike, he returned to work in the Amoskeag until the shutdown.

Peter Theodorakopoulos, a Greek described as one of the "fiercest agitators," was served with injunction papers. He began his career in 1912 and, prior to the strike, had a stable career in the mill as an intermediate hand. He was a prominent speaker at union meetings and active in organizing Greek workers. He was not rehired after the strike, despite the intervention on his behalf of Costas Xolougiane of No. 4 Lower Spinning Department, who wrote to Swallow of the employment office:

> Mr. Theodorakopoulos now recognizes that he had done a big mistake [as agitator in strike] and desires to return to work for the company again . . . he will perform his duties hereafter sincerely and faithfully and will never again repeat the mistakes he had done in 1922 when he was ill-advised by the leaders of the union.[12]

Strikers Thomas and Anna Tomasik were Polish. Thomas, who had worked as a bleach hand from 1917, gassed himself to death in June 1922 in Lowell, "despondent over the strike."[13] Anna, who began as a weaver in 1913, returned after the strike and continued to work until she moved to New York.

Herman Hellmich, a German, worked as a weaver and a loomfixer from 1909 to 1935. He was identified in a picture published in the paper as a "strike sympathizer" and was purportedly a member of a group who were annoying workers returning to their homes. His sworn affidavit against Police Chief Healey and his department for not allowing the strikers to picket was attached to his personnel file.

Vasilo Koloyerpoulou, a Greek, was employed as a spinner in the mill from 1911 to 1935. She participated in the strike but was not served with an injunction. She was sentenced, however, for an alleged assault against fellow worker Olympia Kaldora and was described by the corporation as a strike leader. She left the Amoskeag to work at the Amory Mill but returned within seven months.

Arthur Allen and Ralph Morse, both American-born, were employed as wiremen. Arthur Allen had worked for only one year prior to the strike. He was served with injunction papers and described as a "red-hot" agitator and disturber. He did not return to the mill after the strike. Ralph Morse, who was arrested for inciting a riot, was a member of the Textile and Metal Board of the UTW. He began working in the Amoskeag at age 25 in 1909. He did not return immediately after the strike but did work from 1933 until the mill shut down.

English-born James Heron, another ubiquitous strike committee member, was employed in the mill from 1913 to 1922. First hired as a napper and inspector, he was demoted because the job "was too much for him." He then worked in various low-skilled positions, such as window washer, yarn hand, oiler, kettle hand, and finally kettleman. The employment office described him as one of the most active labor agitators during the 1922 strike. He was an "organizing type" whose hobby was speaking to groups of people, particularly political and religious groups or factory workers. The employment office was notified by management that he was not to be rehired. His poem "Keep On Keeping On" was published in *The Textile Worker*:

> Say, you're broke and busted
> And tired and disgusted
>   And everything seems out of gear,
> And the friends that you had
> All declare that you're mad
>   And say that you're nutty and queer.
> As you struggle and scheme
> In unfolding the dream
>   That you have put all your faith in
> If you set your own pace
> With a smile on your face
>   And KEEP ON KEEPING ON! you'll win.

Say, if business is bad
Don't look glum or feel sad
  Or knock the conditions of trade.
Ten to one, you will find,
By adjusting your mind –
  Increasing your service and grade
You will profit far more
Of goods in your store
  Than the grouch that you once had been:
So keep smiling away
And improving each day
  And KEEP ON KEEPING ON! you'll win.

Every failure in life,
Every trouble and strife
  That comes to you, average man
Is caused by your shifting
And heedlessly drifting
  Far off from your God-given plan:
For the dreams of your youth
Are all founded on truth,
  If kept from pollution of sin
Will start your thought right
For life's strenuous fight,
  So KEEP ON KEEPING ON! you'll win.

French-Canadian Eugene Gelinas began working in 1919 as a doffer but returned to Canada after two months. He came back to the Amoskeag in 1921 to learn how to weave and worked as a weaver until the strike. He was arrested for allegedly "inciting a riot."

Charles Beaumier, a French-Canadian worker who had a more "typical" Amoskeag career, began work at age 16 and stayed for three years, changing jobs nine times. He started as a part-time cleaner, left to return to school, came back to work as an oiler, left to look for "a better job," and then returned to work as a weaver. Later he had a series of menial jobs until he was rehired once again as a weaver.

As the profile of the "activists" suggests, with some exceptions, the majority were members of the stable core of the Amoskeag's labor force. Only 17 of the 94 had had somewhat erratic careers of less than a year. Only 28 career records suggested discontent, listing such reasons for leaving as "dissatisfied," "didn't like the job," "work too hard." Even fewer experienced disciplinary problems,

although several were dismissed at some point in their careers because of "drinking" or because they "stayed out" or "took fits."
Theophile Langevin, for example, an exception among the activists,
was discharged frequently, and even twice within a five-year period, for the following reasons: "lazy," "sleeps well here," "walked
out once," "unreliable," "not wanted," "no good," "very fresh,"
"can't keep up his work," "doesn't care about working." Records of
this kind were not unusual, however, and most of the people leaving for such reasons were rehired.

Most strike activists had been enthusiastic union members in the
years preceding the strike. They had served as union committee
members, employee representatives, safety committee members,
and official collectors of union dues. For example, Yvonne Baker
(née Harbour) was first employed at age 16. She worked for forty-
five months, from 1913 until 1919, as a weaver and was a member of
the union's grievance committee in 1919, a delegate to the weavers'
convention in 1918, and a dues collector in the UTW until 1922,
identifying herself as a "business agent" on her marriage record.
As an active strike committee member, she represented the strikers
at the meeting in which Mayor Trudel was accused of being an
agent of the Amoskeag. On June 8, 1922, she was served with injunction papers.

The activists were not marginal workers. Most had had long careers in the Amoskeag and were committed to the corporation.
They also had served apprenticeships with the union as grievance
committee members or as dues collectors. The violation of their
rights as workers was one concern. The destruction of the delicate
equilibrium that had existed between the workers and the corporation was another concern. When the Amoskeag moved to destroy
that equilibrium, they felt betrayed.

Of the twenty agitators who returned to the Amoskeag after the
strike, four immediately resumed their original jobs, four found
jobs slightly higher in status than their pre-strike jobs, and some
recovered their original jobs within a year. For example, a clerk
worked after the strike as an oiler but returned to his former job
within a year; a piper returned as a piper helper but later became a
pipe fitter. About four obtained entirely different jobs, not always
lower in status.

Assignment to a low-status job was not necessarily a deliberate
penalty for agitators. Because of the lower and more erratic production levels that prevailed after the strike, a number of workers were
unable to recover their former jobs, regardless of their strike activi-

ties. Maria Lacasse's husband, for example, a "trained hand" before the strike, was rehired as a runner boy:

> His pay went down, and we had to pay back all the summer rent [which was in arrears because of the strike]. So I kept on working. I was earning more than he was at that time, and besides, I liked to work. I liked to meet the people [Lacasse, *Amoskeag*, p. 261].

Some interviewees also claimed that the more conspicuous and active union members were the first to return after the strike: "That gang that belonged to the union was the first gang to come in when they opened up. They were the first ones" (Antoine Roberge, interview).

The strike as a watershed

The strike cost the workers over $11 million in lost wages, or about $50,000 per day. The company lost over $10 million due to the strike (*Manchester Union*, Nov. 27, 1922). By late November 1922, 1,000 workers had still not been rehired, despite the corporation's promise as part of the settlement to rehire former strikers. Starr claimed that a number of these workers had been blacklisted: "None of the corporations against which we went on strike one year ago have been so mean and inhumane as the Amoskeag," wrote Starr in the *Textile Worker* (Valade 1959:71).

The strike represented a watershed for the corporation and the workers. It marked the breakdown of an unwritten social contract between the two, destroying a balance based upon internal corporate traditions, mutual respect, and the workers' identification with the abstract notion of the "Amoskeag" as an entity in itself, separate from the people who owned it. For the first time, the traditional institutional structure of the corporation was exposed, and a large number of workers came in direct contact with the absentee "owners" – most notably the controversial treasurer, F. C. Dumaine. Even though most of the corporation's uncompromising announcements had been issued by Straw, the workers focused their blame for the corporation's unbending attitude during the strike on Dumaine. Unaware that Dumaine had been in control of the company before the strike, many interviewees believed that it was his "takeover" of the company that caused the strike and the subsequent decline of the Amoskeag. Their basic loyalty and civility toward Straw persisted, and when W. P. Straw's young daughter died at the depths of the strike, picketing was suspended for a day and a wreath was sent to the agent's house.

To a large extent, the strike destroyed the spirit of the Amoskeag. A former weaver recalled meeting her boss on the street during the strike: "We were looking up at the mill and he said, 'Elizabeth, that was heaven and we didn't know it!' It was true" (Miller, interview). "Up until that time it seemed to me that Manchester was just at its peak, and from that time on it seemed as though for a long time everything was sort of depressed. Everybody was depressed" (Irene Wilson, interview). After the strike, as Omer Proulx recalled, "we all worked, but just in appearance . . . They didn't work for the company. They worked against it" (*Amoskeag*, p. 71). "It didn't go well afterwards," recalled Donat Carignan. "There was always entanglements" (interview). "It was never steady after that, never!" recalled another worker. "The Amoskeag was never the same old place" (Adam Laliberte, interview).

The conflicts that surfaced during the strike further undermined the workers' sense of pride, which had begun to waver earlier with the imposition of increased work loads, frequent wage reductions, and longer hours. The trauma of the strike was so severe, however, that earlier dissatisfactions and disputes paled in comparison.

Most workers viewed the strike as a complete failure. Because of its bitter consequences, the true nature of their involvement is difficult to gauge. Some workers who had initially favored the strike claimed, that in retrospect, they had no choice. The majority stayed out because they did not want to be called scabs and were afraid of violence. It is difficult to reconstruct their level of commitment, to separate the enthusiasts from those who consented reluctantly to the mandate of their union out of fear. With few exceptions, hundreds of interviewees claimed that fear of the pickets had forced them to participate or that they had stayed on strike only as long as the mills were shut. It is possible, of course, that they are now like those former radicals of the thirties who no longer want to acknowledge the "sins" of their youth.

Although fear may have been a potent factor in preventing workers from entering the mill during the height of the picketing, intimidation alone does not explain the fact that more workers did not return after June 5, as additional mills began to open. The strikers were clearly divided. Some, like Paul Morin, continued to stay out because of fear: "I wasn't for the strike. I was mad about it. But what could you do? If you went in to work, you got your head bashed in!" (*Amoskeag*, p. 309). And some, like Cora Pellerin, insisted that no matter what, they would not retreat:

> I was not going to be a scab. I went to Canada and I worked there until the strike was over. My sister went [to the Coolidge Mill], her husband went in, my brother, my sister-in-law went in, not at first. They went in when there was no chance of winning . . . but I didn't want to come back until it said in the paper that it was all over. I felt so strongly. Well, after losing seven or eight months, why not wait till the end? [interview].

And some, like Cora's relatives, whose initial commitment to the strike was eroded by deprivation, reentered the mills as soon as they were reopened.

The strike also discredited the union, leaving the workers with the feeling that they had been used, that the union leaders had sold them "down the river." Some interviewees even now attribute the failure of the strike to the callousness of its leaders. Indeed, many workers felt that a special deal between Rivière and management had settled the strike. Alexandre Bolvin was one of many who claimed that such a deal was made: "We had a big meeting of the union at Mt. Carmel Hall. It was terrible that Mr. Rivière would do this [agree to end the strike]. It was done under the carpet at the Amoskeag. They told us" (interview). Although even F. C. Dumaine's son hinted at such a deal when he said, "Horace Rivière and I settled the 1922 strike in the men's room" (interview), his elaboration clarified the picture:

> He was in his early twenties and French like myself – though I don't think he could have been more French than the Dumaines. Anyway, he was typically French: somewhat hotheaded yet very friendly with me. He suggested to Dad and me how the strike could be settled, while Dad and the others were sitting around the table, working with Bishop Peterson. They wanted to get the people back to work, but they weren't getting anywhere . . .
>
> Horace and I couldn't stand by while these people were not working, so Horace went out and made some suggestions for settling the strike, and the old man grabbed them. I hadn't even said a word to Dad; Horace didn't give in. He just got sick and tired of the employees being idle while all the other mills were running at Amoskeag's expense. The other mills had all agreed to cut wages 10 percent, and none of them did. They just didn't live

up to what they had agreed. So Amoskeag settled: they agreed to give a little and take a little. We had no reason for staying out except that we couldn't make any money! [F. C. Dumaine, Jr., *Amoskeag*, pp. 336–7].

The workers could not identify with the strike leaders – Starr, Fleming, and Rivière – because these men were "outsiders." They could not identify with the union in general because the strike erupted before they had had the opportunity to understand the union's functions and ideology and its likely benefits to them. They blamed Rivière for what went wrong even though he was just an organizer rather than the top leader, because they had known him as an organizer prior to the strike.

In the workers' minds, the 1922 strike was the harbinger of the Amoskeag's subsequent shutdown. "The strike was the beginning of the end," concluded one former worker. His assessment echoed F. C. Dumaine's earlier threat that "grass will grow on the streets of Manchester unless the workers agree to terms." Fourteen years later, the shutdown seemed to fulfill that prophecy. "If they hadn't been always ready to strike," recalled Amelia Gazaille, "maybe the Amoskeag would still be here . . . There was always somebody that wanted to strike for more money and more and more" (interview). "That is when the Amoskeag started to go down, when we had the strike," concluded Dorothy Moore. "Before that, we had the world knocking on our doors for cloth. During the strike, nine months with no cloth, they lost the market. The strike had not accomplished anything for Amoskeag, nor did it for the workers, because the mills [eventually] closed up" (interview). When Marie Proulx was asked "Why do you think the mills shut down?" she answered, "By going on strike" (interview). And Elizabeth Miller said: "It closed down during the strike, and it never really started up. When it started up it never did any good afterwards" (interview).

In reality, the same forces that provoked the strike eventually led to the shutdown; but because of the strike's cataclysmic character, it crystallized for many workers the collapse of the delicate balance in their relationship with the corporation. With the passage of time, some workers confused the strike of 1922, in which little violence occurred, with the violent strike of 1933. In their minds, these two strikes and the subsequent one in 1934 merged into one traumatic sequence, even though they were a decade apart.

The company union and the collapse of labor relations

During the decade following the strike, the corporation established a company union as a substitute for the UTW, which had officially ceased activity in the Amoskeag. Similar to other corporations that had introduced company unions, the Amoskeag's Plan of Representation was intended to avoid conflict by giving the workers an illusion of collective bargaining. In reality, it became, in the corporation's hands, an instrument for negotiating and forcing wage reductions.

The plan was introduced in 1923 through the formation of a committee of 48 members selected by management, most of whom had continued to work during the strike or had been brought in as strikebreakers. Management then convened 244 delegates elected by the operatives according to each department. At this meeting twelve members were elected to work in conjunction with an equal number representing management in drawing up a plan for the company union.

Although the corporation tried to give the impression that the workers wanted the Plan of Representation, in reality it was imposed upon them through the corporation's coercive tactics. When the plan was brought before the workers for a vote, a majority of the cotton and worsted operators rejected it. They were "persuaded," however, to accept it after a temporary shutdown of the cotton division, which was an obvious threat. In other departments, whenever the workers refused the plan, management kept reintroducing and resubmitting it for a vote until it was approved. Usually the workers were pressured to vote in the presence of overseers, thus leaving them little choice. Creamer and Coulter termed the plan a "semblance with or without reality of democratic participation of the employees in the management of labor relations" (Creamer and Coulter 1939:210).[14]

The plan established a complex hierarchy of committees for handling grievances, consisting primarily of joint committees with management and workers having equal voice and representation. Employee representatives were selected by secret ballot by all workers; the employer's representatives were selected by management. Unlike a regular union, the workers paid no dues. Representatives were compensated for the time devoted to committee work.

The grievance mechanism instituted under this plan was far more elaborate than that in the late 1910s and early 1920s. Grievances were presented first to the overseer; if not resolved satisfactorily, they were then sent up through a hierarchy of committees, first to the joint departmental committee and then to the departmental superintendent, to the joint sectional committee on adjustment, and to the agent. The matter was considered settled if a unanimous decision was rendered by any of these committtees. Of the 200 cases that were docketed during the company union's existence, 77 were decided in favor of the employees and 123 against them. Favorable decisions for employees exceeded unfavorable ones only in terms of working conditions, whereas only from one-fourth to one-third of the complaints involving individual wage adjustments; alleged discrimination in discharges, layoffs, or transfers; or increases in the work load were decided in the workers' favor. In analyzing these cases, Creamer observed that he wondered whether it was merely a poor knowledge of English on the part of the French-Canadian secretary of the Joint Departmental Committee for Picking and Carding that led him to record in the minutes "that the complaint be referred back for a better misunderstanding" (Creamer and Coulter 1939:214).

In addition to the grievance committees, the Plan of Representation had a General Joint Council composed of representatives of the three joint sectional committees, which could be called together at any time by management or at the request of a majority of employee representatives on the joint sectional committees to consider matters of common interest to all the employees in the mill. In 1930, the General Joint Council was replaced by a General Employees Council, which came to be the executive committee of the Convention. Management always appointed its representatives after workers' representatives were elected; thus, supervisors of workers who were representatives could be chosen to serve with them on the same committee. This policy increased the corporation's power over employee representatives, because by serving with their superior on the same committees, the workers faced the danger of being discriminated against or losing their jobs if they disagreed with management. Some representatives were also intimidated by their bosses when they were trying to expose the flaws of the company union to fellow workers. Marie-Ann Senechal recalled how as a representative she had to return to the weavers and inform them that their wages would be cut:

> [I was instructed to] get on the chair and tell them, "Boys and girls, you've got to work for $11.00 or $15.00 a week." I came back and told the people what was really going on at the meetings. The boss, Bert Molloy, didn't like it. I was telling the work-

ers what to do. So he said, "I'm going to get rid of her." It wasn't fair. He wasn't using the weavers right [Senechal, *Amoskeag*, p. 327].

General wage reductions were voted upon by the Joint Convention of Employee Representatives, which could call for a referendum of all operatives. The management was not bound to respect – and on occasion did not respect – the decisions of the Convention on the referendums. During the ten years that the Plan of Representation was in effect, the employee representatives were forced to vote a total wage reduction of 40%, whereas the cost of living declined by only 20%. Although the early wage cuts were approved by the employee representatives, the later cuts were not. Following the lead of other textile mills, the Amoskeag raised wages by 12.5% in April 1923, but the work load was increased by "doubling up." In September 1924 a 20% wage cut "to stimulate business and allow the company to compete with other mills in other sections of the country" was unanimously rejected (Creamer and Coulter 1939:215). Several months later, however, the workers agreed to the cut for a six-month period. Subsequently, under pressure from the agent, the workers' representatives repeatedly extended the wage cut for additional periods.

An anonymous Amoskeag worker writing to the editor of the *Textile Worker* expressed his frustration with the Plan of Representation:

> This plan has been in effect for two years, and the only thing that has happened is that they forced a ten percent cut on us, and also doubled up our work . . . and under this wonderful plan there is not one chance for the workers to get anything done for us . . . The only thing that can be done now is for us to get back in our unions . . .[15]

For the next three years management continued to cope with a declining market by cutting production costs through curtailments, speedups, and wage cuts. Each time the workers' representatives sought a 10% wage increase, they were pressured into extending the existing wage agreement. In December 1927, W. P. Straw imposed a 10% wage reduction without the approval of the representatives. The speedups were justified, according to the agent, because they enabled the workers to earn enough despite the wage reductions: "I am glad that those people have got back so much, but it is by working harder. The management has put the work up so as to enable the operative to get so much back."[16] In 1928 the management refused a workers' petition to increase wages by 5.5% to match increases granted by mills in New Bedford and Fall River. Amoskeag workers were so squeezed that the employee representatives requested of the mayor that he find ways to reduce the high cost of living, but without much success.

Henry Rauch, who in 1928 replaced William Parker Straw as agent, was generally remembered more as a "numbers man" than as an expert in textiles. He initiated a game of "divide and rule" by forcing the various mills within the Amoskeag to compete with each other for a given order.[17] To obtain an order, a mill had to manufacture the product at the lowest cost. To achieve the lowest cost, a mill had to cut wages. This policy brought about wage reductions in individual departments, rather than across the board. In 1931, for example, management told the representatives of the cotton section that the "employees of the Bag Mill agree to work a whole year on the present wage schedule" (Creamer and Coulter 1939: 234). Management threatened to close down a mill (and actually did so) when the employee representatives refused to approve a wage reduction. A reduction that was to remain in effect for a limited time was frequently extended with repeat orders.

Collective bargaining became a farce. The agent pushed through another wage cut at the beginning of the Great Depression despite the employee representatives' initial defeat of this measure in a referendum, with 1,708 votes in favor and 3,127 opposing. The agent did not believe "that the 6,000 workers in the Amoskeag would want to see this concern go out of business, but," he threatened, "if that is the sentiment of the workers [I am] absolutely helpless."[18] Following this, workers presented petitions to the Convention to reconsider the vote. The Convention authorized another referendum and also waived the requirement that the reduction had to be accepted by a two-thirds majority in order to take effect. The origin of the petition was suspect. The waiver of the two-thirds majority requirement was necessary, since less than two-thirds of the employees actually voted in favor of the reduction (Creamer and Coulter 1939:238–9).

Despite the corporation's attempt to use the company union to rubber stamp the wage reductions, the union was more active and often more insistent than in other establishments, because of the membership of former UTW activists. The boldness of the company union was expressed in one delegate's request that the treasurer of the Amoskeag resign, since "he is to blame for present conditions" (Creamer and Coulter 1939:218–19).

Nevertheless, the union's resistance crumbled between 1929 and

1933, as each agent's request for new wage reductions or for the extension of the existing reduction was presented as an ultimatum: Accept or the mills will close. In April 1932, when the employee representatives met with F. C. Dumaine at their own request, he said that "personally he thought that if this plant ever closed completely, he doubted if it would be opened again" (Dumaine quoted in Creamer and Coulter 1939: 241).

The threat of a complete shutdown was driven home to the workers through various tricks. William Spencer,[19] who in 1933 and 1934 had worked as Dumaine's troubleshooter in the Amoskeag, recalled that Dumaine would store large cotton supplies in the Billerica car shop of the Boston and Maine Railroad.

> He would then send to Manchester a truckload at a time. The theory was that labor would see just a little bit of cotton coming in and would think that they are running out of orders. It was to give the workers the impression that the mill was in bad straits and was just barely getting by, so they better not cause any disturbances or the mills would have to close [*Amoskeag*, p. 349].

With employment reduced by 28% and overall wage reductions, many workers were forced to seek relief from other quarters. Because the city was unable to shoulder the burden, the Amoskeag agreed to match every dollar that the workers contributed for the relief of those who were unemployed. Between the first week in December 1930 and April 11, 1931, the Employees' Relief Committee collected and expended more than $7,800, including the company's contribution. In addition to the collection of money, the workers also insisted on sharing the work, but they encountered resistance from the overseers. In two weave rooms, for example, the overseers refused to alternate the work, because they felt this procedure would result in many "seconds," as workers would be blaming mistakes on each other rather than taking responsibility for them directly. But the employee representatives insisted that the alternating system was correct and should be enforced.

Wage reductions and layoffs continued in the following two years, although such layoffs were now called permanent, according to the agent's new ruling that laid-off workers should not be rehired. Fewer then 4,200 workers were employed in the Amoskeag in the last week of June 1932. Business began to pick up, however; by the middle of August the number of employees had increased to 5,500, by the end of September to 6,000, and by the end of the year to 6,800, although a considerable number of those workers were recruited from other towns.

The final blow to the company union came in December 1933. When Dumaine informed the employee representatives that a wage reduction of 25% would be required in order to keep the mills running, the employees voted to request a restoration of the wage scale in effect prior to October 3, 1931. The agent not only upheld the existing wage plan but announced the cancellation of overtime and hour agreements; instead, he instituted overtime payments at a straight rate. He further insisted that he had "the right to break agreements if he saw fit without consulting anyone."[20] The employee representatives voted to dissolve the Plan of Representation following a ninety-day notice, unless the agent withdrew the ultimatum. After a final desperate effort on the part of the employee representatives to compromise, which was rejected by management, they voted 5 to 1 in favor of discontinuing the Plan of Representation on January 18, 1933.

The most important legacy the company union had left behind was preparing the way for the reentry of the UTW. Some of those who had been active in the UTW prior to the 1922 strike had managed to become elected to the company union, and thus maintained contact with large numbers of workers. The company union also taught the workers to function through elected representatives in common councils rather than in separate organizations according to each craft, as they had done under the UTW before 1922. Even though issues were rarely resolved to their satisfaction in the company union, the workers learned that most problems affected all of them, regardless of craft, and could be discussed most effectively in a combined convention (Creamer and Coulter 1939). The former union leaders' continued contact with the employees, and the workers' growing discontent and feelings of helplessness caused by the Amoskeag's frequent blacklisting of workers who rejected company policy and the absence of a fair grievance mechanism, led to the reemergence of the UTW in the Amoskeag after the company union was dissolved.

The employees' mood was no secret to the corporation. In 1933, only nine days before the first strike led by the new union, overseers and second hands surveyed the attitudes in the different departments and reported a general spirit of dissatisfaction, particularly over low wages and high work loads. The general sentiment reported seemed to have been that workers were prepared not to strike if government legislation (then pending in Washington) would bring about an increase in wages. The overseer of the Stark Mill's weaving department, for example, reported, "The employees are more or less discouraged. The small amount of wages received makes it difficult to meet their domestic obligations." Workers in the Stark Mill Carding department expressed dissatisfaction with their low wages while the company made a profit. But they were willing to wait for legislation. In several departments, however, the workers made it clear that they were prepared to strike or quit. Similarly, the overseer of No. 1 and No. 3 Carding concluded that the "help was wavering. They don't want trouble. Not convinced that they could not be led."[21]

On May 19, 1933, the first strike since 1922 erupted in the Amoskeag. Its immediate cause was the corporation's announcement that the mills would close from May 26 to July 31 to all employees who did not wish to continue on the existing wage scale. The company did announce a 15% increase in wages to become effective on July 29, but the workers wanted the raise to be retroactive to February, when a cut had been taken. After several departments walked out, the Amoskeag closed on May 19.

Unlike its predecessor in 1922, the strike was short and violent. Trouble broke out on May 23, when 3,000 workers gathered at the mill gates, causing an uncontrolled demonstration. Some of the demonstrators attacked overseers, second hands, and clerks as they were about to leave the mill. Forty workers were reported hurt by mob violence, and fifty people were arrested the next day. Horace Rivière, general organizer for the UTW, claimed, however, that those arrested were not union members, and not even Amoskeag workers. After the dispersal of the crowd, the mayor and Chief Healey conferred and decided to ask the governor to dispatch four companies of the New Hampshire National Guard to Manchester. This step was taken, although the city was not placed under martial law. At the same time, the Manchester Parks and Playgrounds Commission revoked the permit granted earlier to the strikers to hold a gathering, since "the most unfortunate occurrences of last night would indicate that however good his intentions are, he [Mr. Rivière] is unable to control his followers" (*Manchester Leader*, May 23, 1933). After their arrival, the National Guardsmen were quartered in the mill. The police were to guard the entire city, and the militia was assigned specifically to the millyard.

The calling of the state militia on so little provocation is puzzling, since the disturbances did not approach widespread violence. Attacks on strikebreakers exiting the mill had taken place during the strike of 1922 as well, without such drastic responses. It is possible in this instance that the agitation surrounding a two-month shoeworkers strike in Manchester gave special cause for alarm. It is also possible that the authorities rushed the state militia into the city in an attempt to exaggerate the impression and threat of labor violence. Protesting this act, Councillor Alphonse Roy of Manchester wired Governor Winant, "vigorously protesting this unwarranted action in calling out the National Guard" (*Manchester Leader*, May 23, 1933).

The strike was settled following a meeting of the mill officials, the mayor, the governor, Horace Rivière, and Bishop John P. Peterson of Manchester. The union won the retroactive 15% wage increase, as well as a recognition from the management of the right to be represented by a business agent and the establishment of a shop committee to handle grievances. The company did not concede a check-off of dues and a closed shop, but the union gained the corporation's acceptance of seniority of layoffs, although with qualifications. With the promulgation six weeks later of the textile codes under the National Recovery Administration (NRA), which guaranteed the right of collective bargaining, the union was well entrenched, but not in a position to fully control its membership (Creamer and Coulter 1939).

The strike of 1933 deserves special attention because it was *sui generis*. It originated in the Amoskeag, unlike the national textile strike that was to occur in 1934, in which Amoskeag workers participated but were "placid"; they joined more out of solidarity with workers in other towns. The intensity in 1933 expressed a culmination of anger and grievances related directly to the Amoskeag rather than to a national labor struggle. In a sense, the 1933 strike was a precursor of a series of union-led, as well as wildcat, strikes that occurred in the Amoskeag in 1933 and 1934 under the NRA.

The provisions of the cotton textile code of the NRA became operative in the Amoskeag on July 17, 1933, establishing a 40-hour week with wages to equal the amount earned in the 54-hour week. It also set a minimum wage of $13 in the cotton division and $14 in the worsted division, except for the cleaners, sweepers, and learners. On July 14, 1933, Dumaine announced to company officials the Amoskeag's endorsement of the NRA code and an agreement with the union. He hailed the NRA as a "new experiment in industrial relations." Dumaine stated earlier:

> The parties [the Amoskeag and the union] have exchanged assurances that they will give [the plan] sincere and unqualified support and that they will seek to bury all differences that may have arisen from misunderstandings in the past. That they will

aim in good faith to promote efficiency in the mill and a spirit of good will between management, men and the community.
He went on to say in his address to company officials:

> If through this arrangement we are able to inspire the spirit of contact, conference, confidence, and cooperation, the management will never regret the significant step it has taken [*Manchester Leader*, July 14, 1933].

Ironically, although the NRA code brought into the Amoskeag a partial increase in production and therefore employment, as well as an increase in hourly wages, it also provided the setting for a series of labor disputes and strikes unprecedented in the Amoskeag's history. Although the Amoskeag's wage rates were relatively higher than in the south, they were lower in comparison to other New England mills, even after the NRA had led to some narrowing of wage differentials. With the exception of weavers, differentials between the Amoskeag and other New England mills were widened in each occupation. Since the NRA code required payment equal to that paid by competitors, departments in the Amoskeag claimed that they were earning less compared with other mills and threatened work stoppages. Moreover, with the increase of wage rates under the NRA code, the Amoskeag introduced speedups and increased the work load. As Creamer points out, however, the most numerous grievances still revolved around the issue of interpretation of the seniority principle in laying off. After having resisted a commitment to seniority in all its earlier negotiations with the union, the Amoskeag now agreed that "in time of slackness in a department, the oldest person employed from the point of service has the preference of employment . . ." However, the qualification that that person be "conversant and qualified to do work that remains in operation" left the ultimate interpretation to the overseer (Creamer and Coulter 1939:255).

In August 1933, many departments threatened stoppages if their demands for higher wage rates were not satisfied. Management stalled in handling this request until November, and finally turned the matter over to the National Industrial Relations Board (NIRB) for cotton textiles. Although the Board granted increases of 5% to 10% in certain classifications, a strike was called that lasted for 3 days.

On April 2, 1934, the weavers and ancillary workers in the Bag Mill stopped all looms in protest over the stretchout. The entire mill went out on strike. Management agreed to NIRB arbitration on the same day, without insisting on a return to work as a condition for negotiations. The dispute was settled by a unanimous acceptance of the recommendations by a committee of three persons appointed one each by the employer, the employees, and the National Industrial Relations Board. The corporation accepted the recommendations for the reduction in the work loads, and the workers returned.

On May 7, 1934, officials of the worsted union declared a "recess" rather than a strike, without official union authorization, which resulted in the walkout of 7,000 workers who were dissatisfied over the latest wage and hour agreement. The NIRB arbitration had granted 5% to 10% wage increases only to certain occupations. The unaffected workers were the ones who walked out (*Manchester Leader*, May 7, 1934). On May 8, the mill closed until the tenth of the month. Rivière, calling for "intelligent thinking rather than rash action," reminded the workers of their oath to abide by the NIRB's decision no matter what (*Manchester Leader*, May 8, 1934). About 50% of the worsted and woolen operatives returned by the morning of May 8. Considerably less of the cotton section returned. By May 10, the workers returned, and Rivière blamed the triggering of the strike on "communists and a group of young workers who have been visiting communist headquarters quite frequently. He promised to purge them from the UTW" (*Manchester Leader*, May 11, 1934).

The protests expressed in the sporadic strikes and walkouts in the Amoskeag revealed the discontent prevalent industry-wide; this discontent culminated in the national strike of 1934. When the UTW called a strike for September, it demanded a 30-hour week with the same wage rate as a 40-hour week, application of the wage differential to semiskilled and highly skilled workers, and reduction of the work load. Amoskeag workers were apathetic because they felt they stood to gain little from a national strike. The specific grievances they expressed when calling the strike were the inhumanity of the stretch-out system, the immediate and steady decline in the volume of employment after the cotton textile code went into effect, the decline in average weekly earnings under the code, and the permanent layoff of union members before other workers (*Manchester Leader*, September 4, 1934). Because the company did not try to operate, picketing was not necessary and no violence occurred. The strike was called off after three weeks and the workers returned without any gains.

"Chinese strikes" or "sitdowns" began in the Amoskeag in August 1933 and extended through most of 1934. Such stoppages were in violation of the bylaws of the union's constitution, which provided for a two-thirds vote of all the operatives and the sanction of the National Textile Council before machinery could be stopped. In April 1934, when a number of cases were in the process of arbitration, the president of the UTW local had to issue a request to all members "to be patient and not participate in the stoppage of work" (Creamer and Coulter 1939:261).

In addition to the long-term causes underlying this strike behavior, particularly workers' pent-up anger that may have accumulated under the Plan of Representation, Creamer and Coulter identified some immediate ones: Workers' naive interpretation of the labor guarantees of the NRA; the lack of judgment and responsibility among some union business agents; and workers' expression of frustration with management's long delays in handling disputes (Creamer and Coulter 1939:261).

The frequency of sitdown strikes also expresses, however, the final collapse in labor relations in the Amoskeag and the loss of any hope for the settlement of disputes through established channels. The strikes represent the workers' bitterness about the deterioration of the plant and management's violation of codes of behavior that had been mutually accepted earlier within the mill. Most importantly, they expressed the loss of any sense of trust on the part of the workers and their deep feeling of betrayal by the corporation. This sense of betrayal was intensified by the contrast between the insecurity and difficulties the workers were experiencing on the job and the high promises that the NRA would usher in a new chapter in industrial relations – promises reinforced by Dumaine's own declaration in 1933 that a new era in labor relations in the Amoskeag would begin.

The grim reality stood in sharp contrast to those promises, however. William Spencer, despite being Dumaine's special representative to investigate labor and management relations in Manchester, was appalled by the hopelessness of the situation and disagreed with Dumaine's policy. He complained bitterly about the disappointment he had to inflict each day on the workers standing in line at the employment office: "The workers in Manchester were the most courteous lot, because every morning, when they came down there to get a job and I had to tell them there were no more jobs, they believed me" (*Amoskeag*, p. 350). As Bishop Peterson explained to Spencer, when he was wondering at first why the workers were so angry: "These people are speaking from an empty plate. They did not get even three days' work a week" (*Amoskeag*, p. 350).

The worst betrayal the workers felt was the transfer of assets from the Amoskeag Manufacturing Company to the holding company during the Plan of Reorganization in 1925. As Spencer observed: "Labor knew as much about accounting as anybody else. The workers' argument to me was: 'My grandmother and my grandfather worked hard to establish this surplus. We really earned it for the Amoskeag Manufacturing Company. Now, in the Depression, why can't they at least pay me a living wage and keep the mill operating? That surplus is really ours, but they've taken it away" (*Amoskeag,* pp. 347–8).

In handling grievances, Spencer felt that management would not respect the workers' rights even when it should have:

> I gathered that Dumaine and the New York office didn't like that type of thing – they didn't want me to concede that labor was right, even in that one respect . . . If Dumaine could have afforded to pay higher wages, maybe the workers would have turned out more. But because he was so penurious, they would do just enough to hold on to their jobs. This was the era of what they called sit-down strikes. They would sit down on the job and wouldn't go back until somebody came and listened to their complaint [*Amoskeag,* pp. 348–9].

Spencer resigned before the year was up. He felt he was unable to get Dumaine's support in meeting the Union's heavy demands. In addition, Spencer could not drive home to Dumaine that much of the workers' anger and hatred was directed at Dumaine personally. He tried to persuade Dumaine: "If you're willing to hand over the reins to somebody else, you might be able to pull through." But Dumaine replied in rage: "No! I'll blow the God damn place to pieces before I see somebody else operate that mill" (*Amoskeag,* p. 352).

The frequency of the sitdown strikes and the union's inability to contol the workers led management to consider breaking off relations with the UTW. In a confidential memo to F. C. Dumaine, Michael Ahern of the personnel office warned in December 1934 that on the basis of past experience it was clear that union leaders could not control certain groups of workers and that "by not having the control necessary, the experiment of our association with the U.T.W. has been costly." He advised, however, that Dumaine should not bypass the UTW and deal directly with the workers. He insisted that despite its weaknesses, the union carried an important advantage for management: its ability to mediate a group dispute when it would not be possible for the group affected and management to arrive at a solution. Without a union, Ahern warned that "instead of centralizing a medium of settling disputes it would cause a scattering of the workers into so many group organizations." He concluded, therefore, that "knowing that the Company will have to deal with some form of organized workers under present laws, I believe we can make as much progress and be as sure of uninterrupted production under the U.T.W. as we can if we would sever our relations and cause all sorts of groups to contend without any executive agency to make decisions or rulings."[22] Instead he advised Dumaine to embark upon a policy to establish more friendly relations between employees and overseers and to improve public relations in the city in the interest of the company and the whole community. As Creamer observed, "It is somewhat ironical that the best working conditions enjoyed by the Amoskeag workers in a decade and a half should have been in the last year or so of the company's existence" (Creamer and Coulter 1939:264).

Thus, in the final years leading to the Amoskeag's demise, workers' behavior had gone full route, from submissiveness earlier in the century to volatility. Ironically, to control the workers, management had to resort to the union it had previously so strongly opposed. Both management and the union had to admit their helplessness in the face of the workers' uncontrolled anger and despair.

In December 1935, management filed a petition for reorganization in bankruptcy court. On July 9, 1936, the court recommended the liquidation of the company. But for all practical purposes the mill had ceased existence the previous September, when the labor force had dwindled to less than 1,000.

Despite the shutdown and the flood, Amoskeag workers still expected the mill to reopen. An Amoskeag representative who surveyed 931 residents in the corporation tenements in December 1935 reported that "the occupants of tenements made the usual inquiries as to when the mills would reopen. 'Will they be closed all winter?' 'Are the unions to blame for the condition?' 'When they start, will it be longer hours?' Approximately 801 of those interviewed inquired as to when the mills would reopen." Some unemployed workers were using their time to repair the tenements at their own expense; others "were indifferent as to what was in store for the future . . . These persons are in debt, and their hope of ever getting out of the red is forlorn. They appeared to take the attitude of letting things take their course and drift along. All ambition in these families appeared to be gone."[23]

By March 1936, workers were even willing to sacrifice wages in order to see the mill reopen. On March 7, 1936, the Citizens' Com-

SAMPLE BALLOT

All Former Employees of the Amoskeag Manufacturing Co. as appear on 1935 Payroll

Conducted by the Citizens Committee of the City of Manchester and The Manchester Textile Council.

ARE YOU WILLING TO WORK UNDER ADJUSTED WAGES AND CONDITIONS WHICH WILL PERMIT PERMANENT AND PEACEFUL OPERATIONS ON A COMPETITIVE COST BASIS AS DETERMINED BY THE MANAGEMENT AND REPRESENTATIVES OF THE WORKERS AND APPROVED FOR SUBMISSION TO THE WORKERS BY THE CHAIRMAN OF THE NEW HAMPSHIRE TEXTILE COMMISSION (THE MOST REVEREND JOHN B. PETERSON, D. D. BISHOP OF MANCHESTER) AND THE CHAIRMAN OF THE CITIZENS' COMMITTEE (HON. ARTHUR E. MOREAU)?

Total 6828

YES	NO
3669	*3133*

(Mark X in One of the above Squares)
21 Abstentions 5 Blank

Figure 12.1. Sample ballot of the 1936 poll taken by the Citizens' Committee of Manchester and the Manchester Textile Council, Amoskeag Records, BLH.

mittee of Manchester and the Manchester Textile Council polled the
Amoskeag employees who had been on the 1935 payroll, asking
them whether they were willing to work for reduced wages and
under conditions that would allow "permanent and peaceful operations on a competitive cost basis as determined by the management
and representatives of the workers."[24] Of the 6,800 valid ballots,
54% were affirmative.

The mill never reopened. An entire generation of workers was
stranded and the economic base of a city of 75,000 was destroyed.
Mary Perkins recalled later the sense of desolation:

> I was one of the last to leave the spinning room in the Amoskeag.
> It was weird. It was haunted . . . People panicked when the
> Amoskeag closed because they knew nothing else. I think that a
> lot of them would have taken the river if they'd known how long
> it would be before Manchester would get on its feet again [inter-
> view].

13   *Conclusion: Generations in historical time*

> Every man is born, lives, and dies in historic time. As he runs
> through the life-cycle characteristic of our species, each phase of
> it joins in the events of the world . . . some men come to the age
> of work when there is no work; others when there are wars.
>
> Everett Hughes (1971:124)

The essence of the historical process is the meeting between an individual's or a group's life history and the historical moment. People's responses to the historical conditions they encounter are
shaped both by the point in their lives at which they encounter
these conditions and by the "equipment" they bring with them
from earlier life experiences.[1]

The lives of the people studied in this book illustrate these inter-
sections with historical forces in the context of the rapid changes
within the Amoskeag. In one sense the broad economic shifts cul-
minating in the shutdown of the mills cut across all these people's
lives. But their ability to adapt to the historical changes in their
world of work varied in accordance with their earlier life and work
experiences.

As earlier chapters suggest, the lives of the Amoskeag workers
studied here can be grouped into three major periods that corres-
pond to historical changes in the corporation. The first group includes those who migrated to Manchester sometime between 1900
and 1918 and entered the mills when the Amoskeag was still at its
peak. The corporation's demand for labor was such that this group
could choose among different jobs and even transfer easily from
one workroom to another. These workers identified with the Amoskeag and with their jobs, even though they were well aware of being exploited. They formed strong attachments to the corporation,
which provided the context for most of their adult lives. Most remember their work as difficult but not oppressive. The sociability
and humane treatment encountered in the mill left memories that
tended to mellow the bitterness of the subsequent decline.

The second group, who began their careers during the twenties
and early thirties, knew an entirely different Amoskeag than had

355

the first group, some of whom were their parents. The commencement of their work lives coincided with an increase in work loads
and speedups and a reduction in wages. These new conditions diminished the earlier sociability and in its place engendered fear and
insecurity. Although getting a job had been merely routine for
workers of the first group, for the second group, the employment
office became a nightmare. As the Amoskeag continued to curtail
production, successively larger numbers of individuals found
themselves standing in the employment line day after day in the
hope of finding work. Job insecurity also undermined their chances
for occupational advancement. The second group had to accept
temporary jobs in anticipation of periods of unemployment, being
pushed around from one job to another, and less-skilled and lower-
paying jobs. The promise of basic security that had made the
Amoskeag attractive to the workers was beginning to disappear.

Following the strike in 1922, the Amoskeag world was never the
same. The decline of the mill and the deterioration of work relations
hurt the workers of the twenties and thirties not only because of the
personal impact it had on their lives but also because it represented
the loss of a world they had respected.

To the third group, whose work lives started shortly before the
1936 shutdown, the Amoskeag's grandeur was known only from
accounts of parents, grandparents, and other relatives. For them,
the Amoskeag was a place where one was lucky if one could "buy a
job." Yet despite the difficulties and insecurities of the industry,
many were caught unaware by the shutdown and were over-
whelmed by the depression before they had acquired skills and experienced a normal work sequence. They remembered the Amoskeag as a sinking ship – dirty, its morale broken, and stripped of its
earlier fame and sense of purpose and strength.

Timing was crucial in the lives of the Amoskeag workers at the
points at which they intersected with the different periods in the
mill's history. Their adaptation to the changing circumstances in
the Amoskeag affected their subsequent lives and those of their
children. But their adaptability to the consequence of the
Amoskeag's decline and shutdown was conditioned by their earlier
career histories and by the extent to which they were "prepared"
for those conditions.

In their analysis of the careers of former Amoskeag employees
shortly after the mill shut down, Creamer and Coulter (1939) were
able to capture the immediacy of the impact of the shutdown on the
workers' lives. They found that earlier work histories, age and mar-

ital status, and especially gender played important roles in determining the workers' responses to unemployment. Both married men and unmarried men and women who had been regularly employed were more likely to find employment after the shutdown than married women, who had made up the bulk of the Amoskeag's reserve labor force. Married men were more likely to find employment than single men, a reflection of family needs pressing upon them to find work under any circumstances. Workers who had low-skilled jobs had less difficulty finding employment after the shutdown than workers who had had more highly skilled or specialized jobs. The majority of former Amoskeag workers did not find employment in textiles. Indeed, in the subsequent decade, as the textile industry in the Northeast declined and mills gradually shut down, a whole generation of workers would discover that their skills had become obsolete.

The most surprising pattern found by Creamer and Coulter was the relationship between workers' career continuity and subsequent employability. Workers who had had intermittent careers in the Amoskeag were more likely to find employment after the shutdown than those with stable careers. The former may have had greater experience in seeking out other jobs and may also have had the kinds of connections outside the mill and the community that enabled them to do so. Perhaps the important variable was their greater adaptability, a result of their previous experience in coping with job changes and irregular employment.

Workers who had experienced the 1922 strike, depleted of resources and savings, were even more vulnerable to the shutdown, because they had already lost their cushion. In another sense, however, they were somewhat better prepared for the struggle for survival. The various methods for coping that they had developed during the strike served as a rehearsal for the devastating effects of the shutdown and the Great Depression.

The age at which a person encounters critical historical conditions also influences the impression of those events on a person's life history. Those who came of age in the later period of the Amoskeag's history experienced neither the initial smooth transition into a stable work life nor the margin of security that would have enabled them to experiment with employment opportunities outside the mill. Paradoxically, the Amoskeag's peak period was more conducive to young workers' efforts to locate a better job outside the mill than the period of subsequent decline. Thus the group that came of age during the final period of the Amoskeag's history

was caught more tightly in the historical squeeze. Without the employment experience of previous cohorts, the children of the shutdown had no chance to develop skills or accumulate savings or
property. Kin assistance was also less forthcoming because they too
were facing hard times. This group had to start once again at the
level of insecurity at which its parents and grandparents had begun
as immigrants.

The Amoskeag's decline had an even more devasting effect on
workers who encountered it in mid-life or later. Because they had
families to support, these workers had even less flexibility to search
for other jobs. Shuttling back and forth betwen jobs was always
more difficult for older workers because of the industry's general
preference for younger workers, and especially since by the late
1920s the company had embarked on a policy to eliminate many
older workers. Thus, the Amoskeag's decline almost entirely undermined older workers' chances for stability and especially for recovery after the shutdown.

For most of those who started work in the 1920s or later, the
dream of stability and greater opportunities for their children never
materialized. The dismal consequences of the strike relegated many
workers to a level below subsistence. In many cases savings and
homes lost during the strike could not be retrieved. The persistence
of job insecurity, which afflicted their children even more, confronted them with conditions not unlike those that triggered migration to Manchester in the first place. Finally, the shutdown, the
culmination of a decade-long siege of insecurity and instability,
dealt an irreversible blow to the Amoskeag workers' economic and
social lives and to the community. Coming in the midst of the Great
Depression, its impact was all the more devasting.

For those coming of age in the 1930s the shutdown upset the sce-
nario of the "American dream" workers had hoped to follow – escape from the mills by achieving a higher level of education, working their way up to a middle-class occupation, or becoming the
owner of a grocery store or restaurant. The generation that was
caught in the depression and shutdown in its teens was denied the
opportunity to follow this sequence.[2] Graduation from high school
and college and entrance into the world of white-collar work was
not to be achieved until the third generation or the fourth. Progression into the middle class was set back by an entire generation.

Following the shutdown, the unemployed Amoskeag workers
wandered about New England looking for work. They went to
Lawrence and Lowell, Massachusetts, to Biddeford, Maine, to New

Hampshire and Connecticut mill towns. Others returned to Canada. Women went into domestic service or worked as maids in hotels. Many worked in shoe factories; still others worked in the smaller textile companies that took over several of the empty mills of the Amoskeag. After the worst of the depression had subsided, former Amoskeag workers still had difficulty finding employment. Some found jobs in the Chicopee Mill. Some of the people who had never worked in the Amoskeag formed an attachment to the Chicopee that was similar to that felt by the Amoskeag workers in the pre-strike period. As Mary Perkins recalls, "When Chicopee shut down I felt as though I'd lost a friend, but I didn't feel that with the Amoskeag. Of course I was younger" (interview). Chicopee workers expressed the significance of this attachment when they were interviewed immediately following the unexpected shutdown of the Chicopee in 1975. These persons, mostly in their fifties, were again unemployed. Their skills were no longer wanted anywhere in New England. Their industry had died.

The circuitous route in quest for job security kept winding back to the mill, and despite the fickleness of the textile industry, the Depression generation still associated work in the mill with their personal identity and security. As Betty Skrzyszowski put it the day the Chicopee, the last mill in Manchester, shut down:

> If you gave me my choice, if you said today, "Which would you rather have, a thousand dollars right here or the mills starting up tomorrow?" I'd rather have the mills start up. I'd feel secure then; I'd have a job. I'd know what I was going to do. I'd know that I could handle it [Amoskeag, pp. 388–9].

Both first and second generations of immigrant workers at the Amoskeag had a clear sense of expectations and plans and priorities for their lives. Even though these "life plans" were thwarted by historical circumstances, an understanding of them should shed some light on the nature of both historical change and working-class identity.

A life plan – a concept that has not yet received sufficient attention from historians – encompasses a wide range of goals and aspirations around which an individual or family organizes its life. The phenomenon resembles closely what William Thomas referred to as "life organization" (Thomas and Znaniecki 1918–20). According to Robert Park's interpretation of this concept an individual makes life into a "project." "Eventually he formulates principles of action and organizes his life in ways which seem likely to further his life aim." In short, life organization is the individual's conception of his aims and the "codes and rules by which the individual seeks to maintain this conception and this project in a changing workld." Ideally, an individual would learn "to adapt his purpose to the continually increasing sphere of social reality" (Park 1931:170–1). A life organization constantly changes over the life course in relation to other family members and in response to new challenges, crises, and different historical circumstances. As people encounter new conditions, they modify and reshape their life plans, but they always do so in the context of their own customs and traditions.

In the case of the people studied here, two types of life plans can be identified: a "defensive" plan designed to cope with recurring crises and insecurities and a long-range plan, often spanning two or three generations, designed to assure basic security and achieve advancement. Underlying the defensive plan was the fear of losing self-respect that often results from public welfare and support from charitable agencies – something to be avoided at all costs (Modell 1978). The only recourse in times of need was family members. To survive, to fulfill the long-range plan, a family pooled resources and enforced strong discipline among the members.

Long-range planning, although not completely separate from crisis response, involved strategies pertaining to all aspects of life. Migration is an obvious example of a long-range life plan. For most interviewees in this study, the decision to migrate was an act of deliberate planning. In preparation, they contacted kin for assistance in finding jobs and housing, and after migrating they settled in the neighborhoods of kin to help each other – all integral to the plan. Home ownership was also part of their plan. To achieve it, wives and children went to work, and families took boarders into the household. Like the Irish immigrants in Newburyport, Massachusetts (Thernstrom 1964), more than half a century earlier, the first-generation immigrants to Manchester ranked owning a home higher than completion of schooling for their children. The desire for home security was so great that during the strike of 1922, some workers crossed picket lines rather than lose their homes.

To implement their plan to achieve a middle-class life-style, first-generation immigrants were prepared to make the necessary trade-offs: Children were sent to work to help families purchase homes; daughters dropped out of school early and went to work to allow sons to search for better jobs outside the mills. When necessary, families were temporarily divided to allow members to find jobs in other towns.

Life plans were revised and readjusted with each development, internal or external. Although economic forces and constraints were crucial in shaping or handicapping these plans, they did not necessarily determine the style of response. Responses were shaped by the degree to which individuals held on to their culture of origin and family traditions. For example, to the first-generation immigrants, married women's employment was acceptable, whereas the second generation had begun to follow the standards of the native-born that dictated a wife's place was in the home.

In terms of their life goals, most people in this study viewed themselves as being in a transitional stage from their farm background to an urban middle-class life-style. They did not identify themselves as "working class," even though their behavior might suggest it. Their immediate goal was economic security; their long-range goals were for middle-class occupations and life-styles. The seasonal unpredictability and poverty of rural life spurred their migration to a place where the entire family could find work and stay together. Inevitably, they entered the factory – the only employment opportunity available to them. Some viewed their life in Manchester as temporary. Even those who intended to settle permanently often claimed their condition was temporary.

Although mill workers developed attachments to their jobs and took pride in their work, they did not necessarily give up their aspirations to move into better occupations. Nor did they want their children to become mill workers. Their ultimate goals were to be able to afford to keep women and children out of the labor force, to educate their children, to own a home, and eventually to achieve middle-class occupations – if not for themselves, at least for their children. Some accomplished these goals in their own lifetimes; but the majority took one or more generations to achieve them.

Parents reared their children to become steady, reliable workers; but they also taught them to use their connections in the mills, the city, and even other towns to escape mill work. The second generation born in this country had more opportunity than the first to learn industrial work habits and to develop a collective identification with other workers. Although they, more than their parents, developed collective working-class behavior in the mill, they also had higher aspiratons and were better prepared than their parents to leave mill work should the opportunity arise. That they behaved more collectively as workers does not suggest that they considered themselves members of the working class permanently. In a survey

of the residents in the Amoskeag tenements conducted by a personnel officer in 1935, parents as well as the younger generation expressed a lack of interest in mill work:

> The tenement occupants show great interest and make every sac-
> rifice to further the education of their children. The young wom-
> en have their minds set on training to be beauty specialists,
> nurses, school teachers, musicians, dancers, stenographers and
> nuns.
>
> A very small percentage of the heads of families display any
> interest in having their children employed in the mills perma-
> nently.
>
> I venture that 75% of the young men and women under 21
> years of age living in the company tenements have no intention
> or desire to work in the mills.[3]

It is not surprising that mill workers and their children felt like this
in 1935 when the mill let them down. Similar attitudes were
present, however, in the peak period. For example, as one French-
Canadian woman recalled: "but I know one thing, my father said
we'd never work in the mills. That's one thing that my father didn't
want us to do, to work in the mills" (Jeanne Hebert, interview).
And the son of Swedish immigrants remembered his father's admonition:

> My father said to me: "No mills for you down there." So my
> brother was a postal inspector. I was a cost accountant . . . we
> went to school. In those days, there was a very small percentage
> that went to college, and had a high school education. You were
> just a little cut above the average [Oscar Johanson, interview].

Mitchell Skrzyszowski – whose immigrant parents from Poland
worked in the mills at the beginning of the century – had hoped as a
child not to follow in their footsteps. Although he worked in the
Amoskeag temporarily as a teen-ager, he embarked at his parents'
urging on a search for another type of job in Boston in the early
1930s. The onset of the Great Depression deprived him of any opportunity for employment, however, and after seeking work
throughout New England, he finally returned to Manchester. He
eventually found stable work in the Waumbec Mill, which opened
shortly before the outbreak of World War II, where he worked until
his retirement. Both he and his wife continued to value textile work
as a source of stability even though the industry let them down in
the early 1970s when the Chicopee Mill, where his wife was working, shut down suddenly and once again in 1981 when the Waumbec Mill, where his wife subsequently worked, also shut down.

They did send their children to college, however, so that they would not repeat their parents' and grandparents' careers (interview).

The Amoskeag workers' identification with their jobs, whether first, second, or third generation, and even their circuitous return to employment should not mislead us to assume that they intended to remain permanently in the "working class." They were a people in transition who, during their episode in the mill, displayed what could be identified as working-class behavior. At times it would be difficult, though, to distinguish between working-class and ethnic behavior, especially when the two were mutually reinforcing.

A fuller understanding of the Amoskeag workers' and their families' behavior in the larger historical process can be achieved by examining how the conditions described here fit into the broader picture of historical change in American society.

From family time and industrial time to historical time

In its interaction with the factory system, the family both shaped its environment and was shaped by it. As this study shows, the structure of the family, its economic conditions, and the changes it experienced during the life course of its members affected its response to industrial time and historical time. Externally, its ability to retain some control over employment and work processes depended on business cycles, the structural conditions in the factory, and the social, economic, and cultural forces in the larger society.

The Amoskeag case illustrates not only the active role that the workers' families fulfilled in their interaction with the industrial corporation but also their role in coping with insecurities when the tenuous balance with the factory collapsed. Most important, it shows the ways in which the family devised new responses to cope with the adversities it encountered, even when it lost control.

Mutuality characterized the relationship between the workers' families and the corporation. The corporation drew on workers' relatives as a source of labor and used them as training and disciplining agents. Reaching beyond the factory gates, the corporation used the family as a means of socializing workers and fostering loyalty and corporate identification. The workers, in turn, used the corporation as a source of employment and economic stability and as an initial training ground for their children as workers.

The family not only prepared its members for industrial work; it also cushioned them from potential shocks and disruptions in the workplace. In its effort to protect its members from such exposures, the family developed its own defenses and brought its cultural traditions to bear on work processes and relations within the industrial plant.

The workers' use of their kinship and ethnic ties for brokerage clashed with both the corporation's efficiency efforts and the emerging union's goals. When the corporation tried to centralize the personnel system by introducing the employment office, the family's entrenched influence over hiring and placement could not be entirely overcome. Ironically, the employment office eventually incorporated informal family hiring patterns into its formal practices. The family patronage system also conflicted with the principle of seniority upheld by the union. Thus, the family obstructed, at least initially, the development of collective bargaining through the union and delayed the emergence of workers' solidarity, which cut across family loyalty.

Although the balance in the relationship between the family and the corporation constantly shifted, power was always on the corporation's side. In the earlier period in the Amoskeag's history, family brokerage in job placement and transfers, and use of kinship ties to exercise job controls, was the only recourse available to workers. Later, efficiency measures, speedups, and stretch-outs made it increasingly difficult for kin to manipulate work processes. The dependence of entire family units on the same employer rendered individuals and families vulnerable. During periods of labor shortage the family was able to exert a greater influence on the placement of its members and on work procedures but found itself at a disadvantage during periods of labor surplus and industrial crises. The family's strength became its weakness. As Smelser and Halpern observed in their commentary on this study, "it has not been the steady or continued growth of industrial capitalism so much as its crises that have put strains on modern kinship networks" (1978:292).

Under the historical conditions examined here, the family most fit to interact with the factory system was not an isolated nuclear type but rather one of extended kinship ties. Both the corporation and the workers recognized and utilized kin as key agents in their interaction. The flexible relations between nuclear family members and extended kin enabled relatives to fulfill the salient roles discussed earlier. At the same time, in cushioning their adaptation without excessively restricting the mobility of individual workers, kin were instrumental in serving the industrial employer and, at the same time, in advancing the interest of their own members and trying to protect them.

These functions that kin fulfilled were not merely an archaic carry-over from rural society but a selective use of premigration kinship patterns in response to needs dictated by modern industrial conditions. As this study suggests, two types of kin organization, those in the community of settlement and those left behind in the communities of origin, are both effective, each under different conditions. Community-based kinship ties are most effective in interaction with local institutions and in cushioning relatives in critical life situations; long-distance kinship networks reaching across a wider geographic region are most effective when local kin are unable to cope. The strength of the former lies in its stability and local availability; the latter's utility is drawn from its fluidity and continuous reorganization. Kinship ties can be latent at one point in time and revived at some later point. Under certain historical conditions or at certain periods over the life course, local kinship networks are more valuable. Under other conditions, especially severe local disruptions, long-distance kinship ties are the more salient. Any understanding of the role of kin in industrial society must take into consideration both types and view adaptation as a continuous process.

The question must be raised now as to what extent the patterns of the family's interaction with the factory are a product of circumstances unique to the Amoskeag and to Manchester. There is no doubt that the Amoskeag's scale and the diversity of its workrooms, as well as its conscious paternalistic policy, may have increased the opportunity for active intervention on the family's part. In the absence of cumulative employee files similar to those of the Amoskeag for other corporations and in the absence of the reconstruction of kinship networks in other historical studies, it would be impossible to achieve more precise comparisons. Nevertheless, Manchester's comparability could be assessed more specifically in the following areas of kin behavior: First, the active role of kin in migration has been amply documented in other studies (historical as well as contemporary). Chain migration among French Canadians may have been more intense, because their proximity to the communities of origin facilitated back-and-forth migration and communication with long-distance kin. This pattern was not limited, however, to French Canadians but was also common among Appalachian migrants to Ohio (Schwarzweller, Brown, and Mangalam 1971) and more recently among Mexicans and Puerto Ricans (Lewis 1959, 1966). Thus, migration and labor recruitment under the auspices of kin and the continuity of kinship ties between the communities of origin and settlement as part of the same social system are not unique to Manchester. Nor is the central role of kin assistance in critical life situations unique to the people studied here. Kin assistance as the almost exclusive source of social security has been identified as a pervasive pattern in urban working-class populations ranging from nineteenth-century Lancashire's textile workers to the contemporary residents of East London and Italian residents in Boston's West End (Anderson 1971; Gans 1962; Bott 1957; Young and Willmott 1957).

The area of uniqueness or comparability that needs to be examined most closely is that of kin influence on work processes within the factory. In this respect two factors may have intensified the Amoskeag's influence on the involvement of kin with labor relations and work processes: the Amoskeag's paternalism and the nature of the textile industry itself. As explained earlier, the Amoskeag's size and diversity and its earlier policy of family recruitment set the stage for greater family control over the work process, an influence that kin groupings tried to perpetuate even after the corporation had decided to curtail it. As numerous studies of labor history have shown, the efforts of workers to shape work relations and exercise job controls in the factory by bringing their own ties and traditions to bear on it were common in a variety of industries. The Amoskeag's case, however, demonstrates specifically the central role that the family had in this process.

To what extent were these family influences limited to the textile industry? Would these patterns of family integration with the workplace and the active role of kin as brokers hold up in industries that were predominantly or totally based on male employment? At this point, we lack sufficient studies of kin involvement in other industries to provide a more precise comparison. Some existing studies about steel towns, such as Pittsburgh, where the labor force was predominantly male, suggest different patterns in the family's relationship to the workplace (Kleinberg 1977; Byington 1910). Here families did not work as units. But male relatives often tended to work together and to assist each other in ways similar to those exercised in the Amoskeag. Nevertheless, it would be difficult to determine whether male kin in these enterprises had as extensive an influence as in the Amoskeag. In male-dominated industries there was a more specific segregation in the functions of kin along sex lines. Whereas male kin influenced the workplace, female kin assisted each other in handling personal and family crises and in securing employment wherever it was available for women in the community. A fuller understanding of the family's interaction with the industrial process will depend, therefore, on future systematic comparisons of the role of kin in different types of industry.

Whether industries were family-intensive or male-intensive, whether an entire family group worked for the same employer or for different employers, the common pattern in working-class life during the first two decades of this century was one of a commitment to a collective family economy. In this respect, the patterns of family and household structure and of the timing of life transitions found in Manchester were similar to those of other working-class communities with similar ethnic backgrounds in this period (Chudacoff and Hareven 1978, 1979; Hareven 1978; Modell, Furstenberg, and Hershberg 1976; Modell and Hareven 1973). Although the participation of teen-agers and married women in the labor force in Manchester was higher than that reported in other industrial communities, even those engaged in textiles (Mason, Vinovskis, and Hareven 1978), the view of the family as a collective economic unit and the expectation that family members would forego or change their own careers in the service of their families was true of working-class life in general in the time period studied here. What the Manchester experience provides is an intensification of patterns evident in other communities. It also offers a prism through which both of these patterns of behavior and experience can be viewed at a depth that has not been possible in other studies because of the paucity of data. This in-depth investigation was possible in the Manchester case because of the opportunity to follow careers over a significant portion of the workers' lives, to reconstruct their kinship ties, and most significantly, because interviewees opened a window for us to view their perceptions of their own lives.

How do the patterns discussed in this book fit into the larger picture of changes in American family life? The general trend of change that scholars have identified has been the transfer of functions previously performed within the family to other social institutions (Smelser 1959). Indeed, the preindustrial family embraced a variety of functions: It was a workshop, church, reformatory school, and asylum (Demos 1970). Over the past century and a half, these various familial functions have become the responsibility of other institutions. The family has withdrawn from the world of work, insisting on its own privacy and separation, and the workplace has generally become impersonal and bureaucratic. Once considered an asset, familial involvement in the workplace is now denigrated as nepotism. The home is viewed increasingly as a retreat from the outside world. The family has turned inward and assumed domesticity, intimacy, and privacy as its major characteristics. The privacy of the home and its separation from the workplace have been guarded jealously as an essential feature of American family life. The commitment to the domesticity of the family is itself the outcome of a long historical process, which commenced in the early modern period in Western Europe, a process characterized by Philippe Ariès as:

> The modern family . . . cuts itself off from the world and opposes to society the isolated groups of parents and children. All the energy of the group is expended in helping the children to rise in the world, individually and without any collective ambition, the children rather than the family [Ariès 1962:404].

By contrast, writes Ariès, the "premodern family was distinguished by the enormous mass of sociability which it retained. Both family and the household were the foundation of the community." Under the impact of economic growth and industrialization, the family became a specialized unit, its tasks limited primarily to comsumption, procreation, and childrearing.

Although these patterns predominate overall, they are more typical of the urban middle classes. Among working-class and ethnic families, some preindustrial family characteristics persisted, although in modified form. In the case of the people studied here, although the workplace had been separated from the household, the family continued to function as a work unit. Even if all members did not work in the same place, the family experienced a continuity between work outside the home and household production, especially where women were involved. Similarly, the survival of important functions of kin in the workplace suggests that the historical pattern of the separation of family and work had not been consummated across the entire society.

The Amoskeag workers' conduct in both the workplace and the family, particularly their selective use of their cultural traditions as a resource, casts serious doubt on any assumptions of simple linear historical change. Their encounter with the modern factory system led neither to the abandonment of nor to the rigid adherence to, premigration traditions. Rather, they adapted their customs and social organization to the new conditions they confronted, and in doing so, they addressed the factory system on its own terms.

Selectivity was the key principle in their adaptation. The family selected those aspects of traditional culture that were most useful in coping with new conditions. Family traditions were buttressed by ethnic heritage, and conversely, ethnic traditions were reinforced and transmitted by the family. At home, children were taught traditional family ways as well as industrial work habits. Thus, in both the family and the workplace premigration culture was a major resource rather than a handicap.

The traditional customs and beliefs through which family and ethnicity were reinforced did not represent a simple carry-over to American soil but rather a continuing process of adaptation. Although the behavior of ethnic groups in American society resembled that in the communities of origin, it was by no means identical (Hareven and Modell 1980). The observation of Robert E. Park and Herbert Mill concerning the transplantation of Old World traits to American society also holds true for family and work, namely, that the mutual-aid associations of immigrants "are not, in fact, pure heritages, but the products of the immigrants' efforts to adapt their heritages to American conditions" (1921:120). During the transitional stage in their adaptation to industrial life, immigrants modified their attitudes and behavior patterns in relation to mainstream American culture and created a new synthesis between the old and the new.

These patterns of selectivity in the transmission of ethnic and family culture to the industrial system described here call into question the linear view of social change advanced by modernization theory. In their study, Inkeles and Smith (1974) view the factory as a modernizing agent and claim that modernity in the factory led to modernity at home, a generalization based on the assumption that modernization in one part of life affects all others. Historically, however, modernization at the workplace did not automatically "modernize" family behavior. Although the family underwent significant changes in its adaption to new work roles and urban living, and although workers adapted to "modern" work processes within the factory, family behavior did not modernize at the same pace as workers' conduct in the factory. Workers adapted to industrial schedules and work processes more rapidly, whereas changes in family life occurred more gradually. But in both cases, traditional ways of life were neither preserved in their entirety nor obliterated.

The family was both a custodian of tradition and an agent of change. As a guardian of traditional culture, the family provided its members with continuity, a resource to draw upon in confronting industrial conditions. Familial and industrial adaptation processes were not merely parallel but interrelated as a part of a personal and historical continuum.

Appendix A

The subjective reconstruction of past lives

In reconstructing historical experience, the following sources have been consulted: commonly used written documents such as corporation records and newspapers, corporation employment files, demographic records, and oral histories of former workers. Ideally, information drawn from such a variety of sources would converge in the reconstruction of both people's behavior and the perceptions of their lives. Indeed, in many instances the quantitative analysis of the employment files and demographic records coincided with the oral-history accounts. In other instances, certain historical patterns were reconstructed from either quantitative sources or oral-history sources.

Whereas the quantitative analysis provides structural evidence concerning the organization and behavior of kin, the oral-history interviews offer insight into the nature of relationships and their significance to the participants. The empirical analysis reported here – although attempting to weld both types of evidence – at times presents two different levels of historical reality, each derived from a distinct type of data. For example, both the quantitative and the qualitative data provide documentation for the effectiveness of kin in initiating workers into the factory but only the qualitative data provide insight into personal conflicts between siblings or between children and parents resulting from the pressures of joint work situations.

Because oral history is an important component in this book, its role as a source should be explained. Oral history has recently inspired enthusiasm for its unique role in recovering the experiences of anonymous people that would otherwise remain obscured. At the same time, however, oral history has been criticized as a historical tool because of its distance from the events recalled. Hindsight, clearly the source of its strength, is also a potential source of weakness.

When using oral history for the reconstruction of historical experience it must be remembered that the interviewees are survivors. Only people who can be tracked down and who are willing to share

371

their memories can be interviewed. Thus, by its very nature, oral history raises serious questions of representativeness.

Some problems of representativeness were dealt with in this study by comparing the career and family histories of the individuals interviewed with those of the entire sample. This allowed identification of those individual accounts that were unique and those that represented a more general experience. Because most of the people studied here worked in the same corporation, various accounts, despite their individual differences, converged. Moreover, a careful comparison of interviewees' factual accounts of their work and family histories with information from written records provided some test of accuracy. Although many factual contradictions emerged from this comparison – dates, sequences of events, and individuals involved – the important result was not the authentication of the record, but the augmentation and complementarity of the oral-history accounts and factual records. The oral histories provided insights and perceptions that could not have been obtained in any other way.

As a cultural phenomenon, oral history is part of a long oral tradition, which has partly survived in American folk life and the culture of the communities of origin of the various immigrant groups in American society. As a research tool, oral history emerges from several distinct areas of research, including the anthropological study of folk cultures and the psychological study of "lives" through interviews and personal documents, which was developed by John Dollard, Gordon Allport, and others in the 1930s and 1940s. More recently, Oscar Lewis and Robert Coles in their respective works have demonstrated the power of this method when applied to the reconstruction of the lives of Puerto Rican and Mexican families, the urban poor, and the children of migrant workers and sharecroppers. Inspired by this approach, radical historians have used the oral-history technique in recording the experiences of workers, activists, and participants in social protest movements not only to retrieve and record information but to form group consciousness through the process of interviewing itself.

Along these lines, oral history has been used in communities to fire a collective historical consciousness through the discovery of a common past. Some recent oral-history efforts are filiopietistic and attach a mystique to the process because of the encounter with the living past that it represents. The American Bicentennial, in particular, gave an impetus to oral-history projects that are intended to stimulate "community awareness" and "identity."

The widespread use of the cassette tape recording machine over the past decade has contributed considerably to the popularization of oral-history interviewing. Like the computer, the recorder has not only facilitated the gathering and preservation of data; it has also generated a mystique of authenticity, which is attributed to technological means. In the preface to one of his books, Oscar Lewis somewhat glorified its role:

> The tape recorder used in taking down the life stories in this book has made possible the beginning of a new kind of literature of social realism. With the aid of the tape recorder, unskilled, uneducated and even illiterate persons can talk about themselves and relate their observations and experiences in an uninhibited, spontaneous and natural manner [1966:2].

People employing the tape recorder, like those using the computer, quickly discover that it does not have intrinsic magic. Without a historical and sociological imagination to guide the process, only hours of meaningless information are obtained.

Two aspects of oral history are central to its role: the nature of the interview process and the function of oral traditions in a modern, literate society.

In interviewing for this book, it became apparent that oral history is not strictly a means for retrieving information but rather a process for generating knowledge. An oral-history narrative is the product of an interaction between interviewer and interviewee. It is a process of "life review." With the stimulation and assistance of the interviewer, people relive their past lives. The interviewer is like a medium, conjuring memories through his or her own presence, interests, and questions. The very process is intrusive, even when the interviewer tries to remain inconspicuous.

Oral history is a subjective process. It provides insight into how people think about their lives as well as outside events and how they perceive their role in the course of historical events. "A testimony is no more than a mirage of the reality it describes," writes Jan Vansina (1965), the leading scholar of oral tradition in Africa. "The initial informant in an oral tradition gives either consciously or unconsciously a distorted account of what has really happened, because he sees only what he has seen." More than being a source of factual evidence, a reconstruction of reality, oral history is a re-creation of people's memories and perceptions – it teaches us what people remember, why they remember it, and how they remember. Sometimes the subjectivity of oral history is individual in nature, other times it is collective, depending on whether the interviewees are several members of the same family or several participants in the same event. In both cases, however, it is a result of both an individual's personal attitude and the set of cultural values and collective ideology that guides his or her life.

Historians have long been accustomed to employing such subjective documents as diaries, letters, and investigative reports in the reconstruction of past events. In this respect, oral history fits into a wider context, namely, the use of personal documents for historical and sociological research. An oral-history account is essentially a subjective, personal document. In a systematic scrutiny of the reliability of personal documents for psychological research, Gordon Allport defined personal documents as

> *any self-revealing record that intentionally or unintentionally yields information regarding the structure, dynamics, and functioning of the author's mental life.* It may record the participant's view of experiences in which he has been involved, it may devote itself deliberately to self-scrutiny and self-description; or it may be only incidentally and unwittingly self-revealing [1942:xii].

Oral history is an expression of the personality of the interviewees, their cultural values, and the particular historical circumstances that shaped their outlook. Indeed, this subjectivity is its great value. Diaries and personal letters are also highly subjective, though their bias is of a different nature. A diary or a letter reflects a person's individual experiences or observations, whereas an oral-history account consists of the individual's past experiences as evoked by an interviewer who has an intentional or unintentional influence on what is remembered and the way in which it is recounted. This is a result of the interviewer's intervention, as well as of the interviewee's sense of communication with posterity through the interview process. Diaries and letters are acutely connected to the specific event that generated them. Oral history, by contrast, is handicapped by the time distance from the event recounted. The accuracy of the account could be limited by faulty memory or changes in people's own perceptions of their lives. Ironically, this handicap is also a source of strength. It offers the advantage of reconstructing past events from a larger vantage point and interpreting earlier events in the context of subsequent developments. The time perspective gained through oral history creates a different scale of importance by which to judge past events in the light of changes in one's own point of view. The careful listener gains insight into how people reconstruct their life histories, how they order events of their past lives, and how they articulate the meaning of their lives.

Thus, oral history offers a glimpse not only into the sequence of events in people's lives but also into how, in their search for a pattern, the different pieces of their lives are reassembled and disassembled as in a kaleidoscope, losing meaning, changing meaning, disappearing, and reappearing in different configurations at different points in time. A great difficulty in the interview process lies in the listener's inability to discern the specific meaning that an event held earlier as opposed to the significance that the interviewee attributes to it subsequently. Certain occurrences that seem valuable to the historian may be forgotten because their original meaning has been lost for the actor, whereas other events are often elevated out of proportion to their past role in people's lives because subsequent events in that person's life have placed them in a new perspective.

The dynamic interplay between past and present in an individual's reminiscences takes different forms. At times, interviewees temporarily immerse themselves in a past episode as they recount it. This is especially true for childhood memories. On such occasions, the individual slips back into the past and vibrantly recounts earlier episodes without any consciousness of the present. The interviewee becomes an actor fully playing a past role. For example, in recounting a specific scene of conflict with a boss, interviewees often reenacted the scene without any self-consciousness, staging a dialogue with the other characters involved, mimicking themselves as they might have been in the past as well as the other person. To re-create the scene, elderly interviewees even left their seats, sometimes pacing back and forth, sometimes standing in one place. When interviewees were asked to describe their jobs, their detailed descriptions were often accompanied by an actual reenactment of the specific operations involved in handling the machinery. On most occasions, the person retained a conscious separation between the historical account and the present and offered a contemporary perspective on past experience.

On other occasions, however, interviewees found it difficult to distinguish past from present or earlier from subsequent events. Sometimes people just forgot experiences, or they chose to forget, or if they remembered, they did not want to talk about them. According to Gunhild Hagestadt, in many families there are prohibited zones that are avoided, as if by unspoken agreement (personal communication 1979). Although interviewers can sense the invisible electrified fences when approaching such areas, they can do little about them.

Actual events or situations are sometimes misrepresented or reinterpreted because of a faulty memory or a repression of difficult experiences. Traumatic experiences especially lead to the repression or reinterpretation of events. For example, some former workers said they stopped working in the Amoskeag in 1922. When it was pointed out that their work records indicated they had worked until 1930 or later, the typical reply was "Oh yes, but that was after the strike. Things were not the same any more." The strike of 1922 represented to the majority of workers the deterioration of their "world." Even though they returned to work after the strike, they associated the strike with the end of their careers. The strike of 1922 and the shutdown of the mill in 1936, the two great traumatic events in the community, emerged as the two major signposts for reckoning time. Thus, when asked to reconstruct their career histories, interviewees said "I took this job before the great strike" or "after the strike, and before my second baby was born."

In assessing the reliability of oral history, one needs to distinguish, however, between faulty memory and lack of perspective. People who forget certain experiences or events do not necessarily suffer from a lack of perspective or hindsight on the events they do remember. The memory of early life events, although limited by distance in time or colored by fantasy, can still be remarkably clear in old age. Older people interviewed for this study remembered earlier life events with great clarity and elaborate detail. Actually, most of the people interviewed had a clear sense of their own lives and were able to place their past in perspective, observing how they interpreted certain events at the time of their occurrence and how they changed their point of view as the years passed.

Mary Dancause, for example, after decribing her work in the mill and claiming she had gotten some pleasure from it, said she would rather stay old than go through the same jobs again. "If someone said, 'I can give you something to make you young again,' I'd say, 'Oh, no . . . I'm old and I want to stay old'" (Amoskeag, p. 57). She also contrasted the current tendency of people to be sentimental with the sparse emotions and self-restraint that were common earlier in her life. When she was summoned back by her parents to Manchester from Quebec to take care of her younger siblings, she was heartbroken (Amoskeag, p. 53). But during the interview when her daughter asked her why she had not done anything about it, she admitted with a sense of resignation: "That's the way we lived at the time. What could you do? We had no choice."

Marie-Ann Senchal devoted her life to caring for her family. Throughout the interview she insisted on the rightness and timeliness of her dedication, the sacrifice of her personal life, but at the end she admitted, from hindsight: "But it wasn't right of me, because I should have decided for my own self, and married and forgot about everybody else. I knew I wasn't living my own life, but I couldn't make up my mind" (*Amoskeag*, p. 282).

Some interviewees also dramatized the difference between past times and present conditions. The contrast between then and now was sometimes so great that even the interviewees' children found differences incredible. Cora Pellerin remarked with amusement: "When I talk about my work in the mill, to my daughters especially, they think it's a story; and when I say something about living on a farm, to them it's a story. They don't believe it's true that we were that backward" (*Amoskeag*, pp. 201–2). The ability to recount a past experience, to recall the original feelings, and then contradict or reinterpret those feelings from the vantage point of the present are critical to an evaluation of oral history as a source.

Does the retrospective character of oral history render it useless to historians? Most historical information drawn from traditional written sources is also fragmented and biased. The most elaborate letter, diary, or court record still represents only a small fragment of reality, colored by people's perceptions at one point in time. Even quantitative data, recently hailed as "scientific" or "objective," are biased. As historians frequently point out, the census itself is a record of perceptions – that of an individual or family group defining its household status, occupational status, literacy, ethnic origin, family relationships, as well as many other characteristics; the census may even represent the census taker's personal perceptions rather than those of the individuals being counted. Similarly, occupational records, such as the Amoskeag's employee files, reflect the biases of employment clerks or bosses. Historians have developed a variety of methods and approaches to allow a critical assessment of written documentary sources. Similarly, special methods will have to be developed to examine the accuracy of oral-history accounts.

Beyond any doubt, oral history is a record of perceptions; it is not a re-creation of historical events. It can be employed as a factual source only if corroborated. The necessity of cross-checking information does not detract, however, from the value of oral history in understanding perceptions and recovering levels of experiences not normally available to historians.

The major strength of oral history lies not in the accuracy or objectivity of the account; it lies, rather, in its ability to reveal an essence of past lives that allows a connection of isolated events into a sequence that permits some interpretation. A valuable historical experience in itself, oral history offers almost the only feasible route for the retrieval of perceptions and experiences of whole groups who did not normally leave written records.

People who have not been "famous" or who have not participated jointly in a common cause, such as a labor movement, a strike, or an organized political or social activity, experience great difficulty in making the connection between their own lives and the historical process. Without such linkages, in most instances in the United States oral-history interviewing remains a private exercise. In Africa, by contrast, as Vansina points out, "Every testimony and every tradition has a purpose and fulfills a function. It is because of this function that they exist at all" (1965). In nonliterate societies the functions of an oral tradition are socially defined and recognized by all members. In modern America there is no such established tradition, except in the regional oral traditions that survive in individual localities. Within the larger community, the public role and social significance of oral history are not automatically understood.

In societies where the oral narrative is part of the formal culture, the significance of a certain story does not need explanation. The time-honored practice and the setting within which the oral tradition takes place lend it strength and meaning. In modern America, except for historically conscious individuals or groups and unusually articulate and interested individuals, most people do not see an immediate significance in the interview. Although they might reminisce privately, telling stories to their grandchildren or sharing memories of past experiences, most people are rather bewildered when strangers ask about their life histories. The former Amoskeag workers frequently replied with "Why ask me? My story is not special" or "What is so important about my life?" They had never experienced a structured interview situation. With a few exceptions, interviewees consented to the interrogation not because they understood the importance of their life story but because, prompted by their own work ethic, they wanted to help us do "our job."

Attitudes changed drastically, however, after the exhibit "Amoskeag: A Sense of Place, A Way of Life" opened in Manchester in 1975. Although this primarily architectural exhibit was aimed at professionals and preservationists rather than the larger public, it evoked an unexpected response from former and current textile workers in the community. It provided the workers with a public collective identification with their old workplace and symbolized the historical significance of their work lives. Thousands of people, mostly former mill workers and their families, came to see the exhibit. Former workers, now elderly, searched the huge historic group portraits for their relatives; grandparents led their grandchildren through the exhibit, often describing how they did their jobs of thirty to forty years earlier. Although they privately cherished many memories associated with their work experience, they had felt previously that industrial work, especially textile work, was generally looked down upon. The sudden opportunity to view their own lives as part of a significant historical experience provided a setting for collective identification. Under these circumstances, interviewing ceased to be an isolated individual experience. It turned, instead, into a shared community event. Former mill workers recognized each other at the exhibit, some not having seen each other for thirty years. Although the exhibit was not designed to serve this purpose, it became a catalyst.

The oral-history interviews that followed the exhibit were of an entirely different character: now workers were enthusiastic about the prospect of being interviewed. They related their work and life histories with a sense of pride. Hearing about the project, many individuals volunteered to be interviewed. Identification with the history and architecture of their workplace both stimulated memory and inspired a willingness to participate. The exhibit laid the foundation for a continuing series of interviews with the same individuals. This is not to suggest that every successful oral-history project requires an exhibit or some other external device to engender identification. It does suggest, however, the tenuousness of oral history in a society that does not recognize oral tradition as a central element in the culture. Thus, the interview process itself emerged as an important historical tool in linking private life histories to the larger historical process.

Through oral history, the student can better understand how people construct meaning for their lives, and most important, how people interpret their past lives in the context of their own culture. As Everett Hughes puts it, oral history involves the "moving perspective in which a person sees his life as a whole and interprets the meaning of his various attributes, actions and the things which happen to him" (1971b). Such a "moving perspective" is derived not only from one's personal experience but also from a person's own culture. Because memory is selective, past events and experiences are remembered only when they are significant, by virtue of either their intrinsic value in people's lives or the external historical circumstances associated with them and the cultural constraints that give them meaning.

Work, family, and sociability were the three major sources of meaning and importance for the interviewees. They attributed meaning to their work as a source of stability and security. They viewed their work as a primary source of satisfaction, personal accomplishment, and pride. In discussing the meaning of work in their lives, they drew on both their personal experience and the significance conveyed by the corporate setting. Personal satisfaction was reinforced by the sense of continuity and stability that the work process provided. Work was also proof of a personal sense of competence and adaptability to new conditions. But work also drew its meaning from the corporate sense of pride and perfection, its image as a grand, paternalistic institution.

Because the interviewees shared a common workplace and social environment, special meaning was given to the reconstruction of the former workers' experiences. The work experience in the Amoskeag served as the common context for the oral-history interviews. The people sought for this project were those who had worked at the Amoskeag Company. Most interviews were initiated with a request for a description of their work in the Amoskeag. The explanations were remarkably elaborate and included much technological detail, despite the long time lapse since their last job. Some acted out the movements entailed in the operations. In many respects, the job description, more than any other aspect of their past lives, projected workers back into the historical setting and eventually evoked other memories as well.

The interviewees' commitment to a communal sense of survival also stimulated reminiscence. Survival of one's family despite dislocation by immigration or disruption by death was a special source of meaning and achievement. Related to this was their sense of success as children in keeping their families solvent and their subsequent accomplishment as parents in rearing their children and launching them into adult roles. The persistence of family ties, the continuity of loyalty and devotion, and especially the availability of family support in moments of loneliness and isolation were important sources of meaning, particularly to old people. Finally, the interviewees' sense of having triumphed over difficult circumstances – strikes, depressions, and the shutdown – inspired not merely a litany of hardship but also a description of their own strategies for coping. Their sense of humor prevailed as they mused over how they had survived. When they themselves had been defeated, their children's success provided a special source of meaning. Most interviewees emphasized that their children's advancement out of factory work into middle-class occupations and homeownership in better neighborhoods gave their lives a special sense of accomplishment.

Survival, success, advancement, self-respect in old age, familial sociability and loyalty – all were essential criteria by which people judged their past and present lives and assessed them within a larger generational context.

The workers' stories did not follow a linear progression of advancement. Their lives were not individual epics of survival and success, glorifying triumph over circumstances. Rather, they reported the good and the bad, often understating the crises and the suffering they had endured. People did not hesitate to discuss failures or setbacks. Many past experiences were considered important in their own right, even when they involved failure or seemed pointless. Their entire mill careers, even those steeped in drudgery and routine, were perceived as meaningful because they had encompassed a major portion of their lives. "When you work 12 hours a day, you have to find pleasure in work. There's nowhere else to find it" (*Amoskeag*, p. 231).

Most interviewees emphasized that joy and happiness, or personal fulfillment, were not conscious goals. They rarely measured their own lives in terms of personal happiness.

Sociability made the long hours of drudgery bearable. Family celebrations reaffirmed mutual ties and obligations and the shared common heritage. Street celebrations and pageants made city life enjoyable. Parades and circuses occasionally broke up the tediousness of a long workday. Many interviewees contrasted the present-day drabness and emptiness of the streets and their own isolation in little flats or nursing homes with yesterday's lively, and at times boisterous, public life on the city's main streets. In retrospect, entertainment and leisure took on meaning as public and community events. Family celebrations, dances, and outings were enjoyed publicly and collectively. The continuity between public life and private life provided a sense of being part of a larger social context.

By its very nature, the oral-history interview allows the development of two levels of meaning. The interviewees are able to reconstruct their past lives and assess their meaning. The interviewer is permitted to study both the narrative itself and the meaning attributed to it. Although interrelated, the two levels of meaning are not always identical. Aspects that are significant to the interviewee are often less important to the interviewer and vice versa. The interview sometimes provides not only an opportunity for recalling the past but also for reviewing one's life in light of the present. Thus, an interview becomes at times an occasion for squaring accounts with the past, for clearing up earlier misunderstandings, and, at times, for self-justification. Consequently, the historical pictures of the interviewee and the interviewer that emerge may be quite different. One family interviewed for the project resented the publication of personal family details even though they had shared those at great length and initially gave permission for their publication. When they protested the printed, edited interview, they insisted that their private family story was of no interest: "Why didn't you just stick to the mill experience?"

In summary then, oral history is a powerful, indispensable source; it provides a depth of insight that can rarely be retrieved from other sources. It is unique in offering the opportunity for a subjective reconstruction of past lives. Like surveys, it recalls attitudes and perceptions, but, unlike surveys, it places these perceptions in the context of an individual's life history. These perceptions are exceptionally valuable not as individual case histories but as historical, cultural testimonies. Each interview reflects the common cultural frame of reference that shapes the reconstruction of individual lives, that is, individual lives gain their sense and meaning from the collective culture. As Robert Levine puts it: "The subjective career can be dealt with in both collective and individual representations and individual representations of it are permeated with cultural meanings" (Levine 1978).

Appendix B
Description of data

Amoskeag Company Records Collection at the Manchester Historic Association

Amoskeag employee files

Approximately seventy thousand employee files maintained by the employment office from 1911 until the shutdown of the company in 1936. Each file contains a worker's hiring and separation slips, which were prepared by the employment office in conjunction with the departmental overseer. Because workers left and were rehired many times, each file contains a number of such slips.

The hiring slips listed the worker's name, sex, age, nationality, date of hiring, job assigned, pay rate, marital status, number of children, and number of dependents. The separation slips listed the worker's job classification, the department he or she worked in, the reason the worker gave for leaving, and evaluations of the worker's performance and conduct. Newspaper clippings about the worker were sometimes added to the file even after he or she had left the Amoskeag.

Other Amoskeag records

Tenement rental books, workers' letters to bosses, and other correspondence, which appeared most frequently in the Dumaine Records.

Amoskeag Company Records at the Baker Library

Important documents pertaining to wages, production, and labor relations. Most important for this study were the wage records (which survived in samples only), planning office records, employment office records, labor records, and adjustments, which reported on grievances filed by the union and their resolution by the Adjustment Board.

Other sources used in the data linkage process

Vital records, Office of the City Clerk, Manchester
Marriage and birth records.

Manchester city directories

The city directories listed each adult male's address and occupation, or place of employment. For the period studied, employed women were also listed in the directory. The directories were used for tracing occupational careers and for linking workers' addresses to their places of residence (see Appendix C).

Insurance records

The records at the Association Canado-Américaine, a fraternal insurance company whose headquarters are in Manchester, provided the names of beneficiaries, or next of kin, of those workers who were insured.

United States Federal Census Manuscript Schedules

A random sampling of every fortieth dwelling (580) recorded in the 1900 Census for Manchester was used. The sample consisted of 2,948 individuals (1,400 men and 1,548 women). For each individual, the census recorded address, age, sex, relationship to the head of household, marital status, place of nativity and parents' place of nativity, literacy, number of years in the United States, naturalization, number of months employed, school attendance, ability to speak English, and disabilities. For heads of household, the census also listed home ownership or rental and whether the home was mortgaged. For women, it listed number of years married, number of children, and number of living children.

Appendix C

The construction of individual work and life histories and the linkage of kinship networks

The analysis of work careers and kinship networks is based on 1,816 randomly selected individual Amoskeag Company employee files, or a sample of 2.5% of the total. The individual files also served in the construction of kinship networks.

Construction of work histories

We traced each individual in the employee file sample in the Manchester City Directory, which recorded all changes of address and the worker's employment in the city prior to and after termination of work in the Amoskeag, if the individual resided in Manchester. It was possible, therefore, to identify the jobs an individual held in the city during career interruptions, as well as second jobs that a person held while working in the Amoskeag. Fortunately, the Manchester directory listed women as well if they had an occupation.

Following the trace in the city directory, the information in each individual career file – age, sex, marital status, ethnic origin, and so on – was coded for the computer. It was thus possible to reconstruct each worker's career sequence in the Amoskeag, including each job and department change within the mill, as well as each separation and rehiring, including the reason given for each separation. Wherever available, additional career information from the city directories was linked to the person's work history. The individual files were traced to identify relatives, who were then added to the file. The linkage process rendered an additional 1,072 individuals related to the workers in the sample. To avoid bias, however, these relatives were not included in the analysis.

Construction of kinship networks

Although kinship networks were constructed for the entire sample, the kinship analysis in this study is based only on the French Canadians because only their kinship ties could be verified with some certainty.

385

Vital records

After locating the individual from the original sample in the city directory, we culled all those of the same last name as the original individual listed at the same address. We then traced the original person from the file as well as those individuals found in the directory to the vital records at the City Clerk's office in Manchester, especially through marriage and birth records. For this trace, an alphabetical index file was used and individuals in the sample and the city directory who were located in the marriage and birth records were added to the kinship file. Kin relationships were verified on the basis of age, birth date, name of parents, and address. Whenever relatives thus located were also found in the Amoskeag's employee files, their life and work histories were reconstructed in the same manner as the original sample. The linked kinship clusters are a result of this back-and-forth trace.

Parish records

All doubtful French-Canadian kin relationships were cross-checked in the records of St. Marie Parish in Manchester, thus correcting inaccuracies and omissions in the city's records and the misspelling and Anglicizing of French-Canadian names. The parish records also revealed additional members of the kin cluster, who were also traced back to the original employee file. Kin could not be traced in other parishes, because the records were not available.

Insurance records

The Association Canado-Américaine, a French-Canadian fraternal insurance organization that served Catholics of French, French-Canadian, and Franco-American descent, identified insured individuals and their relationship to their beneficiaries. This trace provided a further check on kin relations and also revealed additional relatives not retrieved in the previous search.

Linkage with the 1900 census

The 1900 census is the last accessible census for the analysis of manuscript household schedules. Through the Soundex System, all individuals in the sample who were alive in 1900 or later were traced to the census. Individuals found in the census (linkage only through males) were added to the household data for that individual in 1900.

Kinship clusters were thus reconstructed for the individuals in the sample, although every member of the group may not have been retrieved. The reconstruction of more extensive networks was impossible because the identification of female kin in the employee files was obscured by name changes after marriage (only partially overcome through linkage with marriage records) and because kin whose work careers ended before 1900 could not be identified (employee files commenced in 1911). Finally, couples who were married in a different location were, of course, not identifiable.

In reconstructing kinship networks, only those relationships confirmed through two or more sources were included. Cases involving an ambiguity in names were excluded. Because the major sources for the identification of relatives were the employee files and the vital records, the resulting clusters are weighted toward nuclear units and adult siblings and their families. The clusters also contain, however, significant extensions of lateral kin over two or three generations.

Appendix D

Occupational classification of sample jobs in the Amoskeag Company

Clerical

Skilled
Blacksmiths
Card grinders
Card tenders and millwrights
Construction, maintenance, and
    other mechanical occupations
    not elsewhere classified
  Beltmen
  Boilermakers
  Coremakers
  Drillers
  Masons
  Molders
  Painters
  Plasterers
  Riggers
  Tinsmiths
  Water tenders
  Welders
Electricians
Engineers
  Hoisting
  Stationary
Foremen and overseers
Loom fixers
Machine fixers
Machinists and automobile
    mechanics
Plumbers
Second hands and gang bosses
Section hands
Stationmen
Weavers
Wiremen

Semiskilled
Apprentices and learners
Back tenders, warpmen, rollmen,
    and beam changers
Battery hands

Semiskilled (cont.)
Beamers (chain)
Bleach-house workers
Bobbin boys and girls
Calender men and pressmen
Card strippers
Card tenders
Cloth burlers
Color mixers
Comber tenders
Creelers and tie-over girls
Cutters (cloth)
Doffers
  Filling and warp
  Yarders
Drawers-in (girls)
Drawing-frame tenders
Dressers
Dry-can tenders (cloth)
Dyers (chain beam and top)
Finishers and dandy hands (yarn)
Firemen (stationary)
Folders, winders, and doublers
    (cloth)
Fullers
Graders
Harnessmakers
Helpers not elsewhere classified
Inspectors, trimmers, sorters, and
    examiners
Knot- and warp-tying operators
Machinists' helpers
Menders, darners, and speckers
Oilers
Packers and wrappers
Perchers
Picker tenders
Piecers
Quillers
Reelers and stringers
Sewing-machine operators
Sliver tenders and frame tenders

Semiskilled (cont.)
Slubber hands
Spare hands
Spear hands and nappers
Spindle gagers and setters
Spinners
Spoolers
Steamer hands
Stretchers and tenter-frame tenders
Testers
Truck drivers and chauffeurs
Truckers, handlers, etc.
Twisters
Warpers and beamers
Warp fitters
Washer tenders (cloth and wool)
Weighers
Winders and doublers (yarn)

Semiskilled (cont.)
Wool scourers
Wool sorters
Others not elsewhere classified

Unskilled
Balers
Dye-house workers
Elevator hands
Filling boys
Handy men
Laborers, etc.
Roll-shop workers
Roving boys
Scrubbers and janitors
Sweepers
Watchmen
Yarn boys and girls

Source: Daniel Creamer and Charles W. Coulter, *Labor and the Shutdown of the Amoskeag Textile Mills* (Philadelphia: Works Projects Administration, 1939), pp. 332–3.

Appendix E

Documents illustrating the Amoskeag Company's paternalism and efficiency program

Regulations for the boarding-houses and tenements belonging to the Amoskeag Manufacturing Company

All persons, on taking a tenement, are to sign the lease for the same, and agree, while they occupy the tenement, to conform to the terms of the lease, and abide strictly by such regulations as may have been or shall be established by the Agent of the company for the orderly conducting and management of the tenement.

The tenants of the Boarding Houses will be held answerable for any disorderly or improper conduct on their premises; their doors are to be closed at ten o'clock in the evening, and no person admitted after that time, without some reasonable excuse.

They must not board any persons who are not employed by the Company, unless by special permission from the Agent, and in no case are Males and Females to be allowed to board in the same tenement, and the standard price of board must not be changed by the Boarding House keeper, except by consent of the Agent of the Company.

The keepers of Boarding Houses must give an account of the number, names and employment of their boarders, when required, and report to the Agent the names of such as are guilty of any improper conduct.

The buildings, and yards about them, must be kept clean and in good order; no horses, cattle or swine are to be kept on the premises; and if they are injured otherwise than from ordinary use, all necessary repairs will be made, and charged to the occupant; also the sidewalks in front of the houses must be kept clean and free from snow. It is desirable that the families of those who live in the houses, as well as the boarders, who have not the kine pox, should be vaccinated immediately, the expense of which will be paid by the company for all who are in their employment.

The habitual use of ARDENT SPIRITS as a beverage, or of Profane or Indecent Language by the keepers of boarding houses, or permitting others addicted to the use of either to remain in their houses, will in all cases be considered a sufficient cause for their discharge, and will be required forthwith to leave the Corporation.

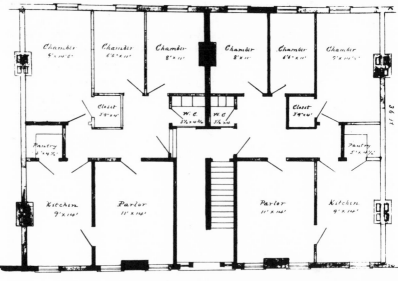

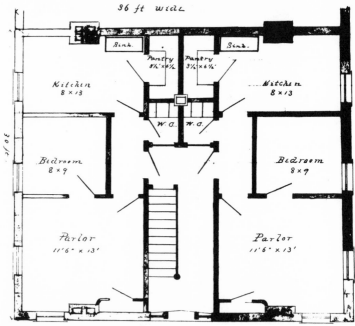

Figure E.1. Block No. 9, plan of first floor. Top: Middle tenements. Bottom: End tenements. Second, third, and fourth floors are like first, substituting two windows for outside door. Cellar is divided into eight compartments, one to each tenement. Compartments are 11' x 14' and 9' x 14' for middle tenements, 6' x 11½' and 8' x 11½' for end tenements. (*Source:* Amoskeag Company Tenement Book: Floor Plans – 1870–1880, MHA.)

NAME Abbott, Sadie
Write last name first

Dept. Dressing   Mill No.   3   Div. Cen.

Nationality American

Address   400 Manchester St.

Date Employed   Aug., 1882

Kind of Work Drawing in girl

Male   Female   X   Age   45 yrs.

REPORTED FOR WORK
FEB. 13 1922

Name *Abbott - Sadie* T2 40yrs
Write last name first
Nationality *American* | Pass No. — | Pay Roll No. 514
Employed as *Drawing in girl* Payment Ending *Jan. 5/23*
Dept. *Dress* Mill *No 3* Div. *Cen*

| Is | Leaving / Discharged | X | because | *Working elsewhere* |

Stated

CHARACTER OF SERVICE | 1 | 2 | 3

Do you recommend hiring again   Work   X
Remarks :   Conduct   X
                                       Steadiness X

Date *Jan 4" 1923* Signed : *H. A. Berger*
                                        Overseer.B.

Name *Abbott Sadie A.*

Employed as *Framing - in - girl*

Room *Worstd. Harness* Mill No. 10   Div. *South*

| Is | Leaving / Discharged | X | because | *only temp.* |

Do you recommend hiring again

Remarks : *Payroll # 2936*

Date *March 14, 1929*, Signed : *Wm. Grocock*
                                              Overseer.

Figure E.2. Sample employee files for Sadie Abbott. (*Source:* Amoskeag
Company employee files.)

393

Notice of Discharge or Leaving

Name _Thibodeau Arthur_
Write last name first

Nationality _French_ | Pay Roll No. | Week Ending _Aug 4, 1917_

Employed as _Drawing & Roving_ in

Department _Beaching_ Mill _7_ Floor _1_

is | Leaving | x | | because _Could not stand Chlorine_
| Discharged | | |

| | Character of Service | | |
| | 1 | 2 | 3 |

Do you recommend hiring again? _Yes._ Work | / | ... |

Remarks: Conduct | / | |

 Steadiness | / | |

Date _Aug 3_ 1917 _____ Overseer

Name _Thibodeau Arthur - 10_
Write last name first

Nationality _Fr_ Pass No. _617672_ Pay Roll No. _267_

Employed as _Rov. Hand_ Payment Ending _June 14 1918_

Dept. _Spinning_ Mill _#10_ Div _Nor_

Is | Leaving | Discharged | because _he thinks work_
is to hard.

Do you recommend hiring again _Yes_   Work /

Remark _____   Conduct
_____ JAN 1 1 1918   Steadiness

Date _June 10 191 8_ Signed _F. Gagnon_ Overseer

NOTICE OF DISCHARGE OR LEAVING

Name _Thibodeau Arthur_
Write last name first

Nationality _French_ Pay Roll No. Week Ending _Sept 21/18_

Employed as _Card Tender_ In

Department _Carding_ Mill _3_ Floor _2_

is | Leaving | Discharged | because _laziness_

 Character of Service
 1   2   3

Do you recommend hiring again? Work — x

Remarks: Conduct x

 Steadiness x

Date _Sept 21 191 8_ _M.D. Nolet_ Overseer

394

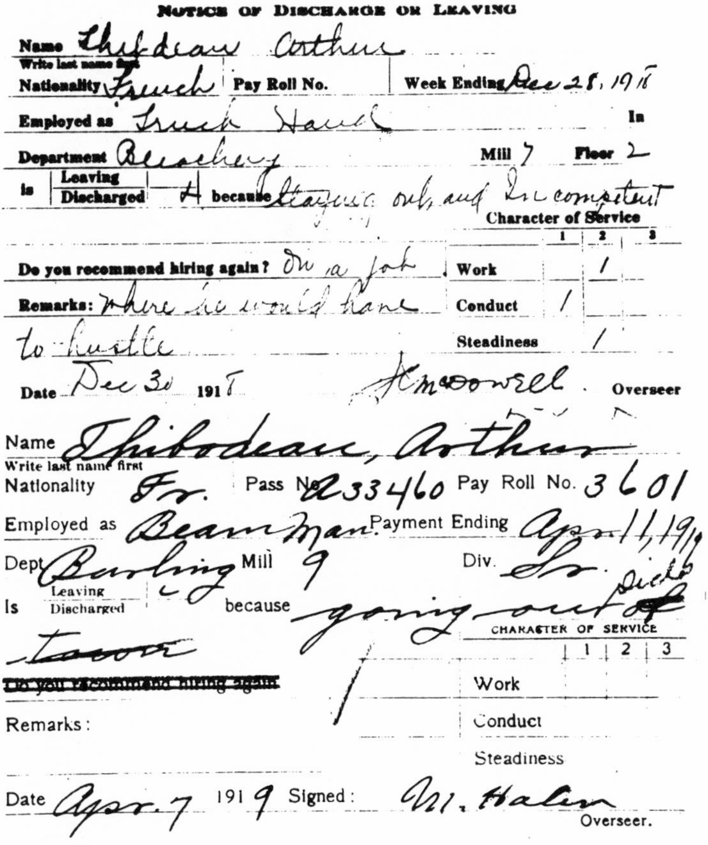

NOTICE OF DISCHARGE OR LEAVING

Name *Thibdeau Arthur*
Write last name
Nationality *French*   Pay Roll No. ___   Week Ending *Dec 28, 1918*
Employed as *Truck Hand*   In ___
Department *Bleachery*   Mill 7   Floor 2
Is   Leaving ___
     Discharged *H* because *leaving ont, and in competent*
                              Character of Service
                                    1 | 2 | 3
Do you recommend hiring again? *On a job*   Work | | / |
Remarks: *where he would have*   Conduct | / | |
to hustle   Steadiness | / | |
Date *Dec 30* 191 *7*   *Mcdowell* .   Overseer

Name *Thibodeau, Arthur*
Write last name first
Nationality *Fr.*   Pass No *33460*   Pay Roll No. *3601*
Employed as *Beam Man*   Payment Ending *Apr 11, 19*
Dept *Burling* Mill 9   Div. *Fr.*
Is   Leaving ___
     Discharged   because *going out of*
                              CHARACTER OF SERVICE
                                    1 | 2 | 3
Do you recommend hiring again   /   Work
Remarks: Conduct
                                    Steadiness
Date *Apr. 7* 191 *9* Signed: *M. Halin*
                                    Overseer.

Figure E.3. Sample employee files for Arthur Thibdeau. (*Source:* Amoskeag
Company employee files.)

395

Appendix F
Descriptions of select major textile occupations

Cotton cloth manufacturing

DOFFER

 Kindred occupation: Doffer, woolen and worsted.

 Description: The doffer takes full bobbins off the spinning frame. The duties are much the same as those of the doffer in wool manufacturing, except that the construction of the spinning frame makes the operation somewhat different. *Qualifications:* Ordinary skill and intelligence; agility. Some time is required to learn the knack of changing the bobbins rapidly.

DRAWER-IN

 Kindred occupation: Drawer-in, woolen and worsted.

 Description: The drawer-in gets the warp ready for the loom by drawing the end of the warp through the eye in the harness. This is a simple operation in which the drawer-in draws through the eye in the harness the thread from the warp, but, since there are hundreds of threads to be drawn one at a time, the work is exacting, and the operative must acquire a certain knack or skill in drawing the threads accurately and rapidly. Men and women are employed.

 Qualifications: Good eyesight. Dexterity.

FIXER, LOOM

 Kindred occupation: Loom fixer, woolen and worsted.

 Description: The loom fixer is probably the most important and skilled worker in the weaving room. When a warp runs out the fixer cuts off the cloth and takes out the empty

Data for this appendix taken from U.S. Bureau of Labor Statistics, "Descriptions of Occupations: Textile and Clothing," prepared for U.S. Employment Service (Washington, D.C.: U.S. Government Printing Office, 1918).

beam, puts in a new beam, and examines the loom to see that it is in proper running condition. When a loom is not running properly it is his duty to fix it. He must also see that the cloth is weaving properly. This is a man's occupation, as the changing of the warp beam is heavy work.

Qualifications: Good strength is necessary. A knowledge of weaving and considerable mechanical ability are required. Must understand construction of a loom. Must know the difference between kinds of cloth by appearance and feel. Must be a dependable man.

GENERAL WORKER, FEMALE

As follows: Folding-machine operator; Harness cleaner; Hooker-machine tender; Knotter; Scrubber; Sliver lap-machine tender; Speeder tender; Spooler tender; Stitcher; Tacker.

INSPECTOR, HAND

Description: The hand inspector examines the cloth for imperfections, and corrects them where possible. It is somewhat of a strain on the eyes. Men and women are employed.

Qualifications: Ordinary strength and good eyesight. Must have been a weaver, or have been trained to know the standards of cloth, the imperfections which may exist, and how to correct them.

SPINNER, MULE

Kindred occupation: Spinner, mule, woolen and worsted.

Description: The duties of the mule spinner are practically the same as those of the mule spinner in woolen manufacturing. The spinner is assisted by piecers, doffers, and back boys, and must direct their activities. Men are always employed because of the mechanical skill and long term of apprenticeship required.

Qualifications: Ordinary strength and considerable mechanical ability. Must know the mechanism of the mule and the operation of spinning.

SPINNER, RING FRAME

Kindred occupation: Spinner, cap frame, woolen and worsted.

Description: The ring frame spinner does much the same work as the cap frame spinner in the woolen manufacturing industry. As in cap frame spinning, the principal knack is in piecing up the ends when they break, with a quick movement, making a joint that will not show. Young girls make the best spinners because of their dexterity in piecing up. Women are usually employed.

Qualifications: Ordinary strength and ability. It requires some time to acquire the deftness necessary to piece ends quickly and properly.

STRIPPER, CARD

Kindred occupation: Card stripper, wool.

Description: The stripper does the work as the card stripper in wool manufacturing. In the case of cotton card stripping a machine is often used which takes the place of the hand brushes, eliminating some of the work. Men are always employed.

Qualifications: Ordinary strength and ability.

TENDER, CARD

Kindred occupation: Card tender, wool.

Description: The card tender does practically the same work as the card tender in wool manufacturing, though the work is somewhat simpler. He feeds the roll of lap into the cards and doffs or takes off the cans of sliver as they become filled. Each worker tends a large number of machines and is kept pretty actively engaged. The work is moderately heavy. Men are always employed.

Qualifications: Ability to do moderately heavy work. Ordinary ability.

TENDER, DRAWING FRAME

Kindred occupation: Drawing-frame tender, wool.

Description: The drawing frame tender does the same work as the drawing frame tender in wool manufacturing.

Qualifications: Ordinary strength and ability.

TENDER, SLASHER

Kindred occupation: Slasher tender, woolen and worsted.

Description: The slasher tender is more responsible than most textile machine tenders. He prepares the yarn for the weaving by strengthening it with a coat of "size" or starch. The yarn is run from one beam to another through the size and over a steam heated drum to dry it. The tender's duty is to see that the yarn is unwinding properly, that there is sufficient size of the proper consistency, that the yarn is dry but not burned, that it is not caked with hard size, that the tension is just enough, and that it is winding properly on the loom beam. He must also put in the back beam and take out the loom beams when full. This is responsible and skilled work. Men are employed exclusively, because the work is very hot and heavy.

Qualifications: Good strength for heavy work and ability to stand heat. Should be a competent, careful man, and have had experience as slasher tender's helper. Must understand enough about steam to keep right pressure in the cylinder. Must be able to tell by feel when the yarn is dry.

WEAVER

Kindred occupation: Weaver, wool manufacturing.

Description: The weaver watches the cloth carefully as it is woven and changes the filling in the shuttles as it runs out, also pieces up threads that break in the warp. In some cases a weaver must oil and clean his own loom. On machines other than the automatic the chief duty is putting fresh bobbins into the empty shuttles and starting the shuttle in the machine. The work is light, but requires the worker to be on his feet most of the time. Close attention is necessary. Both men and women are employed.

Qualifications: Must be able to stand most of the time. The weaver must be able to tell when cloth is not being woven properly, and know how to "pick out" imperfections.

Cotton cloth finishing

COLORIST

Description: The colorist is usually the head of the color-making department. He determines how to get the color desired by the designing department, giving the formula for the different mixes to the color mixers. After the color has been put into the printing machine and a smooth piece of cloth has been printed, the colorist decides finally whether or not the shade and color are correct. Men are always employed.

FOLDER, CLOTH

Description: The folder takes the cloth after it has been folded by the hooker machine and passed through the selector's hands, and doubles it over in different ways to make a neat package, easy to handle, and attractive in appearance. There is a considerable knack in this work to get the folds even and flat and to produce the various types of packages desired by the trade. Men are employed on the heavy goods and women on the light goods.

Qualifications: Considerable strength and ordinary ability. Several months' experience are required to acquire efficiency in folding.

INSPECTOR, CLOTH

Description: The inspector determines the condition of the cloth which is to be finished. He measures it, counts the warp and filling threads, determines the weave, examines the yarn, and tests the strength of the cloth. This work requires a careful, dependable worker. It is light and can be done sitting at a bench. Men are employed, as a rule, but the work can be done by women without detriment to their health.

Qualifications: Several years' experience as an inspector in the weave room or in some position where familiarity with standards of cloth has been acquired. High-grade intelligence; carefulness and dependability.

PRINTER

Description: The printer runs the machine which prints the pattern upon the cloth. He is in complete charge and responsible for the proper printing of the cloth, the adjusting of the machine, and the keeping of it in repair. The most important part of the work is to adjust the machine, which includes fitting in the rollers so that they will print in the proper place, and sharpening and adjusting the "doctor" plates against the roller. The printer must also watch for all sorts of imperfections in the printed cloth and adjust the machine to eliminate them. The printing is the last step in a long and complicated process and the printer must be an experienced and reliable man to complete it properly. Men are always employed.

Qualifications: Ordinary strength and exceptional ability. An apprenticeship of several years.

WINDER

Description: The winder tends a machine which winds the finished cloth around a flat board or upon a roller. He must start and stop the machine, thread in the cloth, and see that it rolls evenly, without creasing. The work is very heavy as the heavy rolls must be lifted from the machine. Men are always employed.

Qualifications: Exceptional strength; ordinary ability.

Woolen and worsted goods

DOFFER

Kindred occupation: Doffer, cotton.

Description: Although "doffing" or removing the finished product is necessary for all the machines in the mill, this is the only place where it is used as an occupation term. The doffer removes the full bobbins of spun yarn from the spindle of the spinning frame. The work is generally done by small boys, as it requires much bending and considerable agility.

Qualifications: Ordinary skill and intelligence: agility. No special skill is required, though some time is required to learn the knack of changing the bobbins rapidly.

DRAWER-IN

Kindred occupation: Drawer-in, cotton.

Description: The drawer-in gets the warp ready for the loom by drawing the end of the warp through the eyes in the harness. This is a simple operation in which the drawer-in draws through the eye in the harness the thread from the warp, but since there are hundreds of threads to be drawn, one at a time, the work is exacting and a certain knack or skill must be acquired to draw the threads accurately and rapidly. Men and women are employed.

Qualifications: Good eyesight; dexterity.

FIXER, LOOM

Kindred occupation: Loom fixer, cotton.

Description: The loom fixer is probably the most important and skilled worker in the weaving room. His principal duties are to put in the new warps and to see that looms are running properly. When a warp runs out, the fixer cuts off the cloth and takes out the empty beam, puts in a new beam, examines the loom to see that it is in proper running condition, and weaves the first few inches of cloth to see whether the loom is running properly. When a loom is not running properly, it is his duty to fix it. He must also

see that cloth is weaving properly. This is a man's occupation, as the changing of the warp beam is heavy work.
Qualifications: Good strength is necessary. A knowledge of weaving and considerable mechanical ability are required. Must understand construction of a loom; must know difference between kinds of cloth by appearance and feel. Must be a dependable man.

GENERAL WORKER, FEMALE

As follows: Coverer, light work; Doubler; Drop-wire operator; Harness cleaner; Leaser; Measurer; Paperer, light work; Porcupine cleaner; Scrubber; Waste picker.
Description: The duties are to tend simple machines, scrub, and to do such work as is indicated by the occupational name or such other work as does not require a long period of training.
Qualifications: Ordinary strength and ability.

GENERAL WORKER, MALE

As follows: Bobbin boy; Card feeder; Cloth winder; Coverer, heavy work; Dolly tender; Drug man; Duster tender; Dye mixer; Extractor tender; Filling carrier; Leaser; Measurer; Opener tender; Paperer, heavy work; Quill boy; Scrubber; Scutcher tender; Sweeper; Top Carrier; Trucker; Washer tender; Waste picker; Weigher, worsted drawing.
Description: The duties are to look after the operation of simple machines, truck, sweep, and to do such other work as is indicated by the occupational name or such other work as does not require a long period of training.
Qualifications: Ordinary strength and ability.

GRINDER, CARD

Kindred occupation: Card grinder, cotton.
Description: The card grinder sharpens the fine teeth on the various cylinders of the cards with a machine, and adjusts them so that the teeth will be the correct distance apart to work the stock properly. He also examines the card for worn-out parts. Men are always employed.
Qualifications: Should have mechanical ability and intelligence higher than that of the average worker. The setting or adjusting of the card requires a responsible and careful man. Considerable experience is necessary to learn how to grind teeth and set the card. Must thoroughly understand the construction of the card.

INSPECTOR

Description: The inspector examines cloth on an inspecting frame for any imperfections in dyeing, and returns cloth not properly dyed, for redyeing.

Qualifications: Ordinary strength and ability. A knowledge of dyeing processes.

OVERSEER, CARDING

Description: Oversees work of carder, card stripper, card grinder, and mixing and oiling tender.

Qualifications: Greater than average ability. Experience in the lower positions.

OVERSEER, COMBING (WORSTED)

Description: Oversees work of carding, of the gill-box tender, preparing-box tender, comber and drawing-frame tender.

Qualifications: Greater than average ability. Experience in the lower positions.

OVERSEER, DYEING

Description: The occupation of boss dyer is primarily one calling for the exercise of trade knowledge rather than the supervision of a large department. The boss dyer has complete responsibility for the dye mixing, matching shades to secure proper colors, and dyeing the wool, yarn, or fabric to the required color. Men are always employed.

OVERSEER, FINISHING

Description: The overseer of the finishing department, or the boss finisher, like the dyer, is usually the only expert in his department. He must know all the processes in his department and how to get the particular finish desired. The arrangement of the process to secure a desired finish and the judgment as to a proper finish are in his hands alone. He oversees the work of the inspectors, the fuller, washer tender, crabber tender, and various other machine tenders, in the wet and dry finishing processes. Men are always employed.

Qualifications: Higher than average ability. Experience in the lower positions.

OVERSEER, GENERAL

Description: Overseers are men in charge of departments. They are responsible directly to the superintendent. Overseers are not only experts in the processes that come directly under their supervision but have rather complete knowledge of all processes in the mill, for a man can not do satisfactory work in one department unless he knows its relation to the other departments. Overseers understand thoroughly all the machines in their departments, and are able to direct changes and repairs on them. Overseers are sometimes called bosses – as boss carder, boss weaver, etc. In most of the departments the position is primarily executive. In the case of the dyeing or finishing departments, however, it has more of a technical character, as there the overseer is the only expert in the process requiring trade knowledge. Men are always employed.

Qualifications: Higher than average ability. Experience in the lower positions.

OVERSEER, SORTING

Description: Oversees work of wool sorter, duster tender, washer tender, drier tender, burr-picker tender, and carbonizer.

Qualifications: Higher than average ability. Experience in the lower positions.

OVERSEER, SPINNING

Description: Oversees work of frame spinner, mule spinner and twister tender, and all minor help.

Qualifications: Higher than average ability. Experience in the lower positions.

OVERSEER, WARP PREPARATION

Description: Oversees work of winder tender, reeler, spooler, dresser tender, slasher tender, and beamer.

Qualifications: Higher than average ability; experience in lower positions.

OVERSEER, WEAVING

Description: Oversees work of drawer-in, hander-in, weaver, loom fixer, harness man, and subsidiary helpers.

Qualifications: Higher than average ability; experience in lower positions.

PIECER

Kindred occupation: Piecer, cotton.

Description: The piecer is a specialized spinner's helper, whose duty it is to help in piecing up or joining the ends of the roving. Also helps in doffing the spun yarn and placing empty bobbins on the spindles for a new doff. Men, boys and women are employed.

Qualifications: Ordinary strength and mechanical ability.

SECOND HAND, GENERAL

Description: Second hands are assistants to the overseers. The work of the second hand is supervisory. He must see that the employees do their work and do it properly; he plans the work and places the workers. The second hand is usually responsible for having the work come off the machines according to the specifications called for. Orders for changes are issued through him and important changes or repairs of machinery are made by him or under his immediate supervision. Men are always employed.

Qualifications: Some executive ability; experience in the various processes.

SECTION HANDS

Description: Section hands are men in supervisory positions directly under the second hands. They have charge of certain sections in which they must supervise the workers and see that the work comes off properly. An important part of the work of a section hand is fixing, i.e., making repairs and changes in machinery. They inspect the machinery to see that no parts are worn out or missing and that the machines are properly oiled and cleaned. The work of a section hand and that of a fixer are practically the same. Where the work of supervision predominates, he is called a section hand; where the fixing is important and supervision incidental, he is called a fixer. Men are always employed.

Qualifications: Some executive ability; experience in the various processes.

SORTER, WOOL

Description: The wool sorter is one of the really skilled workers in textile manufacturing. He takes the fleeces as they are unpacked and divides each one according to the grades of the wool contained in it, since there are several grades of wool in any one fleece. He judges the different grades of wool by the length of fiber and the look and feel of the wool. This work is done mostly by men, but a few women are also employed. It is light, but somewhat dusty, and subjects the worker to danger of infection with anthrax.

Qualifications: Ordinary strength and ability. Several years of experience are necessary to be able to tell the different grades of wool by sight and feel.

SPINNER, MULE

Kindred occupation: Spinner, cap frame, wool: Spinner, mule, cotton.

Description: The mule spinner converts the drawing into yarn. He has full charge of the operation of the spinning mule, and oils, cleans, and makes minor repairs on it. The routine duties in the spinning are "setting in roving," that is, placing the spools of drawing on the mule, piecing up ends, doffing or removing the spools of spun yarn. Though his assistants do most of the work, he is responsible for it and directs them. Because of the mechanical skill and long term of apprenticeship required, men are always employed.

Qualifications: Ordinary strength and considerable mechanical ability. From one to two years of apprenticeship is necesssary to learn the mechanism of the mule and the operation of spinning.

STRIPPER, CARD

Kindred occupation: Stripper, card, cotton.

Description: Usually two men work together in stripping the cards. They remove the fibers, dust, lint, and other foreign substances from the teeth of the card cylinders. This is done by hand with a brush, which is the only thing to differentiate it from card stripping in cotton mills, which is done by machine. This is dusty, dirty, and rather hard work. Men are always employed.

Qualifications: Good strength and intelligence.

TENDER, BEAMER (WARP)

Kindred occupation: Beamer tender, cotton.

Description: The warp beamer tender winds the warp from the spools on to the beam. Her duty is to watch for broken ends and tie them, and to break out poor spots in the yarn. She does not change the spools nor the beam and the machine stops automatically. She must start the new threads on an empty beam. She must clean and oil her own machine. Women are employed almost exclusively.

Qualifications: Ordinary health and strength.

TENDER, COMBER (WORSTED)

Kindred occupation: Comb tender, cotton.

Description: The comber tender tends a machine which is used in the making of worsted yarn to lay the fibers in the yarn parallel. Though the machine is complicated, the duties are simple. The tender must put on new balls of sliver and draw the ends through the conductor which feeds them into the comb. When a can is full of combed "tops" he removes it and sets on an empty can. He has to watch to see that ends are feeding up all right and piece the sliver if it breaks. This is not very hard work. Men or women are employed.

Qualifications: Ordinary strength and ability.

TENDER, DRESSER

Description: The dresser tender is one of the important workers in a woolen and worsted mill. His task is to prepare the warp for the weave room. He sets up the spools of yarn in the creel, counts out the threads of the pattern in the warp, and attends to winding these threads on the loom beam. He must "take a lease," that is, separate by a string or rod the alternate threads of the warp. The important part of the operation is to pick out threads of the patterns properly, and have all the threads at an even tension in winding. When the warp is sized, that is, coated with starch to strengthen the yarn, he must put the size into the size box and run the warp through it. He must oil and clean his machine. When picking the pattern and tying in he may sit, but at all other times is on his feet. Frequently he has a helper. Men are always employed.

Qualifications: He must have average strength, and must be able to distinguish colors of yarn readily. He should be

408   **Appendix F**

a competent, careful, and reliable man, having had experience as helper, or working under close supervision. He must have skill in the various operations of picking the pattern, tying the ends, and keeping proper tension on the yarn.

TENDER, FINISHER

Kindred occupation: Card tender, cotton.

Description: The finisher tender is responsible for the running of the cards. He starts and stops them when necessary and is stationed at the delivery end to watch the ends of roving as they come from the condenser. He must see that the roving is coming off in an even, round strand, free from twists, and mend it when it breaks. Men and women are employed.

Qualifications: Ordinary strength and ability. Must know how to run a set of cards and know when the roving is not up to standard.

TENDER, SLASHER

Kindred occupation: Slasher tender, cotton.

Description: The slasher tender is more responsible than most textile machine tenders. He prepares the yarn for the weaving by strengthening it with a coat of "size" or starch so that it will not be chafed by the loom. The yarn is run from one beam to another through the size and over a steam heated drum to dry it. The tender's duty is to see that the yarn is unwinding properly, that there is sufficient size of the proper consistency, that the yarn is dry but not burned, that it is not caked with hard size, that the tension is just enough and that it is winding properly on the loom beam. He must also put in the back beam and take out the loom beams when full. This is responsible and skilled work. Men are employed exclusively, because the work is very hot and heavy.

Qualifications: Good strength for heavy work and ability to stand heat. He should be a competent, careful man, and have had nine months to a year as slasher tender's helper. Must understand enough about steam to keep the right pressure in the cylinder. Must be able to tell by feel when the yarn is dry.

TENDER, SPOOLER

Kindred occupation: Spooler tender, cotton.

Description: The spooler tender tends the machine which winds the yarn on spools from bobbins. The principal duty is to tie up ends, but when spooling worsted yarn, she must watch the yarn for imperfect places. She must tie in the ends of new bobbins and take off the spools when filled, take out imperfect places in the yarn and tie the ends. Those workers who inspect the yarn while spooling sit at their machines. Those who do not inspect stand most of the time. The work requires constant attention. Women are always employed.

Qualifications: Ordinary strength and ability.

TENDER, TWISTER (WORSTED)

Description: The twister tender operates a machine which twists several plies of yarn together. The duties are to set in the spools of yarn to be twisted, to take off full bobbins, start the yarn on empty ones, and tie ends when they break. The work is not heavy, but requires the operative to stand constantly. This work is usually done by girls over 18 years.

Qualifications: Ordinary strength and intelligence; ability to tie a knot well and rapidly.

TENDER, WINDER

Description: The winder tender transfers the yarn from skein form to spools, or vice versa. The task is to set the yarn in the creel, to start it winding on the spool or skein, and to take off spool or skein when it is wound. She must tie ends when they break. The work is fairly exacting. Young girls over 18 are usually employed.

Qualifications: Ordinary strength and ability. Must be able to move about rapidly.

WEAVER

Kindred occupation: Weaver, cotton.

Description: The weaver operates the loom which produces cloth from warp and filling. The weaver watches the cloth carefully as it is woven and changes the filling in the shuttles as it runs out, also pieces up threads that break in the warp. In some cases a weaver must oil and clean his own loom. On machines other than the automatic the chief duty is changing the filling, that is, putting fresh bobbins into the empty shuttles and starting the shuttles in the machine. The work is light, but requires the worker to be on his feet most of the time. Close attention is necessary. Both men and women are employed.

Qualifications: Must be able to stand on feet most of the time. The weaver must be able to tell when cloth is not being woven properly, and know how to "pick out" imperfections.

Notes

1. The theoretical context

1   The Chicago school of sociology, with which Wirth and Thomas and Znaniecki had been connected, was the major proponent of this theory. Thomas and Znaniecki, in particular, in their massive study of *The Polish Peasant in Europe and America* (1918–20), influenced historical interpretation of the impact of migration and urban life on family and other primary group ties (most notably in Handlin's *The Uprooted*, 1951).

2   The work of French and English historical demographers, subsequently followed by Swedish and American investigations, has consistently documented the persistence of the nuclear household structure in pre-industrial Western society. The most elaborate compendium of these findings cross-culturally is Laslett and Wall (1972). For a historiographic discussion, see Hareven (1971). See also the seminal articles by Greenfield (1961) and Furstenberg (1966), which questioned the sociological assumptions regarding the emergence of a nuclear family type under the impact of industrialization.

3   Anderson (1976) challenged Smelser's (1959) contention that family continuity as a work unit was phased out in the 1830s.

4   The best study of labor recruitment in the early textile industry in New England is by Ware (1931). On the Slater system, see White (1836).

5   On the development of planned New England towns, see Ware (1931), Shlakman (1935), and Green (1939).

6   See Thomas and Znaniecki (1918–20), Handlin (1941), and Erickson (1957). Although Handlin emphasized the disruptive impact of migration on the family, he also documented the continuity in the transmission of assistance among Irish immigrants across the Atlantic. For similar patterns among Italian immigrants, see Yans-McLaughlin (1977).

7   On the "new" labor history, see Gutman (1976) and Montgomery (1979), which are collections of previously published essays. See also Dawley (1976), Walkowitz (1978), and Cumbler (1979). For earlier historiographies, see Faler (1969) and Zieger (1972). On the historiography of the family in the industrial era, see Hareven (1971, 1975b, 1975c, 1977), Anderson (1971), Sennett (1971), and Elder (1974, 1978). Studies by Yans-McLaughlin (1977) and Walkowitz (1978) discuss the relationship between the family and work but do not examine the family's role in the workplace.

411

8   As Parsons himself suggested to his critics (1965), his definition of the "isolated nuclear family" referred to a structural isolation from extended kinship networks, as opposed to the functional isolation of behavioral patterns of exchange and interaction among kin. His critics, on the other hand, emphasized behavioral interaction between the nuclear family and extended kin. See Adams's analysis of the controversy (1968) and Elder's most recent discussion of the distinction between structural and functional isolation (1978).

9   The pioneering cross-sectional studies of household structure for the preindustrial and industrial periods have been criticized because they are restricted to one point in time and thus ignore the possibility of continuous change in household structure and family configurations over the life course; see Berkner (1972) and Hareven (1974), who proposed the family-cycle approach as an alternative. More recently, however, the family-cycle approach has been superseded by the life-course perspective in which the transitions made by families and individuals from one stage to the next are of paramount concern (Elder 1974, 1978, and Hareven, ed., 1978).

10 The term *industrial time* is borrowed from Sorokin and Merton (1937), who use the term to designate industrial and modern time schedules. In this study, however, the term is used more broadly to designate the timing of all aspects of life within a modern industrial framework. For definitions of "family time" and the life-course approach, see Hareven (1977).

2. The historical context

1   The first half of this chapter is adapted from the Introduction to *Amoskeag: Life and Work in an American Factory City* by Tamara K. Hareven and Randolph Langenbach (1978), hereafter cited as *Amoskeag.* I am grateful to Randolph Langenbach for his collaboration in the writing of the description of the urban design of the Amoskeag mill yard and the city of Manchester.

2   On the development of planned New England textile towns, see Ware (1931), Shlakman (1935), Green (1939). On the history of the Amoskeag Company and the development of Manchester, see Potter (1856), Clarke (1875), Browne (1915), and Blood (1948). Browne's book is a company history, published by the Amoskeag.

3   On the planning and development of Manchester, especially the architectural design of the mill yard and the city, see Langenbach (1968).

4   On the transformation of Lowell in the post–Civil War era, see Ware (1931), Coolidge (1942), and Dublin (1979).

5   The Amoskeag Company's specifications were spelled out in the deeds governing the sale and donation of land by the Amoskeag Company. For examples, see Amoskeag Company, Deeds, Manchester Historic

Association (hereafter cited as MHA).

6   For a comparison with Pullman, Illinois, see Buder (1967), and for a comparison with the South, see Herring (1929).

7   The workers' attitude towards the Straws as agents is amply documented in *Amoskeag*. For F. C. Dumaine's rise from humble origins to treasurer of the Amoskeag, see the oral history interview of his son, F. C. Dumaine, Jr., in *Amoskeag*, p. 79.

8   For the local clergy's letters of recommendation on behalf of each girl, see Amoskeag Papers, MHA. See also Mary Cunion in *Amoskeag*, p. 41. Mary's Aunt Susan was one of the original "Scottish girls" recruited in this manner.

9   On the French-Canadian migration to New England, see Vicero (1966), Lavoie (1972), Robert (1975), and Perreault (1976).

10 The first French-Canadian parish – St. Augustine – was founded in Central Manchester in 1871, where the newly arrived French Canadians first settled. The second French parish – St. Marie – was founded in 1880 and became the focus of the developing French-Canadian neighborhood in the West Side.

     Most of the plots on the West Side were sold between 1880 and 1910. Of the 357 persons who bought land, 151 were native-born, English, or Irish, 59 were German, 181 were French, and 19 were from other countries. Each ethnic group settled in a specific West Side area. (This ethnic distribution was derived from a trace of all purchases of Amoskeag plots through the Manchester City Directory.)

11 Manchester City Census, 1882. The unit of enumeration was the household rather than the individual. Ethnicity was defined by that of the head of the household. The Manchester City Census, 1884, is analyzed in Hanlan (1979).

12 This reconstruction of the ethnic composition of city blocks was derived from the Manchester City Census, 1884, by Hanlan (1979:297).

13 The 1894–5 French-Canadian guide for Manchester reported a considerable French-Canadian population. In addition to factory workers, more than 30 other occupations were listed, including insurance agent, grocer, baker, barber, shoemaker, jeweler, and tailor. French Canadians in the municipal administration included 1 municipal magistrate, 4 city councilors, 3 legislative deputies, and several minor officers.

14 Letter to Herman Straw. Amoskeag Records, MHA.

15 The subdivision is clearly demonstrated in the floor plans of the Amoskeag Company's boardinghouses and tenements. See Amoskeag Company Rental Ledgers, MHA. See Appendix E.

16 For a description of growing up in the agent's house near the mill yard, see Mary Flanders, William Parker Straw's daughter, *Amoskeag*, pp. 246–53.

17 For a fuller discussion of these developments, see Chapter 11.

18 In their comparison of wage rates in the Amoskeag with the cost-of-living index in Boston during 1914–18, Creamer and Coulter (1939)

concluded that the wage-rate index did not appreciably exceed the cost-of-living index until 1917. The divergence increased in 1920 and continued to be considerable in 1921 despite the 22.5% wage reduction that year. The resulting index of 203 was some 15% above the cost-of-living index. Concurrent with the putative increase was the reduction of the workweek from 55 hours to 48. In view of the part-time operations and temporary shutdowns however, the improvement must have been minimal. In 1920, the year of the highest wage rates, only about one-third of the workers could earn as much as $1,000, and this opportunity was generally restricted to the most skilled employees (Creamer and Coulter 1939:187–8).

19 Many of the workers left stranded when the Chicopee Mill shut down unexpectedly in 1975 were former Amoskeag workers and their children.

3. The corporation's children

1 On the Ford plant, see Nevins (1954). For a comprehensive discussion of welfare capitalism, see Ozanne (1967), Nelson (1975), and Brandes (1976). On the broader context of managerial reform, see Chandler (1977). For contemporary studies, see Meakin (1905), Boettiger (1923), and Houser (1927). For a comparison of welfare work in the northern and southern textile mills, see Herring (1929).

2 On the activities of the National Civic Federation in stimulating industrial welfare programs, see *The National Civic Federation: Its Methods and Its Aims* (1905), Green (1939), and Brandes (1976).

3 Efficiency and welfare programs were mutually reinforcing in some companies and in conflict or competition in others. In the Amoskeag the two coexisted as part of the same reform. For a case study of conflict between the two and the essential triumph of welfare over efficiency, see Nelson and Campbell (1972).

4 The first personnel department was introduced in the National Cash Register Company after its 1901 strike. Although many companies introduced welfare and efficiency plans between 1911 and 1915, systematic personnel offices did not emerge until after 1915; see Eilbirt (1959) and Nelson (1975). For contemporary accounts of personnel management, see Bloomfield (1922).

5 Amoskeag Records, Manchester Historic Association; hereafter cited as MHA.

6 Amoskeag Records, MHA.

7 Of the workers who purchased plots from the corporation, records for only 36 individuals were found in the employee files. All were males who had been employed for ten years or more, the average number of years being 22.6. Seven workers were employed only prior to 1922; the remainder worked within the period from the beginning of the century

to the shutdown or a fraction of that period. Surprisingly, 32 workers were French Canadians; the remainder included only one native-born, two Irish, and one British. The majority of these men were skilled workers: 16 had worked as loomfixers at some point in their careers, 6 as weavers, and 6 as second hands. Two of the second hands had also been loomfixers earlier in their careers. The remainder included 2 carpenters, 3 unskilled workers, and 3 in semiskilled jobs. This analysis is based on the reconstruction of the career patterns of employees who received company plots, using the individual employee files. Because the dates of purchase were not given, it is impossible to ascertain at what point in their careers they purchased the plots.

8   Some records of the visiting nurses for May 1921 give an indication of the frequency and nature of the visits: During the period of May 5 to May 20 the nurses visited a total of 74 cases, of whom 60 were babies. From May 18 to May 23, they saw 40 cases, of which they visited 6 once a week, 13 daily, 3 twice a week, and 2 three times a week. They also had 16 "social visits," which usually took place once a month. On May 23 the nurses reported having seen 108 cases in two weeks, 69% of whom were babies. The charity cases were summarized from 1920–21 records drawn from the Charity Department (Amoskeag Company records, Baker Library, Harvard University).

9   U.S., Department of Labor, Bureau of Labor Statistics, March 27, 1914: "An Investigation of Labor Conditions in the (Textile) Industry." Manuscript, Amoskeag Records, MHA.

10 On more elaborate Americanization programs in welfare capitalism, see Korman (1967) and Ozanne (1967).

11 Unless otherwise specified, the letters quoted are in the Scrapbook, Amoskeag Company records, MHA.

12 Regulations of Boarding Houses, Lawrence Manufacturing Company, Lowell, Mass., circa 1832–3. Lowell Historical Society Collection.

13 Memorandum of Herman Straw attached to the *Amoskeag New Mills Register of Workers, 1859–1878*. Amoskeag Company records, MHA.

14 I am indebted to Randolph Langenbach (1968) for his insights in this area: He views the continuity of management as the key to the continuation of the Amoskeag's paternalism plan, including the provision of corporation housing into the twentieth century, long after Lowell and most other related cities had abandoned similar policies.

15 F. C. Dumaine, Amoskeag Papers, MHA.

16 Burns Detective Agency, Reports to F. C. Dumaine, Amoskeag Papers, MHA. On the Lawrence strike, see Cole (1963). On the response of Manchester laborers to the Lawrence strike, see Yellen (1936).

17 A. E. Stearns, stockholder, to President, Amoskeag Company, December 22, 1913, Dumaine Papers, MHA.

18 Hayes Robbins, secretary of the Civic Federation, to F. C. Dumaine, July 5, 1906, Amoskeag Papers, MHA.

19 F. C. Dumaine to Gertrude Beeks, March 25, 1908, Dumaine Papers, MHA.
20 Gertrude Beeks to F. C. Dumaine, September 11, 1908, Dumaine Papers, MHA.
21 Settlement House Association to F. C. Dumaine, November 1, 1910, Dumaine Papers, MHA.
22 F. C. Dumaine to Settlement House Association, December 12, 1910, Dumaine Papers, MHA.
23 On the progressive reform and social welfare programs, see Bremner (1956) and Bremner et al. (1968–71).
24 A 1915 survey of the Dental Department shows that the Irish and French Canadians were the heaviest users of the dental service. The proportions of Irish and French-Canadian visitors to the dentist were higher than their proportions in the labor force. Amoskeag Company, Tally of visitors to the dentist's office, MHA.
25 "Happenings," March 28 and April 2, 1912, quoted in Creamer and Coulter (1939:174).
26 *Amoskeag Bulletin*, March 16, 1914.
27 For a critique of Brody's thesis, see Brandes (1976:136–7).

4. The meaning of work

1 For recent condemnations of industrial work as alienating, see Terkel (1972), Braverman (1974), and Edwards (1979). For historical studies along this line, see Thomas (1964) and Thompson (1967). For the most extensive treatment of the work ethic in American society, see Rodgers (1978).
2 The so-called Hawthorne Studies were carried out by a Harvard Business School team headed by Elton Mayo at the Hawthorne Works of the Western Electric Company in Oakbrook, Illinois, between 1924 and 1933. The project was launched under the auspices of the National Research Council of the National Academy of Science and was carried out in collaboration with efficiency engineers from Western Electric. It tried to identify the factors that affect the morale and productivity of workers (Mayo 1933, Roethlisberger and Dickson 1939).
3 See Rodgers (1978). Gutman (1976) has emphasized the tension between the employers' work ethic and that of the employees.
4 Compare with Thompson (1963).

5. The dynamics of kin

1 For a comparison with chain migration patterns among Italian immigrants at the turn of the century, see Yans-McLaughlin (1977). For a

historic comparison in the Midwest, see Bieder (1973). For a contemporary analysis of chain migration and ethnic neighborhood formation, see McDonald and McDonald (1964). On the role of kin in facilitating migration and settlement, see Tilly and Brown (1967). For the most important contemporary parallel of the migration of French Canadians to Manchester, see the study of Appalachian migrants to Beech Creek, Ohio, in Hillery, Brown, and DeJong (1955) and Schwarzweller, Brown, and Mangalam (1971).

2 A picture postcard of the Amoskeag Mills sent to Albert McLeod, 1910, author's private collection.

3 Amoskeag Records, Scrapbook, Manchester Historic Association, hereafter cited as MHA.

4 Amoskeag Records, Scrapbook, MHA.

5 Adjustment, Amoskeag Records, Baker Library, Harvard University; hereafter cited as BLH. These files contain reports on grievances filed by the United Textile Workers Union in the period 1918–22 and again in 1933. For a discussion of the grievance mechanism, see Chapter 11.

6 Adjustments, 1920, 1922, Amoskeag Records, BLH.

7 For a comparison with the contemporary black family, see Stack's (1974) study of the central role of kin in black family survival strategies.

8 Compare Chudacoff's findings for Providence, Rhode Island, in the second half of the nineteenth century, where newlywed children usually lived near their parents if not in the same household (1978). Similarly, Chudacoff and Hareven (1978), in their analysis of select communities in Essex County, Massachusetts, 1880, found that during periods of housing shortage married children coresided with their parents, at least temporarily.

9 These patterns of residence were reconstructed from city directories and addresses listed in the Amoskeag Company's employee files.

10 For definitions and descriptions of traditional kinship systems, see Fox (1967), Arensberg and Kimball (1968), Fortes (1969), and Levi-Strauss (1969). For a historical analysis of legal changes governing American family and kinship organization, see Farber (1973).

11 For a theoretical discussion of the instrumentality of kin in modern society, see also Bennett and Despres (1960).

12 Adjustments, June 26, 1920, Amoskeag Records, BLH.

13 Bott's model has been subsequently applied to a variety of neighborhood and community studies in England and the United States, most notably Michael Young and Peter Willmott's study of East London (1957) and Herbert Gans's study of Boston's West End (1962).

14 Compare also with Litwak's assertion that geographic propinquity is not an essential condition for the maintenance of extended kinship ties (1960).

15 Similarly, in his study of the impact of geographic mobility on middle-class kinship ties, Litwak demonstrated the persistence of kinship ties over a wider geographic space (1960).

16 Recently, the extent to which St. Denis is representative of most rural Quebec communities has been questioned. No comparable studies for other Quebec communities are available, however.

17 A stem family is defined as one in which a married son and his wife reside in the parental household. The pattern was identified and defined by Frederic Le Play (1871). For futher discussion and definition of stem families, see Berkner (1972) and Laslett and Wall (1972:16–18).

18 For a critique of modernization theory in this respect, see Hareven (1976).

6. Adaptation to industrial work

1 See Pollard (1963), Thompson (1963, 1967), and Gutman (1976).

2 Gutman's definition of culture as a resource is based on Sidney Mintz's definition: "Culture is used; and any analysis of its use immediately brings into view the arrangements of persons in societal groups for whom cultural forms confirm, reinforce, maintain, change, or deny particular arrangements of status, power, and identity" (quoted in Gutman 1976:16).

3 See Chapter 5 for a discussion of the selective uses of kinship ties in workers' adaptation.

4 Copies of their employment passes carried a note from their bosses: "Never showed up."

5 Amoskeag Company Accident Records, November 21, 1912, Baker Library, Harvard University.

6 Letter to employment office, January 10, 1935; Amoskeag Company Employment Office File 1930–5, BLH.

7 Report of investigator Coburn to Mr. Hagan, October 9, 1934, Amoskeag Records, BLH.

8 Adjustments, May 28, 1920, Amoskeag Records, BLH.

9 Adjustments, April 6, 1920, Amoskeag Records, BLH. On the activities of the union's grievance committee, see Chapter 11.

10 The grievance mechanism was instituted in 1918 after the entry of the union. For a detailed discussion of its operation, see Chapter 11.

11 Adjustments, October 11, 1933, Amoskeag Records, BLH.

12 Adjustments, March 21, 1919, Amoskeag Records, BLH.

13 The behavior described here as accommodationism partly involves playacting. See Goffman's analysis (1959) of performances and playacting in the workplace, particularly the chapter on "Regions and Region Behavior."

14 Compare with workers' insistence on defining standards in the metal industries in Montgomery (1979:113–34).

15 Adjustments, September 16, 1919, and September 22, 1920, Amoskeag Records, BLH.

16 The task-and-bonus system consisted of two different piece rates: the

base rate (which is below the standard rate) for those who produced below standard and a higher rate for those who produced above standard. In the case of the Amoskeag, several different methods of task-and-bonus payment were introduced between 1911 and 1918 for different jobs. As a result, the system was complicated and provoked complaints among the workers.

Even though the piece-rate base system encompassed almost all major departments and operations, base rates were by no means uniform across departments. In many departments the bosses' tendency to continue to pay workers what they thought they were worth continued. In 1918 the union's grievance committee complained that in No. 11 Cloth Room, "there was no equality in rates and that rates were set promiscuously by the men in charge. They pointed out one instance where some 10 or 12 rates were in operation on the same class of work." Agent Herman Straw agreed that "the older method of paying a man what he was worth might have been all right in years gone by but did not work out now." Wages were standardized upon Straw's instructions, providing a uniform base rate for each job. "The rates had been standardized to such an extent that one was assured of the rate he would be paid in any particular job in which he worked" (adjustments, October 24, 1918, Amoskeag Records, BLH).

Following this adjustment, there were three different methods of pay in the Amoskeag: pay by time rates only, pay by time rates with additional bonuses relative to output, and piece rates. The most common method of pay was by piece rates, which included additional incentives relative to output (task-and-bonus system). Nelson (1975:75) claims that in 1918 Herman Straw, who was acting agent while his son William Parker was in the armed forces, scrapped the task-and-bonus system. Actually, the incentive pay system continued after World War I. I am grateful to Takashi Hikino for his analysis of Amoskeag's wage records and for bringing this contradiction to my attention.

17 See Gantt (1913). On the introduction of scientific management in American industry, see Haber (1964), Braverman (1974), Nelson (1975), Chandler (1977), and Noble (1977). On the textile industry specifically, see Rehn (1934). See also Nadworny (1955).

18 I am indebted to David Montgomery for bringing this difference to my attention.

19 F. M. Caswell report, 1912, Amoskeag Company Planning Office Papers, BLH.

20 F. M. Caswell to W. P. Straw, August 5, 1911; F. M. Caswell to W. P. Straw, July 11, 1912, Amoskeag Records, BLH. Although Gantt did not identify the Amoskeag by name, his breakdown of the burlers' reasons for leaving and the dates match those listed by F. M. Caswell in his report. On Gantt's experience in the textile industry and on women's responses to piece rates, see U.S. Congress, House (1912:583–5).

21 In the piece-rate system a worker was paid for the individual piece, regardless of how many pieces he produced. In the task-and-bonus system a worker was paid a basic rate and an additional bonus for each unit produced. If the worker did not meet a specific quota, he lost the bonus for all the units and received only the basic rate.
22 Adjustments, April 15, 1920, Amoskeag Records, BLH.
23 Adjustments, May 2, 1919, Amoskeag Records, BLH.
24 Adjustments, May 11, 1920, Amoskeag Records, BLH.
25 Adjustments, September 23, 1921, Amoskeag Records, BLH.
26 Adjustments, December 31, 1919, Amoskeag Records, BLH.
27 F. M. Caswell report, June 10, 1914, Amoskeag Company Planning Office Papers, BLH.
28 F. M. Caswell report, April 15, 1914, Amoskeag Company Planning Office Papers, BLH.
29 Adjustments, July 12, 1920, Amoskeag Records, BLH.
30 F. M. Caswell report, April 24, 1914, Amoskeag Company Planning Office Papers, BLH.
31 Adjustments, April 5, 1919, Amoskeag Records, BLH.
32 On the collective responses of workers to scientific management and job control, compare Montgomery (1979). I am grateful to Professor Montgomery for drawing my attention to these types of workers' responses in other industries. For an example of collective restriction on output among workers, see Collins, Dalton, and Roy (1946).
33 Adjustments, November 19, 1921, and February 14, 1921, Amoskeag Records, BLH.
34 Adjustments, November 7, 1919, Amoskeag Records, BLH.

7. Household organization

1 The definition for living alone is membership in a single family household. The exact percentage fluctuated in the second half of the nineteenth century and the early twentieth century from about 1% to 3%. On the emergence of solitary residence as a recent phenomenon, see Kobrin (1976).
2 On the historiography of the household, see Chapter 1.
3 The census sample consists of 580 households drawn randomly from the 1900 individual manuscript schedules of the U.S. Census for Manchester. Every fortieth dwelling was sampled and all households within the dwelling were coded to capture relatives who might be living in separate households within the same building. A comparison of this sample with the aggregate figures for the city's entire population shows its representativeness. The age and sex structure of the sample and the city were similar, except for marital status, where a slightly higher proportion of married men appeared in the aggregate figures for the city than in the sample. Another slight difference between the

sample and the aggregate figures for the city was in labor-force participation – women in the sample had slightly higher participation rates
than those in the city and men had lower rates than women. Generally,
then, the sample was representative of the overall population in the
city.

4   The terms *boarder* and *lodger* are used in the census interchangeably.
    Lodgers usually just slept in the household; boarders both slept and
    ate in the household. Because it is impossible to distinguish between
    them, both categories are employed here.

5   The following classification of household types has been used for this
    analysis: *Nuclear* – parents and children, a couple without children, or
    one parent with children; *extended* – the nuclear family plus one or
    more relatives, such as parents of the head or wife, siblings, cousins,
    etc.; *single-member* – a household unit containing only one member;
    augmented – the family unit plus such nonrelatives as boarders and
    lodgers, servants, apprentices, etc. Each household type would be de-
    fined as "augmented" if one or more nonrelatives were present. For
    example, a nuclear household with non-kin would be "nuclear aug-
    mented" or an extended household with non-kin would be "extended
    augmented." There were also other forms of residence such as a unit in
    which two unrelated individuals lived together and hotels and institu-
    tions, but they were so few that they were not included in this calcula-
    tion. Although this classification embodies the same definitions and
    principles as Laslett and Wall's (1972), it is not identical.

6   For comparison, see Modell and Hareven (1973) and Chudacoff (1978).

7   It is quite possible that the census designation of "boarders" obscures
    relatives who were actually paying board.

8   Although Canadian heads of household constituted 38.6% of total
    household heads in Manchester, they constituted 90.4% of migrants
    who were in the United States less than one year and 75% of migrants
    who were in the United States two to four years. Viewed as a propor-
    tion of recent immigrants within the Canadian group, 41.6% of all Ca-
    nadians were in the United States less than one year and 17.3% of all
    Canadians were in the United States two to four years. The census
    does not distinguish between French and English Canadians. How-
    ever, most of the Canadians in Manchester were French.

9   The mean number of children for households headed by textile work-
    ers was 2.5; for nontextile workers it was 2.3.

10 This comparison is based on an analysis of all (369) households in
    Ward 5, which immediately surrounded the mill district and contained
    the corporation housing.

11 The three Quebec communities analyzed are Franham, St. Sebastian,
    and St. Luc. Analysis includes the entire population of these com-
    munities as recorded in the manuscript census schedules for Quebec in
    1871 with a total of 377 households. This comparison suffers from sev-

eral flaws and can be used, therefore, only for the identification of a general trend, rather than for the identification of specific differences. One flaw concerns the time distance between 1871 and 1900. Another flaw results because the relationship of each individual to the head of the household was not listed. Thus, it is impossible to distinguish between extended kin and strangers in the household. Identification is also difficult when nuclear family members and extended kin have the same family name, but, in reality, such cases were few.

12 In the context discussed here, timing is identified by the age at which an individual makes a given transition and is measured by the time it takes a certain cohort to accomplish such a transition; see Modell, Furstenberg, and Hershberg (1976).

13 It would be impossible to reconstruct a complete sequence of age at leaving home. Because the census does not record those children who had already left home, those enumerated in the household are clearly the last ones to remain. About 8% of the boarders were younger than age 10, either children of working mothers or of distant relatives who were boarding alone or along with their own parents as subfamilies in other people's households.

14 Incomplete vital statistics records for Manchester indicate an excess of births over deaths of about 100 to 200 per year during the 1890s. Net migration was thus about 10,000 from 1880 to 1890 and over 11,000 in the next decade.

15 Adapted from Modell and Hareven (1973). This initial study of boarding and lodging in American industrial communities in the late nineteenth century was based on data from select neighborhoods in the 1880 Census for Boston and the U.S. Bureau of Labor (1892). Numerous other studies of urban household structure in the nineteenth century have identified similar patterns of boarding as a life-course process (e.g., Katz 1975 and Glasco 1977).

16 Among boarders and lodgers in the sample, 63% of those in the country one year or less and 86% of those in the country two to four years were from 15 to 29 years old.

17 Among those aged 10 to 30, 24% of male boarders and 72.5% of sons living at home were under age 20. The corresponding figures for women are 34.7% and 68.5%, respectively.

18 Native-born men and women were underrepresented among the boarders: only 40% of the boarders and lodgers were native-born, whereas they constituted about 54.5% of the entire population in the sample. The Canadians, however, constituted 31.3% of the entire population and 42% of the boarders/lodgers. The Irish were also overrepresented among boarders and lodgers in relation to the overall population (7% of the sample were Irish, but 11% of the boarders were Irish; see Table 7.7).

19 Despite this rise in the rates of widowhood, the proportion of married women in the population did not decline until their sixties. This may

result from the tendency of single women in their forties to get married, as evidenced by the decline in the proportion of single women in the late forties age group.

20 This analysis of later life transitions and household arrangements of older people replicates in part the analysis by Chudacoff and Hareven (1979) for a population sample based on three census decades for Providence, Rhode Island, which was assembled by Professor Chudacoff. I am grateful to him for his collaboration on that article. The patterns found in the Manchester analysis almost completely parallel the Providence patterns.

21 Most of the parents residing in their children's households were older than 59. In this age group 23.2% of all families and 9.6% of all males lived in a household of a married son or daughter.

22 Of the 13 women in the sample who were widowed household heads over age 54, 12 were in the labor force. Because this data is cross-sectional, it is impossible to determine whether these widows had actually worked continuously or whether they returned to work at the time of their widowhood.

23 Compare with Smith (1979), where an analysis of a national census sample for 1900 rendered similar patterns.

24 Smith (1979) found a similar pattern in his study of a sample of the entire United States population in 1900.

25 Emphasis here is on *a* process of adaptation, not *the* process, because individual and family strategies often involve relationships that reach beyond the physical limits of the household unit, a dimension that is very difficult to perceive from census records alone. For ramifications of extra household strategies, see Townsend (1957), Young and Willmott (1957), Anderson (1971), and Chudacoff and Hareven (1978).

26 Calculated from Table 7.10.

27 The probability of ever-married women older than 54 living with children by number of surviving children, Manchester 1900, is as follows:

Number surviving children	% Living with children	N
0	9.5 [a]	21
1	78.0	9
2	60.0	20
3	71.0	14
4	100.0	6
5+	97.0	29

Note: Includes only wives with husbands present and ever-married women who were household heads.
[a] Includes stepchildren, adopted children, etc. Surviving children refers to biological children only.

28 A comparison of the Manchester data in this sample with the three Quebec communities reveals a tendency in Quebec to leave home earlier and to marry earlier than in Manchester. Most men married in their late twenties and most women in their early twenties.

8. Family work strategies

1 Although only half the married women in the labor force were employed in textiles, the proportion of women was much higher than that of men.

2 For a comparison with contemporary patterns, see Oppenheimer (1970) and Sweet (1973).

3 The pattern was less clear-cut for wives in their thirties.

4 "Cost of Living in the Year Ending November 30th, 1918." Manuscript Schedule. Record Group No. 257. U.S. Department of Labor, Bureau of Labor Statistics. National Archives, Washington, D.C.

5 To offset any effect on the pattern that might have resulted from the number of children in the household, this phenomenon was also tested by identifying the proportion of a household in the labor force. There was a correlation between a working wife and the percentage of the entire household in the labor force: In 54% of the households in which the wife worked, at least 41% of the other family members, mostly children, also worked. By comparison, in 69% of the households in which the wife did not work, less than 21% of the other family members worked.

6 The oldest child of 45% of textile household heads worked; the corresponding figure for nontextile heads was 34%.

7 Textile workers had a mean of 2.5 children; nontextile workers averaged 2.3 children.

8 Of male-headed households in which the head was in his forties, 15.2% had one or more children under 14 in the labor force. By contrast, only 12.5% of heads in their fifties had a child under 14 in the labor force.

9. Work lives

1 For a summary of the U.S. Bureau of Labor Statistics studies of labor turnover, see Brissenden and Frankel (1922).

2 For an example of the Amoskeag's annual analysis of turnover, see Figure 9.2.

3 Studies of occupational mobility have reconstructed career patterns by comparing individual job listings in city directories and census schedules over time; see Thernstrom and Knights (1971). But such studies were unable to measure career continuity or discontinuity. This analysis is based on reconstructed work histories from the individual career files that the Amoskeag accumulated for each worker.

4   In the cotton division about one-fifth of the employment periods of the
    men and one-fourth to one-third of the employment periods of women
    were from 1 to 4 weeks' duration in one year. In the three depression
    years a full half of the employment periods for men were from 1 to 2
    weeks; half the employment periods for women were from a mere 1 to
    8 weeks. Only a very small proportion of employment periods for men
    or women was as long as 37 to 52 weeks. In terms of weeks of no
    employment, the picture is even more dismal. After 1923, from one-
    fifth to one-third of the total weeks of potential employment were peri-
    ods of no employment, as a result of production curtailments and the
    complete shutdown of certain workrooms.
        A distribution of male cotton-section workers showed that 22% to
    50% experienced 4 or fewer weeks of no employment, depending on
    the phase of the mill cycle; 17% to 40% (except in 1923) experienced
    from 5 to 13 weeks of no employment, apparently unrelated to the mill
    cycle; 11% to 24% experienced from 14 to 26 weeks of no employment
    (the larger percentage coincides with the depressed years); and 12% to
    27% experienced 27 or more weeks of no employment. The duration of
    periods of no employment was the same for women, but the number of
    periods of no employment within a given year was larger. See Creamer
    and Coulter (1939:265–7).

5   The state of New Hampshire has had child labor laws since 1846. The
    last major revision before the 1911 law took place in 1891. It prohibited
    the employment of women and minors under 18 in manufacturing or
    mechanical establishments for more than ten hours a day and for more
    than sixty hours a week (Chapter 180, Section 14, New Hampshire
    General Laws). Another act in the same year prohibited minors under
    10 from working at all. It also required certificates from local school
    boards to prove fulfillment of enrollment and literacy requirements;
    see Chapter 93, Sections 10, 11, and 12 of the New Hampshire General
    Laws.

6   The year 1912 was selected as the beginning year for analysis to avoid
    including workers already at the tail end of their careers who were
    listed as *starting* work in 1910 when record keeping started. Although
    some files include a date of first employment that preceded 1910, this
    information was based on memory and is, therefore, unreliable. Con-
    sequently, approximately 440 individuals employed before 1912 were
    eliminated from the original sample. In addition, to assure proper cov-
    erage of the labor force, it was important to allow the employment
    office one year in which to get organized. For a description of the indi-
    vidual employee files, see Appendix B. Unless otherwise specified, all
    tables were tested for statistical significance.

7   This distribution of the entire sample working in the mill each year
    suggests a smaller proportion in 1912 because the sample excludes all
    those who did not actually start work in 1912; for other years the sam-
    ple includes those who had started in previous years and reflects the

production curtailments and the corresponding layoffs and hiring slowdowns.

8   Of course, this does not consider the possibility that many people were already wage earners when they arrived in the city. This measure is based on the total number of years from 1912, when these work files begin, until 1936, when the mill shut down, or on a portion of this period if a person was either too young or too old to have worked during the entire period. (The age limits used were 14 and up for commencement of work and 70 for termination of work.)

9   The elapsed time of work interruptions totaled no more than one year for the majority (69%) of workers who were hired more than once. Men tended to experience less total interruption time than women. A smaller proportion of men than women was concentrated among those whose "time out" was from 2 to 5 years, and a still smaller proportion was concentrated among those whose "time out" exceeded 6 years. Because this measure combines all the gaps in a person's career, the actual size of individual career gaps was even smaller. Of those with gaps of known length, about 64% experienced an average gap of less than 1 year and only 15% experienced an average gap of longer than 2 years (Tables 9.5 and 9.6). The employment office defined separations as follows: A worker absent during two pay periods was considered as having left the company's employ. If he wanted to be rehired, he would have to reapply through the employment office, and a new hiring slip would be filled out for him.

10   Work-related reasons include work performance, which is the predominant category, working conditions, and authority conflict.

11   In 6% of the cases the final reason for leaving was the same as all previous reasons; in 18% of cases the final reason matched some, but not all, previous reasons.

12   This analysis was able to capture members of the spare labor force only when they were actually working, because employment files rather than lists were used. Empirically, it would be difficult to distinguish between the reserve labor force and regular repeaters, because for the majority of the workers in the sample the time they actually worked was included in the time they were related to the company. Some of them thought of themselves as regulars, whereas the company treated them as a reserve, and vice versa. However, whereas the group regularly employed was equally divided between men and women, Creamer and Coulter (1939) found that the reserve labor force consisted of 69% women and 31% men. Among regularly employed men, 70% were between 35 and 64 and 20% were older than 65, whereas the reserve men were equally distributed among ages 20 to 64. Among the regular women, 27.7% fell in the age group 25 to 34 and 41% in the age group 35 to 44. The higher concentration of women in this age group may be related to the fact that they were in the peak of their childrearing period. The proportion of women older than 55 was about the same in the two groups. The reserve labor force also contained a

smaller proportion of single women and a larger proportion of married women with dependents. Of the regular women employees, 35% were single, whereas 9.5% of the reserve women were single.

To compare this sample with Creamer and Coulter's it is important to realize the following difference: First, they did not pick a random sample of the entire labor force; second, their sample was heavily weighted toward still employed workers who had started work prior to 1911. (For reasons discussed earlier, such workers are absent from the sample used here.) Therefore, the length of work time Creamer and Coulter captured was, overall, much longer. This is reflected in their definition of a spare labor force: Assuming that a normal work career consisted of 39 weeks of employment in a given year, the regular labor force was defined as those who had 39 weeks of employment in 4 out of 6 years and the spare labor force as all those who had less employment during the same period.

In their comparison of a sample of the reserve labor force with the regular labor force in the Amoskeag between 1923 and 1931, Creamer and Coulter found no major differences in the length of employment and the level of skill, although they did find differences in age, marital status, and sex.

13 This relationship could not be measured for the entire sample because kinship data have been reconstructed only for the French Canadians. That French Canadians were more likely to be repeaters and less likely to be temporaries than members of other ethnic groups suggests, however, that the effect of kinship ties on career continuity was primarily a function of ethnicity.

14 Of the white-collar employees, 13.5% were repeaters and 24.3% were persisters; about one-third and four times, respectively, the corresponding percentages for other employees.

10. Career advancement

1 For analyses of occupational and social mobility following Thernstrom's pioneer study, see Sennett (1971), Chudacoff (1972), Katz (1975), and Griffen and Griffen (1978), among many others. Most of these studies trace occupations from first to last job as recorded in city directories and the census. Unfortunately, women's careers could not be traced in the same manner because city directories rarely listed women's occupations unless they were widows.

2 For definitions of historical and vertical mobility, see Thernstrom (1964), Blau and Duncan (1967), Katz (1975), and Griffen and Griffen (1978). I am indebted to Howard Chudacoff for his insights on the comparison between occupational hierarchies in the textile industry and other types of occupations.

3 Amoskeag Company wage lists in Time and Wages, Baker Library, Harvard University.

Average wages in the Amoskeag Company by occupation

			Dollars per week	
Occupation	Fall 1913 (58 hours)	June 2, 1919 (48 hours)	December 12, 1921 (48 hours)	July 24, 1933 (54 hours) before the code
Weaving room				
Overseers	23.70	40.70		
Second hands		30.62	30.50	
Section hands		29.95	30.00	
Loomfixers	14.79			17.28
Weavers	10.28	22.46	20.02	13.86
Room girls	8.93	18.00	18.05	9.23
Filling boys	8.12	15.46	15.63	8.10
Clerk		16.82	16.90	12.66

Source: "Overseer and Second Hand Wages," and "Production and Labor," Amoskeag Records, Baker Library, Harvard University.

On the classification of textile jobs in the Amoskeag, see Creamer and Coulter (1939:332–3). On wage ranking and occupational classification in the textile industry, see U.S., Bureau of Labor Statistics (1929:32 and especially 1938:101), Hinrichs and Clem (1935), and Lahne (1944).

4   Adjustments, June 16, 1919, and February 2, 1920, Amoskeag Records, Baker Library, Harvard University.

5   Wages for cotton weavers, Amoskeag Company, Southern Division, March 3, 1928, are as follows:

Room	Number Male	Number Female	Hours worked Male	Hours worked Female	Total weekly wage Male	Total weekly wage Female	Average hourly wage per worker Male	Average hourly wage per worker Female
#1	5	6	270	270	$98.72	$103.95	$.366	$.3913
#2	4	4	216	216	$97.72	$87.44	$.452	$.405
#3	3	6	162	304	$51.53	$99.67	$.318	$.328
#4	4	4	216	216	$58.92	$71.00	$.277	$.329
Total	16	20	864	1,100	$306.89	$362.06	$.355	$.361

Note: The instances of higher average wages for women may be explained by greater experience or higher levels of skills, in weaving, e.g., where knowledge of particular types of looms may have been required.
Source: Amoskeag Company, Time and Wages, Baker Library, Harvard University.

6   "Mill Life 50 Years Ago," *Amoskeag Bulletin*, Vol. 1 (November 7, 1913), p. 7, MHA.
7   *Amoskeag Bulletin*, Vol. 6, No. 12 (June 15, 1918), p. 7.
8   "Some Amoskeag Men," *Amoskeag Bulletin*, Vol. 5 (January 15, 1917), p. 6, MHA.
9   The analysis is based on the same sample of the Amoskeag's labor force (drawn from the individual employee files) as in Chapter 9. Job mobility is defined as "upward," "downward," or "no change" by comparing a worker's first job in the Amoskeag with the last one cited. "No change" designates the absence of status changes between the first and the last job in the mill. It does not mean absence of change in jobs within certain ranks. All tables analyzing career advancement, e.g., using the job mobility variables, exclude temporaries and fluctuators from the sample because they worked less than one year.

   Several classification schemes were used to rank the occupations in this study: All occupations – those pertaining specifically to textile production as well as those concerned with other skills in the mill (mechanics, carpentry, construction, trucking, service, etc.) – were ranked in accordance with the scheme used by Thernstrom for twentieth-century Boston (1973); more detailed categories were compared with the "Five City Scheme" employed by the Philadelphia Social History Project. To deal with the great variety of textile jobs, a more specialized classification was used, that devised by the economist Daniel Creamer for his and Coulter's major study (1939) of the Amoskeag's labor force in 1937 after the shutdown of the mill, in which he used the U.S. Bureau of Labor Statistics classification and the Amoskeag's payroll rankings. To allow for additional jobs listed for this sample but not included in Creamer's list, I consulted the Amoskeag's payroll lists and interviewed Charles Parsons, an efficiency expert and former vice president of the Chicopee Mills in Manchester (a Johnson & Johnson plant), who had determined levels of skill and pay rates for occupations since the 1930s. I also consulted Gordon Osborne, president of Warwick Mills, who checked the occupational rankings on my lists. For the ranking of textile occupations, see Appendix F and the U.S. Department of Labor, *Descriptions of Occupations: Textiles and Clothing* (1918); U.S., Department of Labor, *Job Specifications for the Cotton Textile Industry* (1935). For a historical discussion of wage changes and changes in the skill status of jobs, see Hinrichs and Clem (1935).
10 The remaining 36 people could not be counted because their final occupations are not given. However, 30 of these 36 could be counted in measuring mobility because it is known that they changed occupations at some point even though their final occupation is not known. Thus, the 475 persons for whom mobility is measured do not include those whose occupations never changed but do include those 30 workers whose occupations dropped even though their final occupation is not known.

11 Status and occupational structure do not necessarily explain these differences. Many young men started in unskilled menial jobs requiring physical exertion because, perhaps, women were physically incapable of performing such jobs.

12 For the definition and distribution of career typologies, see Chapter 9 and Table 9.11.

13 That a high concentration of the very youngest workers ended up in unskilled jobs reflects their work history: Young beginners worked for a short time and left.

14 A table on the relationship between ethnicity and occupational advancement is not included, because the correlation was insignificant.

15 This reflects the impact of kin presence, rather than of "French Canadians," because the correlation between ethnicity and career advancement was not significant.

16 That these workers were French Canadian does not bias the analysis, because the correlation between ethnicity and career advancement was not significant. That upward mobility was enhanced by kinship ties within the mill cannot be explained as a function of long-term employment, which showed little correlation with career advancement (Chapter 9).

17 To identify the jobs workers held in the city after leaving the mills, we traced workers from the individual employee file to the city directories. This trace turned up only one-quarter of the workers in the Amoskeag sample. We used Thernstrom's (1973) ranking in the occupational classification and the ranking of jobs in the city. We left the shoe workers as a separate category because one-quarter of the Amoskeag workers who could be traced went into the shoe industry. The shoe-worker category also included several levels of skills, but because the city directories did not define these jobs specifically, shoe workers could not be classified by level of skill. The overall proportions of skilled, semiskilled, and unskilled workers would have increased, of course, if shoe workers were included in their respective categories of skill.

11. The struggle to maintain the balance

1 Herman Straw as quoted by Henry Carignan (interview). The account was subsequently repeated independently by several other interviewees.

2 Adjustments, November 14, 1921, Amoskeag Records, Baker Library, Harvard University.

3 Adjustments, January 3 and 31, 1921, Amoskeag Records, BLH. See also Creamer and Coulter (1939:190–1).

4 Adjustments, January 31, 1921, Amoskeag Records, BLH.

5 See, e.g., Adjustments, December 29, 1919, and October 4, 1921, Amoskeag Records, BLH.

6 Adjustments, December 31, 1919, Amoskeag Records, BLH.
7 Adjustments, January 20, 1919, Amoskeag Records, BLH.
8 Adjustments, February 20, 1920, Amoskeag Records, BLH.
9 A breakdown of the grievances heard by the grievance committee and adjustment board during the period 1919–22 includes:

Pay adjustments	140
Violation of individual rights	45
Work processes	27
Rights of the union	15
Change in work pace	5
Miscellaneous, including misconduct, unfair promotion, ethnic prejudice by second hand, shift in schedules, seniority	6

10 Adjustments, April 3, 1919, Amoskeag Records, BLH.
11 This is based on an analysis of all the grievances, 1919–22, Adjustments, Amoskeag Records, BLH.
12 Adjustments, July 6, 1921, Amoskeag Records, BLH.
13 Adjustments, February 18, 1920, Amoskeag Records, BLH.
14 Adjustments, October 6, 1921, Amoskeag Records, BLH.
15 Adjustments, July 6, 1921, Amoskeag Records, BLH.
16 Adjustments, January 29, 1919, Amoskeag Records, BLH.
17 Adjustments, October 25, 1921, Amoskeag Records, BLH.
18 Adjustments, October 17, 1921, Amoskeag Records, BLH.
19 Adjustments, February 19, 1920, Amoskeag Records, BLH.
20 Adjustments, February 17, 1920, Amoskeag Records, BLH.
21 Adjustments, December 13, 1921, Amoskeag Records, BLH.
22 Adjustments, December 18, 1921, Amoskeag Records, BLH.
23 Adjustments, May 1, 1920, Amoskeag Records, BLH.
24 Adjustments, November 28, 1919, Amoskeag Records, BLH.
25 Adjustments, June 12, 1920, Amoskeag Records, BLH.
26 Adjustments, November 15 and 20, 1919, Amoskeag Records, BLH.
27 Adjustments, September 16 and 17, 1919, Amoskeag Records, BLH.
28 Adjustments, March 5, 1919, Amoskeag Records, BLH.
29 Adjustments, May 1, 1920, Amoskeag Records, BLH.
30 Adjustments, October 14, 1919, Amoskeag Records, BLH.
31 Adjustments, November 3, 1921, Amoskeag Records, BLH.
32 Adjustments, October 1919, Amoskeag Records, BLH.
33 Adjustments, September 17, 1919, Amoskeag Records, BLH.
34 Adjustments, November 7, 1919, Amoskeag Records, BLH.
35 Adjustments, September 17, 1919, Amoskeag Records, BLH.
36 Adjustments, May 18, 1920, Amoskeag Records, BLH.
37 Adjustments, October 6, 1919, Amoskeag Records, BLH.
38 Adjustments, December 16, 1921, Amoskeag Records, BLH.
39 Adjustments, February 25, 1920, and April 17, 1920, Amoskeag Records, BLH.

12. The collapse of the balance

1 "Happenings," Amoskeag Co., Manchester Historic Association; hereafter cited as MHA.

2 The Stark mill, the last independent mill in Manchester, was subsequently annexed by the Amoskeag during the strike.

3 The chronological narrative of the events of the strike used in this chapter is based on *The History of the Amoskeag Strike During the Year 1922* (1924), which was commissioned by the Amoskeag Manufacturing Company.

4 "Happening," Amoskeag Co., MHA.

5 For an analysis of strike patterns in the United States in the 1920s and 1930s, see Hiller (1928).

6 *Survey*, August 1, 1922, p. 585.

7 *Textile Worker* 10, No. 12:730. The total number of strike participants analyzed in this sample was 108 males and 63 females. This analysis is based on the reconstruction of career histories of those in the sample of individual employees who participated in the strike.

8 Their various names were culled from newspaper accounts of strike activities and from the Amoskeag's own lists.

9 Their distribution was: native-born, 18; Irish, 36; French Canadians, 20; English and Scottish, 9; Polish, 7; German, 6; others, 7.

10 Information was not available for 4 workers on this list.

11 *Textile Worker* 10, No. 10 (January 1923): 559–600.

12 Amoskeag Co. Employee Files, MHA.

13 This was cited as the reason for his suicide in a note attached to his employee file.

14 Since Creamer and Coulter have offered an elaborate description of the workings of the plan from its inception to its demise, this discussion will draw on their narrative in an effort to illustrate the final struggle in the Amoskeag's declining years.

15 *Textile Worker* 13, No. 2 (May, 1925):79.

16 W. P. Straw, quoted in Creamer and Coulter (1939:27).

17 Rauch was repeatedly characterized as a "numbers" man in several interviews.

18 Minutes of the Joint Convention of Employee Representatives, September 14, 1931, Amoskeag Records, BLH.

19 William Spencer is a fictitious name.

20 Minutes of the Joint Convention of Employee Representatives, January 16, 1933, Amoskeag Records, BLH.

21 Report of Overseers and Second Hands, May 10, 1933, Amoskeag Records, BLH.

22 Michael Ahern to F. C. Dumaine, December 1934, Amoskeag Company Records, BLH.

23 Tenement Survey, Employment Office records, Amoskeag Records, BLH.

24 Amoskeag Records, BLH.

13. Conclusion: Generations in historical time

1 For formulation of the life-course approach, see Elder (1974, 1978) and Hareven (1977, 1978).
2 The term *generation* is used loosely. Actually, the group is an age cohort as distinguished from "generation" in the sense of "second" or "third" generation.
3 Amoskeag Tenement Survey, November 18, 1935, Amoskeag Records, BLH.

References

Abbott, Edith. 1910. *Women in Industry*. New York: Appleton.

Adams, Bert. 1968. *Kinship in an Urban Setting*. Chicago: Markham.

Alford, L. P. 1934. *Henry Lawrence Gantt, Leader in Industry*. New York: Harper & Brothers.

Allport, Gordon. 1942. *The Use of Personal Documents in Psychological Science*, Bulletin 49. New York: Social Science Research Council.

Anderson, Michael. 1971. *Family Structure in Nineteenth-Century Lancashire*. Cambridge: Cambridge University Press.

——— 1976. "Sociological History and the Working-Class Family: Smelser Revisited." *Social History* 1 (October):317–34.

Andrée, Michel. 1970. "La Famille urbaine et la parenté en France." In Reuben Hill and Rene Konig, eds. *Families in East and West: Socialization Process and Kinship Ties*. Paris: Mouton.

Appleton, Nathan. 1858. *Introduction of the Power Loom and Origin of Lowell*. Lowell, Mass.: B. U. Penhallow.

Arensberg, Conrad M. 1951. "Behavior of Organization: Industrial Studies." In John H. Rohrer and Muzafer Sherif, eds. *Social Psychology at the Crossroads*. New York: Harper & Brothers.

——— 1965. "The American Family in the Perspective of Other Cultures." In Conrad M. Arensberg and Solon T. Kimball, eds. *Culture and Community*, pp. 226–39. New York: Harcourt, Brace & World.

Arensberg, Conrad M., and Kimball, S. T. 1968. *Family and Community in Ireland*, 2nd ed. Cambridge, Mass.: Harvard University Press.

Ariès, Philippe. 1962. *Centuries of Childhood*. Translated by R. Baldick. New York: Knopf.

Armstrong, John B. 1968. *Factory Under the Elms: A History of Harrisville, N.H., 1774–1969*. Cambridge, Mass.: M.I.T. Press.

Bagnell, William R. 1890. *Samuel Slater and the Early Development of the Cotton Manufacture*. Middletown, Conn.: J. B. Stewart.

Bell, Daniel. 1976. *The Cultural Contradictions of Capitalism*. New York: Basic Books.

Bennett, John W., and Despres, Leo A. 1960. "Kinship and Instrumental Activities." *American Anthropologist* 62 (April):254–67.

Berger, Peter L.; Berger, Brigitte; and Keller, Hansfried. 1973. *The Homeless Mind: Modernization and Consciousness*. New York: Random House.

Berkner, Lutz K. 1972. "The Stem Family and the Developmental Cycle of the Peasant Household: An Eighteenth Century Austrian Exam-

434

ple." *American Historical Review* 77 (April):398–418.

1975. "The Use and Misuse of Census Data for the Historical Analysis of Family Structure: A Review of Household and Family in Past Time." *Journal of Interdisciplinary History* 4 (Spring):398–418.

Bernstein, Irving. 1960. *The Lean Years: A History of the American Worker, 1920–1933*. Boston: Houghton Mifflin.

1970. *The Turbulent Years: A History of the American Worker, 1933–1941*. Boston: Houghton Mifflin.

Bidwell, Percy. 1925. "The Agricultural Revolution in New England." In Louis Bernard Schmidt and Earle Dudley Ross, eds. *Readings in the Economic History of American Agriculture*. New York: Macmillan.

Bieder, Robert E. 1973. "Kinship as a Factor in Migration." *Journal of Marriage and the Family* 35 (August):429–39.

Blau, Peter, and Duncan, Otis Dudley. 1967. *The American Occupational Structure*. New York: Wiley.

Blauner, Robert. 1964. *Alienation and Freedom: The Factory Worker and His Industry*. Chicago: University of Chicago Press.

Blood, Grace Holbrook. 1948. *Manchester on the Merrimack*. Manchester, N.H.: privately published.

Bloomfield, Daniel, ed. 1922. *Selected Articles on Employment Management*. New York: H. W. Wilson.

Boettiger, Louis A. 1923. *Employee Welfare Work: A Critical and Historical Study*. New York: Ronald Press.

Bott, Elizabeth. 1957. *Family and Social Network: Roles, Norms, and External Relationships in Ordinary Urban Families*. London: Tavistock.

Bouchard, Gerard. 1977. "Family Structure and Geographic Mobility at Laterrière, 1851–1935." *Journal of Family History* 2 (December):350–69.

Bowen, William G., and Finegan, T. Aldrich. 1969. *The Economics of Labor Force Participation*. Princeton, N.J.: Princeton University Press.

Bradney, Pamela. 1957. "Quasi-familial Relationships in Industry." *Human Relations* 10:271–8.

Brandes, Stuart D. 1976. *American Welfare Capitalism, 1880–1940*. Chicago: University of Chicago Press.

Braverman, Harry. 1974. *Labor and Monopoly Capital*. New York: Monthly Review Press.

Bremner, Robert. 1956. *From the Depth: The Discovery of Poverty in the United States*. New York: New York University Press.

Bremner, Robert; Barnard, John; Hareven, Tamara K.; and Mennel, Robert, eds. 1968–71. *Children and Youth in America: A Documentary History*, 3 vols. Cambridge, Mass.: Harvard University Press.

Brissenden, Paul F., and Frankel, Emil. 1922. *Labor Turnover in Industry*. New York: Macmillan.

Brody, David. 1960. *Steelworkers in America: The Nonunion Era*. Cambridge, Mass.: Harvard University Press.

1965. *Labor in Crisis: The Steel Strike of 1919*. Philadelphia: Lippincott.

1968. "The Rise and Decline of Welfare Capitalism." In John Braeman, Robert H. Bremner, and David Brody, eds. *Change and Continuity in Twentieth-Century America: The 1920s.* Columbus: Ohio State University Press.

Brooks, Robert Romano Rave. 1965. United Textile Workers of America. Ph.D. dissertation, Yale University, 1935. Ann Arbor, Mich.: University Microfilms.

Brown, Richard D. 1971. "Modernization and the Modern Personality in Early America, 1600–1865: A Sketch of a Synthesis." *Journal of Interdisciplinary History* 2 (winter):201–28.

Browne, George Waldo. 1915. *The Amoskeag Manufacturing Co. of Manchester, New Hampshire.* Manchester, N.H.: Amoskeag Manufacturing Company.

Bruere, Robert W. 1926. "West Lynn." Survey 56 (April):21–7, 49.

Buder, Stanley. 1967. *Pullman: An Experiment in Industrial Order and Community Planning, 1880–1930.* New York: Oxford University Press.

Burton, Ernest Richmond. 1926. *Employee Representation.* Baltimore: Williams and Wilkins.

Butler, Elizabeth Beardsley. 1911. *Women and the Trades: Pittsburgh, 1907–1908.* New York: Russell Sage Foundation.

Byington, Margaret F. 1910. *Homestead: The Households of a Mill Town.* Vol. 5, *The Pittsburgh Survey.* New York: Russell Sage Foundation, Charities Publication Committee.

Cantor, Milton, and Laurie, Bruce, eds. 1977. *Class, Sex, and the Woman Worker.* Westport, Conn.: Greenwood Press.

Caplow, Theodore. 1954. *The Sociology of Work.* Minneapolis: University of Minnesota Press.

Chandler, Alfred D. 1977. *The Visible Hand: The Managerial Revolution in American Business.* Cambridge, Mass.: Harvard University Press, Belknap Press.

Chapman, Stanley D. 1974. "The Textile Factory before Arkwright: A Typology of Factory Development." *Business History Review* 48 (Winter): 451–78.

Chevalier, Florence Mark. 1972. "The Role of French National Societies in the Socio-Cultural Evolution of the Franco-Americans of New England from 1860 to the Present. An Analytical Macro-sociological Case Study in Ethnic Integration Based on Current Social System Models." Ph.D. dissertation, Catholic University of America.

Chombart de Lauwe, Paul Henry. 1956. *La Vie quotidienne des familles ouvrières; recherches sur les comportements sociaux de consommation.* Paris: Centre National de la Recherche Scientifique.

Chudacoff, Howard P. 1972. *Mobile Americans: Residential and Social Mobility in Omaha, 1880–1920.* New York: Oxford University Press.

1974. "Mobility Studies at a Crossroads." *Reviews in American History* 2 (June):180–6.

1978. "Newlyweds and Family Extension: First Stages of the Family Cycle in Providence, Rhode Island." In Tamara K. Hareven and Maris A. Vinovskis, eds. *Family and Population in Nineteenth-Century America.* Princeton, N.J.: Princeton University Press.

Chudacoff, Howard, and Hareven, Tamara K. 1978. "Family Transitions and Household Structure in the Later Years of Life." In Tamara K. Hareven, ed. *Transitions: The Family Life and the Life Course in Historical Perspective,* pp. 217–44. New York: Academic Press.

1979. "From the Empty Nest to Family Dissolution." *Journal of Family History* 4 (Spring):59–63.

Clark, Sue Ainslie, and Wyatt, Edith. 1911. *Making Both Ends Meet: The Income and Outlay of New York Working Girls.* New York: Macmillan.

Clark, Victor S. 1949. *History of Manufactures in the United States,* vol. 1. New York: Peter Smith. Originally published in 1916.

Clarke, John B. 1875. *Manchester: A Brief Record of Its Past and a Picture of Its Present.* Manchester, N.H.: privately published.

Clarke, John B., ed. 1894. *Le Guide Canadien-Français de Manchester, N.H., pour 1894–95.* Manchester, N.H.: privately published.

Cole, Donald B. 1963. *Immigrant City: Lawrence, Massachusetts, 1849–1921.* Chapel Hill: University of North Carolina Press.

Coles, Robert. 1967. *Migrants, Sharecroppers, Mountaineers.* Boston: Little, Brown.

Collins, Orvis. 1946. "Ethnic Behavior in Industry: Sponsorship and Rejection in a New England Factory." *American Journal of Sociology* 51 (January):293–8.

Collins, Orvis; Dalton, Melville; and Roy, Donald. 1946. "Restriction of Output and Social Cleavage in Industry." *Applied Anthropology* 5 (Summer): 1–14.

Commons, John R. 1903. " 'Welfare Work' in a Great Industrial Plant." *Review of Reviews* 28 (July):79.

1907. *Races and Immigrants in America.* New York: Macmillan.

Coolidge, John. 1942. *Mill and Mansion: A Study of Architecture and Society in Lowell, Massachusetts, 1820–1865.* New York: Columbia University Press.

Creamer, Daniel, and Coulter, Charles W. 1939. *Labor and the Shutdown of the Amoskeag Textile Mills.* Philadelphia: Works Projects Administration.

Cumbler, John T. 1979. *Working Class Community in Industrial America: Work, Leisure, and Struggle in Two Industrial Cities, 1880–1930.* Westport, Conn.: Greenwood Press.

Dalzell, Robert F. 1975. "The Rise of the Waltham-Lowell System and Some Thoughts on the Political Economy of Modernization in Antebellum Massachusetts." *Perspectives in American History* 9:229–68.

Davis, Jessie [pseud.]. 1918. "My Vacation in a Woolen Mill." *Survey* 40 (August 10):538–41.

Dawley, Alan. 1976. *Class and Community: The Industrial Revolution in Lynn.* Cambridge, Mass.: Harvard University Press.

Demos, John. 1970. *A Little Commonwealth: Family Life in Plymouth Colony.* New York: Oxford University Press.

Derber, Milton. 1970. *The American Idea of Industrial Democracy, 1865– 1965.* Urbana: University of Illinois Press.

Dexter, Henry M. 1848. *Discourse Delivered at the Dedication of the Franklin Street Club, Manchester, No. 14.* Andover, Mass.: privately published.

Dollard, John. 1935. *Criteria for the Life History.* New Haven, Conn.: Yale University Press.

Douglas, Paul H. 1921. *American Apprenticeship and Industrial Education.* New York: Columbia University Press.

1930. *Real Wages in the United States, 1890–1926.* Boston: Houghton Mifflin.

1934. *The Theory of Wages.* New York: Macmillan.

Dublin, Thomas. 1979. *Women at Work.* New York: Columbia University Press.

Dugré, Adelard. 1925. *Le Campagne Canadienne: croquis et leçons.* Montreal: Imprimerie du Messager.

Dumont-Johnson, Micheline. 1971. "Histoire de la condition de la femme dans la province de Québec." *Tradition culturelle et histoire politique de la femme au Canada.* Study No. 8 prepared for the Royal Commission of Investigation into the Situation of Women in Canada. Ottawa: Information Canada.

Dunn, Robert W., and Hardy, Jack. 1931. *Labor and Textiles: A Study of Cotton and Wool Manufacturing.* New York: International Publishers.

Durkheim, Emile. 1933. *On the Division of Labor in Society.* Translated by George Simpson. New York: Free Press.

Edwards, Richard. 1979. *Contested Terrain: The Transformation of the Workplace in the Twentieth Century.* New York: Basic Books.

Eilbirt, Henry. 1959. "The Development of Personnel Management in the United States." *Business History Review* 33 (Autumn):345–64.

Elder, Glen H., Jr. 1974. *Children of the Great Depression: Social Change in Life Experience.* Chicago: University of Chicago Press.

1978. "Family History and the Life Course." In Tamara K. Hareven, ed. *Transitions: The Family and the Life Course in Historical Perspective,* pp. 17–69. New York: Academic Press.

Ely, Richard T. 1885. "Pullman: A Social Study." *Harper's Monthly* 70 (June):452.

1902. "Industrial Betterment." *Harper's Monthly* 105 (September):548– 53.

Epstein, Abraham. 1926. "Industrial Welfare Movement Sapping American Trade Unions." *Current History Magazine* 24 (July):520.

Erickson, Charlotte. 1957. *American Industry and the European Immigrant, 1860–1885*. Cambridge, Mass.: Harvard University Press.

Erikson, Erik. 1968. *Identity, Youth and Crisis*. New York: Norton.

1975. *Life History and the Historical Moment*. New York: Norton.

Faler, Paul. 1969. "Working Class Historiography." *Radical America* 3 (March-April):56–8.

Farber, Bernard. 1973. *Family and Kinship in Modern Society*. Glenview, Ill.: Scott, Foresman.

Fawcett, James T., and Bornstein, Marc H. 1973. "Modernization, Individual Modernity and Family." In James T. Fawcett, ed. *Psychological Perspectives on Population*. New York: Basic Books.

Fortes, Meyer. 1969. *Kinship and the Social Order: The Legacy of Lewis Henry Morgan*. Chicago: University of Chicago Press.

Fosdick, Raymond B. 1956. *John D. Rockefeller Jr.: A Portrait*. New York: Harper & Brothers.

Fox, Robin. 1967. *Kinship and Marriage*. Baltimore: Penguin Books.

Fried, Marc, with Ellen Fitzgerald, Peggy Gleicher, and Chester Hoffman. 1973. *The World of the Urban Working Class*. Cambridge, Mass.: Harvard University Press.

Friedmann, Georges, 1961. *The Anatomy of Work*. New York: Free Press of Glencoe.

Furstenberg, Frank F., Jr. 1966. "Industrialization and the American Family: A Look Backward." *American Sociological Review* 31 (June):326–37.

Gans, Herbert. 1962. *The Urban Villagers: Group and Class in the Life of Italian-Americans*. New York: Free Press of Glencoe.

Gantt, H. L. 1910. "The Mechanical Engineer and the Textile Industry." *ASME Transactions* 32:504–5.

1913. *Work, Wages and Profits*. New York: Engineering Magazine Company.

Garigue, Philippe. 1956. "French-Canadian Kinship and Urban Life." *American Anthropologist* 58 (December):1090–1101.

1967. *La Vie familiale des Canadiens Français*. Montreal: Les Presses de l'Université de Montréal.

Garson, Barbara. 1975. *All the Livelong Day: The Meaning and Demeaning of Routine Work*. Garden City, N.Y.: Doubleday.

Gersuny, Carl. 1973. *Punishment and Redress in a Modern Factory*. Lexington, Mass.: Lexington Books.

1976. "A Devil in Petticoats and Just Cause: Patterns of Punishment in Two New England Textile Factories." *Business History Review* 50 (Summer): 131–52.

Gitelman, Howard M. 1974. *Workingmen of Waltham: Mobility in American Urban Industrial Development, 1850–1890*. Baltimore: Johns Hopkins University Press.

Glasco, Laurence A. 1977. "The Life Cycles and Household Structure of American Ethnic Groups: Irish, Germans and Native-born Whites in

Buffalo, New York, 1885." In Tamara Hareven, ed. *Family and Kin in American Urban Communities, 1700–1930*, pp. 122–43. New York: Franklin Watts, New Viewpoints.

Glick, Paul. 1947. "The Family Cycle." *American Sociological Review* 12 (April):164–74.

1955. "The Life Cycle of the Family." *Marriage and Family Living* 17 (February):3–9.

1977. "Updating the Life Cycle of Family." *Journal of Marriage and the Family* 39 (February):5–13.

Glick, Paul C., and Norton, Arthur J. 1977. "Marrying, Divorcing and Living Together in the U.S. Today." *Population Bulletin* 32 (October):1–39.

Glick, Paul C., and Parke, Robert, Jr. 1965. "New Approaches in Studying the Life Cycle of the Family." *Demography* 2:187–212.

Goffman, Erving. 1959. *The Presentation of Self in Everyday Life.* Garden City, N.Y.: Doubleday.

Golden, John. 1911. " 'Scientific Management' in the Textile Industry." *American Federationist* 18 (August):603–4.

Goldin, Claudia. 1978. "Household and Market Production of Families in a Late-Nineteenth-Century American City." Working Paper No. 115, Industrial Relations Section, Princeton University.

Goldmark, Josephine Clara. 1912. *Fatigue and Efficiency: A Study in Industry.* New York: Russell Sage Foundation, Charities Publication Committee.

Goode, William. 1963. *World Revolution and Family Patterns.* New York: Macmillan, Free Press.

1968. "The Theory and Measurement of Family Change." In Eleanor B. Sheldon and Wilbert Moore, eds. *Indicators of Social Change: Concepts and Measurements.* New York: Russell Sage Foundation.

Gouldner, Alvin. 1954. *Patterns of Industrial Bureaucracy.* Glencoe, Ill.: Free Press.

Green, Constance McLaughlin. 1939. *Holyoke, Massachusetts: A Case History of the Industrial Revolution in America.* New Haven, Conn.: Yale University Press.

Greenfield, Sidney. 1961. "Industrialization and the Family in Sociological Theory." *American Journal of Sociology* 67 (November):312–22.

Greven, Philip. 1970. *Four Generations: Population, Land, and Family in Colonial Andover, Massachusetts.* Ithaca, N.Y.: Cornell University Press.

Griffen, Clyde, and Griffen, Sally. 1978. *Natives and Newcomers: The Ordering of Opportunity in Mid-Nineteenth-Century Poughkeepsie.* Cambridge, Mass.: Harvard University Press.

Groneman, Carol. 1977. " 'She Earns as a Child; She Pays as a Man': Women Workers in a Mid-Nineteenth-Century New York City Community." In Milton Cantor and Bruce Laurie, eds. *Class, Sex, and the Woman Worker*, pp. 83–100. Westport, Conn.: Greenwood Press.

Gutman, Herbert. 1976. *Work, Culture and Society in Industrializing America, 1815–1919.* New York: Knopf.

Haber, Samuel. 1964. *Efficiency and Uplift: Scientific Management in the Progressive Era, 1890–1920.* Chicago: University of Chicago Press.

Handlin, Oscar. 1941. *Boston's Immigrants, 1790–1865: A Study in Acculturation.* Cambridge, Mass.: Harvard University Press.

———. 1951. *The Uprooted.* Boston: Little, Brown.

Hanlan, James P. 1979. "The Working Population of Manchester, N.H., 1840–1886." Ph.D. dissertation, Clark University.

Hareven, Tamara K. 1971. "The History of the Family as an Interdisciplinary Field." *Journal of Interdisciplinary History* 2 (Autumn):399–414.

———. 1974. "The Family as Process: The Historical Study of the Family Cycle." *Journal of Social History* 7 (Spring):322–9.

———. 1975a. "The Laborers of Manchester, New Hampshire, 1900–1940: The Role of Family and Ethnicity in Adjustment to Industrial Life." *Labor History* 16 (Spring):249–65.

———. 1975b. "Family Time and Industrial Time: Family and Work in a Planned Corporation Town, 1900–1924." *Journal of Urban History* 1 (May):365–89.

———. 1975c. "The Historical Study of the Family in Urban Society." *Journal of Urban History* 1 (May):259–67.

———. 1975d. "The Family in Historical Perspective: The Development of a New Field, Report on Work in Progress in England and the United States." *Geschichte und Gesellschaft* 1 (April):370–86.

———. 1976. "Modernization and Family History: Perspectives on Social Change." *Signs* 2 (Autumn):190–206.

———. 1977. "Family Time and Historical Time." *Daedalus* 106 (Spring):57–70.

———. 1978a. "The Dynamics of Kin in an Industrial Community." In John Demos and Sarane Boocock, eds. *Turning Points: Historical and Sociological Essays on the Family.* Chicago: American Journal of Sociology, Supplement, 84:S151–82.

———. 1978b. "Cycles, Course, and Cohorts: Reflections on the Theoretical and Methodological Approaches to the Historical Study of Family Development." *Journal of Social History* 12 (September):97–109.

Hareven, Tamara K., and Langenbach, Randolph. 1978. *Amoskeag: Life and Work in an American Factory-City.* New York: Pantheon.

Hareven, Tamara K., and Modell, John. 1980. "Family Patterns." In Stephan Thernstrom, ed. *Harvard Encyclopedia of American Ethnic Groups.* Cambridge, Mass.: Harvard University Press, Belknap Press.

Hareven, Tamara K., and Tilly, Louise. Forthcoming 1982. "Solitary Women and Family Mediation in Two Textile Cities: Manchester, New Hampshire and Roubaix, France." *Annales de Démographie Historique.*

Hareven, Tamara K., and Vinovskis, Maris A. 1975. "Marital Fertility, Ethnicity and Occupation in Urban Families: An Analysis of South

Boston and the South End in 1880." *Journal of Social History* 18 (Spring):69–93.

Hareven, Tamara K., ed. 1977. *Family and Kin in American Urban Communities, 1700–1930.* New York: Franklin Watts, New Viewpoints.

1978. *Transitions: The Family and the Life Course in Historical Perspective.* New York: Academic Press.

Harrison, Shelby M., in collaboration with Bradley Buell and others. 1924. *Public Employment Offices.* New York: Russell Sage Foundation.

Harvey, Fernand. 1973. *Aspéts historiques du mouvement ouvrier au Québec.* Montreal: Boréal Express.

1978. *Révolution industrielle et travailleurs: une enquête sur les rapports entre le capital et le travail au Québec à la fin du 19e siècle.* Montreal: Boréal Express.

Hazard, Blanche. 1921. *The Organization of the Boot and Shoe Industry in Massachusetts before 1875.* Cambridge, Mass.: Harvard University Press.

Heald, Morrell. 1970. *The Social Responsibilities of Business: Company and Community, 1900–1960.* Cleveland, Ohio: Press of Case Western Reserve University.

Heer, David M. 1958. "Dominance and the Working Wife." *Social Forces* 36 (May):341–7.

Henripin, J., and Peron, Y. 1973. "La Transition démographique de la Province de Québec" and "Evolution démographique récente du Québec." In H. Charbonneau, ed. *La Population du Québec: études retrospectives,* pp. 23–44, 45–72. Montreal: Boréal Express.

Herring, Harriet L. 1929. *Welfare Work in Mill Villages: The Story of Extra-Mill Activities in North Carolina.* Chapel Hill: University of North Carolina Press.

Hill, Reuben. 1964. "Methodological Issues in Family Development Research." *Family Process* 3 (March):186–206.

1970. *Family Development in Three Generations.* Cambridge, Mass.: Schenkman.

Hiller, Ernest T. 1928. *The Strike: A Study in Collective Action.* Chicago: University of Chicago Press.

Hillery, George A.; Brown, James S.; and DeJong, Gordon F. 1965. "Migration Systems of the Southern Appalachians: Some Demographic Observations." *Rural Sociology* 30 (March):33–48.

Hinrichs, A. F., and Clem, Ruth. 1935. "Historical Review of Wage Rates in the Cotton-Textile Industry." *Monthly Labor Review* 40 (May):1170–80.

History of the Amoskeag Strike During the Year 1922, The. 1924. Manchester, N.H.: Amoskeag Manufacturing Company.

Hobsbawm, Eric J. 1959. *Primitive Rebels: Studies in Archaic Forms of Social Movement in the 19th and 20th Centuries.* New York: Norton.

1964. "Custom, Wages and Workload in Nineteenth-Century Industry." In Eric J. Hobsbawm, ed. *Labouring Men*. London: Weidenfeld and Nicolson.

Hoffman, Lois Wladis. 1963. "The Decision to Work." In F. Ivan Nye and Lois W. Hoffman, eds. *The Employed Mother in America*. Chicago: Rand McNally.

Homans, George. 1964. "Bringing Men Back In." *American Sociological Review* 29 (December):809–18.

Houser, David J. 1927. *What the Employer Thinks: Executive Attitude Toward Employees*. Cambridge, Mass.: Harvard University Press.

Hoxie, Robert Franklin. 1915. *Scientific Management and Labor*. New York: Appleton.

Hughes, Everett Cherrington. 1951. "Work and the Self." In John H. Rohrer and Muzafer Sherif, eds. *Social Psychology at the Crossroads*. New York: Harper & Brothers.

    1958. *Men and Their Work*. Glencoe, Ill.: Free Press.

    1971a. "Cycles, Turning Points and Careers." In Everett C. Hughes, ed. *The Sociological Eye: Selected Papers*, vol. 1. Chicago: Aldine-Atherton.

    1971b. *French Canada in Transition*. Chicago: University of Chicago Press. Originally published in 1943.

Hughes, Everett, ed. 1971. *The Sociological Eye: Selected Papers*, vol. 1. Chicago: Aldine-Atherton.

Inkeles, Alex, and Smith, David H. 1974. *Becoming Modern: Individual Change in Six Developing Countries*. Cambridge, Mass.: Harvard University Press.

Jacques, Elliot. 1951. *The Changing Culture of a Factory*. London: Tavistock.

Jeffrey, Kirk. 1972. "Family History: The Middle-Class American Family in the Urban Context." Ph.D. dissertation, Stanford University.

Jephcott, Agnes P.; Seear, Nancy; and Smith, John H. 1962. *Married Women Working*. London: Allen and Unwin.

Josephson, Hannah. 1949. *The Golden Threads: New England's Mill Girls and Magnates*. New York: Russell and Russell.

Jump, Herbert Atchinson. 1922. "Six Months in a Strike City." *Survey* 48 (August 1):555–7.

Kahn, Lawrence. 1975. "Unions and Labor Market Segmentation." Ph.D. dissertation, University of California at Berkeley.

Kanter, Rosabeth Moss. 1977. *Work and Family in the United States*. New York: Russell Sage Foundation.

    1978. "Families, Family Process, and Economic Life: Toward Systematic Analysis of Social Historical Research." In John Demos and Sarane Boocock, eds. *Turning Points: Historical and Sociological Essays on the Family*. Supplement, *American Journal of Sociology* 84:S316–S39. Chicago: University of Chicago Press.

Katz, Michael B. 1975. *The People of Hamilton, Canada West: Family and*

Class in a Mid-Nineteenth-Century City. Cambridge, Mass.: Harvard University Press.

Kellogg, Paul Underwood, ed. 1914. *Wage-Earning Pittsburgh*. New York: Survey Associates.

Kennedy, John C. 1914. *Wages and Family Budgets in the Chicago Stockyards District*. Chicago: University of Chicago Press.

Kenngott, George F. 1912. *The Record of a City: A Social Survey of Lowell, Mass*. New York: Macmillan.

Kett, Joseph. 1977. *Rites of Passage: Adolescence in America 1790 to the Present*. New York: Basic Books.

Kleinberg, Susan J. 1977. "The Systematic Study of Urban Women." In Milton Cantor and Bruce Laurie, eds. *Class, Sex, and the Woman Worker*, pp. 20–42. Westport, Conn.: Greenwood Press.

Kobrin, Frances. 1976. "The Fall in Household Size and the Rise of the Primary Individual in the United States." *Demography* 13:127–38.

Kohn, Melvin. 1969. *Class and Conformity*. Homewood, Ill.: Dorsey Press.

Komarovsky, Mirra. 1940. *The Unemployed Man and His Family*. New York: Dryden Press.

———. 1962. *Blue-Collar Marriage*. New York: Random House.

Korman, A. Gerd. 1967. *Industrialization, Immigrants and Americanizers: The View from Milwaukee, 1866–1921*. Madison: State Historical Society of Wisconsin.

Kuczynski, R. R. 1901. "The Fecundity of the Native Born and Foreign Born Population in Massachusetts." *Quarterly Journal of Economics* 16 (November):1–36 and 16 (February):141–86.

Lahne, Herbert J. 1944. *The Cotton Mill Worker*. New York and Toronto: Farrar & Rinehart.

Langenbach, Randolph. 1968. "The Amoskeag Millyard: An Epic in Urban Design." *Harvard Alumni Bulletin*, April:18–28.

Laslett, Peter. 1965. *The World We Have Lost*. London: Methuen.

Laslett, Peter, and Wall, Richard, eds. 1972. *Household and Family in Past Time*. Cambridge: Cambridge University Press.

Latimer, Murray Webb. 1932. *Industrial Pension Systems in the United States and Canada*. New York: Industrial Relations Counselors.

Lauck, W. Jett, and Sydenstricker, Edgar. 1917. *Conditions of Labor in American Industries*. New York: Funk & Wagnalls.

Lavoie, Yolande. 1972. *L'Emigration des Canadiens aux Etats-Unis avant 1930*. Montreal: Les Presses de l'Université de Montréal.

Layer, Robert G. 1955. *Earnings of Cotton Mill Operatives, 1825–1914*. Cambridge, Mass.: Harvard University Press.

Lebergott, Stanley. 1964. *Manpower in Economic Growth: The American Record Since 1800*. New York: McGraw-Hill.

———. 1968. "Labor Force and Employment Trends." Eleanor Bernert Sheldon and Wilbert E. Moore, eds. *Indicators of Social Change*. New York: Russell Sage Foundation.

Le Play, Frédéric. 1871. *L'Organisation de la famille selon le vrai modèle signalé par l'histoire de toutes les races et de tous les temps.* Paris: Téqui, bibliothécaire de l'Oeuvre Saint-Michel.

Lerner, Daniel. 1963. *The Passing of Traditional Society: Modernizing the Middle East.* Glencoe, Ill.: Free Press.

Lerner, Gerda. 1969. "The Lady and the Mill Girl: Changes in the Status of Women in the Age of Jackson." *Mid-Continent American Studies Journal* 10 (Spring):5–15.

Levasseur, Emile. 1900. *The American Workman.* Baltimore: Johns Hopkins University Press.

Levine, Robert A. 1978. "Comparative Notes on the Life Course." In Tamara K. Hareven, ed. *Transitions: The Family and the Life Course in Historical Perspective.* New York: Academic Press.

Levi-Strauss, Claude. 1969. *The Elementary Structures of Kinship.* Boston: Beacon Press.

Lewis, Oscar. 1959. *Five Families: Mexican Case Studies in the Culture of Poverty.* New York: Basic Books.

1966. *La Vida: A Puerto Rican Family in the Culture of Poverty – San Juan and New York.* New York: Random House.

Lindert, Peter H. 1978. *Fertility and Scarcity in America.* Princeton, N.J.: Princeton University Press.

Linteau, Paul-André. 1976. "Quelques réflexions autour de la bourgeoisie québecoise, 1850–1914." *Revue d'histoire de l'Amérique française* 30 (June):55–66.

Linton, Robert. 1959. "The Natural History of the Family." In Ruth N. Anshen, ed. *The Family: Its Function and Destiny,* rev. ed., pp. 30–52. New York: Harper & Row.

Lipset, Seymour M., and Reinhard, Bendix. 1960. *Social Mobility in Industrial Society.* Berkeley: University of California Press.

Litwak, Eugene. 1960. "Geographical Mobility and Extended Family Cohesion." *American Sociological Review* 25 (June):385–94.

1965. "Extended Kin Relations in an Industrial Democratic Society." In Ethel Shanas and Gordon F. Streib, eds. *Social Structure and Generational Relations,*pp. 290–325. Englewood Cliffs, N.J.: Prentice-Hall.

Lopata, Helena. 1972. *Occupation: Housewife.* New York: Oxford University Press.

MacDonald, John S., and MacDonald, Leatrice. 1964. "Chain Migration, Ethnic Neighborhood Formation and Social Networks." *Milbank Memorial Fund Quarterly* 42 (January):82–97.

Magnusson, Leifur. 1920. *Housing by Employers in the United States.* Bulletin 263. U.S., Bureau of Labor Statistics. Washington, D. C.: U.S. Government Printing Office.

Mannheim, Karl. 1940. *Man and Society in an Age of Reconstruction: Studies in Modern Social Structure.* Translated by E. A. Shils. New York: Harcourt Brace.

Mason, Karen O.; Vinovskis, Maris A.; and Hareven, Tamara. 1978. "Women's Work and the Life Course in Essex County, Massachusetts, 1880." In Tamara K. Hareven, ed. *Transitions: The Family and the Life Course in Historical Perspective*. New York: Academic Press.

Mayo, Elton. 1933. *The Human Problems of an Industrial Civilization*. Cambridge, Mass.: Harvard University Press.

Meakin, Budgett. 1905. *Model Factories and Villages: Ideal Conditions of Labour and Housing*. Philadelphia: George W. Jacobs.

Miller, S. M., and Riessman, Frank. 1961. "Are Workers Middle Class?" *Dissent* 8 (Autumn):507–13.

Miner, Horace. 1939. *St. Denis, French-Canadian Parish*. Chicago: University of Chicago Press.

⸻. 1952. "The Folk-Urban Continuum." *American Sociological Review* 17 (October):529–37.

Mintz, Sidney. 1953. "The Folk-Urban Continuum and the Rural Proletarian Community." *American Journal of Sociology* 59 (September):136–43.

Modell, John. 1978. "Patterns of Consumption, Acculturation, and Family Income Strategy in Late-Nineteenth-Century America." In Tamara K. Hareven and Maris A. Vinovskis, eds. *Family and Population in Nineteenth-Century America*. Princeton, N.J.: Princeton University Press.

Modell, John; Furstenberg, Frank; and Hershberg, Theodore. 1976. "Social Change and Transition to Adulthood in Historical Perspective." *Journal of Family History* 1 (Autumn):7–32.

Modell, John, and Hareven, Tamara K. 1973. "Urbanization and the Malleable Household: An Examination of Boarding and Lodging in American Families." *Journal of Marriage and the Family* 35 (August):467–79.

⸻. 1978. "Transitions: Patterns of Timing." In Tamara K. Hareven, ed. *Transitions: The Family and the Life Course in Historical Perspective*, pp. 245–69. New York: Academic Press.

Montgomery, David. 1967. *Beyond Equality: Labor and the Radical Republicans, 1862–1872*. New York: Knopf.

⸻. 1979. *Workers' Control in America*. Cambridge: Cambridge University Press.

Moore, Charles W. 1945. *Timing a Century: History of the Waltham Watch Co.* Cambridge, Mass.: Harvard University Press.

Moore, Wilbert E. 1965. *Industrialization and Labor: Social Aspects of Economic Development*. New York: Russell and Russell.

Morgan, Myffanny, and Golden, Hilda H. 1979. "Immigrant Families in an Industrial City: A Study of Households in Holyoke, 1880." *Journal of Family History* 4 (Spring):59–63.

Morrow, Ellis. 1921. *The Lynn Plan of Representation*. Lynn, Mass.: General Electric Company.

Münsterberg, Hugo. 1913. *Psychology and Industrial Efficiency.* Boston:
    Houghton Mifflin.
Nadworny, Milton. 1955. *Scientific Management and the Unions, 1900 –
    1932.* Cambridge, Mass.: Harvard University Press.
National Civic Federation. 1905. *The National Civic Federation: Its Meth-
    ods and Its Aims.* New York: National Civic Federation.
National Industrial Conference Board. 1933. *Collective Bargaining Through
    Employee Representation.* New York: National Industrial Conference
    Board.
Nelson, Daniel. 1975. *Managers and Workers: Origins of the New Factory
    System in the United States, 1880–1920.* Madison: University of Wis-
    consin Press.
Nelson, Daniel, and Campbell, Stuart. 1972. "Taylorism versus Welfare
    Work in American Industry: H. L. Gantt and the Bancrofts." *Busi-
    ness History Review* 46 (Spring):12–43.
Nevins, Allan. 1954. *Ford: The Times, The Man and The Company.* New
    York: Scribner.
Noble, David. 1977. *America by Design.* New York: Knopf.
Oakley, Ann. 1974. *The Sociology of Housework.* New York: Pantheon.
Oppenheimer, Valerie K. 1970. *The Female Labor Force in the United
    States.* Population Monograph Series, No. 5. Berkeley: Institute of
    International Studies, University of California.
Otey, Elizabeth Lewis. 1928. *Health and Recreation Activities in Industrial
    Establishments, 1926.* Bulletin 458. U.S., Bureau of Labor Statistics.
    Washington, D. C.: U.S. Government Printing Office.
Ozanne, Robert. 1967. *A Century of Labor-Management Relations at Mc-
    Cormick and International Harvester.* Madison: University of Wiscon-
    sin Press.
Palmer, Bryan. 1975. "Class, Conception and Conflict: The Thrust for Ef-
    ficiency, Managerial Views of Labor, and the Working Class Rebel-
    lion, 1903–1922." *Review of Radical Political Economics* 7 (Summer):
    31–49.
Palmer, Gladys L. 1932. *Union Tactics and Economic Change: A Case Study
    of Three Philadelphia Textile Unions.* Philadelphia: University of
    Pennsylvania Press.
Park, Robert E. 1931. "The Sociological Methods of William Graham
    Sumner, and of William I. Thomas and Florian Znaniecki." In Stuart
    E. Rice, ed. *Methods in Social Science: A Case Book.* Chicago: Univer-
    sity of Chicago Press.
Park, Robert E., and Miller, Herbert A. 1921. *Old World Traits Transplant-
    ed.* New York: Harper & Brothers.
Parsons, Talcott. 1943. "The Kinship System of the Contemporary United
    States." *American Anthropologist* 45 (January-March):22–38.
    1959. "The Social Structure of the Family." In Ruth Anshen, ed. *The
    Family: Its Functions and Destiny,* rev. ed., pp. 241–74. New York:
    Harper & Row.

1965. "The Normal American Family." In Seymour Farber, Piero Mustacchi, and Roger H. Wilson, eds. *Man and Civilization*, pp. 31–50. New York: McGraw-Hill.

Parsons, Talcott, and Bales, Robert. 1955. *Family, Socialization and Interaction Process.* Glencoe, Ill.: Free Press.

Patten, Thomas H., Jr. 1968. *The Foreman: Forgotten Man of Management.* New York: American Management Association.

Perreault, Robert. 1976. "One Piece in the Great American Mosaic: The Franco-Americans of New England." *Le Canado-Américaine* 2 (April-May):1–43.

Perrot, Michelle. 1974. *Les Ouvriers en grève, France 1871–1890,* 2 vols. Paris: Mouton.

Pitt-Rivers, Julian. 1973. "The Kith and the Kin." In Jack Goody, ed. *The Character of Kinship.* Cambridge: Cambridge University Press.

Pleck, Elizabeth H. 1978. "A Mother's Wages: Income Earning Among Married Black and Indian Women, 1896–1911." In Michael Gordon, ed. *The American Family in Social Historical Perspective,* 2nd ed., pp. 490–510. New York: St. Martin's Press.

Pollard, Sidney. 1963. "Factory Discipline in the Industrial Revolution." *Economic History Review,* 2nd ser. 16 (December):254–71.

Potter, C. E. 1856. *The History of Manchester in New Hampshire.* Manchester, N.H.: C. E. Potter.

Rainwater, Lee. 1965. *Family Design, Marital Sexuality, Family Size and Contraception.* Chicago: Aldine.

1966. "Work and Identity in the Lower Class." In Sam B. Warner, Jr., ed. *Planning for a Nation of Cities,* pp. 105–23. Cambridge, Mass.: M.I.T. Press.

Rainwater, Lee; Coleman, Richard P.; and Handel, Gerald. 1959. *Workingman's Wife: Her Personality, World and Life Style.* New York: Oceana.

Ramirez, Bruno. 1978. *When Workers Fight: The Politics of Industrial Relations in the Progressive Era, 1898–1916.* Westport, Conn.: Greenwood Press.

Rayback, Joseph H. 1959. *A History of American Labor.* New York: Macmillan.

Regulations for the Boarding Houses and Tenements Belonging to the Amoskeag Manufacturing Company, 1855–1861. Amoskeag Company records, Manchester Historic Association, Manchester, N.H.

Rehn, Henry J. 1934. *Scientific Management and the Cotton Textile Industry.* Chicago: privately published.

Reynolds, Lloyd G., and Taft, Cynthia H. 1956. *The Evolution of Wage Structure.* New Haven, Conn.: Yale University Press.

Riley, Matilda White; Johnson, M. E.; and Foner, A., eds. 1972 *Aging and Society: A Sociology of Age Stratification,* 3 vols. New York: Russell Sage Foundation.

Ripley, Charles M. 1919. *Life in a Large Manufacturing Plant.* Schenectady, N.Y.: General Electric Company.

Robert, Jean-Claude. 1975. *Du Canado-Français au Québec libre.* France: Flammarion.

Rodgers, Daniel T. 1978. *The Work Ethic in America.* Chicago: University of Chicago Press.

Rodman, Hyman. 1965. "Talcott Parsons' View of the Changing American Family." In Hyman Rodman, ed. *Marriage, Family and Society: A Reader,* pp. 262–86. New York: Random House.

Roethlisberger, Frederic J., and Dickson, William J. 1939. *Management and the Worker.* Cambridge, Mass.: Harvard University Press.

Rossi, Alice. 1968. "Transition to Parenthood." *Journal of Marriage and the Family* 30 (February):26–40.

Rothman, David J. 1971. *The Discovery of the Asylum: Social Order and Disorder in the New Republic.* Boston: Little, Brown.

Rouillard, Jacques. 1974. *Les Travailleurs du coton au Québec, 1900–1915.* Montreal: Les Presses de l'Université du Québec.

Rowntree, E. Seebohm. 1901. *Poverty: A Study of Town Life.* London: Longmans, Green.

Rubinow, I. M. 1913. *Social Insurance, with Special Reference to American Conditions.* New York: Holt.

Rudolph, Lloyd I., and Rudolph, Susanne Hoeber. 1967. *The Modernity of Tradition: Political Developments in India.* Chicago: University of Chicago Press.

Ryan, Mary. 1975. *Womanhood in America from Colonial Times to the Present.* New York: Franklin Watts, New Viewpoints.

Ryder, Norman B. 1965. "The Cohort as a Conception in the Study of Social Change." *American Sociological Review* 30 (December):843–61.

Sayles, Leonard Robert. 1963. *Behavior of Industrial Work Groups: Prediction and Control.* New York: Wiley.

Scheffler, Harold W. 1976. "The Meaning of Kinship in American Culture: Another View." In Keith H. Basso and Henry A. Selby, eds. *The Meaning of Kinship in American Culture,* pp. 57–92. Albuquerque: University of New Mexico Press.

Schneider, David M. 1968. *American Kinship: A Cultural Account.* Englewood Cliffs, N.J.: Prentice-Hall.

——— 1972. "What Is Kinship All About?" In P. Reining, ed. *Kinship Studies in the Morgan Centennial Year,* pp. 32–63. Washington, D.C.: Anthropological Society of Washington.

——— 1979. "Kinship, Community and Locality in American Culture." In Alan J. Lichtman and Joan R. Challinor, eds. *Kin and Communities: Families in America,* pp. 155–74. Washington, D.C.: Smithsonian Institution Press.

Schneider, David M., and Smith, Raymond C. 1978. *Class Difference in American Kinship.* Ann Arbor: University of Michigan Press.

Schwarzweller, Harry K.; Brown, James S.; and Mangalam, J. J. 1971. *Mountain Families in Transition: A Case Study of Appalachian Migration*. University Park: Pennsylvania State University Press.

Scott, Joan, and Tilly, Louise. 1975. "Women's Work and Family in Nineteenth-Century Europe." *Comparative Studies in Society and History* 17 (January):36–64.

Sennett, Richard. 1971. *Families Against the City: Middle-Class Homes of Industrial Chicago, 1872–1890*. Cambridge, Mass.: Harvard University Press.

Shanas, Ethel. 1965. "The Family Arrangements of Older People." In Ethel Shanas and Gordon F. Streib, eds. *Social Structure and Generational Relations*. Englewood Cliffs, N.J.: Prentice-Hall.

Shlakman, Vera. 1935. *Economic History of a Factory Town: Chicopee, Massachusetts*. New York: Octagon.

Shorter, Edward. 1971. "Illegitimacy, Sexual Revolution and Social Change in Europe: 1750–1900." *Journal of Interdisciplinary History* 2 (Autumn):237–72.

———. 1972. "Capitalism, Culture and Sexuality: Some Competing Models." *Social Science Quarterly* 53 (September):338–56.

———. 1973. "Female Emancipation, Birth Control and Fertility in European History." *American Historical Review* 78:605–40.

Skolnick, Arlene. 1974–5. "The Family Revisited: Themes in Recent Social Science Research." *Journal of Interdisciplinary History* 5:703–19.

Slichter, Sumner H. 1919. *The Turnover of Factory Labor*. London and New York: Appleton.

Smelser, Neil J. 1959. *Social Change and the Industrial Revolution*. Chicago: University of Chicago Press.

———. 1966. "The Modernization of Social Relations." In Myron Weiner, ed. *Modernization: The Dynamics of Growth*. New York: Basic Books.

Smelser, Neil J., and Halpern, Sydney. 1978. "The Historical Triangulation of Family, Economy, and Education." In John Demos and Sarane Boocock, eds. *Turning Points: Historical and Sociological Essays on the Family*. Supplement, *American Journal of Sociology* 84:S288–S315.

Smith, Daniel Scott. 1973. "Parental Power and Marriage Patterns: An Analysis of Historical Trends in Hingham, Mass." *Journal of Marriage and the Family* 35 (August):419–28.

———. 1974. "Family Limitation, Sexual Control, and Domestic Feminism in Victorian America." In Mary Hartman and Lois W. Banner, eds. *Clio's Consciousness Raised*, pp. 119–37. New York: Harper & Row.

———. 1979. "Life Course, Norms, and the Family System of Older Americans in 1900." *Journal of Family History* 4 (Fall):285–99.

Smith, Thomas Russell. 1944. *The Cotton Textile Industry of Fall River, Massachusetts: A Study of Industrial Localizations*. New York: King's Crown Press.

Smith-Rosenberg, Carroll. 1975. "The Female World of Love and Ritual: Relations between Women in Nineteenth-Century America." *Signs* 1 (Fall):1–29.

Smuts, Robert W. 1959. *Women and Work in America*. New York: Columbia University Press.

Sorokin, Pitrim A., and Merton, Robert K. 1937. "Social Time: A Methodological and Functional Analysis." *American Journal of Sociology* 42 (March):615–29.

Stack, Carol. 1974. *All Our Kin: Strategies for Survival in a Black Community*. New York: Harper & Row.

Straw, William Parker. 1948. *Amoskeag in New Hampshire: An Epic in American Industry*. New York: Newcomer Society of England, American Branch.

Sumner, Helen. 1910. *History of Women in Industry in the United States*. Washington: U.S. Government Printing Office.

Sussman, Marvin B. 1959. "The Isolated Nuclear Family: Fact or Fiction." *Social Problems* 6 (Spring):333–47.

Sussman, Marvin B., and Burchinal, Lee. 1962. "Kin Family Network: Unheralded Structure in Current Conceptualizations of Family Functioning." *Marriage and Family Living* 24 (August):231–40.

Sweet, James A. 1973. *Women in the Labor Force*. New York: Seminar Press.

Taeuber, Irene B. 1969. "Change and Transition in Family Structures." In *The Family in Transition*. Fogarty International Center Proceedings. Washington, D.C.

Terkel, Studs. 1972. *Working*. New York: Random House.

Thernstrom, Stephan. 1964. *Poverty and Progress: Social Mobility in a Nineteenth-Century City*. Cambridge, Mass.: Harvard University Press.
  1973. *The Other Bostonians: Poverty and Progress in the American Metropolis, 1880–1970*. Cambridge, Mass.: Harvard University Press.

Thernstrom, Stephan, and Knights, Peter. 1971. "Men in Motion: Some Data and Speculations about Urban Population Mobility in Nineteenth-Century America." In Tamara K. Hareven, ed. *Anonymous Americans: Explorations in Nineteenth-Century Social History*. Englewood Cliffs, N.J.: Prentice-Hall.

Thomas, Keith. 1964. "Work and Leisure in Pre-Industrial Society." *Past and Present* 29 (December):50–62.

Thomas, W. I. 1966. *On Social Organization and Social Personality*. Edited by Morris Janowitz. Chicago: University of Chicago Press.

Thomas, William, and Znaniecki, Florian. 1918–20. *The Polish Peasant in Europe and America*, 3 vols. Chicago: University of Chicago Press.

Thompson, E. P. 1963. *The Making of the English Working Class*. New York: Pantheon.
  1967. "Time, Work-Discipline, and Industrial Capitalism." *Past and Present* 38 (December):56–97.

Thompson, Holland. 1906. *From the Cotton Field to the Cotton Mills: A Study of the Industrial Transition in North Carolina.* New York: Macmillan.

Tilden, Leonard E. 1923. "New England Textile Strike." *Monthly Labor Review* 16 (May):13–36.

Tilly, Charles, and Brown, C. Harold. 1974. "On Uprooting, Kinship and the Auspices of Migration." In Charles Tilly, ed. *An Urban World,* pp. 108–33. Boston: Little, Brown.

Tilly, Louise, and Scott, Joan. 1978. *Women, Work, and Family.* New York: Holt, Rinehart and Winston.

Tolman, William Howe. 1909. *Social Engineering: A Record of Things Done by American Industrialists Employing Upwards of One and One-Half Million of People.* New York: McGraw.

Townsend, Peter. 1957. *The Family Life of Old People: An Inquiry in East London.* London: Routledge & Kegan Paul.

Troll, Lillian E. 1971. "The Family of Later Life: A Decade Review." *Journal of Marriage and the Family* 33 (May):263–90.

Tryon, Rolla M. 1917. *Household Manufactures in the United States, 1640–1860: A Study in Industrial History.* Chicago: University of Chicago Press.

Uhlenberg, Peter. 1974. "Cohort Variations in Family Life Cycle Experiences of U.S. Females." *Journal of Marriage and the Family* 36 (May): 284–92.

——— 1978. "Changing Configurations of the Life Course." In Tamara K. Hareven, ed. *Transitions: The Family and the Life Course in Historical Perspective,* pp. 65–95. New York: Academic Press.

Valade, Edmond J. 1959. "The Amoskeag Strike of 1922." Master's thesis, University of New Hampshire.

Vansina, Jan. 1965. *The Oral Tradition: A Study in Historical Methodology.* Chicago: Aldine.

Vicero, Ralph. 1966. "The Immigration of French-Canadians to New England, 1840–1900." Ph.D. dissertation, University of Wisconsin.

Vinovskis, Maris A. 1977. "From Household Size to the Life Course: Some Observations on Recent Trends in Family History." *American Behavioral Scientist* 21 (November):263–87.

Volkart, E. H., ed. 1951. *Social Behavior and Personality. Contributions of W. I. Thomas to Theory and Social Research.* New York: Social Science Research Council.

Walkowitz, Daniel J. 1978. *Worker City, Company Town: Iron and Cotton Worker Protest in Troy and Cohoes, New York, 1855–84.* Urbana: University of Illinois Press.

Ware, Caroline F. 1931. *The Early New England Cotton Manufacture: A Study in Industrial Beginnings.* New York and Boston: Houghton Mifflin.

Warner, William Lloyd. 1947. *The Social System of the Modern Factory.* New Haven, Conn.: Yale University Press.

1959. *The Living and the Dead*. New Haven, Conn.: Yale University Press.

Weber, Max. 1947. *The Theory of Social and Economic Organization*. Translated by A. Henderson and T. Parsons. New York: Oxford University Press.

Weiner, Myron. 1966. *Modernization: The Dynamics of Growth*. New York: Basic Books.

Welter, Barbara. 1966. "The Cult of True Womanhood: 1820–1860." *American Quarterly* 18 (October):151–74.

White, George S. 1836. *Memoirs of Samuel Slater: The Father of American Manufactures, Connected with a History of the Rise and Progress of the Cotton Manufactures in New England and America*. Philadelphia: privately published.

White, Robert Winthrop. 1952. *Lives in Progress: A Study of the Natural Growth in Personality*. New York: Dryden Press.

Whyte, William Foote. 1951. "Small Groups and Large Organizations." In John R. Rohrer and Muzafer Sherif, eds. *Social Psychology at the Crossroads*, pp. 297–313. New York: Harper & Brothers.

Wiebe, Robert H. 1962. *Businessmen and Reform: A Study of the Progressive Movement*. Cambridge, Mass.: Harvard University Press.

Wilensky, Harold L. 1961. "Orderly Careers and Social Participation: The Impact of Work History in the Middle Mass." *American Sociological Review* 26 (August):521–39.

Wirth, Louis. 1938. "Urbanism as a Way of Life." *American Journal of Sociology* 44 (July):1–24.

Wishy, Bernard. 1968. *The Child and the Republic: The Dawn of Modern American Child Nurture*. Philadelphia: University of Pennsylvania Press.

Wright, Carroll. 1883. "The Factory System of the United States." Tenth Census, Manufactures of the United States. Washington, D.C.: U.S., Bureau of the Census.

Wrigley, E. A. 1966. "Family Limitation in Pre-Industrial England." *Economic History Review* 19 (April):82–109.

1972. "The Process of Modernization and the Industrial Revolution in England." *Journal of Interdisciplinary History* 3 (October):225–60.

Yans-McLaughlin, Virginia. 1971–2. "Patterns of Work and Family Organization: Buffalo's Italians." *Journal of Interdisciplinary History* 2 (Autumn):299–314.

1974. "A Flexible Tradition: South Italian Immigrants Confront a New Work Experience." *Journal of Social History* 7 (Summer):429–45.

1977. *Family and Community: Italian Immigrants in Buffalo, 1880–1930*. Ithaca, N.Y.: Cornell University Press.

Yellen, Samuel. 1936. *American Labor Struggles*. New York: Harcourt, Brace.

Young, Michael D., and Willmott, Peter. 1957. *Family and Kinship in East London*. London: Routledge & Kegan Paul.

Young, T. M. 1903. *The American Cotton Industry: A Study of Work and Workers Contributed to the Manchester Guardian.* New York: Scribner.
Zaretsky, Eli. 1976. *Capitalism, the Family and Personal Life.* New York: Harper & Row.
Zieger, Robert H. 1972. "Workers and Scholars: Recent Trends in American Labor Historiography." *Labor History* 13 (Spring):245–66.
Zimmerman, Carl C., and Frampton, Merle E. 1935. *Family and Society: A Study in the Sociology of Reconstruction.* New York: Van Nostrand.

Government publications

Massachusetts Bureau of the Statistics of Labor. 1882. *The Canadian French in New England.* Thirteenth Annual Report. Boston: Commonwealth of Massachusetts.
  1911. *Living Conditions of the Wage-Earning Population.* Boston: Commonwealth of Massachusetts.
"Strikes and Lockouts in the United States." 1918. *Monthly Labor Review* 7 (December):359–63.
U.S., Bureau of Labor. 1891. *Seventh Annual Report of the Commissioner of Labor, 1891,* vol. 2, pt. 3. Washington, D.C.: U.S. Government Printing Office.
  1892. *Conditions of Employment.* Washington, D.C.: U.S. Government Printing Office.
U.S., Bureau of Labor Statistics. 1913. *Employers' Welfare Work.* Prepared by Elizabeth Lewis Otey. Bulletin 123. Washington, D.C.: U.S. Government Printing Office.
  1918. *Descriptions of Occupations: Textile and Clothing.* Prepared for U.S. Employment Service. Washington, D.C.: U.S. Government Printing Office.
"Cost of Living in the Year Ending November 30th, 1918." Manuscript Schedule. Record Group No. 257. National Archives, Washington, D.C.
  1919. *Welfare Work for Employees in Industrial Establishments in the United States.* Bulletin 250. Washington, D.C.: U.S. Government Printing Office.
  1929. "Wages and Hours of Labor in Cotton Goods Manufacturing, 1910–1928." Bulletin 492. Washington, D.C.: U.S. Government Printing Office.
U.S., Congress, House. 1912. *Hearings before the Special Committee of the House of Representatives to Investigate the Taylor and Other Systems of Shop Management.* Washington, D.C.: U.S. Government Printing Office, pp. 583–5.
U.S., Congress, House, Committee on Labor. 1936. *Hearings to Rehabilitate and Stabilize Labor Conditions in the Textile Industry of the United States.* 74th Cong., 2nd sess. Washington, D.C.: U.S. Government Printing Office.

U.S., Congress, Senate, Committee on Education and Labor. 1885. *Report of the Committee of the Senate upon the Relations between Labor and Capital and Testimony Taken by the Committee*. Vol. 5. 48th Cong., 1st sess. Washington, D.C.: U.S. Government Printing Office.

U.S., Department of Labor. 1910–13. *Report on the Condition of Women and Child Wage Earners in the United States*, 19 vols. Prepared under the direction of Charles P. Neill, Commissioner of Labor. 61st Cong., 2nd sess., S. Doc. 65. Washington, D.C.: U.S. Government Printing Office.

    1918. *Descriptions of Occupations: Textiles and Clothing*. Washington, D.C.: U.S. Government Printing Office.

    1935. *Job Specifications for the Cotton Textile Industry*. Washington, D.C.: U.S. Government Printing Office.

U.S., Department of Labor Statistics. 1938. *Characteristics of Company Unions 1935*. Bulletin 634. Washington, D.C.: U.S. Government Printing Office.

U.S., Department of Labor, Employment Service. 1935. *Job Specifications for the Cotton Textile Industry*. Washington, D.C.: U.S. Government Printing Office.

U.S., Department of Labor, Women's Bureau. 1922. *The Family Status of Breadwinning Women*. Bulletin 23. Washington, D.C.: U.S. Government Printing Office.

    1923. *The Share of Wage-Earning Women in Family Support*, pp. 137–40. Bulletin 30. Washington, D.C.: U.S. Government Printing Office.

    1924. *Married Women in Industry*. Bulletin 38. Washington, D.C.: U.S. Government Printing Office.

    1926. *Lost Time and Labor Turnover in Cotton Mills: A Study of Cause and Extent*, Pt. 1:109–13. Bulletin 52. Washington, D.C.: U.S. Government Printing Office.

U.S., Immigration Commission, 1907–10. 1911a. *Immigrants in Industries*. Washington, D.C.: U.S. Government Printing Office.

    1911b. *Reports*. 61st Cong., 2nd sess. Washington D.C.: U.S. Government Printing Office.

U.S., Industrial Commission. 1901. *Reports*, Vol. 15.

Newspapers

L'Avenir National, Manchester, N.H.
Le Canado-Américaine, Manchester, N.H.
The Manchester Leader, Manchester, N.H.
The Manchester Mirror, Manchester, N.H.

Index

accidents, 125–6
adaptation
to historical changes in world of work, 355
to industrial work, 1, 2, 7, 118, 119, 120–53, 368–70
in life plans, 360
of new workers, 76
role of family and household in, 164–5, 182–3
stress in, 121–2, 123, 125, 138
see also traditions, premigration
Adjustment Board, Amoskeag Co., 28, 100, 131, 144, 146
handling grievance complaints, 294, 295, 296, 297, 298, 302, 306, 308
agent, 15, 24, 133
personified paternalistic system, 50, 55
role in grievance mechanism, 144, 294, 295, 298, 302, 305–7
Ahern, Michael, 351, 352
Alger, William (overseer), 265, 268
Allport, Gordon, 372, 374
Amalgamated Textile Workers of America, 310
Amoskeag Baseball Team, 43–4
Amoskeag Bulletin, 27, 44, 67, 262–3
profiles of self-made man, 262–3, 264, 265, 266, 268
Amoskeag Industries, 32
Amoskeag Manufacturing Company, 9–37, 138, 224
Amory Mills, 266, 325
annexations by, 10, 266
attempts to modernize, 29–30
balance in labor relations, 287–309
benevolent image of, 133 (*see also* paternalism)

Boston office, 15, 30
change in, 123–4, 150, 151, 218–26, 239–40
Charity Department, 48–9
Coolidge Mill, 224, 314, 319, 320, 322–3, 324
data sources re, 383–4
decline of, 15, 29–32, 83–4, 113–14, 151, 224, 254–5, 279–81, 284–5, 356
dominated Manchester's economic life, 13–15, 48, 57, 113–14, 249, 315, 316
Employees' Relief Committee, 344
as "family," 24, 61, 84
filed for bankruptcy, 352
flexibility of work arrangements, 77, 101, 126–7, 136, 153, 224, 241, 257, 289 (*see also* hiring)
"Happenings" (bulletin), 27
hired detectives to suppress agitation, 58, 287
institutional structure of, 336
methods of pay, 419
mill yard, 12–13, 32, 38, 40, 93
mills reopened during 1922 strike, 325, 326–7, 329 (*see also* Coolidge Mill)
number of employees, 31
occupational classifications, 388–9
occupational structure, 260
Plan of Reorganization, 1925, 301, 351
Plan of Representation, 340–2, 345, 350 (*see also* union, company)
point in history of, at which worker started, and career advancement, 272, 279–81, 284–5, 355–6

457